I0880994

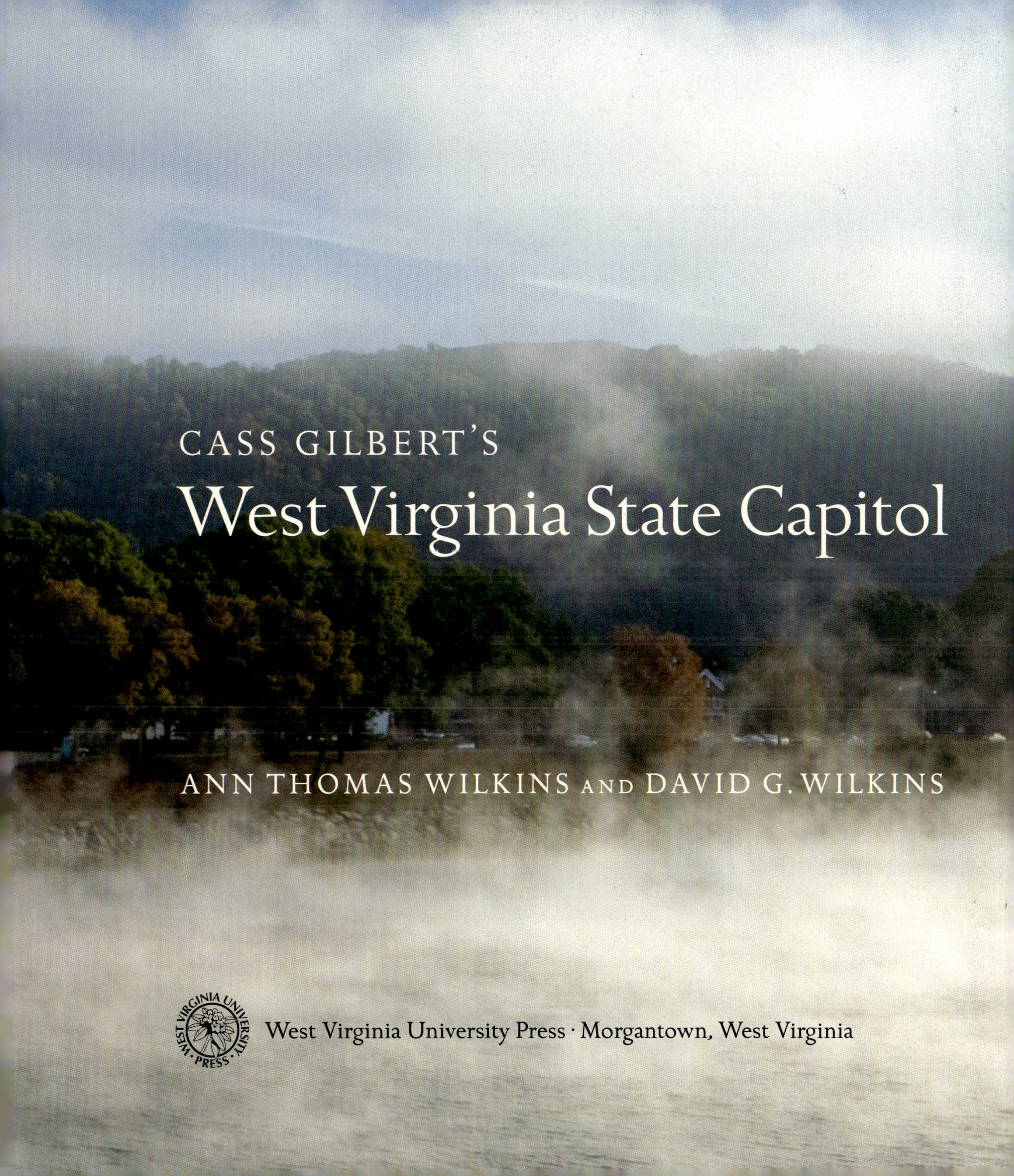

CASS GILBERT'S

# West Virginia State Capitol

ANN THOMAS WILKINS AND DAVID G. WILKINS

West Virginia University Press · Morgantown, West Virginia

Copyright 2014 by West Virginia University Press
All rights reserved
First edition published 2014 by West Virginia University Press
Printed in Canada

20 19 18 17 16 15 14 1 2 3 4 5 6 7 8 9

Library of Congress Cataloging-in-Publication Data

Wilkins, Ann Thomas, 1944– author.
Cass Gilbert's West Virginia State Capitol / by Ann Thomas Wilkins and David G. Wilkins. — First edition.
pages cm
Includes bibliographical references.
ISBN-13: 978-1-938228-46-9 (cloth : alk. paper)
ISBN-10: 1-938228-46-4 (cloth : alk. paper)
1. West Virginia Capitol Complex (Charleston, W. Va.) 2. Gilbert, Cass, 1859–1934—Criticism and interpretation. 3. Charleston (W. Va.)—Buildings, structures, etc. I. Wilkins, David G., author. II. Title.
NA4412.W4W55 2014
725'.110975437—dc23
2013035676

Composed in Golden Cockerel
Book design by Robert L. Wiser, Silver Spring, Maryland
Art direction by Than Saffel, West Virginia University Press

Gallery 1 (page i). Interior of Capitol dome. In this view the chandelier is still in its original position, hanging between the dome and the drum. Photograph by Jeff Lively.

Gallery 2 (pages ii–iii). The Capitol in the morning mist. Photograph by Frank Ceravalo.

Gallery 3 (opposite). The rotunda and dome, with a view toward one of the legislative foyers. This view shows the chandelier in its new, lower position. Note the elaborate chain designed by Gilbert. Photograph by Thorney Lieberman.

Gallery 4. The rotunda, with the statue of Senator Robert Byrd and a view toward one of the legislative foyers. Photograph by Jeff Lively.

Gallery 5. Legislative foyer, looking toward the rotunda. Photograph by Edward Crim.

# Contents



Gallery 6 (opposite). The chamber of the House of Delegates. Photograph by Thorney Lieberman.

*To our family, to the memory of the great architect Cass Gilbert, and to the Gilbert family, who keep his memory strong. And, most of all, to the people of West Virginia, past, present, and future.*

*The West Virginia University Press gratefully acknowledges the financial assistance provided for this book by the State of West Virginia and the West Virginia Division of Culture and History, West Virginia University, and the Myers Foundations.*

Gallery 7. The Senate chamber.
Photograph by Thorney Lieberman.

Gallery 8. The governor's reception room. Photograph by Thorney Lieberman.

Gallery 9. The Doric vestibule. Photograph by Thorney Lieberman.

# Welcome

*Governor Earl Ray Tomblin*

EVERY DAY THAT I WALK into this magnificent masterpiece conceived by Cass Gilbert, I pause and take in its grandeur and beauty. I never tire of looking at it, working in it, or talking to someone who is interested in its history and its genesis.

Because I worked here for nearly four decades as a legislator and am now governor, it would be easy to assume that I could take our Capitol for granted and not consider what it means to me and to the great people I serve. But I don't, and I doubt I ever will. To me, the building represents the noble individuals who settled here and forged from the wilderness a lifestyle that remains special even after a century and a half of statehood.

The pioneers and settlers who came west, crossing mountain peaks in search of a life of freedom and individuality, found it in these hills. Our great Capitol, framed by these same hills, testifies to the ideals of those who braved dangerous trails, fast moving streams, and many other challenges that have now been overcome through education, technology, and hard work. After these rugged individualists had moved the frontier westward, our state was born in the midst of national strife; its great domed Capitol honors them.

Cass Gilbert learned about the people whose Capitol building he was to design, and he created one that was rich in symbolism, suggesting that out of these hills came the greatness that underlies the state's motto: "Montani Semper Liberi," "Mountaineers are Always Free." The mountaineer spirit lives today in these hills and its voice gives rise in the public forum that thrives every day in the great halls envisioned by Gilbert. Here, where public policy is made in an open democratic process, the people of West Virginia continue to explore ways to manifest those same dreams to secure a place of honor in the twenty-first century, as they had in earlier centuries. And in this Capitol built in a time of great national challenges, the people come together, seeking solutions to common challenges.

The nature of the building gives rise to a commitment to maintain it as Gilbert designed it. When I was Senate President, I made every effort to guarantee that we kept Gilbert's concept in mind. During those years more money was spent on preservation and restoration than at any other time in state history; the building today is as close to Gilbert's original design—right down to the style of carpets in the legislative chambers—as we could make it. We also appropriated considerable sums to secure the structure of the building by regrouting, cleaning the stone surface, and protecting the building from leaks. We spared no expense for its maintenance and upkeep.

I want our Capitol to shine so that the state's citizens will continue to take pride in its glory and magnificence. I want the Capitol to continue to be a beacon to those from other states who pull off the interstate to visit it; they often say, "We saw this marvelous building and had to stop and take a look." That's when we know that it is more than just a symbol of a great and noble people; it is a beacon of friendship and fellowship that informs those passing by that this is a special place, these are special people, and a warm welcome for all awaits within.

Thank you, Cass Gilbert, for your priceless gift. We will do our best to respect it and care for it as long as our state and our nation stand.

I hope that through the pages of this beautiful book readers will learn even more about Mr. Gilbert, his building, and the people of West Virginia who cherish it so deeply.

*November 2012*

# Making West Virginia's New Capitol a Reality

*Senator Brooks F. McCabe Jr.*

ANN AND DAVID WILKINS have given the citizens of West Virginia a gift of enduring value with their definitive study, *Cass Gilbert's West Virginia State Capitol.* These scholars have documented how a world-class architect, with the help and support of three governors and a very capable and persistent group of community leaders, was able to conceive, fund, and build a state capitol building that remains one of the great examples of Cass Gilbert's work. The Classical tradition inspired Cass Gilbert, and with a lifetime of training and experience, he was able to create a monumental building that has become a masterpiece. The West Virginia Capitol represents the best of both Cass Gilbert and the Classical architecture of the early 1900s as practiced in the United States.

This magnificent achievement was accomplished by a small, rural state at a time of severe financial trauma preceding and during the Great Depression. The project was conceived following a disastrous fire in January 1921 that destroyed the 1885 Capitol building. As West Virginia was just beginning to feel the adverse impacts of the collapse of the coal industry following World War I, the Capitol Building Commission began planning a new Capitol building. In spite of repeated efforts by others to narrow the scope and limit the quality and scale of the project, the Commission held its own and ultimately selected an architect of international renown, chose a site accentuating the grandeur of a major public edifice, and insisted that the Capitol be a building that would stand the test of time.

The Wilkins's book is a study of a great architect and the Capitol Building Commission that had the foresight to set the bar high and go for the best. It tells of several governors and State Legislatures continually being accosted by local and regional politics, which challenged the selection of the architect, the building site, the funding sources and their amounts as well as the monumental Classical style of the project. Yet through all of this, the one constant was Cass Gilbert. His talent and the force of his personality served him and the State of West Virginia well. The West Virginia State Capitol is a testament to high standards and lofty goals, but also to fortitude, as West Virginia had to navigate rough waters as prosperity gave way to the Depression years.

This is not just a story of an architect and one of his crowning achievements. It is the story of how defining events actually occur. The process was fraught with challenges and disruptions at every turn. The Wilkins's research tells of fortitude, leadership, and vision at a time in West Virginia's development when the world was rapidly changing and long-held conventions were being challenged. It is about a seasoned architect being guided by a clear and unwavering eye focused on the future with a comprehensive understanding of the value and importance of creating a state capitol building that embodies the strength and character of West Virginia. It is about Cass Gilbert's West Virginia State Capitol and "a dome of majestic proportion."

*September 2012*

# Preface: On Re-creating the Past

*Ann Thomas Wilkins and David G. Wilkins*

OUR TOPIC IS RICH—an inspiring American monument designed by one of the nation's great architects—and its presentation made richer by an abundance of quotations and surprising details.

Cass Gilbert was a professional who left an impressive paper trail: telegrams, letters, transcripts of calls and meetings, publications, photographs, sketches, and blueprints, not to mention appointment books, financial records, notes, and diaries. Thanks to his recordkeeping we have access to extensive details about his projects, professional activities, and personal life.

We present the story of West Virginia's Capitol using the voices and words of the historical period whenever possible. Our intent is to re-create a sense of life in the 1920s and early 1930s, when Gilbert was dealing with West Virginia governors, members of the Capitol Building Commission and their hypercritical spokesperson Bonner Hill, contractors, and national and local providers of everything from marble to light fixtures. Quotations from correspondence, newspaper articles, and other sources expose the political jockeying, intrigue, attempts to derail the project, and the ins and outs of planning and construction, as well as, in the end, the exuberance of success.

Having a wealth of sources, particularly Gilbert's writings, has been beneficial; such full documentation does not often survive, and our experience in the archives suggests that few American buildings can be better documented than the West Virginia Capitol. The abundance of primary sources allows us to become part of the interactions, negotiations, and politics that played a role in the evolution of the West Virginia Capitol.

We are also aware of the limitations of our sources. While letters and other written documents offer extensive information, ironically they sometimes raise new questions that cannot be answered. And as abundant and enticing as the materials are, they offer only a partial and particular view of the realities of the period. While we learn much about the architect's, commissioners', and governors' viewpoints, we know less about those of the public, even though West Virginia's newspapers reported facts and rumors alike in a vigorous and often outspoken manner. Furthermore, the archives are so extensive that—even though we have tried to consult every resource with the assistance of archival professionals—it is possible we have overlooked some documents. There is always more to be learned about the Capitol and its architect, more information to be discovered, more connections to be made and ideas to be formulated.

The endnotes provide additional primary source material and commentary on issues discussed in the text. While daunting in number and detail, these notes provide further information for readers who desire it.

As soon as the West Virginia State Capitol was completed, in 1932, its image was distributed nationwide in postcards; some appear here as illustrations to communicate the enthusiasm West Virginia's citizens and travelers felt for the new monument. We are pleased that previously unpublished black and white photographs of the Capitol can appear in this book, thanks to the generosity of the Gilbert family. They date from the 1950s, when Cass Gilbert Jr. was designing his office building for the Capitol complex.

Our chapters differ widely in their content as they present the Capitol's story. Some are detailed and chronological; others are descriptive and comparative as we study the complex as it is now and as it was during the period of its development.

Cass Gilbert and his works were affected by the events, technological advances, and social changes of the times, from the 1893 Columbian Exposition and World War I to economic vicissitudes and the rise of Modernism in architecture. His growth as an artist was closely linked to these developments. By the time he was commissioned to design a new Capitol for West Virginia, he was a well-known architect with prestigious buildings and honors linked to his name, a professional accomplished in design and in running an efficient atelier. He was honest, dedicated, skilled, and proud of his work and his profession.

The Cass Gilbert we see through much of his correspondence is serious, efficient, well organized, fully in control; through other letters and diaries we glimpse a different side. Our first of many quotations—from a letter written to Julia, his wife and confidante, immediately after a visit to Charleston in 1923—reveals a man who appreciated humor and enjoyed lively personal interaction, even with a venerable adversary in the West Virginia Legislature, Septimius Hall:

> I met old Uncle Sept Hall ... who had denounced me in the House and in the newspapers—I greeted him with a loud and hearty welcome—told him that of all the men in West Virginia I would rather meet—he was the man! We talked and argued for an hour until the old devil told me he'd "hear no more of it," he "had heard enough"—I immediately said "You're right! Now you talk!" And you bet he let out a howl.... When old Hall told me "the people" of his county were opposed to the Capitol, I switched around and asked him to tell me about his county, where it is and what it produces—it's Wetzel County up next to the Ohio River—and I told him I was a "sort of a neighbor" of "the folks up there" for I was born not far away in Zanesville. [Letter preserved in the Cass Gilbert archive at the Library of Congress]

This encounter was still business and negotiation, in this case facing an initially hostile legislator, but as we read this account we wonder if Gilbert chuckled to himself as he wrote of the incident to his wife. His personal charm worked; he won the support of Hall and some fellow legislators of "the old devil," and within a week the appropriation for the first wing of the Capitol had been passed. As we observe Gilbert's serious nature and admire his tireless efficiency, we need to remember his lighter side.

One wonders what Gilbert thought the first time he saw the completed Capitol, this magnificent Classical building with its commanding dome set against the West Virginia hills. The Capitol is more than an architectural complex; it is a monument to the state and its people, to the many dedicated individuals who brought it into being, from commissioners to laborers, governors to architect. It is a building of which West Virginians are proud. We are honored to present its story.

# Cass Gilbert's West Virginia State Capitol

# Introduction

It is my desire that the building be of a very dignified and pure type of architecture, something that will last and be permanently approved by the best public taste. Eccentricities of design will be avoided, for I believe that a simple, dignified structure of fine proportions is far more satisfactory in the long run than any amount of elaborate embellishment, or so-called novelty of detail.... The whole structure will be crowned by a dome of majestic proportions.... I want to make this capitol building the crowning work of my life. It is the type of building to which I have devoted the past 25 years of my life, and I feel that the opportunity is now presented to me for a splendid architectural monument. The best is none too good for West Virginia and, therefore, I am anxious to respond to the best of my ability to the responsibility the capitol commission has placed in me.

Cass Gilbert, quoted in the *Charleston Daily Mail*, July 19, 1922

Fig. 1. The West Virginia State Capitol.
Photograph by Frank Ceravalo.

THE GILDED DOME OF THE WEST VIRGINIA STATE CAPITOL, seen against the verdant hills of the Mountain State, is immediately impressive. Its scale and the manner in which it rises above a Classical temple façade reflect the design of the National Capitol in Washington; the members of West Virginia's Capitol Building Commission seem to have wanted the state's new Capitol to be based on this model, probably because of its symbolic and historical significance. Their choice of Cass Gilbert as architect may have been based on his experience designing state houses following the national model. The Capitol he planned, in concert with the commissioners, was intended to convey the dignity of the state it honors and the citizens it serves through dramatic scale, fine materials, and handsome proportions. Architectural elements drawn from Classical antiquity and the Italian Renaissance suggest permanence and stability. This monument to the enduring qualities of American democracy is worthy of an in-depth investigation.

The architectural merit of the Capitol is not the only justification for such a study. Its design and construction engaged West Virginia's governors, legislators, and citizens in an endeavor that exposes the state's history and, in particular, its political, social, and economic fabric. Extensive documentation preserves the role the Capitol played in West Virginia's history during the tumultuous years between Gilbert's appointment in 1921 and the building's dedication in 1932.

The paper trail maintained by Gilbert's office also demonstrates his engagement with every phase of this project, dispelling the rumor that his son, Cass Gilbert Jr., was in charge during design and construction. When evidence from the documents is combined with the lively accounts published in West Virginia's newspapers, the story of the Capitol can be presented through the voices of the main players.

The West Virginia Capitol is, however, seldom mentioned in histories of twentieth-century architecture. The explanation lies largely in its style: by 1932, when the Capitol was dedicated, the Classical style with which Cass Gilbert endowed his public buildings was being rejected in favor of Modernism. The incorporation of earlier architectural traditions at West Virginia meant that the Capitol was soon viewed as a reference to the past rather than a vision of a dynamic future. While such judgments can deny a building a position in the progressive chronology of architecture, they cannot challenge the aesthetic excellence that makes the West Virginia Capitol an outstanding example of the designer's and builder's art.

Modernist architects and critics rejected the architectural motifs drawn from antiquity and the Renaissance that feature so prominently in Gilbert's West Virginia Capitol, substituting pure geometric forms: unadorned planes, rectangles, circles. The modernists also avoided the traditional materials—marble, travertine, bronze, gold—that make such a strong impression at the Charleston Capitol, preferring plaster, local stone, glass, and color. While modernist architects often employed asymmetrical designs, the Classicists preferred the sense of order and control offered by a symmetrical plan.

The ornamental "vocabulary" rejected by the modernists is only one aspect of the Classical style. Equally important is the "grammar"—the sense of balanced proportion within which the traditional elements were ordered. Gilbert emphasized the role proportion played in his design process and, in a 1927 memorandum to the Building Commission, wrote that a building's "principal claim to beauty lies in its proportions, not its adornment."

And so, before delving into a historical narrative that relates design and construction to issues of society, economics, and politics, we must establish the broadest context needed for understanding the West Virginia Capitol: the importance of proportion in the Classical architectural tradition. Founded in antiquity and revived in the buildings and writings of the Renaissance, Classicism endured and flourished in the Beaux-Arts environment that inspired Gilbert. The following essay examines the intellectual tradition within which Cass Gilbert and his West Virginia State Capitol play a role.

PROLOGUE

# Cass Gilbert and the Classical Tradition of Architecture

*Bernard Schultz and Mary L. Soldo Schultz*

But how is a taste in this beautiful art to be formed in our countrymen, unless we avail ourselves of every occasion when public buildings are to be erected, of presenting to them models for their study and imitation? . . . You see I am an enthusiast in the subject of the arts. But it is an enthusiasm of which I am not ashamed, as its object is to improve the taste of my countrymen, to increase their reputation, to reconcile them to the respect of the world, and to procure them its praise.

Thomas Jefferson, Letter to James Madison, 1785

The art of a nation is one of the truest indices of its civilization. It has a great influence on people in many ways. If that influence is fine and pure and noble it is reflected in the development of the nation. . . . The artists, like the poets, blaze this trail of human thought and human endeavor.

Cass Gilbert, Letter to the Honorable Elihu Root, 1929

Fig. 2. Ancient Roman temple known as the "Maison Carrée," Nimes, France, c. 20 BCE, as seen in a painting of 1786–87 by the French painter Hubert Robert at the Musée du Louvre in Paris. The painting shows the temple as it looked when it was admired by Thomas Jefferson in 1787.

ALTHOUGH THEY WERE SEPARATED BY GENERATIONS, CASS GILBERT shared the ideals set forth by Thomas Jefferson in describing the role of art and architecture in nurturing and promoting the values of a nation.[1] Both Jefferson and Gilbert believed that public architecture was a primary vehicle through which to convey and promote the nation's values. Gilbert's elegant West Virginia State Capitol, with its harmonious proportions, classical temple front, commanding dome, and architectural details that recall ancient Rome, bridges the eighteenth and twentieth centuries by faithfully perpetuating the idea that art and architecture could inspire citizens to attain laudable goals through exemplary moral purpose and conduct. This philosophical conviction, held by generations of architects whose works and writings define the Classical tradition in Western architecture, has roots in antiquity. First expressed in the writings of the ancient Roman architect Vitruvius, it became the cornerstone of the theory and practice of Classical architecture. During the Italian Renaissance, the sixteenth-century architect Palladio enabled a continuing revival of the Classical aesthetic in architecture. The writings of Vitruvius and Palladio also bequeathed to later architects insights into the significance of their profession, which encouraged later architects to embrace the same idea: that classicizing architecture could communicate personal values. The West Virginia State Capitol is an outstanding example of that tradition.

The fame of Vitruvius, who worked during the reign of the emperor Augustus at the turn of the first century CE, rests on his Latin treatise *De architectura* (*On Architecture*). His writing enormously influenced Renaissance architects, especially Andrea Palladio, whose illustrated treatise *Quattro libri dell'architettura* (*The Four Books on Architecture*) in turn influenced eighteenth- and nineteenth-century architects, including those engaged in designing public buildings for the young republic of the United States.[2] Gilbert called upon the authority of these architects when he discussed the genesis of the West Virginia State Capitol, writing that the building's exterior and interior were both "designed to give it a noble and distinctive simplicity; to keep it closely within the lines of the great tradition and precedent which were characteristic of the early public buildings of America, lines which were largely influenced by Washington, Jefferson, and their associates, and by architects like Thornton, Bulfinch, and Mills, who were leaders in their profession in the early days of the Republic."[3] The architects Gilbert named, with whom he must have felt a professional kinship, had established the architectural icons of our new nation. When Thomas Jefferson was minister to France, he was awed by Roman ruins. Upon his return, he adapted features of an ancient temple to the design of the Virginia State Capitol, thereby introducing American audiences to the dignity of Classical architecture. William Thornton was awarded in 1793 the commission to design the National Capitol in Washington; Jefferson found Thornton's design to be "simple, noble, beautiful, and excellently distributed." Charles Bulfinch designed the Massachusetts State House in Boston and served as the head architect of the National Capitol from 1817 to 1830. Robert Mills, the first American-born professional architect, designed other

Fig. 3. Thomas Jefferson (architect), Virginia State Capitol, Richmond, 1785–89, as it appeared in a wood engraving by Lawrence Sully published in 1802.

*Behold! a Fabric now to* **Freedom** *rear'd,*
*Approv'd by Friends, and ev'n by Foes rever'd;*
*Where* **Justice**, *too, and* **Peace**, *by us ador'd,*
*Shall heal each Wrong, and keep ensheath'd the sword.*
*Approach then, Concord, fair Columbia's Son;*
*And, faithful Clio, write that* 'WE ARE ONE'.

*sign'd by G.T.* *Trenchard sculp.*

Neo-classical buildings in Washington including the Department of the Treasury building. In citing these men, Gilbert chose predecessors whose designs had helped set the foundation for the Federal style in government buildings and who themselves had been swayed by the works and writings of Palladio.[4]

Beaux-Arts architects of the late nineteenth and early twentieth centuries, including Cass Gilbert, were indebted to Palladio not only for his discussions of buildings and their proportions and ornament but also for the realization that buildings could be inspiring. In considering a temple, for example, Palladio noted that it should be sited so that those who see it will want to "make their salutations and reverences before the front of the temple."[5] In the late eighteenth century, and especially in America, the idea that buildings can be inspirational was extended beyond a religious context to include the structures needed for the new government. Not only did Washington and Jefferson want to associate the republic in a general way with buildings of ancient Greece and Rome, which had witnessed early forms of democratic and republican governments, but they and many other leaders understood that a public building could be interpreted as a symbolic temple of liberty. In 1812, Jefferson described the National Capitol as "the first temple dedicated to the sovereignty of the people, embellishing with Athenian taste the course of a nation looking far beyond the range of Athenian destinies."[6]

Jefferson's understanding of the didactic power of architecture was in keeping with the idealism of the time. In 1788, a print in *The Columbian Magazine* depicted the values of the new American nation as a Classical temple with thirteen columns, symbolizing the original states, and bearing the inscription "Sacred to Liberty, Justice, and Peace." In front, Concord accepts the Constitution from Columbia's winged son, who represents the "genius of the United States." To the right, Cleo, muse of history, writes in her book: "WE ARE ONE."[7] The concept of America as an inspiring "temple of liberty" was repeated by James Wilson of Pennsylvania, a signer of the Declaration of Independence, who argued that his state should ratify the Constitution because "by adopting this system, we shall probably lay a foundation for temples of liberty in every part of the earth."[8]

That architecture could express such abstract concepts, draw emotions from an observer, and inspire a responsive spirit was well understood by Cass Gilbert. Writing in *The American Architect* in 1929, as the design for the West Virginia Capitol was being finalized, Gilbert addressed the didactic virtues of a well-designed state capitol: "It is an inspiration toward patriotism and good citizenship, it encourages just pride in the state, and is an education to ongoing generations to see these things, imponderable elements of life and character, set before the people for their enjoyment and betterment."[9] Gilbert also related these virtues to the more immediate history of American architecture. In a 1927 letter to West Virginia Governor Howard Gore, Gilbert praised the governor's leadership, noting that political stewardship of the Capitol building "needs a man of broad vision and experience like yourself to see beyond the mere momentary utility to its ultimate effect as a work of art.... Architecture and craftsmanship of the right sort always make its impression on the public mind." He added:

Fig. 4. *Classical Temple Sacred to Liberty, Justice, and Peace*, by James Trenchard. Engraving from *The Columbian Magazine*, published in Philadelphia in 1788.

"Great leaders of men like Washington and Jefferson understood this and in the earliest days of the republic encouraged noble architectural designs for the national public buildings. Roosevelt and Root and Taft in their public positions have done likewise and it is my conviction that you in your own way are compatible with the impulse to make the West Virginia Capitol all that it ought to be in every way."[10]

But what was the key element of these "noble architectural designs"? Gilbert's answer: "Speaking purely from the standpoint of design, the greatest element of monumental architecture is good proportion.... No matter now ornate or how simple and plain any structure may be, in the last analysis, its principal claim to beauty lies in its proportions, not in its adornment."[11]

This assertion lies at the heart of the Classical aesthetic, formulated in Classical Greek art of the mid-fifth century BCE. At that time, the sculptor Polykleitos created an ideal figure using a proportional system in which the relationships between the various parts of the body were based on common ratios of whole numbers, such as 1:2, 1:4, 1:8. Polykleitos's sculpture and the book he wrote, the *Canon,* were based on the writings of Pythagoras, the philosopher and mathematician, most famous for his work in geometry, who a century earlier had demonstrated the relationship between musical harmony and simple numerical proportions. The discovery that such ratios governed harmonic proportions was subsequently applied to visual aesthetics, as in the case of Polykleitos's *Doryphorus* and even to the structure of the universe.[12] The theory that beauty is created through the use of mathematical proportions became the essence of the Classical aesthetic in Western culture.

Vitruvius extended these ratios of proportion in the human body to architecture. In *De architectura,* he defined proportion as both a "correspondence" among the dimensions of each part of the building and a correlation between one part "selected as standard" and the whole, like the ratios Polykleitos used. In describing the proportions of the body, he pointed out that the height of the face and the open hand, for example, should be one-tenth of the height of the human body; "the other members, too, have their own symmetrical proportions." He added that, by using this approach to design, "the famous painters and sculptors of antiquity attained to great and endless renown." Vitruvius related symmetry to proportion and noted that without these two elements "there can be no principles in the design of any temple" and that there must also be a "precise relation between its members, as in the case of those of a well shaped man."[13]

Vitruvius also pointed out that the ideal human body can be related to pure geometric shapes: "if a man be placed flat on his back, with his hands and feet extended," his fingers and toes will touch both the perimeter of a square, one side of which equals the measurement from the toe to the top of the head, and the circumference of a circle centered on his navel. The theory that "nature has designed the human body so that its members are duly proportioned to the frame as a whole" (by which Vitruvius meant the circle and the square), led the Greeks to decide that "perfect buildings" were those that had their "members ... in exact symmetrical

Fig. 5. *Doryphoros* ("Spear Carrier"), ancient Roman marble copy after a lost bronze original of c. 450 BCE by the Greek sculptor Polykleitos. National Archaeological Museum, Naples.

relations to the whole general scheme." According to Vitruvius, the ideal proportions of the human body provide the basis from which the Greeks "derived the fundamental ideas of the measures which are obviously necessary in all works."[14]

During the Italian Renaissance, this passage by Vitruvius inspired artists to attempt to capture the harmonious consonances among the human figure, proportions, and geometry. In the late fifteenth century, Leonardo da Vinci created a drawing that illustrated Vitruvius's concept, inscribing a human figure within the two geometric shapes, and thus relating the ideal human body to the universal order through geometry and proportion.[15]

The first artist to show how a work of architecture could be related to an ideal human body was the Italian architect Francesco di Giorgio Martini, who illustrated his *Tratto di architettura civile e militare* (*Treatise on Civil and Military Architecture*, c. 1482) with drawings that demonstrate the connection between figural proportions with specific architectural plans. His integration of human proportions with geometric shapes and building plans and elevations demonstrated the humanist acceptance of the universal interrelationships among these elements. In the upper diagram of figure 7, the body is correlated to the ground plan of a church.[16]

In the sixteenth century, Palladio succinctly restated what Vitruvius had established about the aesthetic relationship between beauty and proportion: "Beauty will result from the form and correspondence of the whole, with respect to the several parts, of the parts with regard to each other, and of these again to the whole; that the structure may appear an entire and complete body, wherein each member agrees with the other, and all necessary to compose what you intend to form."[17]

By the time Cass Gilbert was designing the West Virginia Capitol, his ability to create harmony and beauty through proportions must have been almost intuitive. His many descriptions of the Capitol revealed his sympathy for the practices and writings of those predecessors who had championed the Classical aesthetic. In a passage reminiscent of Jefferson's praise of Thornton's National Capitol design, Gilbert wrote that at Charleston: "Simplicity and good proportion, which are finer characteristics than ornamentation, have been carried out in the rotunda and the principal corridors, and in the rooms of the House and Senate especially, an air of simplicity, amplitude, and dignity has been achieved."[18]

Such an approach to public architecture was more than just an aspect of Gilbert's philosophy; it formed part of his character as well. In a 1927 letter to the *American Architect*, he expressed his position regarding the "possibly radically different views" of some nonmembers of the National Academy of Design who had been invited to participate in the Academy's 102nd Exhibition: "I am by nature a conservative and the extremes shock me. I do not think it is progress to throw away what we have learned by experience, or to make things ugly because we are a bit morbid at times, but I do rejoice in creative work so long as it is pure in thought and honest in expression." He continued: "I detest pose and sensational appeal, but I welcome that broader view which advances to new and higher conceptions of truth and beauty and I am sure the Academy feels the same way."[19]

Fig. 6. *The Relationship of an Ideal Human Figure to a Square and a Circle, as Proposed by the Ancient Roman Architect and Theorist Vitruvius*, drawing of c. 1487 by the Italian Renaissance artist Leonardo da Vinci. Pen and ink, 13½ × 9⅝". Accademia, Venice.

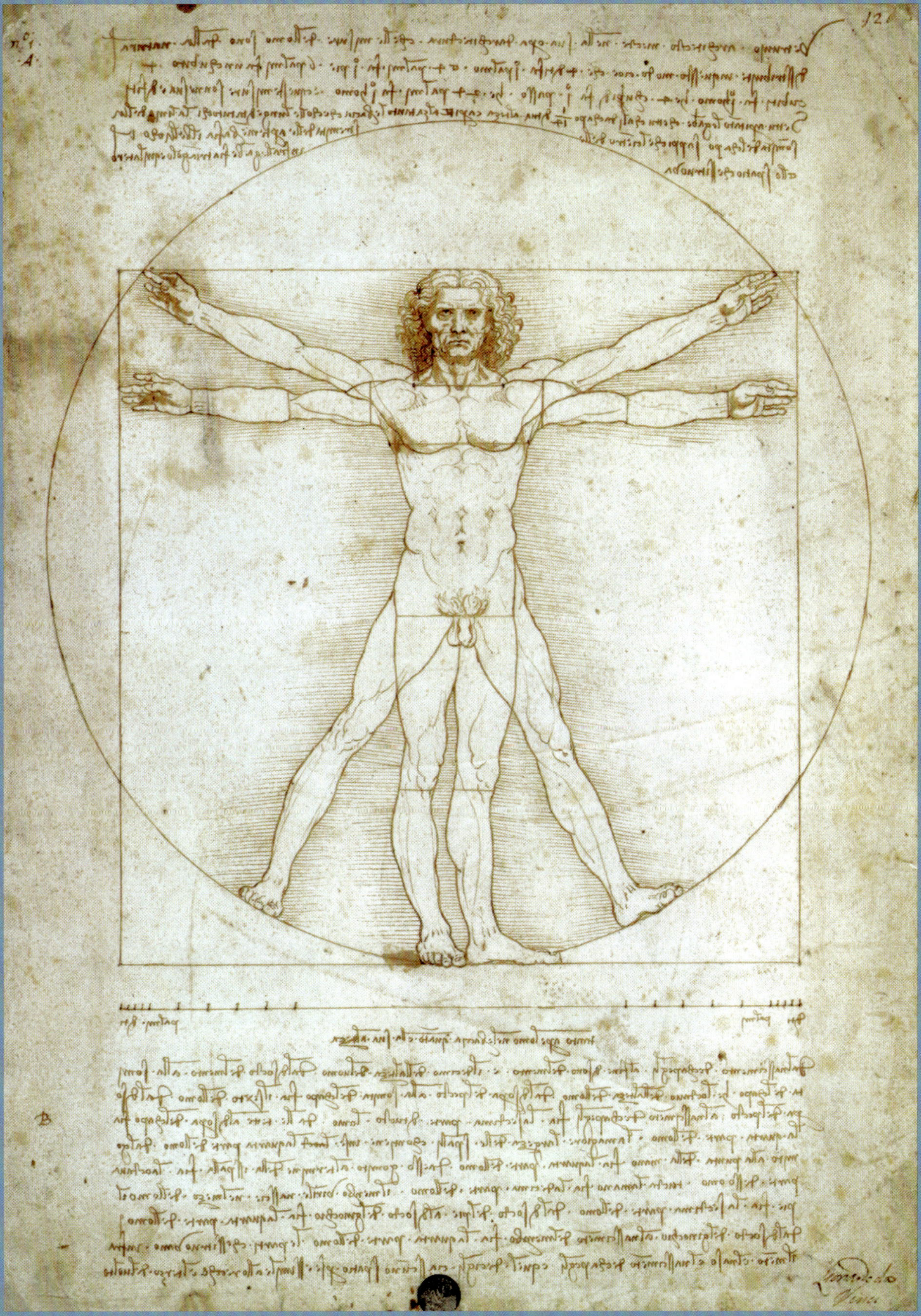

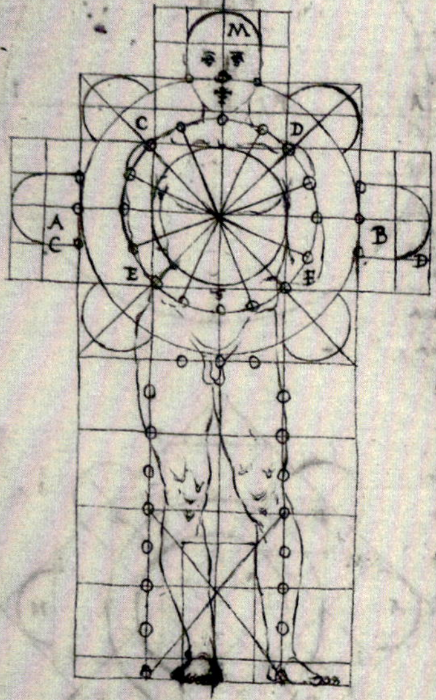


imparare ello corpo ho terminato alquna breue mete dimostrare Imprima e da
Sapere che in due modi Sipuo dividare cioe inparti noue et imparti sette Quello
di parti noue e tutta laltezza della faccia dalla extremita del mento al nasci
mento de capelli & una parte dalla forcina della Gola allo extremo petto
unaltra & daquesta dal nascimento de testicholi & parti due 7 da queste
allastragholo del ginoccio due altre le gambe insino insul collo del pie laltre
due che fanno il numero di octo laltezza del Pie & diametro della Gola fanno laltezza
dela Nona & Questo e ilpartimento ditutto ilcorpo Di Poi Siparti latesta in
tre lequali parti cosi partito Siponghi ilcentro alla linea media extremita
del Petto circu voltando una linea dal naso allo extremo busto lecui extremita
Sara tutta lalarghezza del tempio dalla Quale Sitirara lerecte linee infino
alla Basa linea delli extremi chalchangni laquale Sara quadripartita liquali pa
rtimenti & linee Sitirara insino al Somo Dipoi Sipigli leparti dal naso al Cranio
& Quelle daman dextra & Sinistra dela linea Centrale A B Saratribuischa
le quali tutte partite inparti quattro faranno lacircumferentia delli emicicli &
cusi quelle delli anguli perso lordine loro Sopra le intersechationi dalla circ
umferenzia & cosi tirare tutte lequadrature delle linee & tutti li emi
cicli Sitiri una circulare linea pla naue o Tolo tochando la extremita de
lli anguli delquadrato dmezo chiamato C D E F & simile dentro alminore
Quadrato Sipuo constituire Et qsto Sara partito piglisi una parte dellaltezza
della testa M T overo ilmezo del emiciclo Sedici parti lacircumferentia
del tolo Sitrouara & cosi tutte lenaui & Colonne Sicollocaranno come partita
mente nela presente figura Simanifesta

Altra misura & divisione del corpo pigliandosi laltezza ditutta latesta
in sette equali parti debba essere diviso Dipi Siponghe ilponto del circino
insu limbellicho et intersechatione delle linee una circumferentia dallultimo
mento alastragallo del ginochio & allextremita del circulo Sitiri le linee la
terali terminanti dal Cranio ala Basalinea delli infimi calcangni laqual linea
in quattro parti Sara divisa Dipoi Sitiri uno Semicirculo al Somo del Cranio
terminato A B & ad questo Sara illoco del Simulacro Di poi Sopra limbellicho
Sipigli unaltra centricha circumferentia tochanti le extremita delle linee
medie terminate D E F G & questo e quando accadesse essere lacupola ouero
tolo che lenaui Sanza impedimento possino circumdare si come lafigura
ne manifesto :

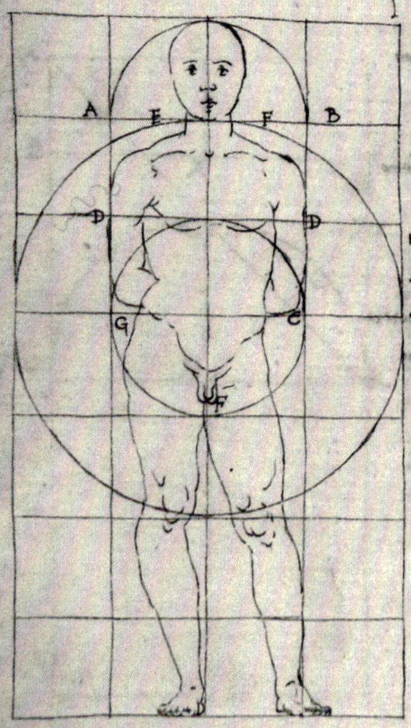

Later that year, Gilbert elaborated on the role of the architect in a letter to the editor of the periodical *Personality*:

> Architecture is a Fine Art, not a trade or a business.... If one would practice an art he must be an artist by nature and by training.... To be an architect in the true sense of the word means that one should be a man of broad culture, he should be able to draw and paint and model, he should understand the art of design in all its phases; color, form, proportion, detail of ornament he should be intimately familiar with. He must master the science of building. He must be able to take great responsibilities and he must be a competent businessman familiar with contracts and a thousand or more details of a technical character. He will have to deal with the strength of materials, with foundation problems, with mechanical equipment and with the constantly changing new materials that are now introduced into modern buildings. It is no job for a man that is looking to make easy money. It requires courage and persistence, skill and resourcefulness and physical endurance. Even then it will have disappointments and trials almost equal to the success. You may say if all of this is so, why do you do it? Well, I suppose for the same reason that inspires anyone to practice a great art, namely that we are bred to it and we *love* it.[20] [Gilbert's emphasis]

In exalting the profession in this way, Cass Gilbert was aware, of course, that he was exalting himself. But this historically grounded understanding of the character and education of the architect and of the value of the architect to humankind was also set deeply in his interpretation of his profession. His views are in line with those expressed by Vitruvius, who in *De architectura* had written: "The architect should be equipped with knowledge of many branches of study and varied kinds of learning, for it is by his judgment that all work done by the other arts is put to test."[21] This concept—that the architect is an educated individual whose knowledge extends to both theory and practice within a broad context of professional expertise and understanding—remained an integral part of the Classical tradition from antiquity onward and was particularly cherished by Cass Gilbert.

Gilbert's final public buildings, the West Virginia State Capitol and the United States Supreme Court Building, however magnificent, belonged to a tradition that was antithetical to the growing enthusiasm for Modernism characteristic of the period. But Gilbert clung to his belief that public buildings should not be measured by practicality and contemporary aesthetic approaches, but by the conviction, as he stated in his letter to Governor Gore, of what public architecture "ought to be in every way."[22]

At the conclusion of his 1929 article in the *American Architect*, Gilbert elucidated the value to the state in creating and promoting this style of architecture: "The educational value alone is worth to the state far more than its cost—it supplements the education furnished by the public school and the university—it is a symbol of the civilization, culture, and ideals of our country."[23]

Working in the late eighteenth century, Jefferson revived the grandeur of ancient Rome by modeling his Virginia State Capitol on a Roman temple (see figs. 2, 3). More than one hundred years later, in his designs for the West Virginia State Capitol (1922–32), Gilbert revisited the same ancient Roman cultural foundations. Using Roman architectural forms and details, combined with symbols of the state's legacy, Cass Gilbert created for West Virginia a Capitol that fulfills the idealistic promise Thomas Jefferson expressed for public architecture in the United States.

Fig. 7. Francesco di Giorgio Martini, *The Relationship between the Ideal Proportions of the Human Figure and the Ground Plan of a Church* (top). Drawing from the *Codice Magliabechiano*, Fondo Nazionale, II.I.141, p. 42. National Library, Florence.

CHAPTER ONE

# West Virginia Needs a Capitol: Selecting the Architect

I perhaps violate no confidence when I say that your name was mentioned in the first meeting as the type of architect we desire to employ for this work.

West Virginia Capitol Building Commissioner Edwin M. Keatley, writing to Cass Gilbert, June 21, 1921

Fig. 8. *Portrait of Cass Gilbert in 1927*, by Ernest L. Ipsen. Smithsonian American Art Museum, Washington, DC. Bequest of Emily Finch Gilbert through Julia Post Bastedo, executor.

IN JULY 1921, CASS GILBERT WAS COMMISSIONED TO DESIGN A NEW Capitol for West Virginia. The story of how Gilbert, who at the time was internationally famous as the architect of the world's tallest building, the Woolworth Building in New York, was convinced to come to Charleston is not without intrigue. To set the stage for his arrival, a brief history of West Virginia's earlier capitols and of the controversy over the location of the state's capital city is necessary.[1]

West Virginia's first capital was Wheeling, where the decision to secede from Virginia was made in 1861 and where, on June 20, 1863, the first governor was inaugurated and the first Legislature convened. The state's first capitol was a rented structure erected as a school for The Linsly Institute in 1858.

It was apparently not presumed that Wheeling would remain the capital, for Governor Arthur I. Boreman, in his 1863 inaugural address, urged the Legislature to "take speedy action for the establishment of a permanent seat of government," advice he repeated in 1866, 1868, and 1869. Finally, in 1870, the Legislature voted to move the capital to Charleston. Its motivation was in part political: by 1869, the Radical Republicans, who were associated with Wheeling, no longer dominated the Legislature. To promote accord, the Legislature chose the more centrally located Charleston, which had offered $50,000 for the erection of public buildings. Construction began immediately on a brick-and-stone building with a 140-foot tower and arched windows in the Italianate style.[2] State officials and records arrived by riverboat, and Charleston became the capital on April 1, 1870. Although chosen in part for its centrality, Charleston proved relatively inaccessible and the city was slow in developing the amenities to support state government; the legislators subsequently voted to return to Wheeling, which again became the capital on May 21, 1875. Some Charleston citizens tried to stop the move by arresting those packing the archives, but state officials left in May and the records followed in September after legal challenges were dismissed.

The Linsly Building was rented again, from May 1875 until December 1876, when the "Third Capitol" was finished. It was Classical in style, with pilasters and pediments marking the entrances and corner pavilions; its clock tower made it the outstanding landmark on the cityscape.[3] Renewed complaints about Wheeling's location convinced legislators to reconsider, and in 1877 they asked the public to choose the state's capital by ballot, limiting the options to Charleston, Clarksburg, and Martinsburg.

Charleston was the people's choice, but it did not become the capital again until May 1, 1885. The new stone-and-brick "Fourth Capitol," in the Victorian Gothic style, eventually proved too small, and by 1903 an Annex, domed and in the Classical style, was built across the street.[4]

The alternation in style witnessed in West Virginia's successive Capitols—Victorian in the first Charleston structure (completed 1870), Classical at Wheeling (1876), Victorian Gothic at Charleston (1885), and Classical again in the Annex (1903)—demonstrates the American struggle to find an appropriate style for public buildings. While Classicism expressed the idea that American democracy was

Fig. 9. West Virginia's "Second Capitol," in Charleston (cornerstone laid November 3, 1869; completed in 1870; in use until 1875). A newspaper of the period referred to the structure as West Virginia's "temporary" Capitol and stated that the contractor's brick machine was producing 15,000 bricks a day. The cost of construction was reported to be $79,000. The contractor was the State House Company, a corporation led by Dr. John P. Hale. Photography courtesy of the Kanawha County Historical Society.

Fig. 10. West Virginia's "Third Capitol" in Wheeling (completed 1876; served as Capitol until 1885), as seen in a postcard mailed from Wheeling in 1912 when it was serving as City Hall. The cost of approximately $120,000 was financed through a bond issued from the City of Wheeling. Later used by local Wheeling agencies, it was demolished in 1956.

STATE CAPITOL AND GROUNDS, CHARLESTON, W. VA., DESTROYED BY FIRE JANUARY 3, 1921.

Fig. 11. West Virginia's "Fourth Capitol" (first occupied in 1885; in use until destroyed by fire in 1921), as seen in a postcard mailed from Charleston in 1922. This Capitol was located on the same Charleston site as the Second Capitol (fig. 9), on the block bounded by Washington, Lee, Capitol, and Dickson Streets. It has been suggested that this structure incorporated part of the Second Capitol but there is no evidence that this was the case. While Charleston had been selected by the state's citizens as capital in 1877, a contract for the new Capitol's construction was not let until 1880. The state staff and records returned to Charleston in 1885, but the interior of the new Capitol was not completely finished until 1887. The clock tower was almost two hundred feet tall. The cost, including land, was $389,923.58.

Fig. 12. The West Virginia Capitol Annex (constructed 1903) at the corner of Hale and Lee Streets, Charleston, as seen in a postcard mailed from Charleston in 1907. Designed by Harrison Albright, it cost more than $225,000. It housed state offices until 1932, when Cass Gilbert's Capitol was completed. At that point, the state sold the land and building, which then became the Kanawha County Library; later it housed Kanawha College and Morris Harvey College. The library moved in 1964 and the building, scheduled to be demolished, burned in 1967.

rooted in traditions then identified with ancient Greece, the "modern" Victorian style appealed to those who wanted to project a progressive image. By 1900, however, the preference for domed public buildings with Classical motifs, as seen in the Charleston Annex and innumerable county courthouses, was obvious in new civic structures across America; the National Capitol in Washington, with its massive dome and expansive wings, became the specific model for state capitols. Perhaps the Annex was West Virginia's attempt to turn its back on the Victorian Gothic style so proudly expressed two decades earlier in the Fourth Capitol.

That Capitol was destroyed in a dramatic fire on January 3, 1921.[5] The State Law Library, State Historical Library, Archives, and State Museum were safe in the Annex, but many state records and the Museum of Agriculture, which was said to be exceptional, were destroyed. Governor John Jacob Cornwell announced that the Senate would probably meet in the local YMCA and the House in the Armory: "There are no vacant buildings or offices in Charleston, but offers are already coming in from private citizens, from churches and elsewhere, and I am quite sure that all departments will be functioning again in a few days." He counseled legislators to erect "a building of modest size and of fitting design ... to contain halls for two houses of the Legislature, a sufficient number of committee rooms, the governor's office and offices for the secretary of state and attorney general, [as well as] a modern office building nearby to house all the boards and departments."[6] Cornwell's support for a "building of modest size" is not surprising; he was a Democrat, and in the debates over the financing of the new Capitol that followed, the Democrats would often accuse the Republicans of extravagance.

Before a decision on buildings could be made, the location of West Virginia's capital had to be fixed, since the fire encouraged some legislators to raise the issue anew. The revival of the debate over the capital's location must have been widely known, for a letter of inquiry from Baltimore architect Josias Pennington to Governor Cornwell dated nine days after the fire noted that "there seems to be some movement with a view of having the Capitol moved from Charleston to some other location." Cornwell reported to Pennington that there was "a sharp struggle" over the question of the location of the capital city. An amendment to a Senate joint resolution proposed that the Commission "not proceed to carry into effect [the resolution to hire an architect and select plans] until after such time as the question of the relocation of the seat of government is finally determined in the regular constitutional manner."[7]

On January 24, however, the Legislature voted that Charleston remain the capital. This made sense, for by 1921, Kanawha was the most populous county, the state's employees were settled there, facilities for state government were in place, five railroads serviced the city, and there were six hospitals, two daily newspapers, and fifty-seven churches representing "practically all of the leading denominations." The offices of the auditor, treasurer, and adjutant general, the Supreme Court of Appeals, and State Archives were satisfactorily housed in the Annex. Once the decision to stay was made, a temporary "clap-and-wallboard" building, the "Pasteboard Capitol," was quickly erected. Nineteen days after the fire, the Senate and House, in session at the YMCA and the Baptist Temple respectively, established a Commission to "secure plans and specifications for a Capitol Building."[8]

The destruction of the Capitol must have been a blow to incoming Governor Ephraim Morgan, a Republican who took office on March 4 in a state already troubled by financial problems. In his inaugural speech, delivered at the Charleston Armory, he noted that the deficit for the fiscal year ending June 30, 1920, was almost $500,000 and that a $1.5 million shortfall was estimated for 1920–21. Even before "the calamitous and utter destruction of the State Capitol," there was a need for a "great building program … called for by the various old and new State institutions, due to the growth of the demands made upon them."[9]

The state's financial status could not have been as dire as Morgan predicted, for the 1921 Legislative Session soon set the maximum price for a new Capitol at $6.5 million plus the insurance settlement the state would receive for the old Capitol and the amount to be gained from the sale of its property in downtown Charleston. Including the value of the land suggests that the legislators thought the new Capitol should be built at a different location in Charleston. The ambiguity of the "$6.5 million plus" figure remained problematic over the decade-long evolution of the new Capitol. Complications arose not only because of the uncertainty of the insurance settlement and the value of the old site, but also because there was a tendency to forget that out of this still unknown total a new site would have to be purchased. In early 1921, the value of the insurance on the old Capitol was undetermined, but the *New York Times* reported that the blanket policy on all West Virginia state buildings totaled $6 million. The value of the former site was also questionable, but at one point it was asserted that this property might sell for as much as $3 million. Yet another imponderable was how much a new site might cost. All these variables explain why the amount that could be spent on designing and building the new Capitol remained unsettled in the minds of West Virginians and their architect. In any case, setting a maximum price of "6.5 million plus" did not mean that $6.5 million was available in 1921. For any funds to be available, the Legislature had to pass an appropriation allowing the governor to spend money and indicate revenue sources to support it. In addition to appropriating money for design and construction, the legislators had to provide funds each year to pay rent for the office space needed until quarters in the new Capitol would become available; this was an expensive proposition as space was scarce in Charleston at the time.[10]

On May 11, 1921, Governor Morgan announced his appointments to the Capitol Building Commission, emphasizing that all candidates were characterized by "unimpeachable character and integrity," and some were experienced "in the construction of large building enterprises."[11] Commission membership could change with a new administration, and replacements were named when members resigned or died. Three of Morgan's appointees—Gohen C. Arnold, Herbert Fitzpatrick, and Edwin M. Keatley—served until the new Capitol was dedicated in 1932.

Because the commissioners chose the architect and approved the design, they might well be considered the patrons of the West Virginia Capitol.

At the Commission's first meeting on June 3, Governor Morgan's Secretary of State, Houston Young, was named Commission secretary. Cass Gilbert was mentioned at this meeting "as the type of architect we desire to employ for this work."[12] Whether this is a reference to Gilbert's fame or to his experience designing public buildings, and state capitols in particular, is not known. Gilbert had written to Governor Morgan two months earlier, "I would be very glad to be the architect of the New Capitol Building." He listed his credentials:

> I have had much experience in the planning and construction of public buildings. I designed and superintended the State Capitol of St. Paul, Minn., and the reconstruction and completion of the State Capitol at Little Rock, Ark. I won the first prize in the competition for the State Capitol of Montana, but owing to political conditions the enterprise was temporarily abandoned and I was again invited to compete, but declined. I won the competition for the State Capitol at Madison, Wis., but here again the Legislature postponed the work for several years and I was again invited to enter a competition, but declined on the ground that having won it in the first instance I was entitled to proceed.[13]

No other architect had such an extensive record designing state capitols. Gilbert had also submitted competition designs for the Capitols of Missouri and Washington and was invited to participate in the competitions for those of Nebraska and Utah. He was consulted when Japan was considering a new Parliament Building and when Cuba was planning a new National Capitol.[14] Gilbert's reputation as a staunch Republican may have been appealing to Governor Morgan, a Republican elected after four years of Democratic control.

The governor and commissioners announced Gilbert's appointment less than six weeks later. While their selection process seems well documented, at certain points it is not transparent and on occasion seems intentionally obscured. Two reports on the selection process were later prepared and a volume of the Commission's correspondence was published because of the criticism of the Commission's actions that was circulating by late 1922. On December 27, for example, headlines in the *Wheeling Daily News* must have alarmed the public: "Architect's Agreement Left Wide Open for Fee To Reach $900,000; NO LIMIT SET TO AMOUNT WHICH DRAWER OF PLANS MAY COLLECT—TO CAUSE INVESTIGATION." The article stated that Gilbert's contract "has drawn the fire of legislators, public spirited citizens and newspapers in all sections of the state. This is the first documentary evidence to be made public showing the alleged extravagant attitude and laxity marking the dealings of the Capitol Commission in matters connected with the project."[15]

That same month, the *Wheeling Intelligencer* published an editorial titled CAUSE FOR INDIGNATION. It declared, "If these provisions of the contract with Mr. Gilbert are true, as reported, it is a criminal waste of the people's money, and every citizen of the State should feel an honest indignation." Such public outrage had to be answered. In January 1923, the West Virginia Senate, which was controlled by

Fig. 13. Cass Gilbert, Minnesota State Capitol, St. Paul, 1895–1905, as seen in a period postcard. Gilbert won the competition in 1895, but ground was not broken until 1896. The cornerstone was set in 1898 and the complex completed in 1905. Gilbert would certainly have shown illustrations of his famous Minnesota Capitol to the West Virginia Capitol Building Commissioners in June 1921.

Fig. 14. Cass Gilbert's design for the Montana State Capitol, Helena, 1896, as reproduced in the British edition of *Architectural Record*, 1899. The role that Gilbert's design(s) played in this competition is unclear. Cass Gilbert may have shown this design to the commissioners in June 1921.

Fig. 15. Cass Gilbert's competition-winning design for the Wisconsin State Capitol, Madison, 1905, as illustrated in *The Architectural Record*, 1905. The caption below the illustration reads "Successful Competitive Design (Now Rejected) for the Wisconsin State Capitol, Front Elevation." Cass Gilbert may have shown this design to the commissioners in June 1921.

Democrats, established a Special Committee to investigate the Commission's activities; the House of Delegates, dominated by Republicans, asked the Commission to prepare a report. Both Senate and House required an accounting of the Commission's finances.[16] A careful analysis of the Commission's report to the House and their correspondence reveals omissions and errors. The commissioners had not suspected they would later be questioned, and precise documentation probably took a backseat to their desire to move quickly. By January 1923, when Gilbert's contract had long since been signed and he had already been paid $35,000, their reconstruction of events may have been flawed because of poor record-keeping or faulty memory. Some gaps can be filled from the archives, but it seems likely there was deliberate falsification. Keeping in mind these suggestions, let us now return to June 1921 and the Commission's deliberations.

The commissioners must have been impressed with the number of inquiries from architects that arrived even before their first meeting. The earliest, written little more than a week after the fire, came from Josias Pennington, designer of the Maryland State House Annex. Governor Cornwall replied, "It is difficult to tell when the question of the construction of the Capitol will be taken up or where the authority will be lodged." Among the others who wrote was the firm of Tracy & Swartwout; this letter, dated April 4, emphasized that Egerton Swartwout was one of the architects of the Missouri State Capitol, the "only Capitol Building ever built within appropriation." The Commission also received letters from other parties. The United Spanish War Veterans of Charleston urged that the new Capitol include a hall honoring veterans, and the Indiana Limestone Quarrymen's Association thanked Houston Young for meeting with its representative.[17] To promote the use of local stone, a bank cashier from Marlinton sent a sample from Pocahontas County to engineers in Brooklyn for analysis and forwarded the results to Governor Morgan.[18]

West Virginia architects hoped to be selected, although some firms understood that completing such a commission on their own would be difficult. On February 21, Egan & Reese of Charleston wrote to Cass Gilbert, "Nothing is in the least settled, but from the most reliable guess we are able to make we believe that the choice might favor a local (West Virginia) firm, backed by the reputation of an Eastern man of your prominence in the profession. It is our hope, therefore, that you may find it possible to collaborate with us." Herbert S. Kyle of Kyle & Wilkins, also of Charleston, wrote to Gilbert on March 30: "As you no doubt know, the State of West Virginia will shortly build a Capitol building.... The matter of awarding this commission is almost entirely in the hands of a legislative committee who very much favor home men." Kyle assured Gilbert that Kyle & Wilkins could win the commission if they could associate "with an architect who has already the organization, preferably a man who has had large experience in work of this character." The West Virginia firm of Wysong & Jones established a relationship with Henry Hornbostel of Pittsburgh, but whether other West Virginia firms tried to connect with architects outside the state is unknown. A week after the commissioners were appointed, US Senator Davis Elkins, Republican of West Virginia, reported to

Gilbert, "I think it is the intention to secure the service of a West Virginia architect, all things being equal."[19]

In his April letter to Governor Morgan, Cass Gilbert said he was motivated to write by a visit from an unnamed West Virginia architect who hoped to collaborate with him. Gilbert also referred to the other letters he had received: "In all these instances, they state … that their reason for calling upon me is that I have had special experience in such buildings." But even before citing his experience, Gilbert underlined his lack of interest in partnering with another architect: "I declined the proposals referred to, as I do not wish to take any step other than in direct communication with yourself or the authorized commissioners." If invited to West Virginia, Gilbert could bring drawings and provide "any information as to dimensions, materials or cost I may have." In reply, Gilbert received a form letter: "Your letter of April 7th relative to the planning of the New State Capitol Building for our State, duly received. The same will be turned over to the Building Committee as soon as one is appointed."[20]

While Gilbert was waiting for this response, he received a letter from Franklin Delano Roosevelt, at the time a lawyer in private practice in New York. Writing on May 20, Roosevelt offered to use his contacts to help the architect obtain an invitation to submit plans for the new Capitol. Across the bottom of Roosevelt's letter, Gilbert annotated: "I did *not* [Gilbert's emphasis] accept this offer of political influence. It was offensive to me. It presumed that I obtained my professional employment by political influence—not by merit." He noted the financial and ethical ramifications of Roosevelt's suggestion: "Had I accepted his offer it would have implied that I should use *my* [Gilbert's emphasis] influence to secure for him the writing of the contractor's bond—the agent's fees on which would probably be at least $100,000.00."[21] Gilbert's documentation of his reaction indicates how important it was for an architect at this time to maintain a careful paper trail. His annotations expose the political and financial intrigue that could surround public architectural commissions. Perhaps Gilbert did not need Roosevelt's assistance, for earlier that month he had asked Minnesota Senator Knute Nelson to deliver a letter indicating his interest in the project to Senator Elkins.

At their first meeting, the commissioners directed Secretary Young to meet with either the American Institute of Architects or the Office of the Supervising Architect of the US Treasury to "secure information as to the rules under which architects are selected and the different methods of selecting the same." In the meantime, the Commission's response to inquiries from architects was: "It has not yet been determined … how the architect will be selected." When one architect asked if he could come to Charleston, the reply was dismissive: "The Commission has letters from probably as many as a hundred firms over the country, and I hardly think that it will be possible for them to see the representatives of the different firms personally."[22]

Letters came from across the eastern United States. Twelve firms, including Gilbert's, were based in New York. Three were in Washington, DC, and three in Pittsburgh. West Virginia applicants included two firms from Huntington,

Richard M. Bates Jr. and Robert L. & Sidney L. Day, and two from Charleston, David Dick & Son (builders of the Pasteboard Capitol) and Wysong & Jones. Other firms wrote from Baltimore, Richmond, Philadelphia, Cincinnati, Columbus, and York, Pennsylvania.[23]

Cass Gilbert advanced his case, writing to the commissioners individually on June 15. Commissioner Keatley replied, "It is needless to say that your reputation ... is such that no introduction to the Commission is necessary ... and I perhaps violate no confidence when I say that your name was mentioned in the first meeting as the type of architect we desire to employ for this work." Commissioner Staunton wrote, "I am only giving you my personal views, but they are in favor of either a limited competition among a half-dozen of the prominent architects of the country, or of selecting an architect to do the work." He continued: "Your name has been suggested to me by a number of people. I might add that there will be no disposition to favor local architects simply because they are local architects. In fact, I rather doubt whether there is one in West Virginia competent to handle the work."[24]

On June 18, while Gilbert was in Vermont, he heard that the current head of McKim, Mead & White was in Charleston. Gilbert wired his New York office: "Telegraph Capitol Commission as follows: I would be glad to appear before Commission on their invitation and I would if desired show plans of various State Capitol Buildings designed by me." He also wired Senator Elkins: "Could you secure for me an invitation to appear before West Virginia State Capitol Commission—I understand other architects are being given hearings." Elkins assured Gilbert that he had "immediately" asked the Commission to invite the architect to Charleston.[25]

On or before June 20, Gilbert asked the following individuals—all but one of whom had been engaged with his state capitol projects—to provide letters of recommendation: Senator Frank B. Kellogg of Minnesota (who had known Gilbert for thirty years), Senator Knute Nelson of Minnesota (governor when Gilbert won the competition for their Capitol), Governor J. A. O. Preus of Minnesota, John I. Moore (chairman of the Arkansas Commission that engaged Gilbert to complete their Capitol), George W. Donaghey (governor of Arkansas when Gilbert completed the Arkansas Capitol), and W. G. McAdoo (who had selected Gilbert to design the US Treasury Annex in Washington when he was secretary of the Treasury). Their recommendations were enthusiastic.[26] Senator Kellogg wrote: "I think he is the greatest architect in the United States. He built the St. Paul Capitol about twenty-five years ago and it is conceded by everybody to be one of the finest gems of architecture in America. He is really not only a great artist, but a builder, and I am sure that your Capitol Commission would make no mistake in selecting him." Governor Preus praised the Minnesota Capitol as "one of the most beautiful buildings in the United States." Ex-Governor Donaghey emphasized, "Cass Gilbert had entire charge of our Capitol during my administration.... As an architectural achievement we have the best piece of work in the south, so attested by all who have seen it." The writers confirmed Gilbert's moral character and administrative abilities, Ex-Governor Donaghey noting, "[He is] a man of high sense of honor, great executive ability, and stands at the top of his profession in America," and Governor Preus reporting, "He is absolutely honest, reliable and I am sure you would make no mistake in selecting him." Moore endorsed Gilbert for "honest and efficient administration, good design and sound construction." Other firms also submitted letters of recommendation, but Gilbert's completed projects for Minnesota and Arkansas enabled him to provide specific references testifying to his experience in state capitol design and construction.[27] While Gilbert waited for his invitation, on June 21 Frederick W. Garber of Garber & Woodward came to Charleston from Cincinnati on his own initiative, where he met with Secretary Young and several commissioners.[28]

There were apparently no Commission meetings between June 3 and 28. A letter of June 23 stated that it had "not been determined what method the Commission will pursue in selecting an architect." A letter that same day from Commissioner Arnold to Senator Elkins reveals, however, that Cass Gilbert "has been most seriously considered by a number of the members of the Commission."

On June 28, Secretary Young reported that the Office of the Supervising Architect of the US Treasury had listed three ways to select an architect—direct selection, limited competition, and unlimited competition—and had recommended hiring Warren P. Laird, an expert on the "matter of employing architects," as a consultant. The Commission must have invited Laird that very day, for he arrived the next. Secretary Young also reported that the Pittsburgh branch of the AIA had recommended direct selection over competition, the latter being "slow and costly; in addition, direct selection meant the architect could advise on selecting the best site."[29]

At this point, Cass Gilbert's standing with the commissioners becomes evident, for he was the first architect invited to Charleston. On June 28, Governor Morgan's secretary called Gilbert's office and asked if he could catch the train to Charleston the next day and meet with the commissioners on June 30. Gilbert's assistant, R. D. Read, who answered the phone, reported that the architect was not expected until the next morning. The governor's secretary then asked Read if he knew "what the subject of the message was." Read replied that he did and asked "if this was an official invitation from the Capitol Commission for Mr. Gilbert to appear before them. [The secretary] said it was." Read assured the caller that Gilbert would arrive on June 30 as proposed. This was the first of more than thirty trips that Gilbert would make to Charleston between 1921 and 1933.[30]

Time-pressured correspondence during this period was usually conducted by telegram; the phone call indicates that Governor Morgan needed to know immediately if Gilbert could be in Charleston soon, perhaps even at the same time as Professor Laird. The commissioners were apparently already considering an offer to Gilbert, since Secretary Young's June 29 response to a letter of inquiry informed the sender that "even before you receive this letter some action may be taken on the selection of an architect."[31]

The commissioners did not publicize their invitation to Gilbert. Although he arrived on June 30, the headlines in the *Charleston Daily Mail* that day read: "ONLY ONE ARCHITECT IS CALLED BY COMMISSION; Warren Laird of University of

Pennsylvania Giving Views on New Capitol." An article in the July 1 *Mail* documents Laird's visit ("New Capitol Site Will Be At Least Ten Acres, Is Unofficial Report; New Plot to Be Selected by Commission; Twice as Large as Location of the Burned Structure; EXPERT ARCHITECT IS HERE FOR MEETING; Advice of Professor Warren Laird of University of Pennsylvania Is Sought as to Best Plan of Procedure"), but makes no reference to Gilbert. The first mention of Gilbert's visit, that afternoon in the *Mail*, suggested he was there to consult on the site: "Capitol Commission is Near Definite Decision; Discussing Site with Cass Gilbert, Prominent New York Architect; Both West Side and East End Under Consideration."[32]

The intrigue that surrounds Gilbert's appointment as architect is exposed by a visit and telephone call he received in New York on June 27, immediately before his June 30–July 3 trip to Charleston. The visitor was Theodore T. Sansbury, an architect from Parkersburg. Gilbert's meticulous transcript documents Sansbury's morning visit and his 4:45 P.M. telephone call.[33] Sansbury identified himself as a "personal friend of Mr. Houston G. Young, Secretary of State and secretary of the Capitol Commission," and informed Gilbert that Young would be willing to confirm the following proposal: If "I [Gilbert] will agree to enter into a joint arrangement ... for the State Capitol then he [Sansbury] can assure me that I will be appointed architect of the building," but, Gilbert noted, "he must know immediately as there is a meeting tomorrow." To demonstrate his connection with Young, Sansbury presented a copy of the telegram Gilbert sent to the Commission on June 18. The West Virginia architect reported that Young had not written but was prepared to speak with Gilbert on the phone. Sansbury's possession of the telegram and his statement that Young would communicate with Gilbert only by telephone hint at the conspiracy that seems to surround this encounter.

Sansbury warned Gilbert that "George B. Post & Sons, McKim, Mead & White, John Russell Pope, Henry Bacon and a Philadelphia concern, not named, are [also] being considered." Sansbury wanted "to forestall and prevent a competition" and believed that if Gilbert would "join with him" the commission would be awarded to Gilbert "by direct selection." Sansbury repeatedly told Gilbert that if a collaboration could be arranged, Sansbury "would telegraph to West Virginia today and that the matter would be settled at the meeting tomorrow."

Gilbert was "not favorably impressed" and counseled Sansbury that he "had been repeatedly approached by different West Virginia architects and by representatives of contractors and engineers in regard to this building." Gilbert emphasized that "I had declined to commit myself in any way and that I had no representatives on the ground nor was I tied up with anybody. That if I should be appointed by the Board I wanted to be free to serve the State to its best interests without prior committal of any kind." Gilbert concluded: "I told him that if I went to Charleston I would probably talk with all the Commissioners, Mr. Young included ... [and I] declined to commit myself or to accept his proposal or give him any encouragement."

Sansbury called that afternoon at 4:45, and a transcript records Gilbert and Sansbury's conversation. Sansbury pressured Gilbert again, saying, "If I [Sansbury] should report by telegram today that you can make this arrangement with me then there is a strong possibility of your being called to Charleston." When Gilbert asked, "Suppose you report that I am non-committal in the matter," Sansbury replied, "then I believe the matter will go to competition." Gilbert replied that he did not think he would enter a competition.

Sansbury was at least in part misinformed, for Gilbert's refusal to partner with him did not lead to a competition, and whether Sansbury was backed by Houston Young remains in doubt. But why would Sansbury travel to New York and make this suggestion if he did not think it could succeed? Perhaps Sansbury had been told by one or more of the commissioners that he and Gilbert would be awarded the job if Gilbert would agree to a partnership, or perhaps Sansbury hoped this would be the case. Possibly Sansbury knew that Gilbert was the leading candidate and hoped that he might be partnered with the New York architect if he could guarantee a connection prior to Gilbert's appointment.

Or were Sansbury's overtures to Gilbert intended to test Gilbert's integrity? Such a possibility cannot be ruled out; Gilbert's careful record of Sansbury's offer can be seen as an attempt to protect himself should questions arise about his selection. If this visit were such a test, Gilbert proved himself immune to the temptation of Sansbury's offer. It is not documented if Sansbury communicated the results of his visit—or Cass Gilbert's reluctance to enter a competition—to Young or other commissioners.

The Capitol Building Commission met on the last three days of June. Professor Laird was in Charleston on June 29 and 30 and presumably attended its meetings on those days.[34] It seems no transcript for Gilbert's June 30 presentation has survived, and it is not known if Laird observed it. Considering Gilbert's meticulous record-keeping, the lack of a transcript suggests he may have been asked to keep the discussion private. Because there is no record that he met again with the commissioners before his selection was announced on July 13, it must have been at this meeting that he showed photographs and drawings of his other capitols and capitol projects, all of which featured domes on high drums (see figs. 13–15).

That Cass Gilbert was the first architect invited to Charleston clearly shows the commissioners' preference for him; he was a persuasive speaker, and his presentation on June 30 most likely consolidated his position. His ability to influence patrons is documented by the draftsman and architect Hugh Ferriss, who worked in Gilbert's office from about 1912 to 1915. Ferriss had watched as Gilbert "fascinated and swayed some large group of clients with his handsome conception of their clubhouse, skyscraper, or state capitol." Ferriss called this "the diplomat's iron hand and silk glove."[35]

The events that followed Gilbert's June 30 presentation suggest that before leaving to return to New York he was told he was the leading candidate; perhaps he was even offered the commission tentatively, contingent on the commissioners' response to presentations by other architects, or perhaps they only wanted to meet with other firms to justify a decision already made. Whatever their motivations, at this point they moved quickly, announcing that architects who wanted "a full and complete hearing" could receive one on July 7. On Tuesday, July 5, several national firms were sent telegrams: "Capitol Building Commission will be in session Thursday, July seventh, for purpose of selecting architect for new Capitol. Will be very glad to have you present. This invitation implies no obligation on part of Commission."[36] The invited firms, which Young called "the best architects in the country," had all designed one or more important public buildings: Henry Bacon, architect of the Lincoln Memorial; Arnold W. Brunner, designer of a group of public buildings for Cleveland; Carrère & Hastings, architects of the New York Public Library; Herts & Robertson, designers of the Brooklyn Academy of Music; McKim, Mead & White, the firm that designed the Boston Public Library; John Russell Pope, designer of Union Station in Richmond, Virginia; and George B. Post & Sons, designers of the Wisconsin Capitol. Asking such firms to appear on such short notice is surprising and suggests the proceedings may have been a formality. Nevertheless, representatives from five of the firms made presentations on July 7: Bacon; Brunner; Herts; McKim, Mead & White; and George B. Post & Sons. Other firms not on the list also presented that day: Richard M. Bates Jr. of Huntington; F. R. Walker of Walker & Weeks of Cleveland; and A. F. Wysong of Princeton, West Virginia.[37]

The minutes record few details, with the exception of a statement by Henry Bacon, who removed himself from consideration. The Commission documented that he advised them "not to select him, as he did not have sufficient organization with which he felt he could do justice to such a large undertaking."[38] By documenting Bacon's reluctance in their later report, the Commission justified their selection of Cass Gilbert, whose experience in successfully managing design, engineering, and construction on such a scale was well documented.

Meanwhile, on July 7, Gilbert was in New York, anticipating an invitation to Charleston:

> About 3 o'clock, daylight savings time, today I called up Mr. Houston Young at Charleston, W. Va., on the long distance telephone and inquired if the Capitol Commission would want to see me there tomorrow. I told him that I had hoped to receive a message from them by this time but if I delayed the call any longer I would not be able to get the 3:40 train but if they would like to see me I could come on the 3:40 train and be there at noon tomorrow. I asked him if they had arrived at any decision. He said they had not arrived at a decision yet and that the Board was now in session. I asked him if he could give me any news about it. He said he could not. I said I hoped that I was going to be successful and he gave a cordial response implying that he hoped so too, or that it would be agreeable to him if I was. I asked him to speak to the Governor and ask if the Governor thought I ought to come down on this afternoon's train or if the Governor wanted to see me. He left the telephone for a couple of minutes and returned and said in effect that the Governor thought it was not necessary for me to come today, that they would let me know tomorrow.[39]

The Commission would have required Gilbert's presence in Charleston for three possible reasons: to conduct a further interview, to negotiate the terms of the contract, or to announce he had been selected as architect. When he had heard nothing by Friday morning, Gilbert wired Young: "If you desire to communicate with me before Monday, I shall be [at my country home] in Ridgefield, Connecticut; my office is closed on Saturday during July and August; hope to hear from you."[40]

The Commission's minutes state that Gilbert was not to be notified of his selection until after he had agreed their terms would be acceptable. On Friday, July 8, Secretary Young sent Gilbert a telegram: "Direct selection of architect will be made by Commission. Commission has determined that six per cent compensation to architect must include all supervisory charges of any kind or character; also engineering and clerk of works; also report on site location and supervisory charges on foundation tests. Wire if such terms would be satisfactory to you."[41]

While the Commission Report published in 1923 gives Wednesday, July 13, as the date of the decision to hire Gilbert, the telegram is dated July 8, 6:15 P.M. The architect received it Saturday morning, July 9, at 11:50 A.M. He replied, "Your telegram July eighth received; terms are satisfactory to me." Accepting these terms was a concession for Gilbert, for it was not customary for the architect to pay engineering fees.[42] About 4:30 P.M. that same day, Gilbert received a call from Houston Young; he repeated the conversation to Cass Junior, who transcribed it:

> Young: The Commission wants to see you. When can you come to Charleston?
> Gilbert: Want to see me? Thursday next at noon?
> Young: Yes.
> I asked him what action had been taken.
> He replied: Can't say. Not at liberty to tell you now.[43]

Although the discussion suggests that Gilbert was not needed until Thursday, July 14, he left New York on July 11. When he arrived in Charleston on Tuesday, July 12, the commissioners were still hearing presentations. Edward B. Franzheim and F. F. Farris, both of Wheeling, presented on July 12; J. W. Cross of Cross & Cross of New York City presented on Wednesday, July 13. At 7:26 that morning—when the Commission had yet to hear the presentation by Cross & Cross—Gilbert sent his wife, Julia, a telegram: "Capital Appointment awarded to me. Contract will be signed tomorrow. Your helpful advice and encouragement brought success. Announcement will be made tomorrow morning's newspapers. All well. Home Saturday. Cass and I send love and congratulations. CG."[44] Gilbert's early morning telegram to Julia on Wednesday reveals that he was offered the commission on Tuesday, July 12, the day he arrived in Charleston.

On Thursday, July 14, the *Charleston Gazette* headlined: "CASS GILBERT, ARCHITECT OF FAME, TO PLAN NEW CAPITOL; Man Who Designed Woolworth Building Picked By Commission To Plan New Home For State Government; SELECTION OF SITE TO FOLLOW SOON; Gilbert Promises To Help Find Place For State House; First Important Step of Commission." The reference to the Woolworth Building was relevant for Charleston's citizens, who had been shopping at an F. W. Woolworth & Company store for years. The national press presumed readers needed neither Gilbert's full name nor a reference to the Woolworth Building. The *Washington Times*, for example, announced: "GILBERT TO DRAW PLANS OF COSTLY W. VA. STATEHOUSE; New York Architect to Assist in Location and Construction of New Capitol," while the *New York Times* reported: "WEST VIRGINIA PICKS GILBERT AS ARCHITECT; He Will Design the New Capitol to Take the Place of Burned Structure."[45] If Governor Morgan and the commissioners intended to draw national attention to West Virginia, hiring Cass Gilbert and budgeting more than $6.5 million for the project had accomplished their goal.

In reporting this "first important action of the state capitol commission," the *Charleston Daily Mail* emphasized Gilbert's reputation and his role in selecting a site: "In the appointment of Cass Gilbert of New York, the commission obtains the services of a man for whom no job of architecture in the country is too big. The capitol commission has other problems to deal with, but the appointment of one of the first [i.e., leading] architects in America gives absolute assurance to the people of this state on one cardinal point: they are going to see erected in Charleston a noble building of SUITABLE DESIGN on a SUITABLE SITE." The editor accentuated the choice of site "because it is certain that the commission will not select a location of which this eminent architect, according to the best of his professional judgment, disapproves."[46]

Before leaving for New York, Gilbert surveyed the Charleston area for potential sites. He returned the following week and on July 21 presented a contract to the commissioners. After discussion and revisions, it was signed on July 23.[47] The contract clarified his roles: "It is agreed that the scope of the Architect's professional employment and authority shall include all architectural and supervisory services of every sort in connection with the grounds and the design and construction of the building or buildings and the embellishment thereof... he shall advise regarding bids and bidders." Furthermore, "he shall supervise the construction in person or by duly authorized agent."

In their 1923 "Report to the House of Delegates," the commissioners justified their direct selection of the architect by pointing out that a competition would have led to a delay of at least six months, cost an additional $30,000 or more, and required them to select the site without the possibility of consulting the architect. Furthermore, most architects had agreed they would enter only competitions managed by the AIA. Also, although the patron was allowed to make the final choice based on the AIA Committee's recommendations, the Commission emphasized it "did not want to place itself in a position where it would be required to employ an architect that was not satisfactory to it, or be obliged to ignore the recommendations of the Committee."[48]

The commissioners had worked quickly and efficiently. In less than three months, they had resolved how to proceed and signed a contract with a leading American architect. Selecting a site, acquiring it, and approving a final design would take considerably longer.

## CASS GILBERT'S CONTRACT: THE FACTS AND THE CONTROVERSY

When the project was completed, the architect's total compensation was to equal 6 percent of the cost of construction. To cover the architect's overhead during the early stages of the project, payments were scheduled according to his progress:

$10,000 when the site was selected;
$25,000 when preliminary sketches were submitted;
$25,000 when preliminary sketches were approved and the architect was directed to proceed with working drawings and specifications;
$50,000 when the working drawings and specifications were certified by the architect to be one-half complete;
$50,000 when the working drawings and specifications were complete and a contract had been let for the building or buildings.
The balance was to be paid in proportional installments as work proceeded thereafter.[49]

In a letter of April 20, 1925, describing his contract, Gilbert cited other clients who were paying the same percentage: "My fee of 6% is my regular and usual charge. It is the *minimum* [Gilbert's emphasis] standard charge recommended by the American Institute of Architects. It is what I am paid by such bodies as the Chamber of Commerce of the United States of America, the Federal Government, the Federal Reserve Bank, ... etc., etc." He made "a special concession at the request of the Capitol Commission and on the understanding that the work would be progressed rapidly and completed in a relatively short time and that the overhead expenses would not be as large as where a work extends over a number of years."

This turned out not to be the case, of course, but no one in 1921 could have suspected that political difficulties would delay the completion of the complex by more than a decade. Gilbert described his concessions: "I was to pay the salary of the local superintendent and furnish at my expense the service of structural engineers, mechanical engineers, electrical engineers, heating and ventilating engineers and such other experts. These charges are customarily borne by the owner. In this case *I* [Gilbert's emphasis] have paid them out of my fee."

This letter, written after the first wing of the complex was completed, was addressed to Gilbert's representative on site, who was being questioned by the Senate Investigating Committee. Gilbert advised him how to reply to the committee's questions: "If this fee question is brought up you might give them some idea of the cost of preparing drawings for a *modern* [Gilbert's emphasis] building—designers, draftsmen, computors, specification writers, accountants, etc.—and how well-prepared drawings enable an owner to get lower and better bids and save money that might otherwise go into 'extras.'" Gilbert advised his supervisor to "Point out [that] in this building the 'extras' were less than the 'credits' and that the building as built actually cost about $30,000 less than the *contracts* [Gilbert's emphasis]. No office in this country or anywhere else renders such effective service."[50] The "computors" listed here probably refer to staff members who calculated the weight of materials, the stresses experienced by arches and supporting members, and so forth.

Gilbert's six percent fee was criticized as excessive, in part because the basis on which it was calculated was misinterpreted. A December 1921 editorial in the *Wheeling Intelligencer* titled "CAUSE FOR INDIGNATION," for example, incorrectly reported the contract's provisions.[51] In response, Cass Gilbert wrote to Secretary Young: "I understand that it has been stated that my fees are based on the cost of the land as well as the cost of the building. It should be made clear that I have nothing to do with the cost of the land and have no fee therein." Gilbert continued:

> I have just seen a clipping . . . which has doubtless come to your attention and it occurs to me to send you duplicate copies of the American Institute of Architects' document "Series A, No. 124," entitled "Professional Practice of Architects," "Details of Service to be Rendered," "Schedule of Proper Minimum Charges," as showing the standard of charges customary and usual for architects' professional services. . . . A careful comparison will show that my contract is based upon the minimum charge, that I assumed the cost of the services of heating, plumbing and ventilating, mechanical engineers, electrical engineers, etc. I advise that my contract be published in full. . . .
>
> There seem to have been some wild statements made to the effect that the building will cost $15,000,000.00. It should be made clear that the building will not cost one-half that amount and probably not exceeding 6½ or $7,000,000.00. . . .
>
> There is nothing in my contract that is not reasonably fair and equitable to the State and I would be pleased to meet the fullest investigation.[52]

Gilbert's contract was still being attacked by members of the Legislature and in the popular West Virginia press in December 1922 and January 1923.[53]

CHAPTER TWO

# "The Most Remarkable Architect of His Generation in America"

I always had the most constant interest in all the buildings that I have designed. I take almost the same interest that a parent would in his children. While my time and other duties do not permit me always to follow them up, I nevertheless have a lively interest in them, and I am most solicitous that the State Capitol of West Virginia should be an example of how a building can be properly developed and preserved, for it will set an example to other states.

Cass Gilbert to Walter E. Clark, editor, *Charleston Daily Mail*, April 8, 1932

Fig. 16. *The Woolworth Building at Night (1910–1913).* Photograph, c. 1913.

WHEN CASS GILBERT DIED IN 1934, THE *LONDON TIMES* TESTIfied, "A list of his most important buildings only would be long enough to prove him the most remarkable architect of his generation in America." Gilbert's own remarks above—in which he expressed his personal connection with and commitment to his buildings, his impressive schedule, self-assurance, and confidence in the lasting importance of his work—suggest additional reasons for his international fame.[1]

Since several accounts of Gilbert's life have recently been published, it is sufficient here to establish a foundation that will elucidate his role as architect of the West Virginia Capitol.[2] Our story moves about from his later life to the formative years, from his education to his many projects and honors, and returns to his most important buildings as needed. It reviews what made him an ideal architect for this Capitol as well as why his fame extended worldwide, was eclipsed, and has been renewed. After the decades in which his work was unappreciated, Cass Gilbert is now recognized as a respected architect who has earned a well-deserved place in the history of American architecture.

The rise and fall of Gilbert's reputation parallel that of the Beaux-Arts architectural movement. His Minnesota State Capitol (1895–1905, see fig. 13), which drew heavily on his Beaux-Arts background, and his Gothic-inspired Woolworth Building in Manhattan (1909–1913) explain his leap to fame; praise abounded and he received many important commissions. By 1932, when the West Virginia Capitol was completed and his US Supreme Court Building under way, however, many European and American architects were turning away from the Beaux-Arts and Classical traditions toward Modernism.

Gilbert wrote the words quoted at the opening of this chapter late in his life. The West Virginia Capitol and Supreme Court Building capped a career that had begun with homes, churches, and public and commercial buildings, and later brought him international fame with the Minnesota Capitol and the Woolworth Building. Gilbert was seldom modest about his accomplishments; in 1915, for example, he made a drawing that juxtaposed his Minnesota Capitol, New York Custom House, St. Louis Art Museum, and the recently completed Woolworth Building to the Parthenon and other renowned structures (see fig. 17).[3]

The state capitol and skyscraper are two distinctive American contributions to the history of architecture; the Minnesota Capitol and Woolworth Building are quintessential examples of each. In choosing Cass Gilbert, West Virginia's governor and Capitol Building Commission revealed their desire for a prestigious architect and building.

Gilbert died just two years after the completion of his West Virginia complex, and his obituaries reflect ongoing admiration. The *London Times* clarified the respect for Gilbert at the time, while the *New York Times* asserted that "New York City lost the prophet of her architectural distinction." *Archi*, published by an undergraduate architectural fraternity, suggested that Gilbert had been unique among the pantheon of American architects: "America has had its Richardsons, its

## KEY DATES: LIFE AND WORKS

| | |
|---|---|
| 1859 | Born in Zanesville, Ohio |
| 1868 | Family moved to St. Paul, Minnesota |
| 1878–1879 | Studied at MIT |
| 1880 | First of many European study tours |
| 1880–1882 | Worked with McKim, Mead & White in New York City |
| 1882 | Returned to St. Paul |
| 1885–1891 | Partnership with James Knox Taylor in St. Paul |
| 1895–1905 | Minnesota State Capitol (fig. 13) |
| 1896 | Won competition for Montana State Capitol; decision overturned (fig. 14) |
| 1899 | Moved to New York City |
| 1899–1907 | United States Custom House, New York |
| 1904 | Won competition for Wisconsin State Capitol; decision overturned (fig. 15) |
| 1909–1913 | Woolworth Building, New York (fig. 16) |
| 1909–1917 | Completed Arkansas State Capitol, begun by George R. Mann |
| 1918–1919 | US Army Supply Base, Brooklyn |
| 1921–1932 | West Virginia State Capitol, Charleston (fig. 21) |
| 1928–1935 | United States Supreme Court Building, Washington, DC (fig. 20) |
| 1934 | Died in Brockenhurst, England |

Fig. 17. Cass Gilbert, *A Selection of His Buildings With Historic Monuments*, 1915. Drawing. Gilbert's buildings include the Minnesota Capitol, the St. Louis Art Museum, the Woolworth Building, and the US Custom House in New York. They are compared with the Egyptian Pyramids at Giza, the Parthenon in Athens, two Gothic Cathedrals (Durham in England, and Notre Dame in Paris), the Church of San Marco in Venice, and the Taj Mahal in India. The only other contemporary building included is St. Thomas Aquinas Church in New York City, designed by Cram, Goodhue, and Ferguson (completed 1913).

McKims, its Sullivans, and its Goodhues, but we may point to but one CASS GILBERT. The very mention of his name will bring a flush of pride to those who knew him."[4]

Yet soon after these days of glory, Gilbert became identified with a bygone era, and his buildings were considered out of date. The neglect and even abuse his reputation suffered in the decades following 1934 were profound; the contemporary architect Robert A. M. Stern notes that "among the many exceptionally accomplished architects of one hundred years ago Cass Gilbert has been until recently, more egregiously overlooked than virtually any other."[5] It was Gilbert's position as a leading proponent of the eclectic Beaux-Arts style that made him and his works vulnerable to criticism by supporters of the modern. A late twentieth-century summary of his life and works concludes not with his Supreme Court Building but with a slightly earlier project, the stone cladding planned for the George Washington Bridge in New York (1926–31): "One of Gilbert's last commissions is today best known for the absence of [his] contribution.... The heavy steel towers and cable anchor pylons were to have been enclosed in masonry designed by Gilbert, but conditions imposed by the worsening business depression prevented completion. Today, ironically, many observers believe the bridge achieves its particular beauty specifically because the structural system is not hidden behind Gilbert's masonry."[6] Such a cavalier rejection would have astounded his contemporaries but not historians of the decades that followed, who dismissed the historical elements on which the Beaux-Arts and other revival styles were based. At the same time, architects who emphasized change and modernity, including Frank Lloyd Wright in the United States and Le Corbusier, Walter Gropius, and Mies van der Rohe in Europe, were thrust into prominence. Although Gilbert's preference for the elaborate ornamentation characteristic of the Beaux-Arts style diminished during the course of his career, as witnessed in a comparison of the Capitols of Minnesota and West Virginia (see figs. 13, 21), he never abandoned his belief in the validity of Classical forms for the design of public buildings. His assessment of Goodhue's Nebraska Capitol (see fig. 88) is revealing: "I do not find myself enthusiastic over the design as it looks to me more like a crematorium than a public building, though I am bound to say that it has certain artistic qualities, which are characteristic of all Goodhue's work." Gilbert rejected Goodhue's design because it was for a "public building," not a functional structure such as a crematorium. Gilbert's US Army Supply Base had demonstrated his understanding of this distinction, for its austere style has nothing in common with the public buildings in which he specialized after the Woolworth Building. Gilbert added: "I have no doubt [Goodhue] will make a very interesting thing of it. Though I greatly doubt if the state will ever build that tower or anything like it."[7] The state did build it, and Gilbert's judgment indicated how uncomfortable he was with the changes affecting architecture in the 1920s. In 1933, he wrote that he hoped his Classically inspired Supreme Court Building would "cause some reaction against the silly modernistic movement that has had such a hold here for the last few years."[8]

The change in architecture is manifested in the reception of Gilbert's two completed state capitols: Minnesota's was widely praised, West Virginia's ignored after the initial flurry of excitement.[9] The temporary structures erected for the 1893 World's Columbian Exposition had demonstrated the possibilities of Beaux-Arts architecture; the Minnesota Capitol was lauded as an early example of how to capture this ebullient style in permanent materials.[10] By 1932, when the West Virginia complex was dedicated, Modernism in architecture was already being celebrated in *The International Style: Architecture Since 1922*, an exhibition at New York's Museum of Modern Art. Even Gilbert's handsome Supreme Court Building, completed in 1935, received negative reports, including scathing words from Frank Lloyd Wright.[11]

With historical perspective, however, as well as new scholarship on the architect and his works, and even popular interest, as seen in the creation of the Cass Gilbert Society, for laypeople and scholars alike, the architect of West Virginia's Capitol has been thrust back into prominence. His buildings and his passion for them are better understood, and the organizational skills needed to produce and document his enormous output are becoming clear as his archives are mined. His dedication to the Classical tradition and his vision of the lasting importance of his works are now appreciated.[12] Perhaps time has afforded a new perspective. We are now better able to recognize, in addition to the excellence of his buildings, the impressive productivity of his atelier, his bold choice to control the quality of production by heading his own firm without partners, his meticulous organization and attention to detail while never losing sight of the broader impression and function of his buildings, and the personal confidence he projected.[13] Cass Gilbert revealed his self-assurance when he replied to a question about how an architect finds clients: "I did not know; . . . I did not solicit business but I supposed it came to me because I was known to build certain classes of buildings well, and that people liked what I did. In short, it came from such general reputation as I might have."[14] Julia Finch Gilbert explained her husband's passion for his profession: "his whole attitude toward life was an eager, impulsive, and enthusiastic desire to express to others the enthusiasm he himself felt for his work."[15] Such zeal communicated his pride and confidence.

How one client viewed Gilbert is evident in comments he made at the dinner for eight hundred people held to celebrate the opening of the Woolworth Building. Although the event was ostensibly to pay tribute to the architect, who had designed, engineered, and managed the construction of "the biggest building ever built for practical use," the ceremonies praised both architect and patron.[16] Woolworth thanked the guests for accepting his invitation "to do honor to one of the greatest architects in this world." He added, "Some of the greatest architects of this country were anxious and ready and willing to do this work." But "it required an extraordinary architect to put up a structure of this nature. I have never regretted my choice of the guest who honors us this evening. . . . He had done great work before he ever touched this building. However, he is a greater architect today than he ever was." Gilbert lauded Woolworth in turn: "He praises me and I praise him. He is a real patron of art as ... were the wool merchants and bankers of Italy who made their cities beautiful."[17]

The Woolworth Building was completed just a year before the beginning of World War I, which profoundly affected American life. A postwar depression was succeeded by the prosperity and exuberance of the later 1920s and then by the difficult years of the Great Depression. The economic collapse and ensuing social problems were felt throughout the country, yet American builders, businessmen, and educators did not shy away from proclaiming themselves in architectural icons. Art Deco and Gothic skyscrapers altered skylines, announcing the continuation of commercial and academic successes. William van Alen's Art Deco Chrysler Building (1929–30) and its rival, William Lamb's Empire State Building (completed in 1931), for instance, vied to replace Gilbert's Woolworth Building as the tallest structure in the world, while Charles Klauder's Cathedral of Learning at the University of Pittsburgh elicited pride as the country's tallest educational building (1921–31). All three were functioning by 1932 when Charleston's Capitol was dedicated. It was in this social and architectural context that the dome of the West Virginia Capitol was constructed. For some of the state's citizens, it must have been a symbol of hope during the days of hardship and an expression of perseverance, state pride, and patriotism. For others, it may well have been a symbol of money denied them and their families in order to create a gilded monument for the state.

The West Virginia Capitol was the last project Gilbert would see completed. He died on May 17, 1934, while his Supreme Court Building was still under construction.

Cass Gilbert was born in Zanesville, Ohio, on November 24, 1859. His father, Samuel Augustus Gilbert, worked for the US Coast and Geodetic Survey as a topographical engineer, owned a foundry in Zanesville, and had served in the Union army. Cass Gilbert spent his early years in Ohio until the family relocated in 1868 to St. Paul, Minnesota, shortly before his father's death. Throughout his life, his family was an important source of support. Long before Gilbert's catapult to international recognition, his mother, Elizabeth Fulton Wheeler Gilbert, played a role in his development as an architect. A steadfast force in his life, she encouraged him and helped pay for the early European travels pivotal to his career.

In addition to European travel, Gilbert's professional training included apprenticeship, formal education, and work in the offices of an important firm—all common educational experiences for architects at the time. It did not include study at the École des Beaux-Arts in Paris, which established one of the styles that influenced his early work. The first American of note to study there was Richard Morris Hunt, one of thirteen men who founded the American Institute of Architects in 1857. Others who followed included H. H. Richardson (whose buildings Gilbert admired), Charles McKim (for whose firm Gilbert worked), Ernest Flagg (architect of the Singer Building, completed in 1908, and, like the later Woolworth

Building, a notable addition to the Manhattan skyline), and Louis Sullivan (theorist and creator of some early tall buildings).

Instead of going to Paris to study, in 1878, after an eighteen-month apprenticeship as a draftsman in the St. Paul office of Abraham Radcliffe, Gilbert enrolled in the two-year program offered by the first American professional school of architecture, at the Massachusetts Institute of Technology. He studied there under Eugène Létang and William Robert Ware, proponents of the Beaux-Arts style and system of architectural education pioneered at the École.[18] Gilbert chose not to return to MIT for the second year, however, deciding instead to observe and sketch on an eight-month study tour through Italy, France, and England.[19] These travels proved crucial for his development, providing inspiration, artistic practice, and a portfolio of drawings he could show prospective employers; the draftsmanship and watercolor skills he honed on this trip served him the rest of his life.[20]

Once Gilbert was an established architect, he returned to Europe almost annually for relaxation, inspiration, and often to work on a particular issue. During the five months he spent there in 1897–98 as he was finalizing plans for his first domed structure, the Minnesota Capitol, he climbed Brunelleschi's Florence Cathedral dome to examine its design, structure, and engineering. As he stated in a letter to his West Virginia patrons in 1921, "It is my purpose to make a quick trip to France and Italy with a special view to studying, and refreshing my impressions of, the great monumental and classical buildings which I can see there." He wanted to bring to West Virginia "the very best work that I can do with a fresh mind and the clear impressions which would arise from just such a trip at this time." After he returned from his European trip in 1929, he reported that he had studied domes in France "with a special view to solving certain details in the design of the dome for the West Virginia Capitol."[21]

In 1880, at the end of his first study tour of European architecture, Gilbert tried to find an apprenticeship or work in London.[22] Unsuccessful, he returned to the United States hoping to work with H. H. Richardson. Instead, he found a position in New York with McKim, Mead & White, the country's foremost practitioners of the Beaux-Arts tradition. This elite firm provided training for many architects of Gilbert's generation, including three who would be considered by the West Virginia Commission in 1921: Henry Bacon, Merven Carrère, and Thomas Hastings.[23] Gilbert worked there with Stanford White, who introduced him to artists and influenced him to follow the Beaux-Arts style.[24] Thus, while he did not study at the École, Gilbert was exposed to its style during two formative phases: his year at MIT and his more than two-year association with McKim, Mead & White. These experiences were reinforced when he worked on the architectural jury for the 1893 World's Columbian Exposition.

In December 1882, Gilbert returned to St. Paul as McKim, Mead & White's representative to preside over the construction of hotels and stations for the Northern Pacific Railroad. When the railroad's financial problems prevented this position from being fully realized, Gilbert established his own practice in St. Paul and in

1885 formed a partnership with James Knox Taylor, whom he had known in Minnesota and at MIT.[25] Until their partnership ended in 1891, they designed city and summer homes, a number of them variations on the popular Shingle style, as well as railroad stations, churches, and public and commercial buildings. Their Endicott Building in St. Paul (1889–91) was praised in the national press.

Cass Gilbert lived during a period when both the architectural profession and American architecture were undergoing great changes. From our twenty-first century perspective, an apprenticeship followed by a year of university study, European travel, and work in the office of a major firm would seem insufficient to master the expertise in design, engineering, and construction required for an architect. Yet in the nineteenth century it was not unusual.[26] Other well-known architects of the period learned their trade through apprenticeships and work, including Bertram Goodhue (whose Nebraska State Capitol, see fig. 88, was planned and constructed at approximately the same time as West Virginia's), Addison Mizner (best known for his South Florida projects), and Frank Lloyd Wright (who apprenticed with J. L. Silsbee and Louis Sullivan).[27] Architects could also achieve a certain amount of self-education through study of the architectural and engineering periodicals established in the late nineteenth century.[28]

Later in life, Gilbert enhanced his credentials with honorary degrees from the Universities of Michigan and Minnesota; Princeton, Columbia, and New York Universities; and Oberlin and Middlebury Colleges. He taught Harvard architecture students in 1911–12 as one of four lecturers for "Architecture 9 (2) Professional Practice Requirements of Special Classes of Buildings." His presentations covered "the organization of an architect's office, the relations of the architect to his client, to the builder and to his brother architect." He also considered "the problems of Government Architecture and the relations of the architect to the government."[29] In 1924, while he was designing the West Virginia Capitol, he became the second person to be named "master architect" by undergraduate architecture students at Alpha Chi Rho; the first was Nathan C. Ricker, who was honored as the first person to receive an architecture degree in the United States. Gilbert received national as well as international awards, and in 1931, as the West Virginia complex was being completed, he was honored with gold medals from the Architectural League of New York and the Society of Arts and Sciences.[30] Gilbert played a leading role in the most important national architectural organization, the American Institute of Architects, organizing the Minnesota chapter in 1892 and serving as national president in 1908–09.[31] In 1906, when the constitution of the National Academy of Design was changed to encourage the election of architects, Gilbert was among the first to be chosen; in 1926 he became the first architect to be elected academy president, and he served until 1933. He also served as a federal appointee on national committees; in 1909, for example, President Roosevelt named him chair of the newly founded Council of Fine Arts.[32]

But these honors were in the future at the time of the 1893 World's Columbian Exposition, which was crucial for the development of Gilbert's career.[33] The grandeur of this "White City" inspired his design for the Minnesota State Capitol (see fig. 13), which boasted a shining white dome and decorative elements characteristic of the Beaux-Arts style seen throughout the fairgrounds.[34]

Winning the Minnesota Capitol competition at the age of thirty-five thrust Cass Gilbert into the national spotlight with a major project that took ten years and an enlarged and well-organized studio to complete. The skills he had learned were certainly challenged by the charge to design and supervise the construction of a public building rich in symbolism and requiring complex structural engineering.[35] In 1896, he took on additional responsibility by accepting the commission for the Brazer Building in Boston (1896–97), his tallest building to date and a major East Coast project. Gilbert's architectural expertise and organizational skills were enabling him to accept a number of prestigious commissions.

In 1899, at the same time as his first New York City project, the Broadway Chambers Building (1899–1900), he won the competition for the United States Custom House in New York (1899–1907), thereby establishing himself as a professional firmly connected with that great metropolis. That his design was chosen over those by Daniel Burnham, George B. Post, Carrère & Hastings, and McKim, Mead & White placed Cass Gilbert in the midst of this elite group less than two decades after he had assisted Stanford White. The Beaux-Arts Custom House marked a turning point in his career, and he decided to move to New York, writing to his wife: "We are rich.... Tell the children my ship really has come in."[36] Cass Gilbert was forty years old when he moved his practice from the Midwest to New York. The next year he received his first international honor when he was awarded a gold medal at the Paris Exposition. His entry included a twelve-foot high model of the Broadway Chambers Building and its steel frame; the exhibit also earned medals for the George A. Fuller Company, the contracting firm that later worked on the West Virginia Capitol, and the engineer Gunvald Aus, who was also instrumental in the Charleston project.

The commissions that followed included the Union Club (1901–03), the West Street Building in Manhattan (1905–07), and the Essex County Courthouse in Newark (1901–02).[37] In St. Louis, Gilbert designed the Festival Hall and the Palace of Fine Arts (now the St. Louis Art Museum) for the Louisiana Purchase Exposition (1901–04); later, he designed the St. Louis Public Library (1907–12). Work on the Chicago and St. Louis Expositions led to projects such as college campuses, which required coordination of multiple buildings. His work at Oberlin College spanned twenty-six years (1905–31), and he created a master plan for the University of Minnesota (1907–10) and served as campus architect for the University of Texas in Austin (1910–22).[38]

Gilbert's collaboration with Frank Woolworth earned immediate fame for both patron and architect. By the completion of the Woolworth Building in 1913, the residents of many American towns, Charleston and Wheeling among them, were well acquainted with the name Woolworth because of his "five-and-dime" stores. When Gilbert was chosen to design the West Virginia Capitol, he was identified in

Fig. 18. Cass Gilbert with members of his studio in St. Paul during the construction of the Minnesota State Capitol, c. 1900.

local newspapers as "Man Who Designed Woolworth Building," establishing recognition and a local connection for West Virginians.[39]

Woolworth had selected Gilbert for his ambitious project in April 1909 because the architect's earlier work in Manhattan convinced him that his vision of a beautiful engineering marvel could be realized. The building that bore his name rose fifty-seven stories (792 feet) and was the tallest functional building in the world from 1913 to 1930; its observation deck attracted tourists from the United States and beyond.[40] Photographs, postcards, and guidebooks encouraged the world to come to New York to see it. Joseph Pennell made etchings of the building, and more than thirty prints and paintings by John Marin, including one based on the view from the observation deck, demonstrated the impression the building made on contemporary artists.[41] It was featured in the first Avant-Garde film made in the United States, Paul Strand and Charles Sheeler's 1920 *Manhattan*.[42] Praise abounded; even Frank Lloyd Wright granted that it could have had "character," which he prized, had it not been burdened with "professional Gothic prejudices and predilection."[43] A *Scientific American* cover depicted the Woolworth Building towering over its neighbors, and a *Popular Mechanics* article addressed its engineering intricacies. Tourists and New Yorkers alike marveled at the terra-cotta tile exterior continuously washed clean by the rain, the sumptuous lobby with its portraits of Woolworth, Gilbert, Aus, and others, and the twenty-nine high-speed elevators. Cass Gilbert had ushered in a new age with his functional and highly ornamented skyscraper.[44]

Perhaps the international success of the Woolworth Building encouraged Gilbert to be vocal about foreign as well as domestic architecture, as evidenced in his 1924 letter to Benito Mussolini. Referring to a newspaper report concerning a proposed building, the decoration of which would incorporate "vertical lines strongly reminiscent of the Woolworth Tower," Gilbert asked the Italian leader to abandon plans for this skyscraper that would have dwarfed Rome's historic monuments. We do not know if Gilbert's words had an impact on the thinking of Mussolini or the architect, but the skyscraper aspect of the design was altered and the project eventually dropped. Gilbert also directed his attention to Greece, where he supported the restoration of the Parthenon and advocated a ban on tall buildings in Athens.[45]

Gilbert's establishment and successes in New York led to memberships in distinguished clubs and connections with people of influence. He belonged to the city's oldest and most prestigious social club, the Union Club, as did McKim and White, and to the Century Association and London Athenaeum, among others.[46] Professionally and socially, then, Gilbert had established himself in New York.

In 1887, Gilbert had married Julia Tappan Finch, the daughter of a Milwaukee lawyer. Julia soon became a part of New York society; she and Cass attended the Metropolitan Opera and other social and cultural events. Gilbert consistently honored her as a partner in their accomplishments; when he received the West Virginia commission he wired her: "Your helpful advice and encouragement

Fig. 19. Julia Finch Gilbert and Cass Gilbert (seated) with their family on Thanksgiving Day, 1928. Back row, left to right: Charles Morgan Post, Julia Gilbert Post, Emily Finch Gilbert, Jarvis Wyeth Gilbert, Cass Gilbert Jr. Children in front row, left to right: Charles Morgan Post Jr., Julia Gilbert Post, Cass Gilbert III, Jarvis Gilbert. Julia is holding Grosvenor Gilbert. Photograph taken by Joseph Hartmann at the Gilbert country home in Ridgefield, Connecticut. Photography courtesy of the Keeler Tavern Preservation Society, Inc., Ridgefield, CT.

brought success."[47] They raised two daughters, Emily and Julia (a third, Elizabeth, died young), and a son, Cass Jr., who followed his father in his profession, held a position in his office, and continued the firm after his father's death. Cass Jr.'s most significant commission may have been Building 3 (the "Department of Motor Vehicles Building") for the West Virginia State Capitol complex (see figs. 95, 96).[48]

Like many of his patrons, Cass Gilbert was a political and social conservative, a fact that was most likely significant for his relationship with his West Virginia patrons. His conservatism was demonstrated when he resigned from the American Institute of Architects in 1919; this was surprising, for Gilbert had served as its president a decade earlier.[49] The AIA was discussed when Gilbert met with George E. Johnson, Nebraska's state engineer, in December 1919. The transcript records Gilbert's words: "I told him I had resigned from the American Institute of Architects because I was out of sympathy with some of their policies and particularly with the radical and socialistic views which had been expressed in the Journal and which had not been repudiated by the body of the Institute although I believed the large majority of the Institute members were sound on these questions." Gilbert also mentioned Thomas R. Kimball, president of the AIA and member of the Nebraska Capitol Commission, who had called on him about the Capitol project the previous month: "[I added that] Mr. Kimball's extreme radical views on such questions were contrary to my own."[50]

It is no surprise that Cass Gilbert was a dedicated member of the Republican Party. For an architect of public buildings in an era when the majority of influential politicians were Republican, this was a pragmatic position; it also fit Gilbert's broader and deeply held philosophical attitudes.[51] In light of this, it seems unexpected that Gilbert was a friend of the irreverent humorist and author Mark Twain. Such an incongruity illustrates how easily the personality of a multifaceted individual can be oversimplified.

Cass Gilbert was also a patriot. In 1917, as the United States entered World War I, he offered to design buildings needed for the war effort. In 1918–19, he designed the US Army Supply Base in Brooklyn, the largest such base in the country (also known as the Brooklyn Army Terminal). It was constructed of reinforced concrete slabs and lacked the extensive decorative elements characteristic of Gilbert's buildings. These departures exemplified his flexibility as he designed an architecturally innovative form intended for utilitarian functions; decades later, during World War II, 85 percent of army equipment and personnel were shipped from the Supply Base. Writers of the period praised it, and its impact on such modernist architects as Le Corbusier and Richard Neutra has been noted.[52] While it may seem ironic that Gilbert's influence on later architecture derived not from the public buildings in which he took such pride but from a functional building quickly designed and constructed at minimal cost, his ability to match form with function in the Supply Base demonstrated the creativity with which he approached each challenge.

In 1921, when West Virginia needed an architect to design its new Capitol—a project that demanded efficiency and both broad and specific symbolism in design and decoration and that needed to be built with public funds—Cass Gilbert must have stood out as a logical choice. His service to the nation in designing the Supply Base had demonstrated his ability to solve functional needs and was an added recommendation. His design and engineering expertise, his business sense, self-assurance, and leadership, his ability to organize complex projects and communicate his vision verbally and visually, and the thoughtful manner in which he viewed each commission all supported his appointment.

While he was preparing his proposal for West Virginia, Gilbert was involved with other projects. Some, such as the US Treasury Department Annex in Washington (1917–22) and the grand Detroit Public Library (1913–21), were nearing completion.[53] Gilbert received the commission for the US Chamber of Commerce Building in Washington in 1922 (1922–25) and was also serving as architect for the University of Texas at Austin and Oberlin College. His payroll records for January 1927 indicate that his office could simultaneously manage fourteen projects, including the West Virginia Capitol.[54]

After completing the Woolworth Building in 1913, Cass Gilbert was clearly in demand. As it became possible for him to be more selective, he chose to focus on noncommercial buildings and to avoid competitions.[55] He also understood that there were limits to how many large projects he could manage at once. In November 1919, when he was invited to compete for the Nebraska State Capitol commission, he declined, stating that he "had a large amount of work under consideration at the present time and that if a considerable portion of it went through immediately it would be impossible for me to give the time to the competition or even if successful to make the long trips necessary to hold conferences with the Commissioners in Omaha."[56] A competition requires a great deal of preparation that is wasted when proposals are not chosen; perhaps the memories of his victories in the Montana and Wisconsin competitions and the subsequent rejection of those designs gave him pause. Furthermore, his disagreements with Thomas R. Kimball, who was a member of the Nebraska Commission and president of the AIA (from which Gilbert had resigned), may have influenced his decision regarding the Nebraska project.

Gilbert also chose not to be among the more than two hundred architects who submitted proposals for the Chicago Tribune Building competition in 1922. In this case, his reluctance may have also been influenced by his exclusion from the list of ten firms invited to enter. It is also possible that he was offended by the manner in which this competition for a commercial skyscraper was being popularized.[57] And he may well have felt consumed by the coveted Charleston project, which was then in its demanding initial stages.

Gilbert won the commission for the West Virginia Capitol—a project that was important in size and scope, in line with his values, and potentially lucrative—without having to enter a competition. After beginning work on this State Capitol in 1921, Gilbert did not accept another large commission for several years. During the second half of the 1920s, however, he agreed to design the New York Life Insurance Building (1925–28); the Federal Courthouse on Foley Square (1929–36); the SJM Building (now the Cass Gilbert Building, completed in 1927 and decorated with Assyrian animal friezes that are unexpectedly Art Deco in style); the R. C. Williams Warehouse (completed in 1928), reminiscent of the US Army Supply Base in design and function; and the New York County Lawyers' Association Building (1930).[58] In 1930, he began the Seaside Sanatorium, for heliotherapy treatment of childhood tuberculosis, in Waterford, Connecticut. It was also during this period that he designed the masonry decoration for the George Washington Bridge (1926–31), but this was never executed.[59] Most importantly, however, during this period he began work on the US Supreme Court (1928–35).

It seems almost impossible that a single firm under the direction of one man could balance the organization, paperwork, and meetings needed for designing and executing these varied and far-flung projects and still maintain a high level of quality. The West Virginia Capitol was the last major work to be completed before Gilbert's death, but despite the continuation of his name and firm under the direction of his son, the death of the elder architect signaled the end of an era.

This review of the work of Cass Gilbert reveals a life that was productive and varied. His career was expansive: domestic, ecclesiastical, academic, commercial, and governmental structures, including homes, tall buildings and skyscrapers, libraries, warehouses, railway stations, private clubs, and public buildings were all designed to function efficiently and many intended to inspire. A number of his

Fig. 20. Cass Gilberts, United States Supreme Court Building, Washington, DC, 1928–35, as seen in a postcard sent from Washington in 1944. The reverse notes: "This building is a magnificent white marble edifice, dedicated to 'Equal Justice Under the Law,'" but the architect is not identified.

Fig. 21. Aerial photograph of the recently completed West Virginia State Capitol, c. 1932. Note the parking lots near the West Wing and in the courtyard near the East Wing. Duffy Street was eliminated and the many homes and other structures in the area behind the Governor's Mansion were demolished during the expansion of the Capitol campus.

projects were not realized, however. He was not chosen to design the campus for the Carnegie Institute of Technology in Pittsburgh, for instance, or the "Minnesota Building" at the 1893 World's Columbian Exposition. His prize-winning designs for the Capitols of Montana and Wisconsin were not built, nor was the public library he designed for Charleston, West Virginia.[60]

Throughout Gilbert's career he seemed never to have wavered from hard work and dedication to beauty. As a young professional, in 1888, he expressed his personal commitment: "To become an Architect in the right sense of the word means that a man shall give his life to it and nothing else, and shall study the work he has to do with enthusiastic interest in every detail pertaining to it, and content himself with nothing less than complete success. He must have also certain gifts of imagination and a natural or a carefully acquired sense of proportion."[61]

Four decades later, in August 1928, Gilbert must have been musing about his career when he created a drawing that united dozens of his monumental buildings into a single cityscape. The West Virginia Capitol, its great dome still on the drawing board, is at the far right. No other living architect could have produced a more impressive panorama. The central structure rising above the others is, of course, the Woolworth Building. In a 1918 promotional publication entitled "The Cathedral of Commerce: The Highest Building in the World," the unnamed author compared the Woolworth Building to three of the great monuments of the past, with credit given to the collaboration of patron and architect: "The man who proposes and the architect who designs a truly great building confer a lasting favor on the race at large. Our indebtedness to those who constructed the Parthenon, the Coliseum in Rome, St. Peter's Cathedral in that city ... is utterly beyond ordinary methods of computation." He added, "These monuments of rare beauty, devotion and civic pride far outlast other achievements of their respective periods. Such ... testimony [is] due to Frank W. Woolworth, whose magnitude of mind originated the scheme, and to Cass Gilbert, whose genius executed it to the last detail." The panegyrist concluded: "To these men, America pays a lasting tribute, and their accomplishment will remain at the heart of the world of trade, a lofty example of the best possibilities in human nature, even when engaged in mercantile pursuits."[62] This was high praise for entrepreneur and architect, albeit within a publication designed to draw attention to their success, but the concluding phrase, "even when engaged in mercantile pursuits," suggests hesitation. Gilbert himself wrote to his fellow architect Ralph Adams Cram: "I sometimes wish I had never built the Woolworth Building because I fear it may be regarded as my only work and you and I both know that whatever it may be in dimension and in certain lines it is after all only a skyscraper."[63]

Fig. 22. Cass Gilbert, *Panoramic Composite of His Buildings*, August, 1928. Drawing. The West Virginia Capitol is pictured on the far right. The tall structure in the middle is the Woolworth Building, with the New York Life Insurance Building directly to the right. The Minnesota Capitol is the domed structure to the right of the Insurance Building. The Arkansas Capitol is the prominent domed structure several buildings to the left of the Woolworth Building. Above Gilbert's signature in the lower right he wrote: "Some of the buildings ... built or designed by me.... Add to this a lot of smaller buildings."

In 1900, Gilbert had defined a skyscraper as "a machine that makes the land pay."[64] On the other hand, he wrote in 1932 that "public buildings, and especially the State Capitol, constitute the best evidences of the character of material, success and solidity, culture and civilization of a state." In creating the West Virginia Capitol he aspired to "set an example to other states": a lofty goal, indeed.[65]

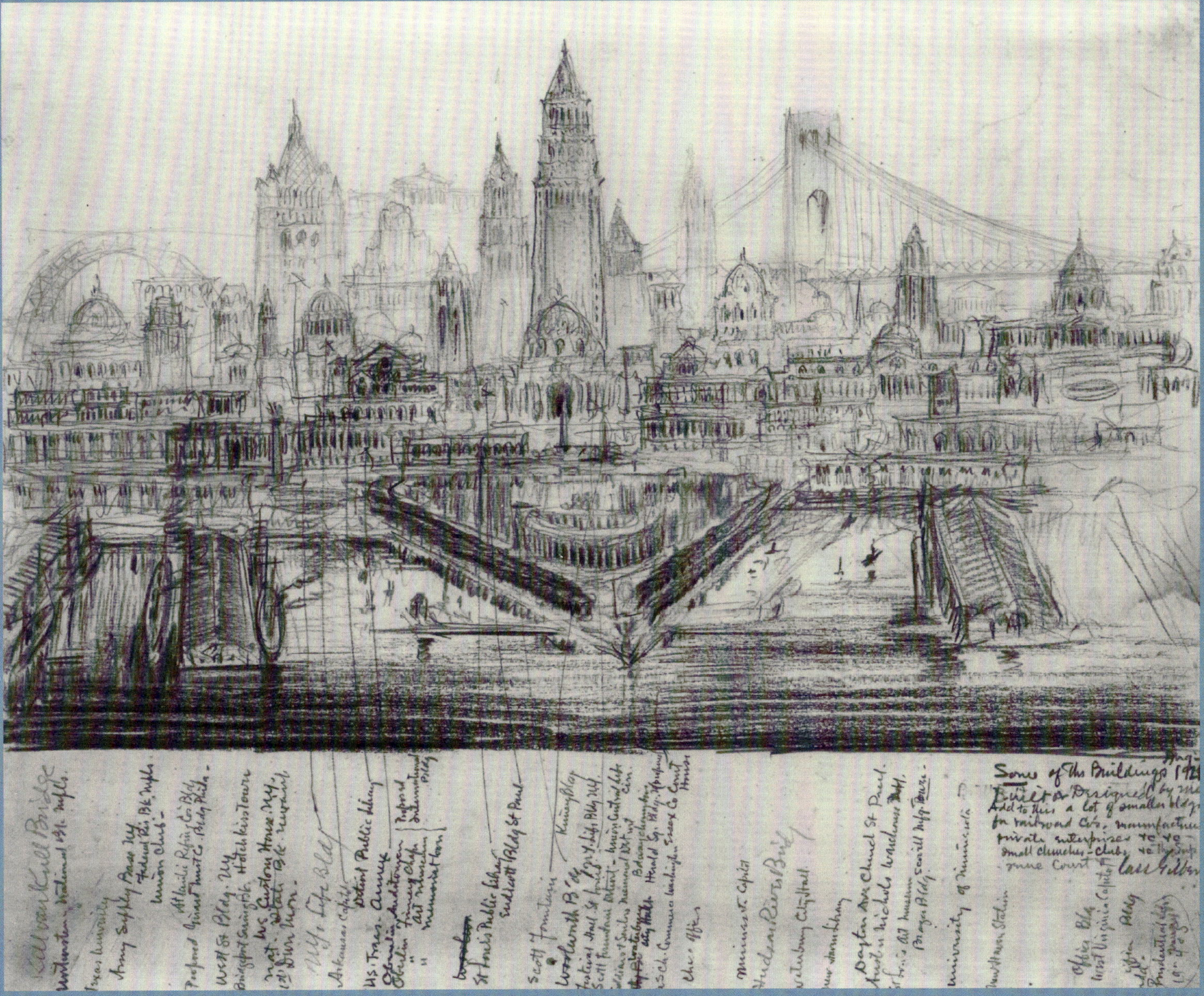
Some of the Buildings
Built & Designed by me
Add to this a lot of smaller bldgs
for railroad Co's, manufacturers
private enterprises &c &c
small churches – clubs &c
Cass Gilbert

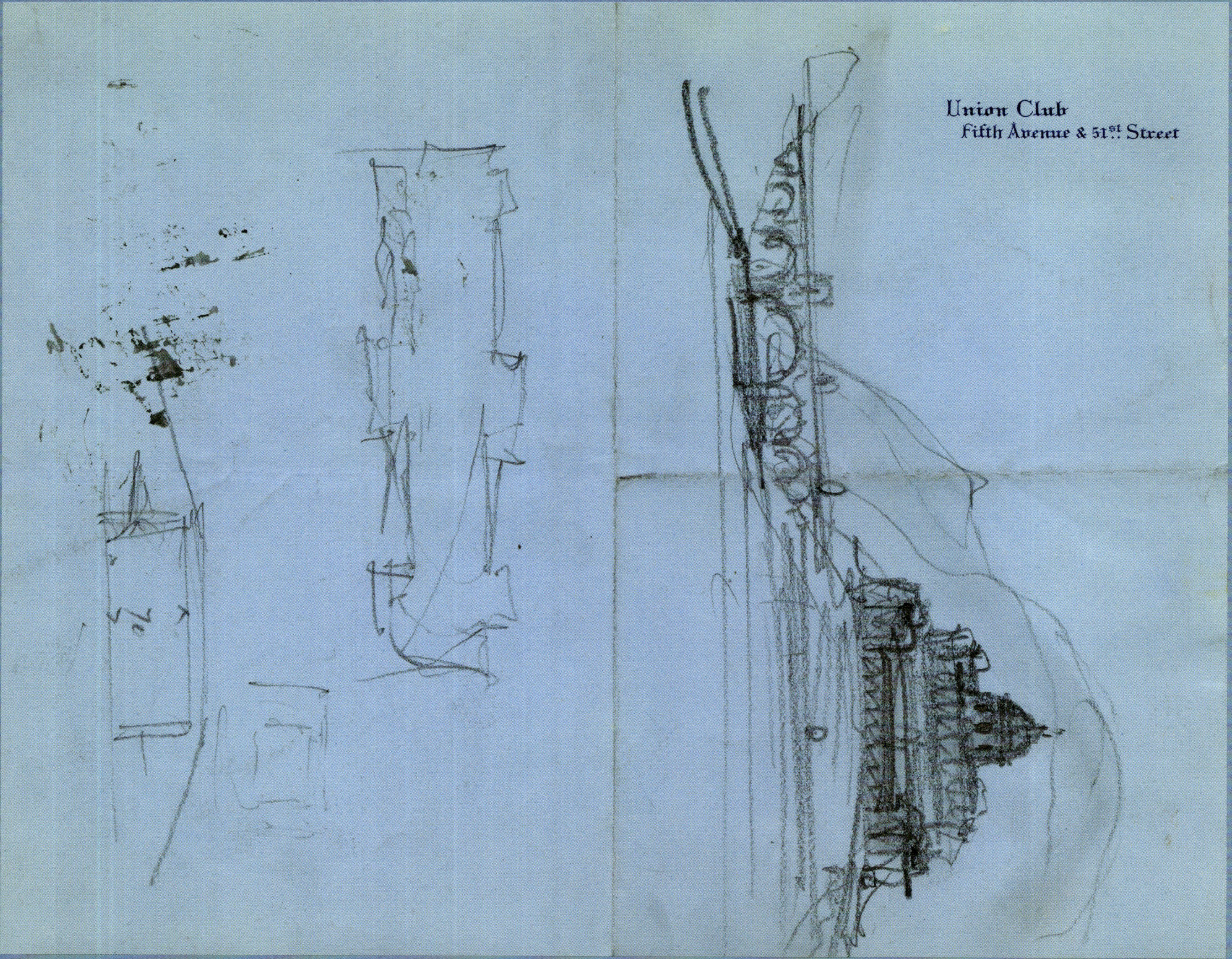
Union Club
Fifth Avenue & 51st Street

CHAPTER THREE

# "Duffy Street Site Is Selected for State House"

The location and topography of Charleston, placed as it is in a narrow valley bordered by steep and beautiful wooded hills, offers opportunities for the location of the Capitol Building which are of unusual beauty and at the same time complicated by practical conditions which cannot be ignored.

Cass Gilbert, "General Memorandum … Advising as to New State Capitol Site," August 1921

Fig. 23. Cass Gilbert, Study for the West Virginia State Capitol, August 11, 1921. The date is on the reverse.

THE JULY 1921 HEADLINES ANNOUNCING GILBERT'S APPOINTMENT emphasized his role in choosing the site: "CASS GILBERT, ARCHITECT OF FAME, TO PLAN NEW CAPITOL ... SELECTION OF SITE TO FOLLOW SOON; Gilbert Promises to Help Find Place for State House; First Important Step of Commission."[1] Charleston's residents had already waited months to learn how the location of the new Capitol might affect their city's development; despite newspaper headlines, the decision would not come soon. Only after more than five months of public meetings, editorial debate, many designs by the architect, and a power struggle that engaged the mayor, local businessmen, property owners, and the commissioners was it decided that the Capitol would be constructed north of the Kanawha River east of downtown.

The Commission called an open meeting for July 19 and one paper headlined: "WOMEN TO TAKE PART IN PUBLIC CAPITOL PARLEY; They Will Join in Making Recommendations to Commission Concerning Location; ... Women of Charleston Are Destined to Play Leading Roles in West Virginia's Latest Drama, 'I'm the State Capitol; Where Do You Want Me to Sit?'" At this meeting ten sites were considered and others proposed as possibilities; one was offered free to the state, but it was too distant from Charleston to be practicable.[2]

The summary offered here concentrates on the four locations that ultimately became most important: (1) the Old Capitol Site, a plot of slightly less than five acres, downtown; (2) the Capitol Hill Site, directly north of the Old Capitol Site; (3) the South Ruffner Site, a large tract outside the city limits, south of the Kanawha River; and (4) the Duffy Street Site, a residential area of approximately 15 acres, east of downtown and north of the Kanawha. On July 21, a newspaper reported a "tendency during the last day or two to narrow the discussion ... to locations south of the Kanawha River"—the South Ruffner Site. At the same time, however, another paper announced: "PROTEST AGAINST SITE ACROSS KANAWHA RIVER; West Side Business Men Enter Formal Protest Against Putting Capitol Outside the City." The motivations of individuals who promoted certain sites should be questioned, but it is not clear who owned which sites and how they might gain or lose in the sale of property to the state. Already on June 30, a series of headlines in the *Charleston Gazette* had ended with the phrase "Hints at Graft."[3]

On August 4, the architect complained that he was "very much handicapped" because of "a lack of information regarding the space requirements of the various departments of the State Government." He had requested this information soon after he was appointed; among those who responded quickly were the judges of West Virginia's Supreme Court of Appeals, who proposed "a separate building to be known as the Temple of Justice or Department of Justice."[4]

Housing the court in a separate building was a possibility, for on August 10, when Gilbert inquired if the list of departments copied from the bulletin board in the Temporary Capitol was complete, he was trying to "estimate the size of the one building, if we have only one, or the sizes of the various buildings." He could then "lay out a diagrammatical plan of the building or group of buildings and plat these rough diagrams on the various proposed sites to determine whether the sites are large enough or not."[5] Although the Old Capitol Site had strong popular support, Gilbert opposed it from the beginning, in part because of its limited size; he may have hoped that office space requirements would demonstrate the Old Site was not sufficient.

Gilbert's earliest known sketches for the West Virginia Capitol, on two sides of a piece of Union Club stationery, show grandiose schemes that culminate in a domed structure high on a hill above a river. He did not specify a location and, because one is not obvious from the designs, these impressionistic drawings may be simply an exploration of what Gilbert hoped might be possible somewhere in Charleston's dramatic river-valley setting. In what seems to be the earlier sketch, the dome is set against hills that rise behind it (see fig. 23). On the reverse, the viewpoint is changed 90 degrees, for the bridge visible to the left in the earlier sketch now leads to a "tunnel to elevators." On the middle level, a U-shaped building provides a visual base for the domed structure crowning the scheme (see fig. 24). On this second version, Gilbert wrote "Ponte Sant'Angelo," revealing that he was inspired by the way the Ponte Sant'Angelo in Rome crosses the Tiber River toward the monumental tomb of the Emperor Hadrian, now known as Castel Sant'Angelo. For West Virginia, Gilbert moved this ancient urban spectacle to Charleston and created an impact even grander than that of the Roman original. Gilbert marked this sheet 1 and dated it; later he developed this scheme for the site known as Capitol Hill (see fig. 26).[6]

Also in August, Gilbert inquired of Secretary Young how he could register as an architect in West Virginia, since a recent law required registration of architects wishing to work there. The law was probably intended to draw public attention to the decision to hire an out-of-state architect; its sponsor was A. F. Wysong, the architect and legislator who had applied to design the Capitol and who would later try to convince his fellow legislators to void Cass Gilbert's contract.[7]

On August 10, Gilbert asked the commissioners to make additions to a list he had compiled of sites proposed to him or mentioned in newspaper articles or letters he had received. He also telegraphed the custodians of certain state capitols requesting the acreage of their grounds. Their responses revealed a range between fifteen to forty acres, figures that could be useful in counteracting support for the Old Capitol Site. On August 17, Gilbert received an expanded list of twenty-four sites from the Commission; corrections followed in a letter from Secretary Young, who pointed out that site 12 had been "suggested by Mr. Gillespie as a joke."[8]

Two days later, the architect announced his intention to travel to Europe: "It will probably take several months to consummate the selection and acquisition of the site to a point wherein I can proceed with the preparation of the designs for the building.... I am, therefore, arranging to take my vacation beginning the latter part of this month and I am to be gone from six to eight weeks." He noted this would be a working holiday: "It is my purpose to make a quick trip to France and Italy with a special view to studying, and refreshing my impressions of, the great monumental

Wall
Tunnel to Elevator
Wall
Roadway
Stations & tracks under viaduct & roadway
Viaduct (Ponte St Angelo)
Study of West Virginia Capitol. Aug 11. 1921

and classical buildings which I can see there," adding "I want to bring to the service of the State of West Virginia the very best work that I can do with a fresh mind and the clear impressions which would arise from just such a trip at this time."[9]

Gilbert offered to cancel if the commissioners objected. Young's August 23 telegraphed reply was amiable—"Capitol Commission very glad to grant your request. Wish we could all go with you"—but on August 25 he clarified: "We hope, however, that we can get your preliminary report this week, so that we can have the site decided before you return."[10] To fulfill the Commission's request, Gilbert delayed his departure until September 3.

On August 31, he sent a "Report Advising as to the New State Capitol Site," which was especially directed to Secretary Young, and a "General Memorandum to Accompany Report Advising as to New State Capitol Site" addressed to the commissioners.[11] The distinction is revealing. The General Memorandum set out the principles by which he reached his conclusions and his thoughts on the viability of certain kinds of sites in Charleston, while the Report listed six specific sites for special consideration. The former provided Gilbert's broad philosophical approach for the commissioners, while the latter was designed to help Young focus the deliberations on Gilbert's preferred sites. Gilbert alerted Young to the dangers of publishing his recommendations: "You will of course use your discretion as to whether any part of [this information] should be made public at this time." He added, "My own view is, and I am sure that you will agree with me, that the public is entitled to the fullest information on all public matters, but that in negotiations for the purchase of property the public interest is better served if the buyer (i.e. the State) is not at a disadvantage by reason of any expressed preference in advance." Gilbert understood that "for perfectly good reasons of economy or public service the Commission may not find it practicable to follow my suggestions in some respects and possibly not at all.... [I] will be content to do the best I can whatever site they select." He complimented the commissioners in advance, noting that their choice would be "made with wisdom and that anything I may say constitutes only a part of the data from which their decisions may be arrived." Gilbert planned to take a copy of these documents with him to Europe, "so that I can refer to it in case correspondence is necessary."

While Gilbert could easily have sent the commissioners a generic description of "how to select a site," his General Memorandum detailed how to assess sites in Charleston, a city rich in natural beauty but with restrictions due to its hilly, river-valley setting. He urged them to remember, for example, that changes in industrialization, transportation, and population would transform the city: "Fifty or a hundred years is a very short time in the history of a state or city. As the buildings now to be erected are to be the permanent official home of the State, we are impelled to consider the matter not only from the standpoint of present conditions but for a period of at least fifty or a hundred years ahead." He thought the Capitol should "be placed where it will be a conspicuous object in the landscape and be visible for a considerable distance," adding that "fine views of the building

Fig. 24. Cass Gilbert, Study for the West Virginia State Capitol, August 11, 1921.

should be obtained from the city" as well. He pointed out that "if a hill site is chosen it should be where it would look down on pleasant surroundings and not upon railroad tracks or factory buildings" but warned that a "commanding" and "picturesque" site should also be "convenient and approachable as well as beautiful." Certain sites raised distinct problems: while some proposed hill sites would demand "leveling off ... to get adequate space and would result in very costly terracing and retaining walls, ... at least two sites suggested in the valley would require extensive filling and protection against flood water."

"If the Capitol could be seen by the hundreds of thousands of people from all over the United States who pass through Charleston by way of the Chesapeake & Ohio R.R.," he summarized, "it would lend distinction both to the State and to the City." Sites on both the southwest and northeast sides of the valley would provide such a view, but "a location on the hills on the northeast side of the valley would be more conspicuous because ... such a location would be very visible from the Chesapeake & Ohio R.R. for a long distance."[12] Because Charleston was on the C&O routes from Washington and Norfolk to Cincinnati, Chicago, and beyond, Gilbert's estimate of "hundreds of thousands" of passengers was, at the time, no exaggeration.

Perhaps Gilbert was remembering his early sketches (see figs. 23, 24) when he pointed out the advantages of sites on the city's hills, emphasizing that they "offer such exceptional and tempting opportunities for picturesque beauty that, if properly developed, they would be unrivalled." These sites had specific advantages: "the extended views of the building which would be obtained from so many points; the beautiful views of hills, rivers and valleys which would be obtained from the Capitol Building and its terraces and gardens; the fresh, pure air and sunlight of the higher location above the heat of the valley as it is in summer." These "would contribute to the charm of such a location and would perhaps outweigh other considerations, such as those of the cost of approaches, retaining walls, and accessibility, which might be urged against a hill site."[13] The memorandum demonstrated the diligence, care, intelligence, and integrity with which Gilbert approached an assignment; his understanding of Charleston and his vision of its future may have seemed even more perceptive and comprehensive than that of his patrons.

In the Report, Gilbert pointed out that he had visited sites, consulted topographical surveys, reviewed flood records, and learned of public opinion through articles forwarded by his clipping service, but he clarified that he had not investigated how much each parcel might cost. He recommended six sites as "the best or the most available (irrespective of cost). My recommendations are based on their architectural possibilities, lines of approach, convenience, practicability and beauty; and I have had in mind the present conditions and future growth and development of the City and State."[14]

The Duffy and two South Ruffner Sites were among Gilbert's six recommendations. He explained why the Old Capitol Site was not: it had been submerged by floods, its use would "interrupt the growth of the city," a capitol built there "would soon be over-topped by private business buildings," and, perhaps most important for him, a new building on this site "could not have the beauty and dignity which the State Capitol should have." He dismissed the argument that it was advantageous to have public buildings in the downtown area: "A business street is more successful where business is continuous." He recommended selling the old site and using the proceeds "for a new site better located and of larger size."

While the Duffy Site was described as rather narrow, it was above the flood plain, and a Capitol built there "would be conspicuous from the river, the railroads and the surrounding hills." The South Ruffner area was listed twice because it offered two sites of different size. Gilbert preferred the "center and southwesterly half thereof," if a bridge and viaduct could be built and a plot of 60 acres (more if possible) acquired.[15]

Of the six he recommended, Gilbert preferred four: the Duffy Site, the two South Ruffner Sites, and another identified as "between Porter's Branch and Lick Branch." He did not include the Capitol Hill Site among the six because it would require removing railroad crossings and switching yards.

In October, while Gilbert was still in Europe, James A. Kane, one of his former assistants, received a letter from F. M. Lange, an architect. Lange was assisting A. F. Wysong, the West Virginia legislator and architect who had failed to gain the commission for the West Virginia Capitol despite his association with Pittsburgh architect Henry Hornbostel.[16] Lange asked Kane, who had worked for Gilbert as an assistant between 1912 and 1919, to confirm that it was actually he (Kane) who had designed the Detroit Public Library and most of the important buildings produced by Gilbert's office during that period. Lange also wanted Kane to corroborate that "Mr. Johnson" (probably Thomas R. Johnson) in the Gilbert office had been the real architect of the Woolworth Building.

Lange implied that Gilbert was claiming credit for buildings designed by others in his office and that he had, therefore, "morally received the commission [for the West Virginia Capitol] through false pretenses." Lange continued: "Architecture is considered as high an art as painting and sculpture. No one would give the commission for a painting or sculpture to a person who is not personally an artist or a sculptor. It is ridiculous to think that Mr. Cass Gilbert will probably become famous as Stanford White in architectural art."

Lange attacked Gilbert: "I think this would be a very interesting case to fight out; it would afford an opportunity to show the public who really are the great architects and who only architectural salesmen or building constructors." He reported that Wysong was "a prominent member of the State Legislature and is determined to make a stiff fight for the revocation of the commission and an open competition." Lange hoped for Kane's help: "I would be obliged to you for any information you possess, also names of others who can help. I believe Mr. Wysong's local prestige and publications of my work will enable us with such help, to carry this fight for fair-play and common decency in our profession beyond the boundaries of this State." He knew that Gilbert was out of the country: "The fact that Mr.

Gilbert is at present in Europe while the preliminary sketches are being prepared for this Capitol Building, to be delivered within two weeks, shows even cynical disregard for appearances. The entire profession of the country will be interested in this case, if we can get 'the goods' on this man."[17]

Kane replied to Lange that he was "astonished" at these "absolutely false" accusations, adding, "West Virginia has been particularly fortunate in the selection of Mr. Gilbert as the Architect for the State Capitol. Without any question of doubt Mr. Gilbert is without any superior in the architectural profession, whether he is judged from the point of view of integrity, intelligence or knowledge of his profession." Kane clearly respected his former boss: "He is a gentleman in whom artistic perception and feeling finds its highest development, and you may be assured that all the remarkable work of his office is his own work in every sense."

Kane forwarded to Gilbert copies of Lange's letter and his response; in his cover letter he reassured Gilbert that he had replied to Lange, "if for no other reason than to let it be known with what respect your old assistants think of you." Gilbert thanked Kane and told him, "I need not characterize his statement as contemptible, for he wrote in ignorance and in a spirit of suspicion, not to say malevolence, which is obvious on the face of his letter." Gilbert reported that "at a recent meeting in Charleston I took occasion to place [Lange's] letter and your reply before the Governor and State Capitol Commissioners so as to fully inform them, as I have no concealments to make on any matters of this kind. Their only comment was to the effect that the letter should not be noticed."

The commissioners adjourned their October 22 meeting, when Gilbert was still away, without a decision. After Gilbert returned and a meeting was set for November 22, Gilbert wrote Young to inform him that Frederick Law Olmsted Jr., "the noted landscape architect," would probably accompany him.[18] Gilbert and Olmsted, whose famous father had pioneered the idea of urban and park planning in America, had developed an urban plan for New Haven, Connecticut, in 1907 and had been in communication about the West Virginia project since August. Gilbert wrote Olmsted a compelling letter inviting him to Charleston:

> I was in Charleston several times during the summer, incident to my appointment as architect of the new State Capitol and, in looking over various locations ... suggested by the citizens ... I was very much impressed with the necessity of there being a definite city plan and, especially, of there being a definite plan for park and boulevard development.
>
> The hills on each side of the valley are very much broken and are very beautiful. They are cut by deep ravines and both the ravines and the hills between them are beautifully wooded. The hills rise to a height of several hundred feet above the city, rather precipitately, and are somewhat difficult of access. Residential sections are being developed on these hills in a somewhat disconnected way.
>
> I advised them that a definite boulevard system should be planned connecting these various hill sites and so as to make a series of beautiful drives and parkways as such a boulevard would make the sites far more accessible and bring into use areas which are not now very available, and also it would help in their consideration of the selection of a Capitol site in case they should determine to build the Capitol upon one of the hills.

In any event, it should be done as a matter of city improvement whether the Capitol is placed on one of the hills or not....

Charleston is a city of about fifty or seventy-five thousand, growing very rapidly, and has very great possibilities of being one of the most attractive and beautiful of the State Capitals in the country....

While I have no authority to expend any money or pay any fee on the matter, I am willing to pay all traveling expenses myself for the sake of helping the matter along, and it is my opinion that it would develop into your being called in professionally, on terms that you and they might agree upon.[19]

Olmsted, unable to accompany Gilbert because of family obligations, ultimately played no role in the West Virginia project.

No decision on the site was made at the November 22 meeting, at which Gilbert probably shared the information he had gathered on the acreage and interior space ("cubical contents") of other state capitols. He showed designs for various sites, including a series of large sketches on lightweight paper that were probably drawn at the meeting. Sketches of complexes for the Capitol Hill Site are marked with elevation numbers from 38 to 238 feet to indicate the terrain one would ascend when approaching the Main Building. Proposals for the Duffy Site showed three, five, or seven structures. Sites on either side of the Elk River were still being considered; all the plans for these sites featured five buildings.[20]

Gilbert's most extravagant complexes were for the South Ruffner sites, which offered virtually unlimited space on a level plain above the river (see fig. 25). Each proposal has a main building at the east end of a large open area paralleling the river. The example shown features eleven buildings: a main building and four subsidiary buildings around a "Grand Court" and six more structures flanking the "Lagoon." Both plan and terminology are reminiscent of the design of the 1893 Chicago Exposition and of other World's Fairs. The consistently odd number of buildings in these sketches (three, five, seven, eleven) reveals Gilbert's adherence to the basic concept of a central structure flanked or surrounded by smaller buildings.[21]

If the inability of the commissioners to select a site or even focus on a single kind of site strained Gilbert's patience, it also inspired his creativity. The proposed sites offered diametrically opposed attributes: limited or unlimited space, level ground or dramatically rising terrain. As a result, Gilbert and his office created a large number of distinctive proposals; so many, in fact, that a book-length study would be needed to assess them all. Gilbert had yet to receive any payment from the state and—although he was due $10,000 "when the site was selected"—this payment remained the same no matter how long the process of site selection took or how many proposals he and his studio had to make in an attempt to expedite it.[22] In addition, the delay in making a decision on the site required Gilbert to make several overnight train trips from New York to Charleston, with a change in Washington. Gilbert left Charleston the day after the November 22 meeting and arrived in New York at 1:30 P.M. on November 24, just in time for Thanksgiving dinner and the celebration of his sixty-second birthday.

The site for their new Capitol was not the only issue being considered by West Virginia's citizens during the fall of 1921. Organized labor was watching the Capitol project closely, and a November 21 letter from the Charleston Building Trades Council to the Commission encouraged the employment of West Virginia workers: "As citizens and taxpayers of this State we are deeply interested in the growth and prosperity of West Virginia, and recognize that through close co-operation of all the people that greater progress in this direction can be made, especially during the present reconstruction period with its attendant unemployment problem which has a general effect upon our entire social fabric." The writer continued, "Under these circumstances it behooves all good citizens to unite in keeping the wheels of progress moving to the greatest possible extent, therefore, we most sincerely urge that your honorable body in considering and letting all contracts in connection with the erection of the new Capitol Building as well as all public improvements made by the State, that the specifications explicitly call for the employment of home or West Virginia labor and that the same proceeding also apply to all materials and supplies as far as possible." A resolution from the Kanawha Valley Central Labor Union of Charleston expressed the same sentiment: "that only [West Virginia workers] be employed and that the material and supplies for the same be products of this State as far as is possible to secure the same, with the view of solving the unemployment of our own State to some extent and keeping the taxpayers' money in circulation within its borders to the general welfare of its citizenship."[23]

During the first two weeks of December, Gilbert and his office prepared drawings for a December 15 meeting in Charleston.[24] The ground plans made at this time were all drawn in a similar style and on the same scale so that the commissioners could easily compare how site affected design. Although few of these plans were accompanied by elevations, one exception is a dramatic proposal for the Capitol Hill Site that features a domed structure based on the National Capitol model with symmetrical subsidiary buildings below. This design bears similarities to the sketches made in August (see figs. 23, 24), but now the location on Capitol Hill makes the viewer's orientation, facing west, clear. This plan required moving the Kanawha & Michigan Railroad tracks at the base of the hill and constructing a tunnel under it from the intersection of Morris Street and Piedmont Road that would lead to "the little stream known as Coal Branch" and then to a bridge across the Elk River. Gilbert had already met with a railroad representative to discuss moving the tracks.[25] While this solution would have provided an imposing setting for Gilbert's structures, the modification of Capitol Hill shown here seems to negate much of the natural beauty of the setting.

For the Old Capitol Site, Gilbert proposed a two-building solution that reveals its limitations. The main building seems shoehorned into an awkwardly shaped plot between Washington and Lee Streets, while a second building across Capitol Street would be needed for additional office space. It must have frustrated Gilbert, who asserted order and symmetry whenever possible, that the two structures could not be axially related.[26]

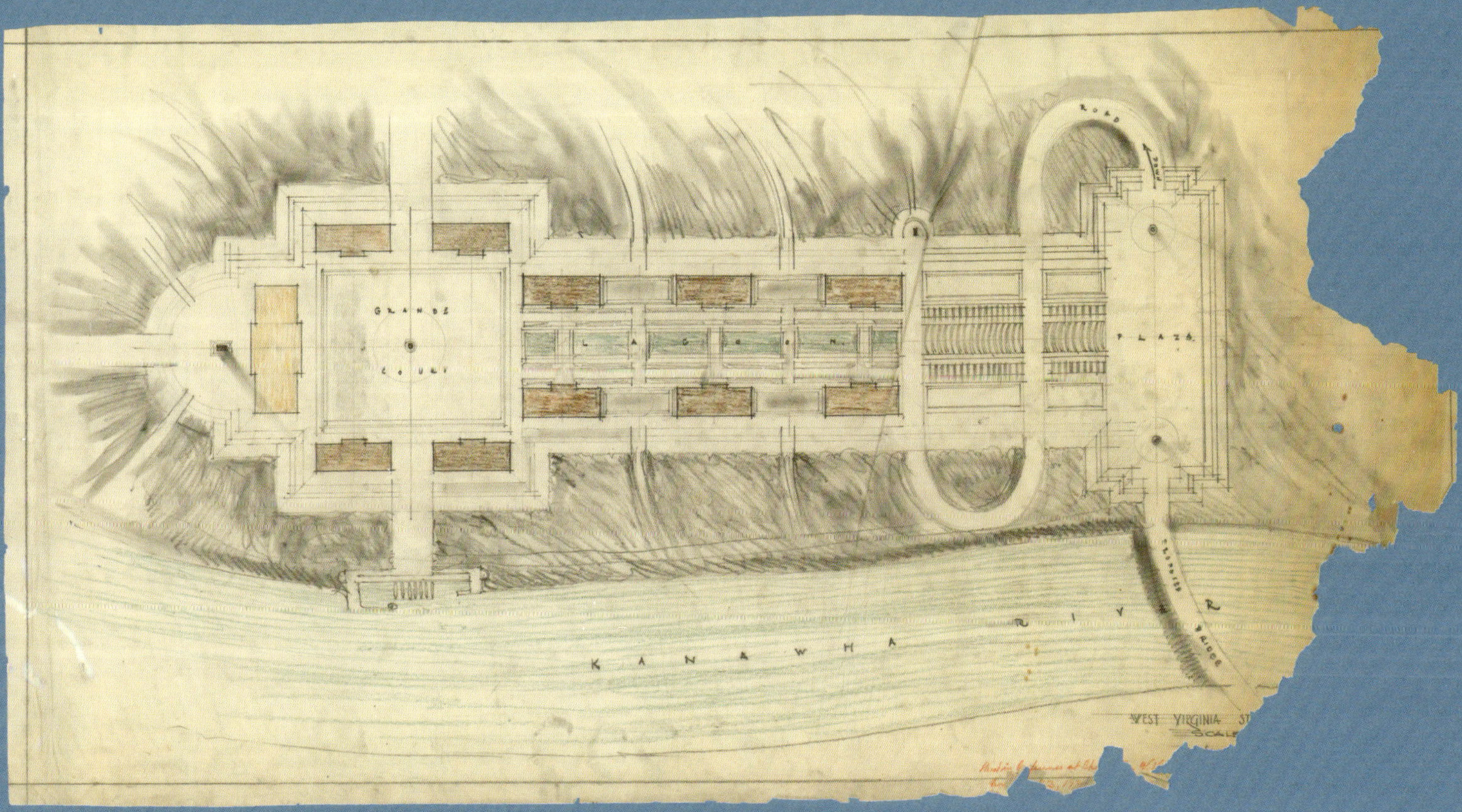


Fig. 25. Cass Gilbert/Studio, Sketch for the South Ruffner site with eleven buildings, August 1921. Marked, as are several others, "Shown at Conference at Charleston, W. Va, Nov. 22–23, 1921."

Fig. 26. Cass Gilbert/Studio, Proposal for the Capitol and subsidiary buildings on the Capitol Hill Site, December 1921.

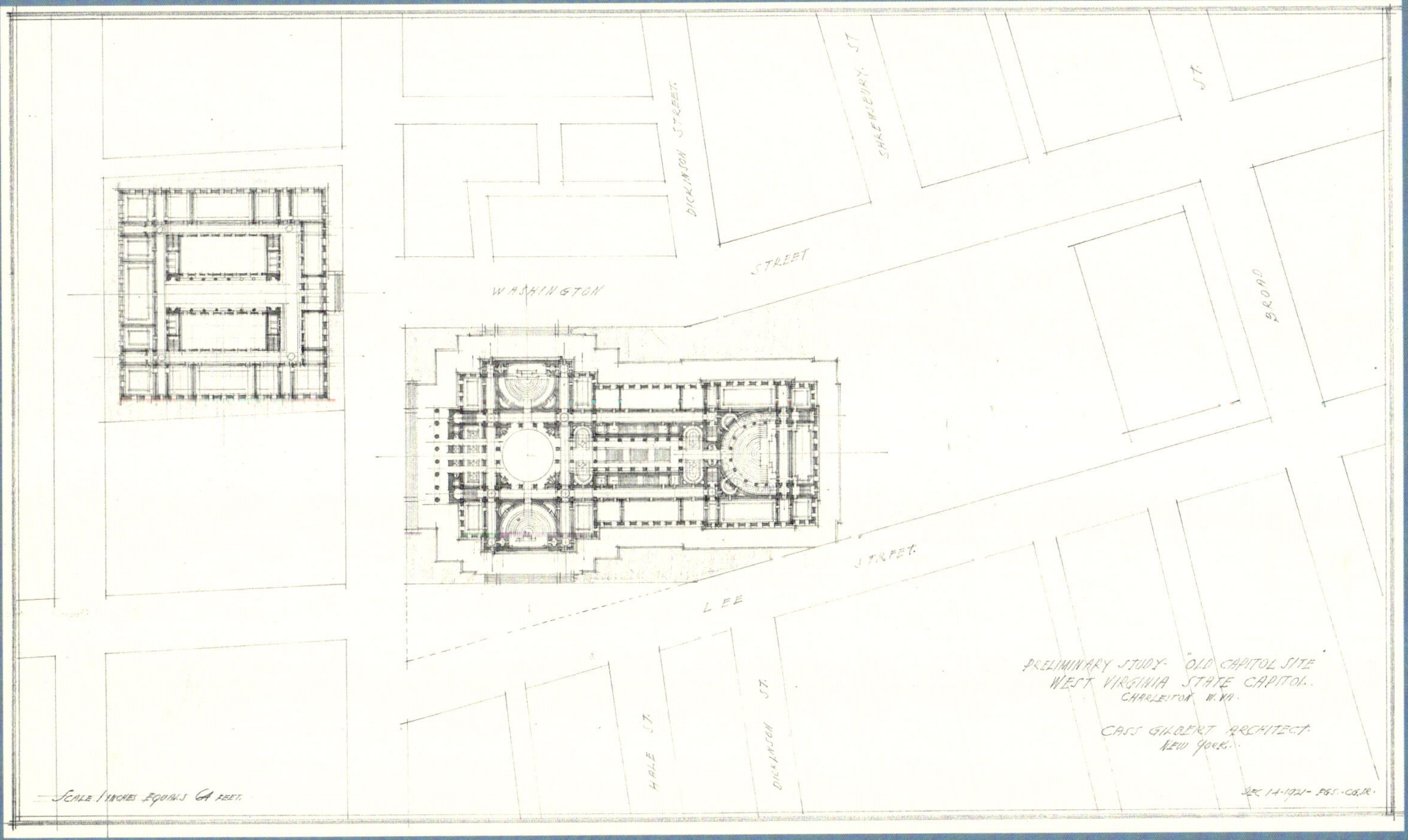


Fig. 27. Cass Gilbert (concept), "Preliminary Study," with ground plan, for the "Old Capitol Site," December 14, 1921. Drawn by Frederick G. Stickel and Cass Gilbert Jr. To the best of our knowledge, this is the only drawing for the West Virginia Capitol in which Cass Gilbert Jr. had a hand.

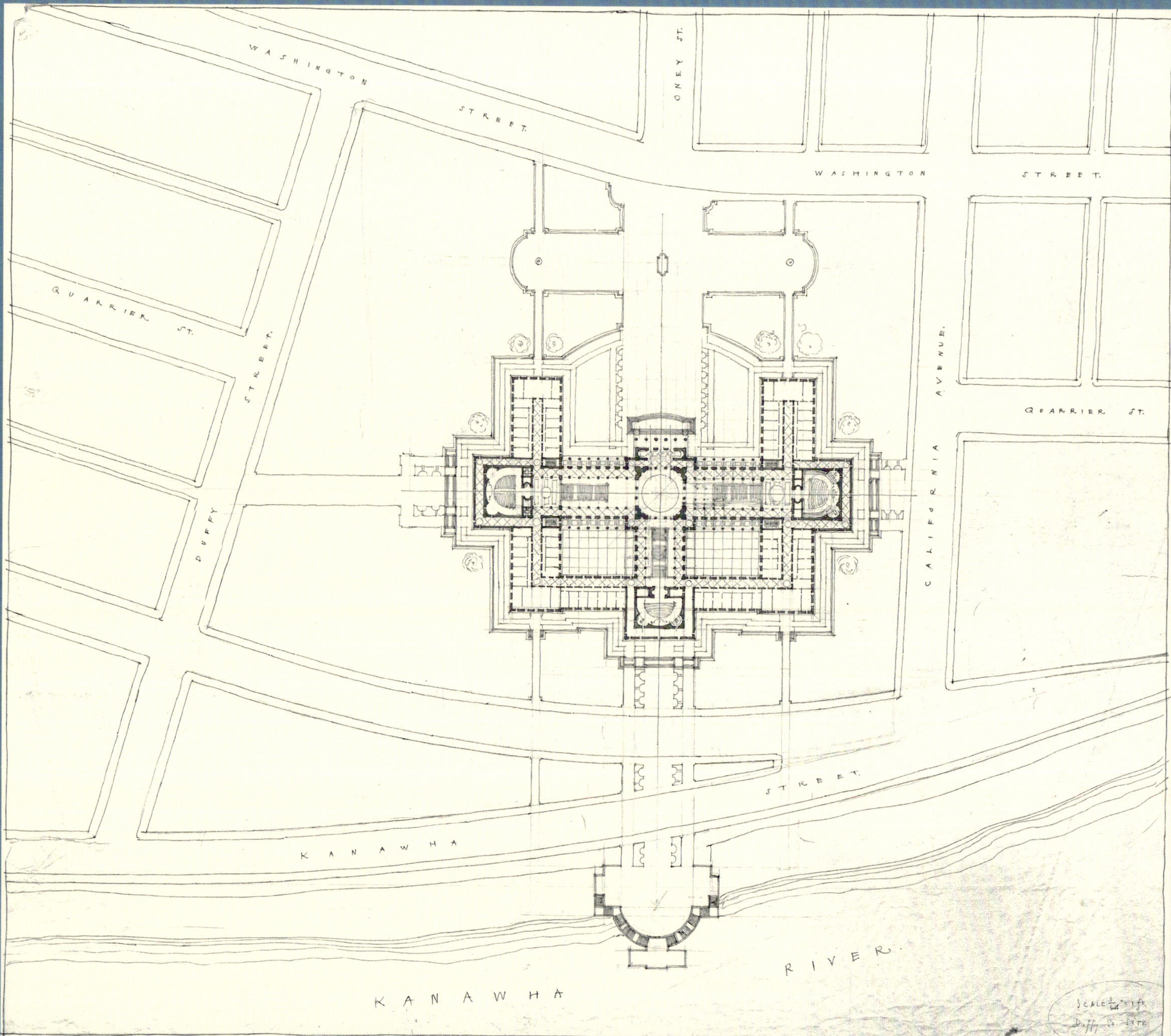


Fig. 28. Cass Gilbert (concept), Proposed ground plan for a single structure for the Duffy Street Site, undated.

The only site for which Gilbert proposed a single structure was Duffy Street. In this plan, semicircular legislative chambers were to the west and east, while a similar, smaller chamber to the south was probably intended for the Supreme Court. The main façade and entrance were to be on the north side of the structure and there was no distinctive entrance on the river side; this design featured a tall dome elevated above two superimposed drums, each with a colonnade of free-standing columns.

In early December, a citizen named Thomas E. Jeffries wrote to the editor of the *Charleston Daily Mail* recommending a skyscraper capitol for the Old Capitol Site. He wanted to replace "ancient and foreign architecture" with "modern and American design and ideas where the sky is the limit for eight miles and the center of the earth is limit for distance below grade." His proposed capitol was to be twenty or more stories high, "large enough to fill all the requirements of the state and small enough to fit the old lot on Capitol Street with a good margin for grass, trees, and parking cars." Jeffries continued, "It could, like the Woolworth Building, be made a beautiful structure that would represent modern American ideas and because we have broken away from the old methods, make West Virginia the talk of the nation and advertise Charleston as nothing else would [and] at the same time satisfy more people than a building in any other location."[27] Jeffries was probably inspired by the plans for the new Nebraska State Capitol, which was receiving nationwide publicity (see fig. 88).

Citizen involvement continued to be important. On December 8, 1921, William G. Conley, a prominent lawyer who resided within the Duffy Street Site, sent a long letter to Governor Morgan with copies to the commissioners and the press.[28] Conley had been West Virginia's Attorney General from 1908 to 1912 and would later serve as governor. He began, "I have heretofore refrained from taking part in the controversy over the location for the new Capitol building. It was my idea that the Commission should be free to decide unhampered by the importunities of persons having selfish interests to serve, but this idea does not now prevail, I am sorry to say." Conley had been inspired to write after he had signed a petition "at the solicitation of three of my neighbors asking that the proposed location at Duffy Street be not selected." He then discovered that "one of the three solicitors has all along been in favor of the proposed location in the country across the Kanawha River at South Ruffner. When I signed the petition I did not know and did not even suspect that any person seriously favored building the Capitol in the country unless it would be those who were financially interested in that location." He continued, "Had I known then, as I have since learned, that there was a strong and well organized effort to locate the Capitol in the country across the Great Kanawha River I would not have signed the petition, and I write this letter to correct my mistake."

When Conley signed the petition, hoping to preserve his home and neighborhood, he assumed that the Old Capitol Site was the obvious alternative. Upon learning that the purpose of the petition was to promote South Ruffner, he decided to express his concern. He began by discussing the impact the South Ruffner Site would have on his neighborhood, pointing out that it would require building an expensive bridge across the river with long and high approaches that would destroy homes, damage others, and "render unfit for high-class residence practically all the homes in that neighborhood." While Conley objected to South Ruffner in part because a Capitol there would be "inaccessible and inconvenient for public use," he feared it would be selected because "the local organization to force the Commission to select the site in the country across the river is a strong and powerful one from a political and financial standpoint."[29] In a choice between South Ruffner and Duffy Street, he was "strongly in favor" of the latter and would "yield [his] selfish interest to the larger interest of the public good, if in the wisdom of the Commission it is to the best interest of the State to take our home."

Conley pointed out that the Acts of the 1877 Legislature, which established the permanent seat of the state government in Charleston, had stated that it "shall never be removed from the place at which the same is located." This, he argued, could be interpreted as meaning the Capitol had to be kept within the city limits; it could even mean that the new Capitol had to be erected "on the site of the destroyed building." He had heard a rumor that "the architect the Commission has employed claims he cannot draw plans to suit the location at the old site even if you purchase additional ground. . . . I dislike to believe this report," Conley added, "but if it be true, then he ought to be discharged as incompetent. I am sure there are hundreds of architects in this country, and some even in this city, who could draw plans and make the building one of beauty and comfort and of which the entire citizenship of this State could be proud." He concluded, "I am taking the liberty of mailing a signed carbon copy of this letter to each of the other members of the Commission and giving it to the press for publication."

What role Conley's letter played in the decision for the Duffy Site a week later is not known, but the bittersweet outcome of Conley's willingness to sacrifice his family home, "with its memories and association," for the good of the state meant that he lost his residence during the development of the site.[30] Later, when Conley was governor, he presided over the construction of the Main Building and the dedication of the Capitol complex in 1932.

Gilbert arrived in Charleston at 11:40 A.M. on December 15 for the meeting that day. According to his diary, he visited the South Ruffner, Duffy, McFarland, and Elk River Sites and went to the hotel, all before meeting the Commission at 2 P.M.[31] Unfortunately, no transcript seems to survive for this meeting.

On December 17, after Gilbert had returned to New York, he penned a draft for an enthusiastic telegram supporting South Ruffner: "I believe the Ruffner site to offer far greater opportunities for artistic development than any other except Capitol Hill, which is apparently out of the question on account of the railroad environment. I have examined and carefully considered twenty-six sites during the past six months without prejudice for or against any and unhesitatingly go on record as advising adopting the Ruffner site because I believe it to be distinctly the

Fig. 29. Cass Gilbert or assistant, Proposed elevation sketch for a single building for the Duffy Street Site, December 1–15, 1921.

best." He supported his conclusion: "It is reasonably accessible now and will become more so as the city grows. It is more consistent with the logical development of the city." In addition, "It is more economical for the State and would provide a superb location for the new Capitol. I believe that we should look to the future as well as the present and that when confronted with two alternatives no mistake is ever made in choosing the larger." Gilbert had second thoughts and revised the draft: "I believe the Ruffner site to be far the best and to offer a superb location for the Capitol and strongly recommend its adoption. I have no hesitation in going on record to this effect and will state my reasons in writing if desired." This also was not sent. In the end, his telegram stated only that the Ruffner Site was "by far the best" and that he could submit a more developed "landscape plan with estimate of cost" if the governor thought it would be helpful.[32] Why Gilbert did not send one of his more enthusiastic drafts is uncertain; perhaps he feared that such an expression could cause trouble for him if the Ruffner site were not chosen, as indeed it was not. It is also possible that one or more members of the Commission had alerted him that there were political or other problems with the Ruffner Site.

The Ruffner Site was promoted at the commissioners' meeting on December 17 by the mayor of Charleston and a number of "our leading business men." In return for a payment of $1.5 million from the State of West Virginia, the group offered to provide 248 acres in this area and build a monumental bridge across the Kanawha. After their presentation, Fred M. Staunton, one of the most active commissioners, moved that the Commission "proceed to ballot on a site and continue until a location for the new State House had been selected."[33] The meeting was adjourned, however, without voting.

The next day Staunton renewed his motion and six ballots were taken; no discussion is documented, but the commissioners' votes reveal their continuing indecision. Because six commissioners and Governor Conley were present, four votes were needed for a majority. Even after months of discussion and consultation with their architect, there was no consensus. On the first three ballots no site received more than two votes. Attention then turned toward the Old Capitol Site, which on the fourth and fifth ballots received three votes. At last, on the sixth, the Old Capitol Site received four votes and the issue was apparently resolved. Discussion, however, revealed that those voting for the Old Capitol Site had presumed the City of Charleston would provide, at no cost to the state, the additional property needed to make it viable. It was not clear if this was the case, and the commissioners requested clarification from the mayor and the chairman of the Capitol Site Committee of the Chamber of Commerce.

On December 19, a commissioner telegraphed Gilbert: "Can you design and build on either the old site extended or the Macfarland street site [a] Capitol and Office Buildings that will in your opinion be adequate, convenient and handsome and keep within the appropriation. Please reply to me, care Governor Morgan ... and your reply will be laid before the Commission Tuesday morning [the twentieth]."

Gilbert's December 20 reply read: "Yes so far as mere physical and working space go, but as you know I regard both McFarland and old capitol sites unsuitable and strongly advise against them."[34]

At the December 20 meeting, the mayor and others reported that the city's offer of free land had been made months earlier, when it was being proposed by some legislators that the capital be moved from Charleston; the offer was, therefore, unrelated to the current question of where to build a new structure in the city.[35] They could not renew the offer, in part because after the discussions of the past months, there was "a very great division of sentiment" among citizens as to where the new capitol should be located.

After a "full discussion" of this response, a seventh ballot was taken and the winner, with four votes, was Duffy Street. The next morning, a sequence of five headlines in the *Charleston Gazette* announced: "Duffy Street Site Is Selected for State House by Commission; Locate Capitol In East End of City, On River; Announcement of Decision of Commission Is Made Public Near Midnight; Site Includes Sixteen Acres in Heart of Residential Section of Charleston; PLOT PURCHASED FOR GOVERNOR'S MANSION ADJOINS THIS PROPERTY."[36] The Duffy Site encompassed land owned by more than forty individuals, who the Commission guaranteed would be paid "fair prices, and no more than fair prices." The "Commission expects the hearty cooperation of the citizens and the City of Charleston in securing the site at prices fair to the State of West Virginia." Public opinion in support of the Old Capitol Site was so strong that the commissioners felt they had to explain why it had not been selected; they pointed out that it was too small to provide for current and expected needs, it was "being rapidly surrounded by business buildings of great height," it was three feet below high water, and to build there would cost approximately $1 million more than the chosen site. The commissioners emphasized that even with additional property, "there would be no outlook which a monumental, as well as useful building should have," and "the opinion of every architect before the Commission was that the old site was not adapted to the proper symmetrical development of a state building."[37] The commissioners' choice of words reveals that even before the site was chosen their preference was for a Capitol building that was "monumental" and "symmetrical."

On December 21, Cass Gilbert telegraphed his "hearty congratulations to the Governor and Capitol Commission" on their choice of the Duffy Site: "It is excellent and will make an admirable location for the new capitol."[38] As an architect who had worked for decades with powerful politicians and businessmen, he understood that cooperation and collegiality should characterize his relationship with patrons.

That the Duffy Site was selected is surprising, for on six previous ballots it never received more than a single vote and its development required displacing the residents of one of Charleston's best neighborhoods. Equally curious is the commissioners' disregard for the South Ruffner proposal, despite the preference the architect had expressed for it. Decades later, Houston Young reported that the commissioners had avoided the Ruffner Site because Commissioner Staunton owned property there and its selection would have been interpreted as a means of enriching a Commission member. This statement is revealing, because soon after the 1922 vote Staunton himself "expressed his sense of disappointment" that South Ruffner had not been chosen.[39] There had clearly been a power struggle, but which actors made their decisions on what grounds remains uncertain; money was surely at the basis of their disagreements, however, because the selection of the site had financial implications for all who would be buying and selling property.[40]

On December 30, Gilbert requested a survey and aerial photographs of the chosen site: "One or two airplane photograph views, if they could be conveniently made, would be useful in this connection.... The negatives of all such photographs should be dated, numbered and titled so as to show the record in the photographic prints." Gilbert underlined the importance of organizing such materials: "Such surveys and record photographs should be in duplicate, one copy for your files and one for mine. They will always be of historical interest and may become very valuable to the Board in letting or negotiating contracts and in litigation that might ensue either in taking possession of the property or in execution of work on the job."[41]

Acquiring the more than sixty properties in the Duffy Street residential area was complex, lengthy, and well documented. More than a year later, in January 1923, only two parcels remained to be purchased.[42] Some homes had been moved, including twelve that were ferried across the Kanawha on barges to South Ruffner; others were rented until they were demolished and a few served as temporary office space for the contractor, the architect's supervisor of construction, and the Commission's secretary.

In January 1922, Gilbert demonstrated his concern for improving the approach to the site in a letter to Commissioner Keatley: "I have just finished reading Charles Moore's 'Life of Daniel H. Burnham' and I am immensely impressed with the importance of a proper setting for the capitol and of a development for the City Plan so the capitol may have an axial line of approach as well as a fine view from the river and the railroads and I hope you will give this your earnest consideration." He emphasized that "the City of Charleston must do *something* to correct the lines of some of the streets so that the site shall be all that we hope to make it. It should be done *now*. It will never cost less. It should be planned and established by law *now*, even if not executed immediately"[43] [Gilbert's emphases].

With the location fixed, Gilbert was optimistic that construction could begin in 1922. Although he wrote on February 24 that the site map he received was "not complete enough to cover the purposes set forth in my letter of December 30th," he was still planning to establish foundations that summer. To raise funds, the sale of the "Old State House Grounds" was planned for April.[44] Gilbert now began to prepare initial design proposals for the Duffy Site, a process that would last until the summer of 1922.

Fig. 30. Houses being moved across the Kanawha River from the New Capitol Site. The high supports were required because of the elevation of both the Duffy Street and South Ruffner locations above the Kanawha River.

ERECTED FOR THE PEOPLE OF WEST VIRGINIA

CHAPTER FOUR

# The Initial Design Phase: "A Simple Dignified Structure of Fine Proportions"

It is my desire that the building be of a very dignified and pure type of architecture, something that will last and be permanently approved by the best public taste. Eccentricities of design will be avoided . . .

Cass Gilbert, quoted in the *Charleston Daily Mail*, July 19, 1922

Fig. 31. Cass Gilbert/Studio, Detail of proposal for the West Virginia Capitol (see fig. 33).

WITH THE LOCATION FIXED AND ACQUISITION OF LAND under way, the design process could begin. At a meeting with Cass Gilbert in June 1922, Governor Morgan and the commissioners seem to have declared their preference for a central structure with a high dome similar to that of the National Capitol in Washington and flanked by two office buildings.

A history of earlier state capitol design explains the enthusiasm of all parties—Gilbert, Morgan, and the commissioners—for a design inspired by that of the National Capitol.[1] The earliest state houses were relatively simple Colonial brick buildings. The first monumental capitols built after independence were those designed for Virginia by Thomas Jefferson (see fig. 3; 1785–98) and for Massachusetts by Charles Bulfinch (1795–98). Both feature a portico with Greco-Roman columns and a pediment, but Bulfinch capped his Massachusetts Capitol with a dome. The Capitols of New Jersey (1792), Connecticut (1792–95/1822), and New Hampshire (1816–18) continued the dome motif with small cupola-domes, while other early state capitols combined Classical porticoes with larger domes (North Carolina, Vermont, and the first Capitols of Mississippi, Illinois, and Florida). By 1850, the dome had become an identifying symbol for state capitols.

Shortly after 1850, a new and highly symbolic model became available: the dome added to the National Capitol by Thomas U. Walter between 1855 and 1866.[2] The idea that the US Capitol should have a dome can be traced back to Pierre L'Enfant, who envisioned a national capitol with an interior rotunda surmounted by a dome in his 1792 plan for Washington. The dome seen in the earliest designs for the National Capitol was transformed in shape and height by various architects. In the wake of the Civil War, Walter's final solution—a tall dome pushed high by a drum surrounded by a ring of magnificent freestanding columns—became the quintessential symbol of national unity.

Not all capitols erected after the Civil War were based on the National Capitol model, however, and not all had domes. Governors and legislators who wanted to suggest their states were progressive chose "modern" styles. New York's Capitol, for example, is Richardsonian Romanesque in style and has no dome. State Houses in Michigan and Connecticut feature the eclectic Victorian style, but even these incorporated small domes. The Victorian Gothic style was chosen for West Virginia's Fourth Capitol (1880–85), but with a tall clock tower as its focal point, not a dome (see fig. 11).

This West Virginia Capitol bucked the trend, for by the end of the nineteenth century the most popular state house design was modeled on the National Capitol. By 1900, seven such capitols had been built and between 1893 and 1899 foundations were laid for seven more, including Gilbert's Minnesota Capitol (see fig. 13).[3] When its cornerstone was laid in 1898, a commissioner noted that the public, "educated by familiarity with the great Capitol building at Washington, required that this should be a domed building, with impressive approaches and an extensive rotunda." In 1901, the Minnesota Capitol Commissioners stated: "public sentiment showed that a central dome and rotunda must be part of the design, and that the people would not be satisfied with any other."[4]

The trend continued in the early twentieth century with the capitols of Mississippi, Kentucky, South Dakota, Idaho, Wisconsin, Utah, Missouri, and Washington.[5] The idea that state capitols needed a dome similar to that of the National Capitol was confirmed in Maine in 1909–11, when the low dome of Bulfinch's 1832 Capitol was replaced with a dome on a high drum.

By 1932, when West Virginia's Capitol was dedicated, more than half of American state houses followed the National Capitol model.[6] Only potent symbolism can explain the popularity of this configuration, for the visual drama of a dome and the grand public space it creates below cannot justify the expense; during discussions in 1923 about how to finance the West Virginia Capitol, Cass Gilbert's office estimated that eliminating the dome would save $1,142,000.[7] The many governors, legislators, and building commissioners who chose designs based on the National Capitol model in the decades after the Civil War may have done so in the belief that this would express their state's unity with the nation. Such a motivation would have been especially appropriate for West Virginia, whose citizens had rejected secessionist infidelity by voting in 1861 to maintain their relationship with the Union.

A modern alternative to the National Capitol model was available to West Virginia's commissioners, for in 1920 the Nebraska Capitol Commission had chosen a design that is often referred to as the nation's first "skyscraper capitol" (see fig. 88).[8] The modern was still a novelty in 1921, however, when Governor Morgan and the commissioners selected a design based on the popular National Capitol model; they must have been confident that their choice would place West Virginia within a venerable symbolic and historic tradition.[9]

In January 1922, Gilbert began refining his designs for the Duffy Street Site. On January 5, he noted in his diary: "I worked on the Tennessee competition for a time, and on the West Va. Capitol sketch plan with Rockart."[10] The next mention was on April 18: "worked on West Va Capitol." His entry for April 20 indicates the variety of work Gilbert pursued in a single day:

> Cold & gloomy weather.
>
> Called at Blashfield's studio this A.M. & spent an hour with him looking at & discussing his great paintings for the stair hall of the Detroit Library. The two end lunettes and the two principal side panels are about finished.
>
> At office on [US Chamber of Congress] & various jobs. In late afternoon I struck what I think will be the motif for the West Virginia State Capitol—Cass Jr., Stickel & Rockart were with me.
>
> I stayed at home in evening.[11]

The accompanying sketch shows a ground plan for the left portion of a capitol with a rotunda entered through columned porticoes on both sides. When completed with symmetrical elements to the right, the rotunda is flanked by columned foyers leading to legislative chambers and two subsidiary buildings

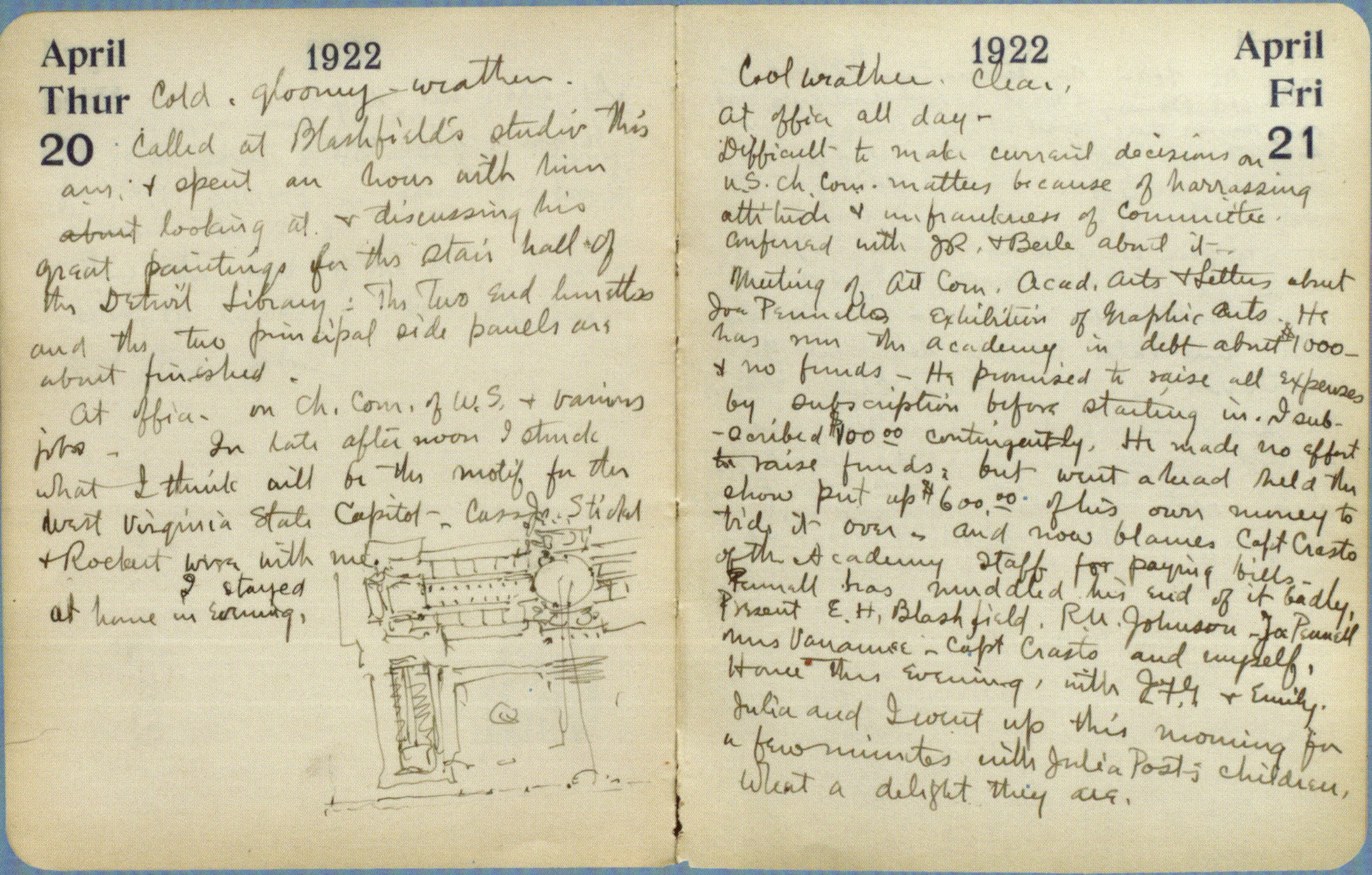


Fig. 32. Cass Gilbert, Diary entry for April 20, 1922, with proposal for the West Virginia Capitol (left). The sketch shows only the central dome/rotunda area and the wings on the left; to complete the plan, add symmetrical wings on the right.

form a U-shaped courtyard. In its general outlines, this "motif" is remarkably similar to later plans and the complex as built (see fig. 38). The chamber at the lower left may have been intended for the Supreme Court of Appeals; if the opposite wing was to house the governor's office in the same position—as seems likely given Gilbert's taste for symmetry—the three branches of state government would be housed in three separate buildings. Gilbert promoted this three-building, three-branches-of-government concept to his patrons at a meeting in New York two months later.

This design was only one of several on which Gilbert was musing. Three days later, he drew a plan for the West Virginia Capitol that was "suggested by the Baths of Diocletian." This design, which is similar to the Palace of Fine Arts Gilbert had designed for the Louisiana Purchase Exposition in St. Louis (1901–04; now the St. Louis Art Museum), incorporates the three branches into a single structure and, like the ancient Roman and St. Louis complexes that inspired it, has no dome.[12] Many other proposals were sketched or more fully prepared as Gilbert finalized plans for meeting with Governor Morgan and the commissioners in New York on June 22, 1922.

This meeting was held at Gilbert's Madison Avenue studio, where the governor and the commissioners could be impressed with the quality, extent, and organization of his office.[13] And, in New York, Gilbert could have at hand all the drawings needed in a setting where he could control their presentation. Perhaps most important was the psychological advantage this location would give the architect over the powerful politicians who were his patrons.

Commissioner Staunton arrived early and, calling on the architect on June 20, brought the disappointing news that land acquisition was taking longer and proving considerably more expensive than anticipated.[14] He feared the Duffy Site would cost as much as $800,000 more than the South Ruffner location, which could lead the public and press to question why it was selected. This overrun would also reduce the amount available for construction. The delay had raised a further problem, for Staunton reported, "Unless work is under way when [the] Legislature meets, the site will be changed to another city."

Gilbert's transcript of his meeting with Staunton reveals that the latter was worried about the plans for the new Governor's Mansion, and that he asked Gilbert "to informally advise him about a design for it, that the local architect [Walter F. Martens] did not seem to be trained in that sort of thing and he feared would not do it well. I said I would help all that I could." Staunton must have brought Martens's tentative plan with him, since Gilbert noted that after the commissioner left: "I made a study of the plan & asked Mr Ward to draw it to scale."[15]

The all-day meeting on June 22 was attended by Governor Morgan, six commissioners, Secretary Young, and Bonner Hill, the recently hired agent for land acquisition.[16] Ultimately they were shown more than eighty drawings, but the transcript of the meeting makes it clear that Gilbert choreographed the presentation to gain acceptance of his preferred design.[17] First, however, the space requests of various departments were discussed. In the architect's opinion, some departments "had asked for a great deal more space than they would require not only for present needs but for their future expansion," and he had reduced these as seemed appropriate.[18] Gilbert then showed proposals for a complex of three buildings, one for each of the branches of state government. The transcript suggests that this complex featured a central structure with a tall dome in the National Capitol model and two buildings perpendicular to it, much like the drawing in his diary and the finished complex.[19] Gilbert located the bicameral Legislature in the central, domed building as an expression of the democratic foundations of American government.

The symbolism of giving each branch its own building is consistent with Gilbert's architectural philosophy. He supported his suggestion with an economic consideration: because the Legislature would not be in continuous session, the Main Building, which Gilbert called "the Capitol," could be "closed up when not in use and would require less up-keep.... With the three buildings the Capitol itself would be built of more elaborate design and finish whereas the office buildings could be finished in cheaper material as office buildings." He explained that he had "tried out one building and found that the expense was so great that he had not developed the scheme." Gilbert then showed renderings of how the complex would look when completed.[20]

Gilbert may have made a misstep, for Governor Morgan seems to have been offended by the location of his office in a building finished in "cheaper material." Morgan argued that his office should be in the "Capitol," as should those of the secretary of state, attorney general, and pardon attorney. One commissioner suggested moving the legislative chambers up one floor to make room for more offices on the main floor. The architect countered that such a change would necessitate grand staircases on the interior, which were expensive and required a great deal of space. Such a move would also demand changes in the exterior because of "the necessity of having the elevation tell the story of the plan.... If the Senate and House were put on the second floor the [exterior] columns or pilasters would have to be raised to that story in order to tell that the main rooms were there." For Gilbert, the symbolic and visual integrity of the Capitol would be compromised if the legislative chambers were moved up without reflecting this on the elevation. Commissioner Camden criticized the dome—which he called the "tower"—as too high, but Gilbert pointed out that an elevation drawing did not represent how the structure would appear when seen in perspective from the ground.[21]

The ballot taken on Gilbert's proposal for a three-building, U-shaped complex dominated by a tall dome passed with a single dissenting vote from Commissioner Camden who, perhaps not coincidentally, was a Democrat. In the partisan debates that followed, it was West Virginia's Democrats who criticized the cost of the new Capitol. Camden's negative vote may have been based on his disapproval of the dome as an expensive symbol.

Gilbert's efficiency in bringing the commissioners to a quick agreement on a design is impressive. This step determined the form of the West Virginia Capitol;

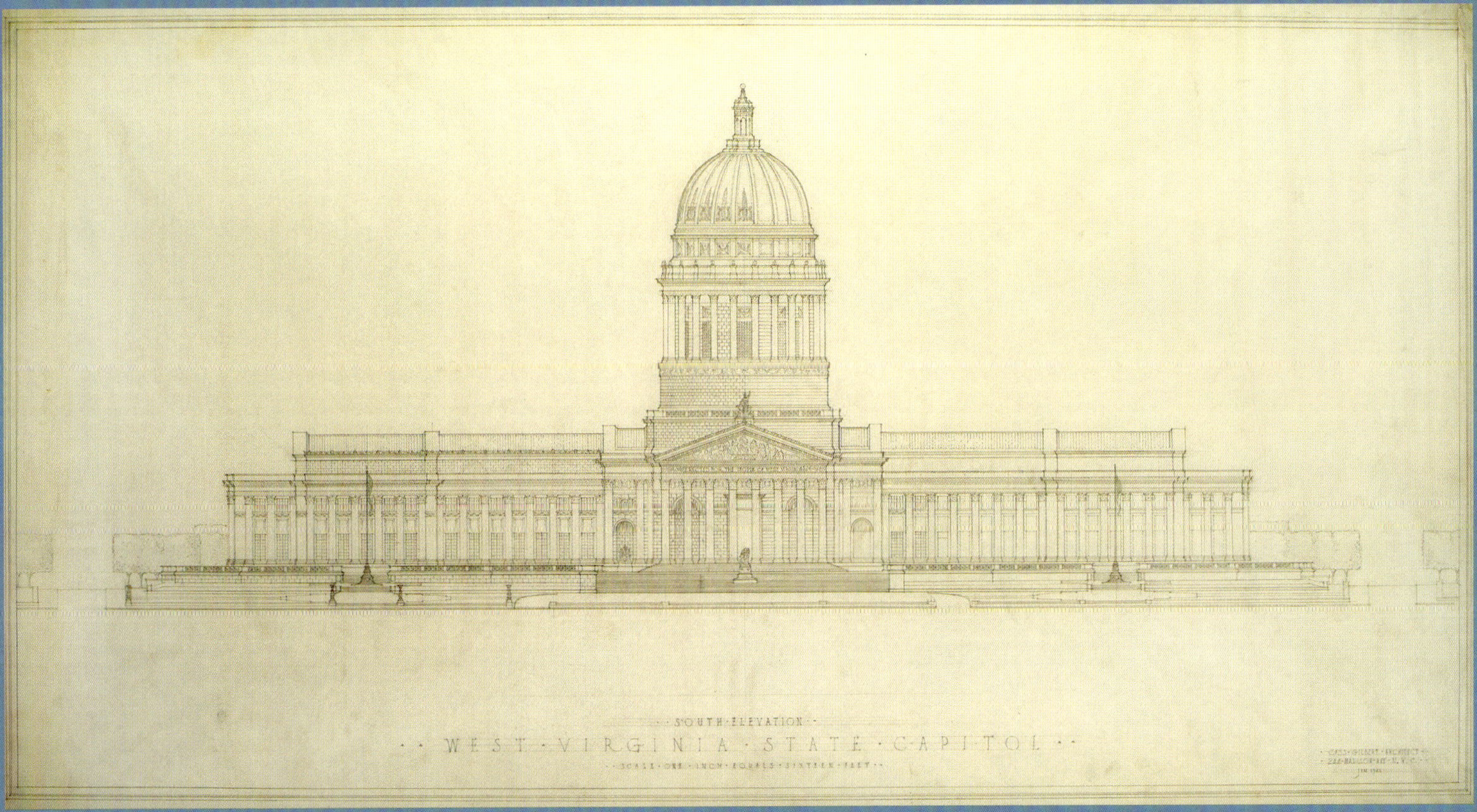


Fig. 33. Cass Gilbert/Studio, Elevation proposal for the West Virginia Capitol, June 1922. This is probably one of the drawings shown to the governor and commissioners at the meeting in New York on June 22, 1922.

despite legislative and public criticism and financial difficulties, the complex dedicated ten years later is the result of decisions made in New York on June 22, 1922.

The meeting was not over at this point, for after the plan was approved Gilbert showed other designs he had prepared. Offering customers alternatives after they have decided which product to buy is an advertising no-no, but Gilbert was no naïve salesman. The delay in picking the site had cost him time and money; now, after more than five months spent envisioning a variety of possibilities for the Duffy Site, his goal at this meeting was to convince his patrons to agree on a design so that planning could move forward. Once agreement was reached, he could present alternatives to confirm the wisdom of their decision. When they selected Gilbert, the commissioners had revealed their preference for a design based on the National Capitol model, and their enthusiasm for this type of capitol had probably been clarified in their initial meetings and discussions of his proposals for various sites. By starting this meeting with a compelling design based on that model and asking them to vote on it, he had limited debate and reached a quick resolution.

Most of Gilbert's alternatives were represented as ground plans, without elevation drawings or renderings, and most do not have a dome. Several are large, rectangular buildings with areas devoted to all three branches of government, and should be related to the architect's statement, made earlier that day, that "he had tried out one building and found that the expense was so great that he had not developed the scheme." Clearly he was encouraging his patrons to find these proposals unacceptable. One plan for a large, single building has a dome at the center, but it was small and would have made little impact when seen from the exterior. The inadequacy of these designs is clear in light of the Commission's preference for a design based on the National Capitol.

One of these alternative plans and a related drawing exemplify the dome-less option. The plan shows a rectangular building with four large public rooms; the two semicircular ones to the left were probably intended as legislative chambers, the square ones to the right for the Supreme Court and governor (see fig. 34). That all four are the same size expresses the American ideal that the branches of government are equal in power; Gilbert consistently allotted the House of Delegates and Senate the same square footage, confirming the balance of power between them despite the disparity in number of members. Two broad porticoes and deep open porches, each with five rows of columns, provided grand entrances but little functional space. A long axial hallway, lined with more columns, was lit through clerestory windows; this aspect of the design can be related to Gilbert's April 23 sketch inspired by the Baths of Diocletian and his St. Louis Art Museum. While this proposal is pleasingly and symbolically symmetrical, a maze of corridors was necessary to gain access to the chambers and offices.

The related elevation appears to have been quickly sketched, suggesting it may have been prepared during the meeting, perhaps at the request of the commissioners (see fig. 35). To create architectural interest for his proposals without domes, Gilbert added columns and pilasters on the exterior; in this case, an impressive row of twelve freestanding columns draw attention to the pair of entrance porches. The arched Diocletian windows that would light the interior are seen above the porches. The exterior columns bring to mind McKim, Mead & White's Pennsylvania Station in New York City (1904–10), which itself was inspired by the bathing structures of Imperial Rome. No other state had a capitol based on an ancient Roman bath complex; had West Virginia's governor and commissioners noted this proposal's similarity to the railroad station where they had arrived in New York, they would certainly have found this suggestion unacceptable.

Although Gilbert didn't note on any of his National Capitol-type drawings that they had been shown on June 22, two superbly detailed elevations are dated "June '22"; figure 33 is one example.[22] Both have the grandeur that would impress patrons who preferred this style of capitol. While the two drawings differ in specific decorative elements, the identical proportions of the portico and use of unfluted columns in both reveal the inspiration of the Pantheon in Rome. A dome with a tall drum crowns both designs; these lofty domes may explain Commissioner Camden's criticism that the "tower" in Gilbert's designs was too high. The pediments have figural decoration, and an impressive multifigured acroterion inspired by ancient precedents rises above the pediment in figure 33. In both drawings the domes are windowless, and each vertical panel is handsomely decorated with a wreath and a tapering form that echoes the curvature of the dome. The tapering form resembles a feather (perhaps a reference to the pens with which the Declaration of Independence was signed?) or the head of a stalk of wheat as a reference to agrarian abundance and prosperity. Garlands based on ancient Roman examples embellish the attic area, as they do in the completed Capitol (see fig. 75). A memo dated June 1922 lists the dimensions of the proposed central building: 550 by 142 feet, with a dome rising 280 feet above street level.[23]

In each drawing a broad exterior staircase leads up to an entrance onto the legislative floor; this is an important change from Gilbert's Minnesota Capitol (see fig. 13), where the exterior staircase leads to doors that open into a lower floor. Once inside the Minnesota Capitol, visitors who wanted to ascend to the legislative level had to use the expensive and space-consuming grand stairways that Gilbert wanted to avoid for West Virginia. But perhaps saving money and space were not Gilbert's most important motivations in suggesting this change. As in the drawings, the exterior steps at the Capitol in Charleston mount directly toward the core of American democracy: the rotunda that opens into the foyers leading to the legislative chambers.

Once the basic design had been determined, the governor and commissioners made suggestions about the plan. They wanted the office buildings connected to the "Capitol," and the architect had accepted Governor Morgan's request that his office be located there.[24] The latter concession forced Gilbert to abandon his idea that each branch be housed in a separate building. In giving this up, he revealed the perennial dilemma faced by architects: how to reconcile personal philosophical or architectural ideals with the desires of patrons.

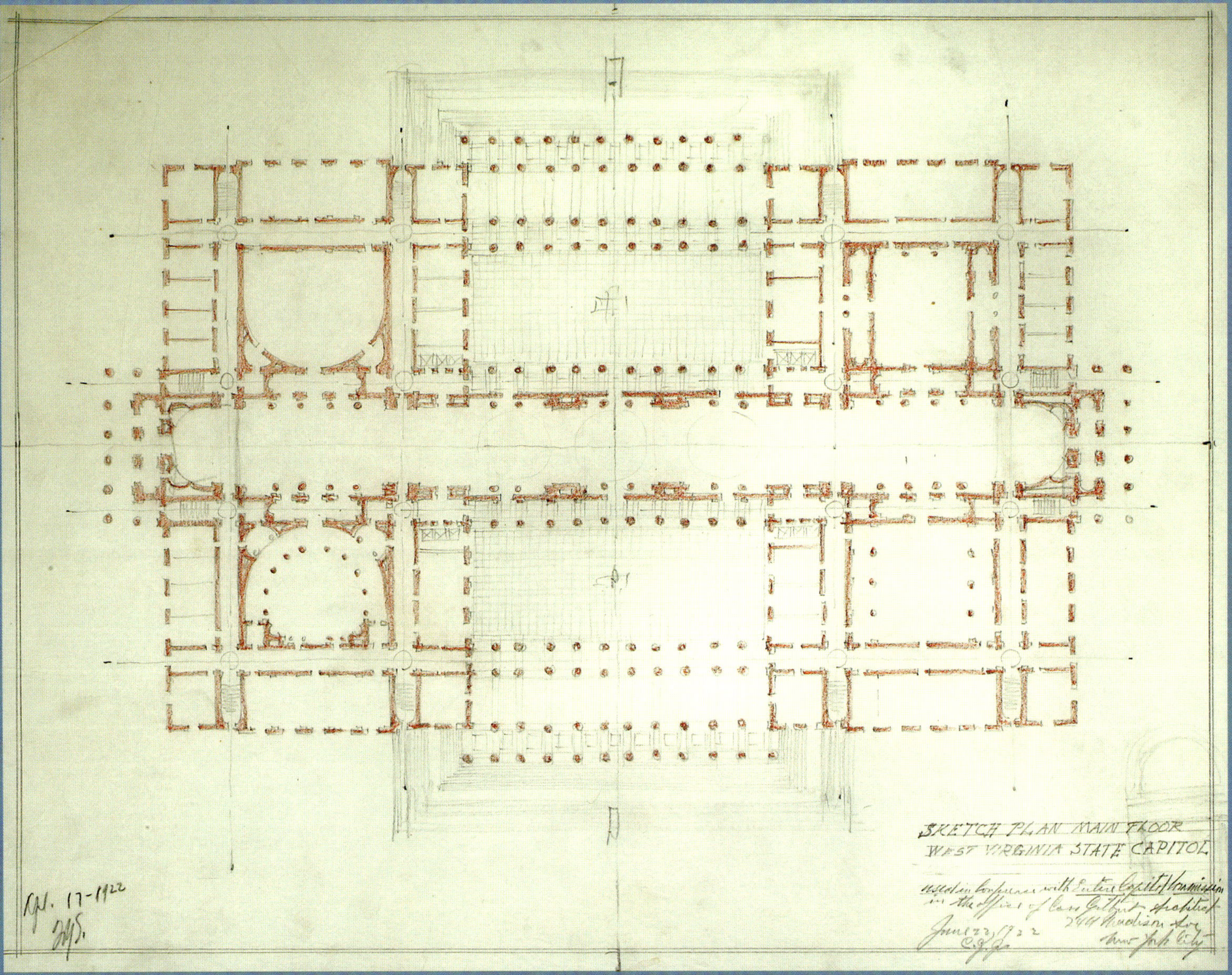


Fig. 34. Cass Gilbert (concept), Ground plan proposal for the West Virginia Capitol, drawing by Frederick G. Stickel, shown on June 22, 1922.

Fig. 35. Cass Gilbert (concept), Elevation proposal for the West Virginia Capitol, dated April 12 and 17, 1922, drawing by Frederick G. Stickel.

Gilbert estimated the cost at approximately seventy-five cents a cubic foot without statuary and decorations.[25] When asked if $700,000 would be sufficient for these additions, Gilbert replied it would be "more than enough." Governor Morgan underlined that it was important that they keep within the appropriation, which Gilbert assured them would be possible. The architect hoped "excavation work could begin by the middle of the summer and ... that some time next winter or early spring, before March [1923]," the contract for the superstructure could be signed.[26] Had an appropriation been available, the whole complex could have been completed by late 1924 or early 1925.

After the meeting, Cass Jr. took Governor Morgan on a tour of the Woolworth Building before returning him to the Waldorf-Astoria Hotel. When Commissioner Staunton arrived to see Cass Sr. the next day, he underlined the suggestion that some offices be in the Main Building and countered Commissioner Camden's suggestion that West Virginia bluestone be considered as a building material with his own preference for marble.

Work continued on refining the design, and on July 11 Gilbert asked: "When does Commission expect me in Charleston? Can be there with new plans any day next week or all week if desired." He offered to stay as long as needed and bring "more complete restudies of design."[27] The meeting was called for July 17.

On July 10, William MacCorkle, ex-governor of West Virginia, visited Cass Gilbert in New York.[28] He was greeted by Cass Jr. and, before Cass Sr. entered the room, MacCorkle told the son that he had come to "strengthen Mr. Gilbert's back-bone." Apparently Gilbert was being criticized in West Virginia, and MacCorkle feared he would face difficulties when he returned to Charleston. Cass Jr. reported, "I told him that Mr. Gilbert's back-bone was about the strongest part and that although he might give it some support he could not strengthen it because it was already very strong. Mr. Gilbert came in as we were laughing at the joke." MacCorkle also wanted Gilbert to design a hotel for Charleston and redo the memorial in Lexington, Virginia, where Robert E. Lee was buried; neither project seems to have reached the drawing board.

MacCorkle informed Cass Sr. he should not weaken his Capitol plan because West Virginia was "very wealthy" and "they could easily raise the money should the estimate run too high." Gilbert reiterated his intent to design a Capitol that could be erected within the appropriation. Gilbert consistently rejected proposals to increase the appropriation: later, when criticism was leveled at the cost, he pointed out that he had always worked within the limits set by the Legislature.

When MacCorkle reported that the Commissioners thought the building was a little larger than expected, Gilbert replied that it was only forty-four feet longer than the Arkansas Capitol. At this point, the architect showed the ex-governor a sketch of a single structure housing all three branches that was probably related to a plan dated three days later for a building measuring 672 by 320 feet. MacCorkle asked about the "beauty" and Gilbert replied "the interior halls would be the finest things in the country," but he regretted "the loss of the big court between the two office buildings of the original scheme." The scale of this structure, which if built would be 114 feet longer and 200 feet wider than the Main Building today, may have been intended to convince the commissioners that a single structure was not feasible.[29]

Gilbert opened the July 17–18 meeting in Charleston by announcing he had moved the governor's office into the Main Building and connected the buildings as requested.[30] After studying eight designs, the commissioners accepted the one they had tentatively approved in June and instructed Gilbert to develop it with minor changes.[31] They informed Gilbert that the funds available for construction would be $7,000,000, from which $500,000 would be set aside for decorations, sculpture, landscaping, and changing the grade of Kanawha Street (now Kanawha Boulevard). Gilbert reported that construction costs had increased to eighty cents per cubic foot, which meant the complex could not exceed eight million cubic feet.[32] When some commissioners proposed asking for an additional appropriation, Gilbert assured them this would not be necessary.

On July 17, headlines in the *Clarksburg Telegram* reported that the Commission was studying plans for a "Group of Three Buildings." Headlines in the July 19 *Charleston Daily Mail* stated: "RENAISSANCE STYLE IS VIRTUALLY DECIDED ON FOR CAPITOL BUILDING; Commission in Session Today Considering Drawings; Cass Gilbert, Architect, Tells of Design He Has Worked Out."[33] It was here that Gilbert identified his design as "Renaissance" in style. In so doing, he was referring to the European Renaissance, which at the time was defined broadly in terms of area and chronology; his inspirations encompassed examples from Italy, France, and England that spanned the fifteenth to the early eighteenth century. Gilbert was quoted in the article: "It is my desire that the building be of a very dignified and pure type of architecture, something that will last and be permanently approved by the best public taste. Eccentricities of design will be avoided, for I believe that a simple, dignified structure of fine proportions is far more satisfactory in the long run than any amount of elaborate embellishment, or so-called novelty of detail." To unify the design, "the whole structure will be crowned by a dome of majestic proportions." Gilbert envisioned the Charleston Capitol as the culmination of his career as an architect of public buildings: "I want to make this capitol building the crowning work of my life. It is the type of building to which I have devoted the past 25 years of my life, and I feel that the opportunity is now presented to me for a splendid architectural monument. The best is none too good for West Virginia and, therefore, I am anxious to respond to the best of my ability to the responsibility the capitol commission has placed in me." Such hyperbole, which surely must have impressed his patrons, is not unexpected from Gilbert, but the West Virginia Capitol would have been the capstone of his already remarkable career had he not subsequently received the commission for the US Supreme Court Building.

Gilbert's diary reports that he and Julia were entertained in Charleston by former Governor MacCorkle and his wife:

7/20: Charleston, West Va. Warm weather, clear. Called up Mr. Keatley—told him river wall should be held off until cost of capitol was known. Had made similar statement to Mr. Staunton & Gov Morgan and all agreed that this is the right course. Called on Houston Young and found Atty Genl there—told them same as to river wall. Both said I was correct. Called on Mr John Thayer and thanked him for putting me up at the Country Club. Gov and Mrs. Morgan came to hotel at 10:30 and took us by motor to Ex Gov MacCorkle's where we met Ex Gov MacCorkle and his wife and Old Tom served us a delicious Mint Julep with the mint standing in great bunches a foot high above the rim of each glass. We sat on the side porch and drank this nectar and ate little sandwiches until it was time to go to the train—MacCorkle has a house full of interesting things especially LaFayette engravings & relics—a bust of Wm Pitt &c &c. Gov & Mrs. Morgan took us to the station & we took the noon train east. Arrived at White Sulphur Springs—Greenbrier hotel about 4:25 PM.

Gilbert described the Greenbrier as "beautiful and very restful." Julia's role in advising on business issues is documented in his diary during this interlude, for they "had a long talk about our financial affairs and figured out our assets. We talked of incorporating my office and various business questions."

Although a design had been tentatively approved, financing was still uncertain. A July 17, 1922, article in the *Clarksburg Telegram* reported that the total cost of the new building, with land, was expected to be $9.5 million, with $6.5 million raised by taxation and $3 million from the sale of the old property. In reality, however, the Legislature had appropriated no funds for construction and no tax supporting construction had been levied.[34]

By August 7, Gilbert was back in New York working on the Capitol, the US Chamber of Commerce Building, and other projects, as indicated by his usual abbreviation in his diaries, "&c." On August 14, Rockart and Cass Jr. presented the final plans to the commissioners in Charleston; Cass Sr. was available for questions by telephone.[35] There was little discussion of the overall design, but Commissioner Fitzpatrick suggested where certain offices should be located. When asked about the cost, Cass Jr. telephoned his father, who told him "that the buildings as shown by the plan could be built inside the appropriation.... [I do] not contemplate a building program in excess of the appropriation."[36] The commissioners approved the design and authorized borings to determine the stability of the ground prior to construction.[37]

Renderings of the new Capitol were published in the *Charleston Daily Mail* on September 2, 1922. The design became national news, as attested by clippings in the architect's scrapbook from the *Manufacturers Record* (Baltimore), the *St. Louis Post-Dispatch*, the *Detroit Free Press*, the *Christian Science Monitor*, the *Philadelphia Public Ledger*, and the *Baltimore American*. The headline in the *Manufacturers Record* read "West Virginia's New Capitol to Be Greatest of Its Kind—Reckoned Among World's Most Beautiful—Cost with Site $9,500,000."[38] The most compelling published design is the night view commissioned by Gilbert from Hugh Ferriss, in which the illuminated dome glows against the night sky and a flood of light from the portico invites the multitudes surging outside to enter. This idealized rendering—what occasion could prompt such a gathering, and what lighting would make such

Fig. 36. Cass Gilbert (concept), Rendering of the accepted design for the West Virginia State Capitol, as released for publication, July 1922. Drawing by Hugh Ferriss. An inscription to the right bears the date July [illegible], 1922.

effects possible?—demonstrates how Gilbert could use a vision of his finished structure to seduce patrons when presenting a proposal.

On September 18, 1922, Commissioner Staunton stopped by Gilbert's New York office during a trip that included visits to "public buildings."[39] Gilbert was out, but Staunton spoke to Rockart, who transcribed their discussion. The commissioner reported on his visit to McKim, Mead & White's Rhode Island Capitol: he had disliked the "four minarets" around the dome and criticized the grand staircases for blocking the vista through the interior. Staunton hoped Gilbert would use white marble for West Virginia's Capitol, adding he would petition the Legislature for an increase of 5 to 10 percent in the appropriation if needed. Staunton even made a stylistic recommendation, stating his desire that both the exterior and the interior should be based on "a simple design with proper proportion" and that the Capitol should impress through "simplicity rather than ornament." Because few comments concerning style are documented from West Virginia's governors and commissioners, Staunton's recommendations document at least one commissioner's preferences. Rockart replied that Gilbert wanted the Capitol to be "as simple as possible but in good proportion and to retain the impressiveness from the latter." Staunton "expressed his sense of disappointment in the choice of the site, feeling that the site across the river should have been selected." Rockart agreed, but emphasized that the chosen site offered the possibility of making "the situation of the buildings very impressive." Staunton's comment on the South Ruffner Site is surprising, given the later report that he had owned some of that property and that the commissioners had worried that selecting South Ruffner might be seen as self-serving.

Once the design was accepted, finished drawings and specifications were prepared so bidding could begin. As the design was being refined, Gilbert realized the budget might preclude the murals and sculptural embellishment characteristic of public buildings at that time. In November 1922, when a Brooklyn Museum of Art curator wrote to recommend a muralist, the architect replied that it was too early to bring this up, adding, "the money available for the Capitol building may not be sufficient to permit of any extensive decoration."[40] Already at this point, then, Gilbert understood that his design, not historical narratives or allegories represented in murals or sculpture, would have to communicate his ideology and express the dignity of West Virginia's statehood.

In December 1922, replying to a letter from Houston Young, Gilbert wrote that while progress on the drawings meant that construction could start in the spring, "several considerations" required a meeting with the Commission.[41] Gilbert probably did not know the extent of the trouble then brewing in West Virginia. In the immediate future, his appointment would be questioned, an investigation would be launched, the Commission would be asked to prepare a report for the House of Delegates, and the possibility of moving the capital away from Charleston would again be raised. In addition, an appropriation for construction was still months away.

Fig. 37. Cass Gilbert (concept), Rendering of the West Virginia State Capitol at night, March 1923, as published in *The American Architect* in 1929. Drawing by Hugh Ferriss. This rendering was also published in the *Christian Science Monitor* on July [illegible], 1923.

CASS GILBERT ARCHITECT MARCH 1923

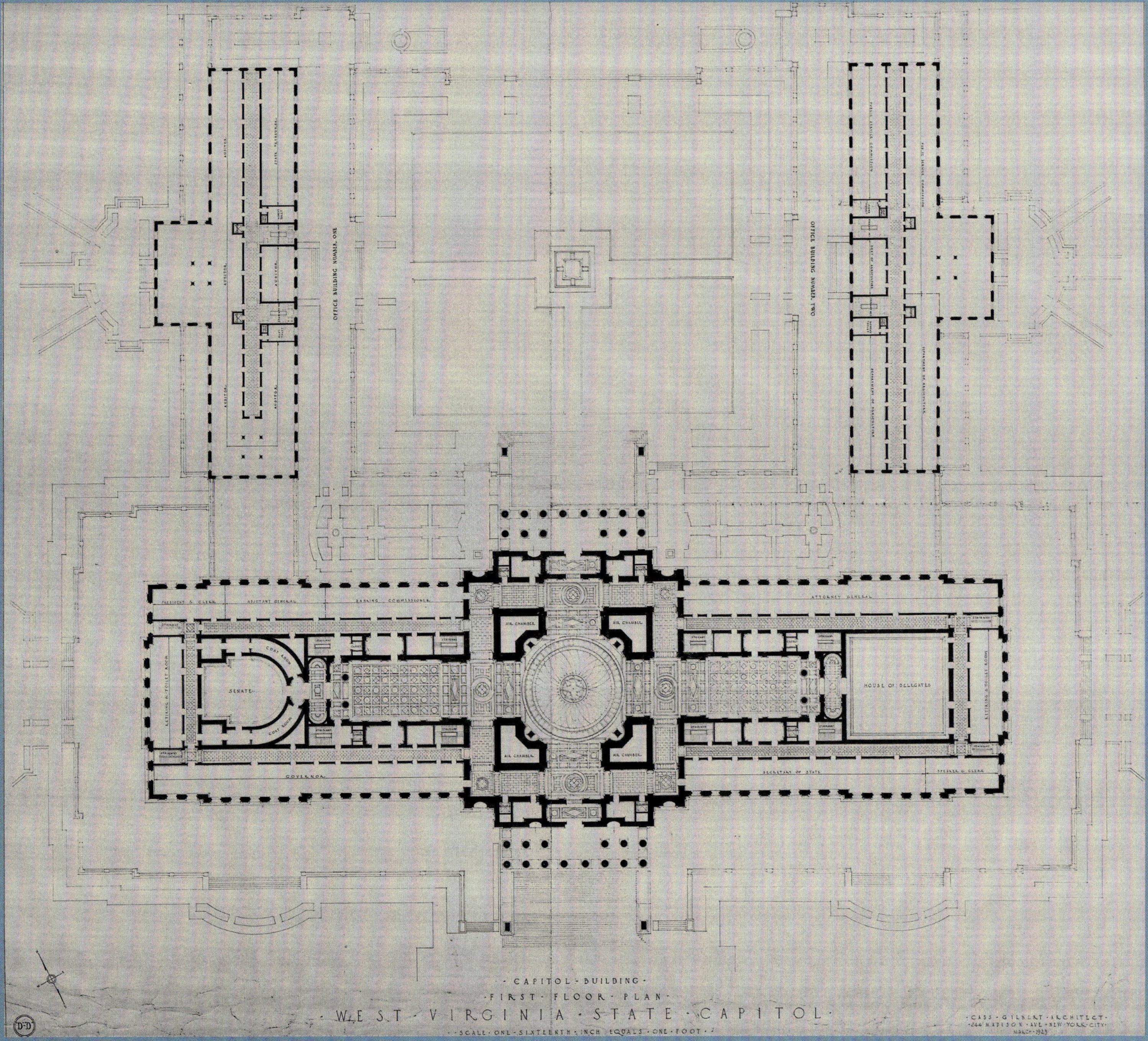

OFFICE BUILDING NUMBER ONE
OFFICE BUILDING NUMBER TWO
SENATE
HOUSE OF DELEGATES
ATTORNEY GENERAL
SECRETARY OF STATE
GOVERNOR
· CAPITOL · BUILDING ·
· FIRST · FLOOR · PLAN ·
· WEST · VIRGINIA · STATE · CAPITOL ·
· SCALE · ONE · SIXTEENTH · INCH · EQUALS · ONE · FOOT ·
· CASS · GILBERT · ARCHITECT ·
· 244 MADISON · AVE · NEW · YORK · CITY ·
MARCH · 1923

CHAPTER FIVE

# The West and East Wings: Politics, Money, Progress

There is unquestionably a great sentiment throughout the state that the state is figuring on spending too much money on a Capitol [and] that the Commission has agreed to give the architect too much money. This is but natural; and, while the members of the Commission naturally feel very keenly the criticism, yet, they know that they have done the only thing that could be done in the building of a Capitol which is intended to last for generations.

Houston Young, secretary of the Capitol Building Commission, to Cass Gilbert, January 4, 1923

Fig. 38. Cass Gilbert/Studio. First floor ground plan for the West Virginia State Capitol, dated March 1923. In its basic outline this plan is similar to what was built between 1924 and 1932, but many of the details are different, and the scale of the finished building was reduced as well. Note the suggested patterns for inlaid-stone floors in the public areas, the broad terraces around the buildings, and Gilbert's suggestions for radiating walkways from the West and East Wings.

LEGISLATIVE ACTION REQUIRED TO FUND STATE CAPITOLS HAS often led to political wrangling and delays; the situation in West Virginia proved no different from that in other states.[1]

By January 1923, eighteen months after Gilbert's appointment, the location had been determined, most of the property acquired, and the plans approved and published. Financing, however, was being delayed by partisan politics. As the architect would later report to his wife, some members of the Legislature wanted to block the project because they hoped to elect a democratic governor in 1924.[2] Newspaper articles provided by Gilbert's clipping service reveal how the West Virginia media tried to form public opinion for or against the Capitol and its architect. Gilbert's frustration at reading some of the misrepresentations cited below can only be imagined.

Statewide criticism of the project that came to a head in early 1923 can be related to the results of the elections of the previous November. While the Republicans retained their majority in the State Senate, they lost the House of Delegates, where the Democrats gained a majority of sixty-five to twenty-nine. A partisan debate over the Capitol erupted, with the Democrats opposing the actions taken by Governor Morgan, the previous Legislature, and the Commission he had appointed.

George Laughlin of the *Wheeling Telegraph* visited Gilbert's New York office in late December 1922. He asked the architect about the criticisms being leveled by Democrats encouraged by H. C. Ogden, a prestigious Wheeling businessman who owned or controlled a number of West Virginia newspapers.[3] Laughlin wanted to know if Gilbert had selected the site and if he would be paid his 6 percent fee on the cost of its land and houses. Gilbert's response was negative in each case.[4] The site had been selected by the commissioners and because his fee was "based on new construction" he would not receive anything on the purchase of land or the value of demolished houses. Gilbert also assured Laughlin that the complex would not cost more than the appropriation. In a letter to Secretary Young, Gilbert reported that Laughlin "was very much pleased ... and very cordial in his expressions of confidence in the Commission and in myself and especially stated that he believed in our charge there 'would be no graft' and I assured him that there would be no graft of any kind." Gilbert added that Laughlin had offered to introduce him to "Mr. Ogden, the owner of one of the other papers, so that Mr. Ogden also would get a clearer understanding of my personal attitude toward the work." The questions raised and the suggestion of graft must have troubled Gilbert, for he asked, "Do you think I could help any by coming to West Virginia at once, or in the near future?"

Young replied that he had submitted the relevant facts to Walter E. Clark, editor of the *Charleston Daily Mail*, who planned to publish an editorial on the subject.[5] Young's summary of the situation for Gilbert is quoted at the opening of this chapter. He continued: "The criticism was started by Mr. H. C. Ogden, of Wheeling, who has been from the beginning a very bitter critic of the present administration. The present Capitol Commission, however, I presume cares as little about criticism as any bunch of men you could get together." None of the commissioners was a candidate for public office and "each and every one knows that the Commission has followed the course set out by the Legislature two years ago.... I have no doubt that every man who sat on the Commission did so realizing that they would be criticized." Young's comments clarify that Ogden's opposition was to the "present administration," suggesting that the Capitol project was collateral damage in a larger dispute.

On January 4, the *Wheeling News*, which was controlled by Ogden, published a report on some of the criticisms being leveled against the Capitol project: "West Virginia architects were completely ignored and rebuffed by the State Capitol Commission when they asked to be permitted to submit plans for the proposed state capitol, it was divulged today by sources close in touch with the operations of the Commission." Without identifying them, the article added: "Three architects from West Virginia cities, recognized as the foremost in the state, spent a week in Charleston seeking a hearing with the Commission. At first they were politely informed that the commission was not ready to consider the architect question, but when they several times during the week sought an interview, ... the Commission flatly informed them that they couldn't do the work." These local architects were ready to accept a fee below 6 percent: "The three architects, it is said, were prepared to offer to plan and supervise the construction of the new capitol at the usual commission of probably five per cent or lower, based on the cost of construction alone." The next paragraph, headed "Could Have Saved Big Sum," pointed out, in contrast: "The contract entered into with Cass Gilbert, New York architect, allows six per cent of the cost of construction of the building and the development of the grounds and the equipment and furnishing of the complete structure." The article continues, "With the employment of West Virginia architects, it is estimated the state would have been saved approximately $300,000 to $500,000 alone in architect's fees." The section that follows misrepresents Gilbert's contract, suggesting that it is exceptional rather than typical and inferring that others may have benefited from the process:

MOTIVES SUSPECTED

Observers are daily becoming more suspicious of the motives that actuated the Commission in its dealings with the New York architect. From questioning directed at various officials and others interested it is now known to be a certainty that no architects other than Cass Gilbert were approached.

This fact, combined with the very effulgent generosity of the Commission in fattening the architect's fee not only in percentage above the average, but in allowing him to base it on the whole cost of the project is adding more strength to the belief that possibly Mr. Gilbert is not the only beneficiary of the document.

Color is lent to this opinion by the rather elaborate schedule of advance fees allowed Gilbert before a tap of work is done on the structure, not to mention the $10,000 he has been paid for his 'advice on the selection of a site.' All in all, Mr. Gilbert gets $160,000 before a pick sinks into the ground.

It is said to be unusual for an architect to secure more than a very nominal fee until actual work has been begun on the building. It is further estimated that the cost of the completed plans, even for the elaborate structure Gilbert and the commission plans, [should be only] about $90,000 to $100,000.[6]

If the proponents of this attack knew they were misrepresenting the contract, they must have felt that the means justified the ends.

Some West Virginia editors tried to defuse the anti-Gilbert, anti-Commission rhetoric. On January 6, the *Charleston Gazette* clarified the basis for Gilbert's fee: "ARCHITECT FOR CAPITOL GETS SIX PER CENT; Cass Gilbert Says Schedule of American Institute of Architects Forms Basis of All Compensation."[7] On January 8, the *Clarksburg Telegram* responded to "THOSE STATE CAPITOL LIES," stating: "These falsehoods have been accumulating in their bulk like a snowball rolled up by a school boy on the commons. Starting from a small bit of exaggeration they have grown and swelled into ridiculous proportions." The writer identifies two "purposes" for the lies: "One is a strict partisan purpose, naturally to be expected in view of the fact that the Democrats have obtained control of one branch of the state legislature. The other is a strictly personal and selfish purpose on the part of a few dissatisfied individuals who ought to know by this time that willfully destructive criticism will get them nowhere and do the state no service." The article continued, "The snowball is still being pushed and doubtless by the time this appears in print the capitol cost will have reached $25,000,000 and the architect's commission $3,000,000 or $4,000,000." The editor explained, "This comes from the fact that some of the snowball pushers have been making it appear that the state capitol commission, which has the governor of the state as its chairman, is going to spend a huge, indefinite sum of money with great abandon and unchecked wantonness." But, he pointed out, the Commission "has no authority to spend so much as ten cents for capitol building purposes unless authorized and instructed to do so by the legislature. It happens that the state legislature has already set the limit of the cost of the capitol." That limit is "$6,500,000—not $20,000,000—plus moneys received from the sales of land, plus insurance moneys on the old state house and minus the cost of the new site." As a result, "the new capitol cannot cost more than around $7,000,000, unless, of course, the new legislature should increase the limit. It is not likely to do so, and there is no likelihood that anybody is going to ask it to do so." The writer clarified the terms of the contract of the architect, "CASS GILBERT, of New York City, one of the ablest and most famous in the country," pointing out that he "is to receive the standard fee of six per cent upon the cost of the building alone—not on the cost of the site nor on the cost of clearing the site. No first class architect in the country charges less. And considering the work that is to be done and the splendid ability of MR. GILBERT, there is nothing out of the way about this." The editor continued:

In fact, the state is to be congratulated that it has been able to obtain the services of MR. GILBERT, one of the foremost men of his profession. It has been generally agreed by all who are conversant with constructive projects, including the architects of the state, that the engagement of MR. GILBERT has been a most fortunate one in that he has had experience with such large structures as the architects of the state have not had.

So, instead of a million or more dollars, MR. GILBERT is to receive at the most around $420,000 for all of his work. To the inexperienced and uninformed this looks like a large fee, but when the facts are taken into consideration there is nothing excessive about it. It should be remembered that in the case of an important public building project such as this, the architect is obliged to give a large part of his time to it for a period of something like five years. Then he has to maintain a large and expensive office. From twelve to fifteen high priced, skilled architects employed in his office are at this moment working on the plans and the specifications for the West Virginia state capitol, and they will have to continue to be so employed for a long period.[8]

The writer continued, "It is high time that the truth be known about it, or rather recognized and realized," adding that the proceedings have been "done out in the open and above board and at the insistence of the regularly constituted delegates of the people," and concluding: "Nobody wants a barn for West Virginia's seat of government, nor a makeshift or unattractive structure. The state can afford as good a capitol as the other states, the majority of which have beautiful and commodious structures of the kind, unless its people feel that it has been reduced to such a condition of penury and backwardness that any old thing will do."[9]

When the Legislature convened in January 1923, both houses moved to investigate the Capitol Building Commission's proceedings and finances. The Democratic-controlled House, on the offense, required the Republican-led Senate to play defense. Eventually three publications documented the process: the report prepared by the Commission in response to a request from the House of Delegates, the report of a Special Senate Committee, and a volume of the Commission's correspondence.[10]

On Thursday, January 18, Secretary Young informed Gilbert by telegram that the "House of Delegates has passed resolution requiring inspection of plans. Commission desires your presence here not later than Monday with such information as possible to bring." For the Commission to require their internationally famous architect to rush to Charleston on short notice reveals the seriousness of the situation. Gilbert left on January 21 and returned to New York five days later. On the first day, Gilbert joked with Governor Morgan about "the possibility of going to jail," he warned the governor that "if his name was libeled he would sue for a large sum and do it at once." Transcripts document this visit, as do drawings marked "used 1/25/23" and "not used 1/25/23."[11] "Not used" reveals that Gilbert did not have to present all the evidence he had prepared. Transcripts suggest that some legislators hoped to reduce the "6.5 million plus" limit on total cost approved in 1921. Such a reduction would require that the project be redesigned.

One commissioner suggested that because plans had been approved, the Commission should let a contract immediately for the construction of all three buildings, and Gilbert had to point out that such an action would be illegal because the cost would exceed the $2,250,000 appropriation approved by the 1921 Legislature. In any case, even that sum was unavailable because no revenue stream supported it.

To start the project, Governor Morgan requested the Legislature appropriate $3.25 million and establish a related revenue stream. In response to the possibility that "contracts be let for portions of the work at a time," Gilbert prepared four proposals, each with an approximate price tag: (1) complete all three buildings but no power plant or mechanical equipment, $4 million to $4.2 million; (2) establish the foundations and walls up to grade and complete the structural steel for all three buildings, $1,500,000 to $1,750,000; (3) do the pilings for the two office buildings plus general construction for the Main Building but no power house or mechanical equipment, $3.2 million; or (4) establish the foundations and structural steel for all three buildings and complete the boiler house, tunnel, and both office buildings, $3,230,000. An appropriation of $3.25 million would mean that the Commission could not afford proposal (1); (2) and (4) raised the specter of forlorn steel skeletons awaiting further legislative action; (3) would provide no relief for the state's ongoing rental costs for office space. Commissioner Staunton suggested a fifth alternative: do everything in (4) but omit the structural steel for the Main Building, saving $450,000 for a total of $2,780,000.

At this point, however, the problems with the Legislature subsided. The report prepared by the commissioners for the House of Delegates justified the 6 percent fee as appropriate for a project of this size and complexity. This was the percentage mentioned by most of the architects interviewed, and it was based on the standards of the AIA. The commissioners had worked within the stipulations of the 1921 Legislature: "The Commission believes that it has secured the services of one of America's greatest architects, and it has faith enough in him, based on what it believes as to his character and ability, to feel that it had adopted as practicable a course as it could be expected to adopt in carrying out the program outlined by the Legislature of 1921."

When the Senate Committee met with Gilbert on March 15, 1923, he told them he could build the new capitol complex "complete and ready for occupancy" for approximately $7 million. The committee members concluded that the terms of Gilbert's contract were advantageous to the state for they "are more liberal than is usual in work of this kind, as he is bound by the terms of the contract to furnish at his own expense all electrical, sanitary, heating and structural engineering." Letters from seventeen leading architects testified that they would not accept a contract in which the fee was less than 6 percent. The Senate Committee recommended that the 1923 Legislature appropriate $3,000,000 to complete both office buildings and commended the Capitol Commission for having chosen such a beautiful site, for having saved at least $1,000,000 through their choice of site, and for selecting "one of the world's greatest architects, who has had experience in building other state capitols and many public buildings."

During this visit Gilbert also met with the Finance Committee of the West Virginia Senate, the Joint Committee of the House and Senate, the Commission, and Governor Morgan. There must have been some hope for an appropriation and revenue stream, for on March 16, the Commission directed Gilbert to "proceed with the plans of the two Office Buildings and the Power House and Tunnel with a view to letting a contract for completion at an early date, and with the plan of the Legislative Building with a view to letting the contract for foundations if the funds were available."[12] A plan dated March 1923 is probably one result of the Commission's request.

Continuing controversy over cost, however, led Young to wire Gilbert on March 22: "Badly need cost other state capitols." Gilbert's response was a "Memoranda as to State Capitol Buildings," which compared ten capitols in terms of approximate cost, cubage, price per cubic foot, acres in the site, dimensions, date, and exterior and interior materials.[13]

Visiting Gilbert in New York on March 31, Young brought good and bad news. The good news was that "the Capitol site will not be moved to Parkersburg but will be retained in Charleston." The bad news was that the total cost for the new Capitol would probably be reduced to $2.5 or $3 million. Gilbert replied, "We would have to do the best we could in the situation," adding that "of course we could not build the capitol and office buildings as planned."[14]

On April 30, Secretary Young informed Gilbert that a House of Delegates resolution proposed to "abolish the present Capitol Commission, abrogate your contract, and appoint a new Commission to report to the Legislature of 1925, limiting the cost of the Capitol to $5,000,000.00." The goal was to have a "fresh start ... except as to the site." The resolution was defeated 62 to 22, but Young warned: "There are many complications ... which weigh heavily in securing an appropriation. We have a very serious situation on our hands regarding it."[15]

Gilbert's next important communication was received from Bonner Hill on May 17. From this point on, Gilbert's correspondence with the Commission more often came from Hill, whose job as the Commission's agent in acquiring Duffy Street properties was virtually finished by late 1922. By May 1923, he had assumed many of the duties previously handled by Houston Young.

On May 17, Hill warned that Governor Morgan was having difficulty convincing the Legislature to pass his budget, which included the appropriation. On May 16, Morgan had extended the session for the third time, until June 30 or until they passed a budget; Hill worried that legislators would eliminate the appropriation in an attempt to pass the budget. He urged Gilbert to finish plans so bids could be presented to the Legislature before June 10. On May 23, Gilbert replied that although he could finish the drawings and obtain estimates from "experienced and responsible contractors," such estimates, being higher than competitive bids, might help discourage legislators from passing the appropriation. Hill was often indifferent to procedure, and Gilbert had to emphasize that he was only responsible for design and supervising the construction; contracts were let not by him but by the Commission, and only after open bidding had taken place. Gilbert offered to travel to Charleston if such a trip would be "necessary or desirable for the progress of the work."[16]

On May 26, Gilbert wrote that the plans and an estimate could be ready by June 4 or shortly thereafter: "In the meantime bearing in mind that the sum of $5,000,000.00 has been suggested as the total cost for the buildings, I will see what can be done by a restudy of the design to reduce the total cost."[17] In asking "Do you think the Commission would be willing to reconsider the whole plan and general design of the buildings?" Gilbert seems to hint that the dome, the focal point of the original plan, might have to be eliminated. He added: "I want to meet the view of those in authority and believe that I can do so and still make a good design though of course we would have to modify the buildings very materially to bring them within the $5,000,000.00 limit."

Hill's May 28 reply suggested that Gilbert should try to adhere to the selected plan, which would have included the dome: "I do not think that the Commission at this time is ready or willing to consent to a change in the whole plan and general design of the Capitol buildings." The commissioners, he reported, were hoping for an appropriation allowing construction of one or both office buildings and the power plant, an outcome that would delay any decision on whether the dome would stay. Even if this Legislature limited the price to $5 million, "we would still be in a position to go before the next legislature with your proposed plans for the main Capitol Building, and also be in a position to say now that the entire proposition could be done for Five Million Dollars by reducing the size or standard of the main Capitol building." On May 28, Governor Morgan wrote that he hoped "with a sufficient amount of publicity that the legislature can be brought to see the light in the proper manner." He added sarcastically, "There is wonderful opposition in the House to the Capitol Commission."[18]

On May 29, Gilbert wrote to Hill, "If the Legislature determines to appropriate only $5,000,000.00 for a State Capitol it is our duty to loyally fill that requirement, but obviously we cannot build a $7,000,000.00 or $8,000,000.00 structure for $5,000,000.00, especially in these times when building costs are at the peak."[19] Gilbert posited using what funds became available to complete the plans and foundations and to hope for lower building prices in the future, but he also recognized the need to provide office space for state agencies. He proposed "condensing the whole project into one building, omitting monumental features as far as possible and reducing the size of the condensed structure so as to meet the wishes of the Legislature," lamenting that "this would probably cause us to omit the dome and reduce the whole project to a rather practical common-place aspect." He knew this would disappoint the commissioners: "I do not urge it because I think none of us will be satisfied with it and I am sure the people of West Virginia would not take the same pride in the building if it was done, but if that is what they want, let us do the best we can with the problem they give us."[20]

Gilbert left New York on June 6 and stopped briefly in Washington to inspect progress on his US Chamber of Commerce Building. He brought to Charleston a "large roll of blueprints and reproductions for the West Virginia State Capitol; they included the working drawings and specifications for the general construction & mech. equipment of both of the Office Buildings and for the Boiler House, also sketch plans of the Capitol and reproductions of the illustrative drawings of the interiors of the principal rooms." Among the latter were probably proposals for the legislative chambers prepared by his head draftsman that capture the grandeur the architect still hoped might be possible. Gilbert also brought a "Revised General Summary, Showing possible changes & omissions to reduce costs." Reducing the length of the office buildings would save $250,000; simplifying the interior finish of the Main Building, $150,000. Omitting the dome would save $1,142,000; making changes to the Power House, $475,000. While the cost of the original plans was approximately $10,444,520 (without the architect's fee and general expenses), the changes listed above would bring the cost down to $8,321,368 ($8,881,368 when the architect's fee and other general expenses were added).[21] While a total price of more than $10.5 million is surprising, the original "$6.5 million plus" budget had always been vague because of the uncertainty of the value of the "plus" and the question of the cost of a new site.

Gilbert wrote two accounts of his Charleston visit, a transcript for the office and a letter to Julia.[22] The latter was composed by the apparently tireless architect the morning after he left, during a layover in Cincinnati on his way to Minneapolis. Both are worth quoting at length because of the contrast between the documentary tone of the transcript and the colorful details of the personal letter. The letter exposes a playful aspect of Gilbert's personality we would hardly suspect were we limited to the office records.

Both documents also reveal the partisan disagreement raging in West Virginia. Gilbert's explanation of the budget stalemate is clearer in the transcript: "The Republicans control the Senate and the Democrats control the House of Delegates. The Governor and administration are Republican. The House refuses to concur in the action of the Senate and is criticizing the Governor and also criticizing my contract for the State Capitol work." He realized that the criticism was directed toward both the Capitol project and the governor: "The opposition to the Capitol and to the Governor is led by a Mr. Byrne of Charleston and very strongly backed up by Mr. Septimius Hall of Wetzel County. He has apparently denounced me on the floor of the House." In other words, the Capitol had become a vehicle for attacking Governor Morgan and his administration. While Gilbert's letter to Julia clarified how deeply the Capitol was embroiled in local politics, the good news was that there had been "no effective legislation against

Fig. 39. Cass Gilbert (concept), Proposed design for the chamber of the House of Delegates for the West Virginia Capitol, March 12, 1923. Drawing by Frederick G. Stickel. There is an equally grand design for the Senate chamber, also drawn by Stickel and dated March 6, 1923 (WVSA). For the House of Delegates as built, see gallery 6.

the capitol project ... though I must say it has had a close call." After noting the partisan nature of the criticism, he added, "I believe there is also an appropriation for militia and for state constabulary, the latter desired by the mine operators and opposed by the labor union crowd, and either they can't agree or they are holding these things out as trading measures." He told Julia that the reason for trying to "oust the Capitol Commission and turn the work over to the Board of Control and the Governor" is because "they expect to elect a democrat for Governor next year and get a democratic Board of Control." This explains why some legislators were so eager to stall funding; were ground broken and foundations laid for the new Capitol, it would be difficult to prevent the completion of the project as designed.

Gilbert wrote Julia that on June 8 Governor Morgan "doubted very much if [the Legislature] would make any appropriation at all and it seemed to be almost an uncontrollable situation." To Gilbert, this appeared "to be the general opinion in Charleston as neither side will give way and nothing can be accomplished unless some compromise is effected." Gilbert told Morgan: "I had filled my contract up to the present time and ... I did not believe the State of West Virginia was going to 'repudiate' its obligation to me." The governor apparently assumed the architect's contract could be broken, for Gilbert alerted him that "the repudiation of my contract would be the same as the repudiation of a contract for bonds with any banking organization and it would be a breach of faith which I did not believe the State of West Virginia would do. In other words, I insisted that my contract should be maintained." Morgan "was apparently a little bit surprised at my firm statement on the subject and then acquiesced in the reasonableness of it."

Governor Morgan had a reputation for crisis-mode leadership, but what role he played in resolving this crisis is uncertain. Although he assessed the situation as virtually "uncontrollable" on June 8, a budget that included an appropriation for the Capitol passed on June 14. The June 30 deadline and threat of another extension may have been factors, but Gilbert's personal charm and persuasiveness also seem to have played a role. He wrote Julia: "There was very strong prejudice being built up 'against Cass Gilbert' but I think my 2½ days in Charleston has largely killed that idea. Personally I received the most cordial and friendly treatment.... I made friends right and left with Dems. and Reps. without distinction." He defused the animosity some legislators held toward him: "There is no more fight there on *me* [Gilbert's emphasis]—My visit covered that. They are after Mr. Staunton and the Governor and it's just rank politics and they are all ashamed of it."

In the office transcript, Gilbert documented his encounters with legislators. On June 8, while at lunch at the Hotel Kanawha, for example, he "chanced to meet several members of the Legislature. There seems to be no personal antipathy toward me but a pretty strong opposition to my contract on the part of the Democratic members of the house." Late that afternoon while he was waiting in the governor's outer office, he met Septimius Hall, a powerful opponent of the Capitol project. Hall, born in 1847 and the oldest member of the House of Delegates, was a member of the West Virginia Constitutional Convention of 1872 and had served in the House of Delegates from 1881 to 1884, when the capital was still in Wheeling. He was reelected to the House in 1907 and served there until his death in 1926. Hall's encounter with the architect was so unexpected and so important for our story—without it perhaps Cass Gilbert's West Virginia State Capitol as we know it might not have been built—that it is worth recounting in full, especially since it is documented twice in the architect's own words. Gilbert's transcript reported:

> I at once told him that I "would rather meet him than any man in West Virginia" and asked if he had read my reply to his recent statement concerning the nature of my contract. He said he had not read it. I said he ought to have read it, it would interest him, that I believed a man in his position would want to know the truth and I proposed to tell him the truth. We sat down then and had a long talk together. Sometimes it was very vigorous and he at one point said he "did not want to hear any more." I told him "that it was all right, I would be glad to hear him talk," and I asked him to state his objections. He said the whole Capitol matter was illegally handled. I told him I believed the Capitol Commission had handled it in accordance with the law passed by the Legislature in 1921. Mr. Hall said, "the people in my County won't stand for it" and my contract must be annulled. I told him I thought the people of his County ought to know the truth and that I was prepared to tell the truth to them or the Legislature, or anybody else, and that I courted the fullest inquiry and was prepared to make the fullest statement, that I had no secrets in the matter, that I had not solicited the work and that my contract was upon a basis quite as favorable and in some respects more favorable than contracts for similar work which I had executed for many important buildings and in fact was substantially a standard contract which was used for the best public buildings all over the country. I then asked him about his County and got him talking about his local people and where he lived. He had apparently a good deal of prejudice against me on the ground of my being a "New York man." I told him he ought not to have prejudice against me on that account as I was really an Ohio man, was a native of Ohio and came not far across the river from his County and he was surprised at this and the conversation took a more friendly tone. He presently asked me if I would walk up to the Hotel with him, which invitation I gladly accepted. On the way to the Hotel he would stop at intervals and make a sort of stump speech to me and then proceed very intimately till finally we reached the Hotel and he introduced me to a number of the members of the Legislature. I sat down with [them] in the lobby and we had a cheery conversation and exchanged stories and quips for a half hour or more. After I left the group, two of them came to me and asked if I would be willing to make an address to the House. I said I would very glad to do so and they said they would let me know the next morning. I agreed to be at the Governor's office at 9:30 the next morning and would wait for them there.[23]

While the transcript exposes Gilbert's conviction in his mission, his letter to Julia reveals a more intimate record of his meeting with "Uncle Joe."

> I met old Uncle Sept Hall (the Uncle Joe of the House) who has denounced me in the House and in the newspapers—I greeted him with a loud and hearty welcome—told him that of all the men in West Virginia I would rather meet—he was the man! We talked and argued for an

hour until the old devil told me he'd "hear no more of it," he "had heard enough"—I immediately said "You're right! Now you talk!" And you bet he let out a howl. (We were in the Governor's outer office and the door was open. Gov. Morgan told me afterward that he heard it all.) When old Hall told me "the people" of his county were opposed to the Capitol, I switched around and asked him to tell me about his county, where it is and what it produces—It's Wetzel County up next to the Ohio River—and I told him I was a "sort of a neighbor" of "the folks up there" for I was born not far away in Zanesville.

It ended to the surprise of my Charleston friends in Uncle Septimius inviting me to walk up to the Hotel with him and there to the amazement of the Republican members of the Senate the old man became my sponsor and introduced me to about a dozen members of both houses—I think he enjoyed it but I don't think he enjoyed it half as much as I did. Before the séance closed I was telling Uncle Joe Cannon's story about Mark Twain asking him the "thanks of Congress" so he could speak from the floor of the House and as I left the party the President of the Senate and a member of the House came up to invite me to speak before the next meeting.

I accepted—

When Gilbert arrived at the governor's office the next morning, he told Morgan, Commissioner Keatley, and Hill "of the suggestion made by several members of the House that I should make a speech to the members and we discussed the outlines of the speech. Mr. Keatley is more optimistic than the others have been and I told them that I was very optimistic. They were all very much surprised at my talk with Mr. Hall and seemed to regard it as a good omen." That morning's newspapers, however, reported the bold announcement by House of Delegates Majority Leader J. S. Zimmerman that "the House will stand for a Capitol, but not for Cass Gilbert." As if in response, another paper referred to Gilbert as "one of the world's greatest living architects," one who builds "structures that live in idealism as long as brick and mortar lasts."[24]

The architect had planned to depart on the 12:30 P.M. train, but the possibility of speaking to the House led him to change his departure to the evening. No invitation arrived, however, and Gilbert summarized the day's events for Julia: "Then the opposition got busy and as the Gov told me they were afraid to hear me speak for I'd tip the scales against them—I waited however all day for the invitation but [W. E. R. Byrne, the Democratic speaker of the House of Delegates] and his crowd blocked it. This left them in the position of not being able to get real facts & figures before the legislature and probably strengthened our side more than though I had spoken."[25]

The transcript documents that at about four o'clock, as Gilbert walked to his hotel, he met "a Democratic member of the House who had been at the Hotel the day before. We met several other members of the House who greeted us cordially. They seemed to have no unfriendly feeling toward me personally though opposed to my contract." Gilbert "invited them to go with me out to the Capitol site. They did not accept as they had all been there. Mr. Lighter [Righter?], however, did accept and he and I walked out to the Capitol site."[26] Gilbert's ability to encourage conversation even with those who opposed him is evident:

> I found him a very straightforward, upright sort of man and working with his party as a party man without much knowledge of the building of the Capitol or the nature of my contract. I did not press the discussion at all, but answered such questions as he asked me. He invited me to take supper with him and I accepted.... In the latter part of our conversation Mr. Lighter told me that he had been there 101 days and that he was getting very tired of the legislative session and of Byrne's leadership and that if something definite was not done in that evening's session he and about thirty others were going to "break away." We met one of his fellow members of the House while walking along the street and a conversation to that effect occurred and he repeated the statement.

Gilbert's account to Julia was more candid: "I took a long walk yesterday afternoon with a lanky farmer democratic member of the house ... and wrote my autograph for his son and daughter at his request & then accepted his invitation to dinner at the cafeteria of the W.C.T.U. [Women's Christian Temperance Union]. We became very good friends, and I liked him and he liked me." Gilbert persuaded Lighter to change his mind: "He has been voting against me—but he is over that now. And as we parted after two hours, he disclosed that he and his farmer friends were sick of the leadership of the smart lawyer Byrnes [*sic*] who has been leading the fight against us and he thought the whole bunch would swing around monday and vote for us. Twill they do it?"

The crisis was resolved by Thursday, when Young telephoned Gilbert's office to report that $2.5 million had been appropriated for the two office buildings and the boiler house. Young asked Gilbert not to release the fact that while the limit for the whole project had been set at $5 million, the commissioners "expected at a later date to have this amount increased in order to complete the whole operation as originally planned." Young asked Gilbert, "if we could build the buildings within that amount." Gilbert replied that he "did not see any reason why it could not be done, at least we would try."[27] Of the scenarios proposed in January, when the governor was still hoping for an appropriation of $3,250,000, none was possible with $2,500,000.

What is notable in retrospect is that the wording of the appropriation did not require that both office buildings and the power plant be built for $2.5 million. While the financial cap was fixed, the bill specified only that "one or two office buildings" be erected for that amount. It is not clear why the bill used this wording; perhaps the legislators were suggesting that a single, large office building replace the two buildings of the approved plan. By November, however, someone—the governor, one of the commissioners, or the architect—realized that "one or two" allowed them to use the $2.5 million to construct only one of the two planned office buildings. By going ahead with one building as the first element in the approved design, the Commission set the course for the future, hoping that the other two buildings of their three-building scheme would be brought to completion. The only alternative would be to leave the first building as an isolated monument in a complex of mismatched structures, denying West Virginia the dignified and commanding Capitol envisioned by the patrons and their architect.

On June 15, before the Commission realized that wording would allow them to build a single building, Governor Morgan had asked Gilbert to submit plans for both office buildings and the power plant as soon as possible so that bids could be let. Hill clarified the governor's intent, saying that the governor had "intimated" to him "that the new plans mentioned in this bill would be a reduction of space in the present plans of the office buildings and as small or cheap [a] power plant as will heat these buildings."[28] Young suggested that perhaps Gilbert could "cut down the two office buildings about fifteen feet and not have to make entirely new plans."

On August 8, Governor Morgan wrote that the Old Capitol Site would be sold for at least $1.1 million and construction could begin.[29] By November it had been determined that the legislative appropriation would be used for one office building, and in December the contract was let for Office Building 1, as it was consistently identified in the documents. On November 22, Houston Young asked Gilbert for a public statement about the cost, to help citizens "slowly realize the facts," and for photos of the design.[30] He emphasized the difficulty of dealing with the local media: "Please remember that half the press in the state is Democratic, and that they will not give us a square deal on the subject, especially in a campaign year. The other half is nominally Republican, but some of the Republican interest is antagonistic and is controlled by H. C. Ogden. His attitude toward everything connected with the State House clearly shows that he will not be fair and will not tell the truth concerning the project." Young's assessment of Ogden's attitude is harsh, but we must remember that Young and Ogden were political adversaries and that Young was writing privately to Gilbert and not making a public statement.

Gilbert took a proactive stance and sent photographs and a letter to H. L. Snyder, publisher of the *Shepherdstown Register*. Snyder's reply was enthusiastic: "Your pleasant letter of a few days ago was received.... I have also received the photographs that you so kindly sent me, and am tremendously impressed by their great beauty. The view of the rotunda interior [probably fig. 86] is simply lovely, and looks like an artist's dream that I hope will come true." He found the complex "entirely satisfying" and thought that it "should appeal to State pride to such a degree as to make the buildings a reality." He planned to frame the photos for his office and "use them as a means of education." He regretted that "what is called the 'extravagance' in planning for these noble buildings will be used by politicians in our next campaign. One of the leading Republican editors of the State is attacking the project, and just this week I had a visit from a Democratic candidate for Governor who began to talk along the same line." When Snyder showed him the photos, however, "and appealed to his State pride and tried to argue that West Virginia ought to have the very best, he had to admit that this was true. At least I have made him think, and he knows now that not all of the people want economy to the extent that so noble an enterprise shall suffer." Snyder planned to write an editorial and hoped "that other papers will use their influence to the same end.

In the meantime, plans for the new governor's mansion on the edge of the Duffy Street Site were proceeding. Hoping to defuse the tension over the appointment of a New York architect for the Capitol by selecting a local professional for this project, Governor Morgan selected Walter F. Martens, who had established a practice in Charleston in 1921. Martens had no formal education as an architect, but he had served as a draftsman in an architect's office in Danville, Illinois, for five years, followed by two years as a junior assistant in the same office. His appointment worried Commissioner Staunton, who in June 1922 showed Martens's first plan for the mansion to Gilbert. At that time, Gilbert had studied it and asked one of his draftsmen to draw a version to scale.

In July 1923, the governor sent Martens to New York for a consultation with Gilbert; they met on July 11 and 12. Martens reported that after he showed Gilbert the sketches he had prepared for a Georgian style mansion, Gilbert reached "into his desk drawer [and] produced a design sketch ... he had made, almost identical with mine."[31] Gilbert showed Martens both "the preliminary sketch plans which were made for the Governor's Mansion at the request of Mr. Staunton about a year ago" and "a small sketch of the exterior" that Gilbert had made "within the last few days." Although both were apparently based on the plan by Martens that Staunton had brought to New York the year before, Gilbert seems not to have informed Martens he had seen his earlier plan. Martens reported that the two architects noted the "marked similarity" between their designs and said that Gilbert "stated that never before had he had such an experience, where designs by two individuals were so thoroughly in agreement." Gilbert made a number of suggestions, some of which were then drawn up by his draftsmen to assist Martens. Gilbert also urged that the building be constructed of brick rather than limestone, the material suggested by the First Lady. Martens had followed her proposals for certain practical aspects of the design, including the placement of the staterooms on the ground floor and the family rooms, including a living room, on the second. Martens based the reception hall and staircase on those of the White House.

Gilbert loaned Martens two books on Georgian architecture and pointed out some features that could be incorporated in the mansion; Martens took these books to Charleston, where he shared them with Mrs. Morgan before returning them. Gilbert's recommendation that Martens model details for the mansion on motifs drawn from historical architecture was an accepted part of the Beaux-Arts approach to design.

In a letter of August 24, Martens wrote Gilbert that he was finishing the design and "Governor and Mrs. Morgan as well as members of the State Board of Control were well pleased with the results of my visit to your office, and the work is

generally following the sketches outlined in your office." Martens confided in Gilbert, however, that he feared "the $85,000.00 appropriation will not be sufficient to complete the Mansion. I venture that it will require nearly $150,000.00 to build the building, to decorate the same, and to carry out the treatment of grounds and garden in keeping with the Mansion."

He concluded: "When the plans are well under way I shall send a print to your office for your criticism. As Governor Morgan stated on my visit to you in July, any charges in connection with your work will be promptly taken care of." Given the documentary record and the fact that Gilbert was being paid for his assistance, the design of West Virginia's Executive Mansion should probably be understood as a collaboration between the two architects. It was completed in early 1925 and an illustrated article in the *Charleston Gazette* on March 15, 1925, announced, "New Executive Mansion Will Blossom Forth In All Glory of Paradise When Grounds Are Finished Around Beautiful Home."[32]

Fig. 40. Governor's Mansion, from a period postcard. On the reverse it states that the mansion "was rushed to completion in 1925 after it had been designed the previous year by Walter F. Martens."

What with partisan prejudice and narrowness of public opinion, however, we will probably have a hard fight to make the project as popular as it ought to be to get it across successfully." He supported the Commission: "If I were a member of the Capitol Commission I would stand for the best in architecture and in contracting, with my own conscience as my guide, and unfearful of a partisan press or of prejudiced, narrow-minded individuals. I hope that our Commission will stand fast."[33]

The project progressed, despite these problems. Bids on Office Building 1, now usually known as the West Wing, were opened on December 21, 1923, with the architect in attendance. Because Gilbert's contract required that he supervise construction, he could monitor the bidding process to guarantee the winning contractors had the experience needed to complete the job satisfactorily. The contract, with the George A. Fuller Company of New York, was signed two days later. Gilbert had used the Fuller Company, one of America's most important contracting companies, for many other projects, and most recently the firm had built Henry Bacon's Lincoln Memorial.[34] The quality of the finished West Wing and the speed with which it was erected resulted from the use of a contractor experienced in constructing large public buildings.

Gilbert's contract stipulated he would select the superintendent of the works (his representative at the site) and pay his salary. The superintendent was directly responsible to Gilbert; the daily reports, telegrams, and requests for advice that he received from his superintendents reveal how Gilbert controlled quality and costs from afar.[35]

Beginning construction with one office building was pragmatic; the appropriation was not sufficient to build the central unit, rental space for state agencies was scarce and expensive, and delaying the construction of the Main Building meant that no decision on the expensive dome had to be made at this time. Perhaps the West Wing was chosen because it did not include the facilities needed for the Supreme Court of Appeals, which was still located in the Annex and did not require rental space.

Ground was broken on January 7, 1924, and the cornerstone laid on May 1; the building—300 by 60 feet, 67 feet tall, with 84,000 square feet of floor space—was completed by April 1925. The cost, $1,218,171.32, included the architect's fee of $68,953.09. The Fuller Company employed more than forty subcontractors, at least some of which were West Virginia companies; the steel, for example, was made in Wheeling.[36]

Figs. 41–44 (pages 121–24). Four views of Office Building # 1—the West Wing—under construction in 1924. Sequentially, the dates are July 1, September 8, September 15, and October 16. Ground had been broken in January, and the interior was complete by March 1925. For photos illustrating earlier steps in the construction process, see the examples chosen for Office Building #2, figs. 46–49. More construction photos are available online at *http://www.wvculture.org/history/wvmemory/*.

Before excavations began, some houses were removed, and a spur of the New York Central Railroad was laid for direct delivery of large equipment and impressive amounts of steel, stone, and other materials. Excavated soil was used to fill the foundation holes of the houses, while trees and shrubs were saved for later use.

Photographs taken at approximately one-week intervals document the construction. The stone of the curtain wall was quickly hung on the exterior of the steel structure, as seen in figs. 41–42. Note the railroad car on its siding on July 1 (fig. 41) and the crane that moved on the same siding on September 8 (fig. 42).

Taken 7-1-24
West Virginia State Capitol
Cass Gilbert, Architect

Fig. 41

Fig. 42

No. 30. Taken 9-15-24
Virginia State Capitol
GEORGE A. FULLER CO BUILDERS

Fig. 43

No. 34 Taken 10-16-24
West Virginia State Capitol
Cass Gilbert, Architect
GEORGE A. FULLER CO. BUILDERS

Fig. 44

By September 8, the drums (cylinders) for the columns of the porch above the courtyard entrance lay on the ground; within a week, they were erected (fig. 43). On October 16 (fig. 44), the crowning balustrade was in place, but the scaffolding around the columns awaited removal. The protruding blocks for the heads over the courtyard entrance were installed by September 8 (fig. 42), but they were not carved until January. A comparison of figures 43 and 44 reveals the role played by one particular element in Gilbert's design. While the balustrade might seem like an expensive historical reference, its importance becomes clear when the views are compared. On September 15, the building looks dull and its proportions ponderous; within a month, the balustrade has transformed the building, which suddenly seems not only finished but elegant.

In October 1924, just as the exterior of the West Wing was nearing completion, Gilbert told the Fuller Company to eliminate all decorative carved detail with the exception of the heads over the courtyard entrance; this would save $35,884. The same measure was later taken for the East Wing, and in 1932, after the Main Building had been completed, Gilbert wrote Governor Conley urging that the "carving of exterior stone work of the east and west wings originally contemplated but omitted should be done." The postponed carvings included rows of small lions' heads above the cornice (note the square blocks along the upper edge of the building in figure 44) and garlands in the panels below the upper-level windows; on the Main Building these motifs were finished (see fig. 99), while on both wings the stone waiting to be carved is obvious once attention is drawn to it. Drawings reveal that raised panels to the left and right of the open porches above the courtyard entrances to the office buildings were to be decorated with Medusa heads and other motifs.[37] In January 1925, craftsmen provided by J. Donnelly and Company, the New York firm that Gilbert traditionally used for sculpture and decorative motifs, mounted temporary wooden scaffolding and carved the heads of Greco-Roman deities and heroes from the blocks of stone above the three arches. Cass Gilbert, Cass Jr., and Samuel McGuire traveled to Charleston in early April to inspect Office Building 1 with superintendent Charles Hequembourg; although the architect noted a few minor problems, the Capitol Commission agreed that the governor should formally accept the building after the completion of required paperwork.[38]

Just as Office Building 1 was being completed, another attack on the Capitol project was mounted. An editorial in the *Fairmont West Virginian*, reprinted in the *Charleston Gazette* under the headline "What West Virginia Editors Say" on April 18, 1925, stated that Robert Permar, managing editor of the *Wheeling Intelligencer*, had asserted that the cost of the new Capitol would be between $9 and 12 million, or $3 to 5 million dollars "in excess of the amount authorized by the legislature, which is $7,000,000."[39] While the author expressed confidence in Governor Gore, he urged an investigation: "The people ought to know it if their officials have been guilty of graft, and these officials ought to have no cloud hanging over them if they have been honest in the administration of their duties." Further information on Permar's accusations appeared in the *Charleston Daily Mail* on April 19: "CAPITOL FRAUD CHARGE AUTHOR FACES PROBERS; Robert Permar Questioned Before Joint Legislative Committee, Admits He Doesn't Know Whether Original Plans Were Changed to Meet New Requirements." Permar, who had alleged "fraud, extravagance and waste," stated that these charges were based on the fact that, despite the $5 million limit established by the 1923 Legislature, the Commission had built one office building without changing the plans, leading to the conclusion that the total cost would "go to $7,000,000 or more." When asked, "Did you inquire of any member of the capitol commission as to whether any changes had been made in the plans?" Permar replied, "I did not myself, but Mr. Ogden [his publisher] did." The investigating committee decided to call Ogden and Hill to testify but had not decided if they would ask the architect as well. This new attack may help explain the delay in starting Office Building 2.[40]

On the same day, Superintendent Hequembourg informed Gilbert he had guided members of the Senate Committee investigating the *Intelligencer* charges and two members of the press through the building, at their request.[41] Hequembourg reported: "Nothing developed this afternoon. I was courteous and found no trouble in answering direct questions and some cross questions regarding the materials of construction, source of same, etc., and my statements in reply were direct, without superfluous words." But when Hequembourg was told he would be summoned before the committee, he informed Gilbert that he did not want to appear unless "ordered to do so by you." He warned, "The committee may go so far as to summon you," and asked, "Please ... telegraph me what you want me to do." Gilbert told Hequembourg "to go before the Committee and give them the *fullest* [Gilbert's emphasis] information—nothing to conceal." A special delivery letter from Gilbert to "My dear Mr. Hequembourg" began: "We have no occasion for the slightest fear or anxiety as to the result of any honest, thorough and fair investigation, no matter how rigid and searching. There is nothing in the transaction from start to present time which I have the slightest wish to conceal." Gilbert continued: "My contract was not procured by politics, influence, misrepresentation, promises, graft or any impropriety of any sort. [It] was published in the daily papers ... with my hearty concurrence." Providing information would demonstrate his integrity: "Finally: I want the Legislature to have all information. The more they know about the job and my part in it, the better it will suit me. We have a good building. We have had honest, skillful contractors. They have done a good job." He added: "My books, correspondence, drawings and data are open to them. If they tell me what they want I will try to supply it." He concluded: "I will do the best I can with whatever appropriation the Legislature makes. I will not do any 'shoddy' building, or try to make galvanized iron look like stone. It's up to the Legislature and I am sure they want the truth."[42]

Other points in Gilbert's letter are worth noting. He warned, for example, that cuts could lead to the elimination of the dome: "All designs, drawings,

Fig. 45. The courtyard entrance of the West Wing on January 22, 1925. By this date, the head of Herakles/Hercules above the left door had been carved, the head of Fortuna above the right door was nearing completion (the plaster model the sculptor was following can be seen on the scaffolding), and the block of stone from which the head of Zeus/Jupiter would be carved was in place above the central door. The plaster models for the heads were probably created by the Donelly Company under Gilbert's supervision.

sketches or illustrations which show a dome or porticoes were made before the legislation of 1923 [which limited the total cost to $5 million] and in accord with the legislation of 1921." He emphasized that there was no question that the 1923 legislation would have meant the loss of the dome: "I have repeatedly stated ... that the original designs ... could not and would not be carried into effect under the legislation of 1923. In other words they must be changed to just the extent that the appropriation was lessened, and that the dome of course would have to be omitted."

Gilbert further clarified: "I have no idea of building anything beyond what is authorized by the Legislature. Neither has the Capitol Commission so far as I know. We could not do so. We could not get a contractor to do the work unless it was authorized by the Legislature. The cost and extent of the work depends on the will of the Legislature." He emphasized the importance of quality: "It is of course assumed that the Legislature would not want a 'shoddy' job, that they want good, sound, honest building and equipment that will last—no matter how plain it may be. It is my duty to tell the Capitol Commission all the facts in the case and not to deceive them as to quality that may be obtained for a fixed sum of money." Because quality should remain high, it was size that would determine cost: "The first estimate of space ... amounted to about 212,000 sq. ft.... This was scaled down to about 145,000 sq. ft., [then] raised to about 156,000 sq. ft. which was approved by the Capitol Commission, each state department chief having OK'd the space assigned to his department." As an assurance that no money had been or would be diverted by graft, Gilbert concluded: "All contracts are let by public advertisement, bids opened in public and awarded to the lowest responsible bidder." This extensive letter was surely designed to provide Hequembourg with quotations from Gilbert that he could use were he called to testify.

Accusations of corruption must have been circulating, for Governor Gore reassured Hequembourg that "the integrity of the Architect was not questioned in any way." Hequembourg reported that Gore's main concern was: "what sort of building (Main) could be built for the balance available after Building No. 2 was erected. In answer to this I simply stated that you would plan this to suit the available funds and you had at no time held any other idea since the Legislature acted in 1923." Hequembourg told Gilbert that he had reassured Gore that the architect "would plan only such construction which would be sound, serviceable and properly equipped for obtaining the desired results as to economy of operation, but in doing this the 'coat must be cut according to the cloth.' I stated you did not care to be misunderstood and that I was here ready to submit any information the committee might desire."

In May 1925, we have the first documented evidence of problems created by Bonner Hill, who took on increased responsibilities after Secretary Young reduced his involvement in October 1922 and who eventually assumed the title of secretary. Hill had served as Charleston city manager and was supposedly selected by the Commission because of his knowledge of construction and administration. Hill was a difficult person, and it is certainly not irrelevant for the role he played at the Capitol after 1925 that he had been Kanawha County sheriff during the 1912 Paint Creek–Cabin Creek mine war. At the time, he was accused of being "another tool of the coal barons." He was on the "Bull Moose Special" armored train and it was possibly he who gave the command to attack the Holly Grove miners' settlement.[43] How his political or other connections functioned while he was the agent/secretary to the Capitol Building Commission is uncertain, but they may have helped to protect him during the years when he quarreled with Gilbert and his superintendents. Despite continuing problems and Gilbert's frequent complaints to the governor, Hill served as secretary of the Commission until at least 1933.

By May 21, 1925, Gilbert was so incensed that he wrote to Governor Gore to ask for "Mr. Hill's instant dismissal."[44] Gilbert summarized: "This is not the first time I have had occasion to take exception to Mr. Hill's activities. During the construction of [the West Wing], Mr. Hill gave me occasion for much annoyance by asserting supervisory authority ... in that he gave instructions to contractors, questioned actions taken by this office ... in a way ... subversive of good discipline and authority." Gilbert's letter was precipitated by a dramatic encounter between Hill and Superintendent Hequembourg, who had asked workmen to store models in a house on state property: "Mr. Hill met me at the house and without the slightest provocation he became very angry and ordered me to remove these models ... immediately. He said that if I did not do so he would throw them out the window." Hill said to Hequembourg: "And you get out of here ... too. ..." (Hequembourg added in parentheses that the omissions represented "abusive language".) "Mr. Hill then forced me to the entrance door and began to shove me out by pushing the door against me. I resisted this for a moment—then Mr. Hill became *furious* [his emphasis] and acted like a crazy man. His face became purple and I feared he would have an attack of apoplexy. I decided to refrain from having a fist fight although Mr. Hill threw back his arm in a threatening manner and would have started a fight in the next moment but I managed somehow to hold my temper and avoid personal combat." Hill then ordered Hequembourg "out of the house at 1804 Quarrier." This was "where the balance of your property (drawings) and some of my things are stored. ... Mr. Hill 'gets this way' every so often and at such times he is impossible to handle." When Hequembourg reported this to Governor Gore, the governor urged him to "keep quiet and be patient and await developments." No matter how bad Hill's behavior became, Governors Gore and Conley seem to have been unwilling to censure him.

In June 1926, Gilbert revealed his displeasure in a letter he penned, but did not send, to Commissioner Fitzpatrick: "I really feel that something must be done about Bonner Hill's attitude toward our work in Charleston. ... I can see the situation developing very much as it did on Building No. 1 and I simply cannot stand it."[45] Such language is startling, as Gilbert's archives reveal a man in careful control of both his emotions and the situation. He continued: "If I am not competent to prepare the specifications and documents incident to my work, it might be well for the Commission to find an architect who is, but with some forty years' experience I am justified in saying that I know the way these things should be done somewhat better than Mr. Hill." There was more: "If Mr. Hill could be instructed to keep his hands off we will get a better building with less trouble and less expense. If we have to go through what we had to endure in Building No. 1, I fear that I will not be able to keep a competent self-respecting superintendent on the job." A hand-written note reveals that this letter was "not sent." Gilbert decided not to bother the commissioners, adding that the "complaint should be addressed to Gov Gore" because of his "promise to keep Hill from interfering." It would be best "to present the matter in conference with him as a letter is so easily misunderstood."

The completion of the West Wing was commemorated with two bronze tablets. One names Governor Morgan and the commissioners, including those who had resigned or died, as well as Bonner Hill and the Fuller Company. The second names the architect and reproduces a "preliminary" elevation of the Main Building and a "preliminary" ground plan of the three-building complex. Naming the officials involved and the contracting company is traditional for public buildings, but the second plaque is unexpected. Its function was most likely to remind legislators and future governors of the grand complex that Governor Morgan, the members of the Commission, and Cass Gilbert had envisioned for West Virginia and to urge them to bring the three-building complex to completion.

Bids on Office Building 2 (now known as the East Wing) were not accepted until the middle of 1926. The delay seems related to the appropriation passed in early June 1925, which limited its cost to $1.4 million and established a timetable for the delivery of the funds. Of the $900,000 appropriated, only $450,000 would be available the first year and the Commission had to wait until the next fiscal year to receive the second $450,000 installment.[46] The additional amount needed to reach $1.3 or $1.4 million was to come "from the sale of the land and buildings now occupied as temporary quarters by some of the State departments."

On October 17, 1925, Hequembourg reported to Gilbert that some officials were urging the governor to let contracts "for an amount of work which could be taken care of by the funds now available," a sum the superintendent believed to be $900,000. By October 28, however, he reported "it does not seem to me, from present indications, that construction work on this Unit will be started for some time to come." The governor had not sold the Temporary Capitol Site, and several energy companies were challenging the Gross Sales Act in the courts, a process that could cost the state revenue and might not be settled quickly.[47]

Finally, in May 1926, Gilbert traveled to Charleston to finalize plans for the East Wing with Governor Gore, after which it was announced that bids would be due on July 12. One bidder was the recently formed James Baird Company, whose founder was almost certainly known to Gilbert through Baird's previous work at the Fuller Company. A representative of the Baird Company was in Charleston on July 12, staying at the Hotel Kanawha, and the architect asked him about the "quantity and quality of work which this Company is doing at this time." The reply was impressive: seven projects with construction costs of approximately $4,380,000, including Aeolian Hall in New York City and an addition to the Corcoran Gallery in Washington. The Commission awarded the contract to the Baird Company on July 19; their acceptance included a guarantee to "complete the building on or before 375 working days from date of contract. ('Working days' shall be construed as being all days excepting Sundays and holidays)."[48]

Excavation began that month, and the East Wing was completed by December 1927, just in time for state offices to move out of rented quarters at the end of the year. Construction was apparently expedited because of the need for office space after the Pasteboard Capitol burned in March 1927. Compared to the West Wing, the construction time was about two months longer and the cost somewhat higher ($1,361,425, including Cass Gilbert's fee of $77,061.79 for the East Wing; $1,218.171.32 included the architect's fee of $68,953.09 for the West Wing). The increases can be credited to the East Wing's new, more secure State Treasurer's Office and the richly appointed courtroom for the Supreme Court of Appeals.[49]

In September 1926, as the foundations of the East Wing were rising, John Rockart was in Charleston and he received a wire from Gilbert asking that he arrange a meeting with Governor Gore, Superintendent Hequembourg, and Secretary Hill for a "full and frank discussion." The purpose was to establish a clear understanding of Hequembourg's and Hill's respective roles: "Make it clear that I have no prejudice or animosity against Mr. Hill and would welcome his friendship, but that he must not attempt to dictate to me or my Superintendent or interfere with my function as architect. Very important that you should be present at such conference and assist Governor Gore in clarifying the situation." Gilbert asked Rockart to call the governor's attention to provisions in Gilbert's contract that defined the architect's specific responsibilities. "Point out that these services cannot be properly performed under Hill's meddlesome interference and request that I be sustained in carrying on the work under conditions named in contract otherwise cannot be responsible for results." Gilbert wanted Rockart to report on the "impropriety of Hill's assumption of authority talking with the workmen and writing letters and reports unfairly damaging to the good reputation of the work and its unfavorable reaction on all concerned." He concluded: "Assure Governor of my most sincere desire to meet his wishes and to cooperate to make the Capitol a credit to his administration and give him my personal assurance thereof. Show him this telegram if you wish." No meeting is documented, and on November 6 things came to a head when Hill accused Hequembourg in

Figs. 46–49 (pages 132–35). Four views of Office Building # 2—the East Wing—under construction in 1926. Sequentially, the dates are October 7, October 21, November 11, and November 30 (laying of the cornerstone). Ground had been broken in July. Note the rough wooden ladders supplying access to the upper levels (October 21), and the wooden forms prepared for pouring the concrete walls of the basement (November 11). The speed in which the steel structure was being erected reveals the coordination with which materials were ordered, delivered, stored, and assembled by the contractor.

No. 24 Taken 10.21.26
West Virginia State Capito
Office Building No. 2
Cass Gilbert, Architect

Fig. 47

No. 30 Taken 11-11-26
West Virginia State Capitol
Office Building No. 2
Cass Gilbert, Architect
JAMES BAIRD COMPANY, BUILDERS

Fig. 48

SPEC. No. 11-30 Taken -26
West Virginia State Capitol
Office Building No. 2
Cass Gilbert, Architect
JAMES BAIRD COMPANY, BUILDERS

Fig. 49

Fig. 50. Chamber for the Supreme Court of Appeals, under construction on May 7, 1927.

writing of being late for work, indulging in a "love affair," taking bribes, and being drunk. Hequembourg sent a copy of the letter to Gilbert and reported that after he had challenged the accuracy of these accusations he and Hill had a talk and were reconciled. Hill assured Hequembourg he would telephone Gilbert in the superintendent's presence to inform the architect that he had not sent a copy of his letter to the governor. Hill requested that Gilbert return the copy of the November 6 letter so that it "would not be on record anywhere." Gilbert apparently complied, but he also had a copy made for his archive. Later, Hequembourg spoke to the architect in Hill's presence, Hill and Hequembourg had lunch together, and Hequembourg reported that "there will be harmony from now on."[50]

Photos document the rapid progress of the East Wing's construction. On October 7, 1926, the foundation was under way; note the temporary railroad spur in the foreground (fig. 46). By October 21, the steel structure of floors one and two was in place (fig. 47), and by November 11, the structure had reached its maximum height (fig. 48). On November 30, the laying of the cornerstone was held (fig. 49).

Simultaneously, attention turned to the details of the interior. The construction of the marble columns for the chamber for the Supreme Court of Appeals is documented in several photographs. Two of the complex specification drawings for this chamber reveal the precise detail with which the Gilbert firm guided the contractors. In November 1926, the justices wrote to their counterparts in other states asking how their courtrooms were arranged; they requested photographs, plans, and descriptions of the furniture used by judges, attorneys, and spectators. In April of 1927, after the results were compiled, they wrote to Gilbert recommending that moveable chairs be used for the spectators, but added that "the Judges are depending on your good taste in the matter." When Gilbert's designs were finalized, on August 12, 1927, he sent them to Hequembourg, asking that he show them to the justices. Gilbert explained his process: "It is perhaps unnecessary to state that I have given very careful thought to the designs of the furniture in order to keep it in harmony with the architectural style of the room and at the same time not overelaborate, which no doubt will be obvious to you and the Judges when examining the designs." He recommended that "benches—not stationary but moveable, be used as they will provide for an orderly arrangement of the furniture and will be in scale with the room also; whereas if chairs are used they will be in the first place out of scale and will not provide for the orderly arrangement that should be obtained in so important a room." It was crucial that the justices decide soon: "I would add that prompt decision in this matter is quite important so that the order can be placed and the furniture delivered in time when the building is completed and ready for occupancy."[51]

The justices were pleased with their new quarters. At the opening of the first session, on January 11, 1928, Justice William N. Miller wrote: "This beautiful court

Fig. 51, 52 (pages 138–41). Cass Gilbert (concept), Specification drawings with sections and elevations for the Supreme Court chamber. The complex detail needed by the contractor is demonstrated in these two drawings, which also include specifications about materials, including the original cork floor with its marble border. For the finished chamber, see fig. 53.

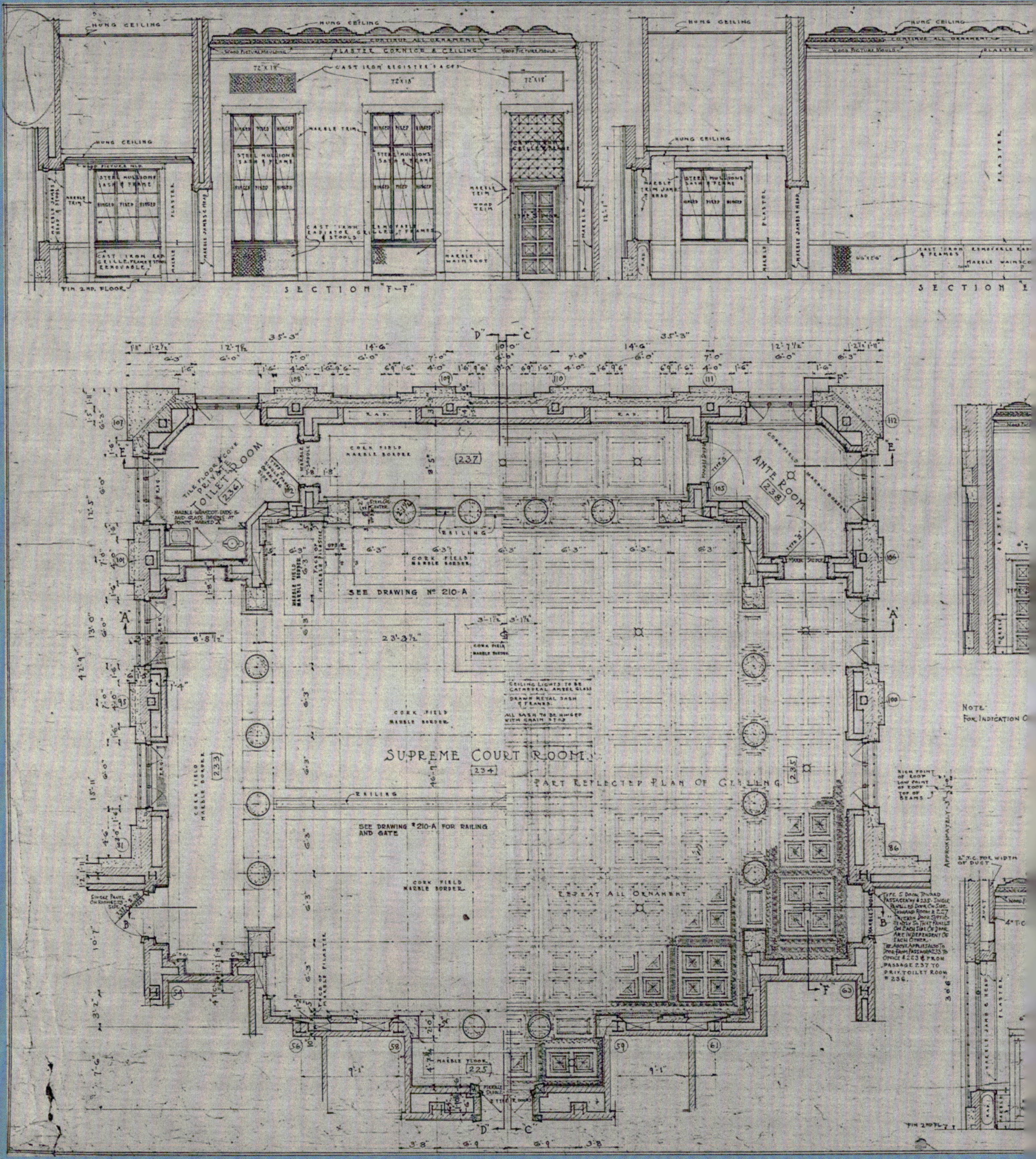

SECTION "F-F"
SUPREME COURT ROOM
234
PART REFLECTED PLAN OF CEILING
PRIVATE TOILET ROOM
236
ANTE ROOM
238
SEE DRAWING Nº 210-A
SEE DRAWING #210-A FOR RAILING AND GATE
CORK FIELD MARBLE BORDER
REPEAT ALL ORNAMENT
HUNG CEILING
PLASTER CORNICE & CEILING
CAST IRON REGISTER FACES
STEEL MULLIONS SASH & FRAME
MARBLE WAINSCOT
MARBLE FLOOR
225
233
235
237


Fig. 51

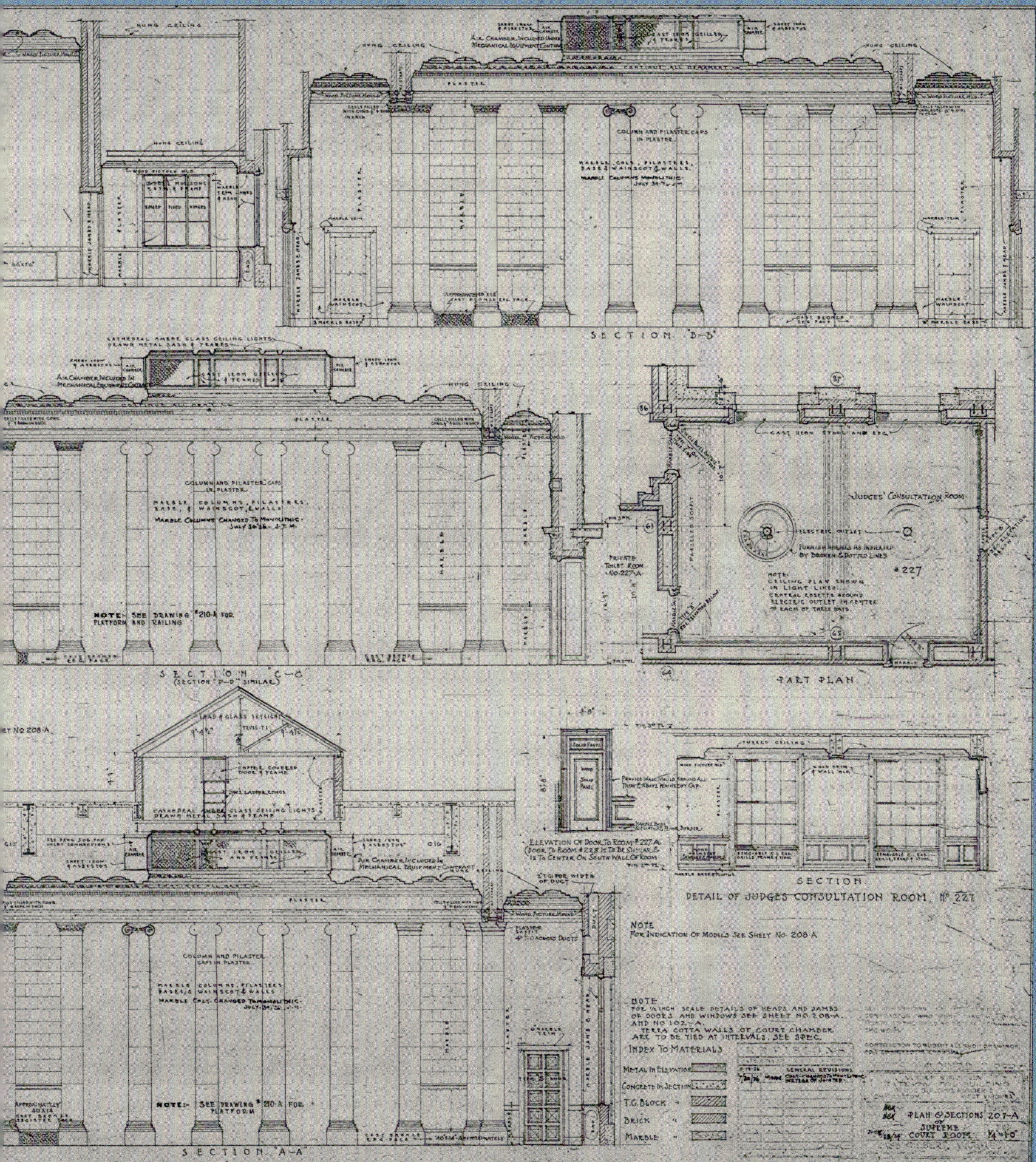
SECTION "B-B"
SECTION "C-C"
(SECTION "D-D" SIMILAR)
PART PLAN
JUDGES' CONSULTATION ROOM
#227
SECTION.
DETAIL OF JUDGES CONSULTATION ROOM, No 227
SECTION "A-A"
NOTE
FOR INDICATION OF MODELS SEE SHEET NO 208-A
NOTE:- SEE DRAWING #210-A FOR PLATFORM AND RAILING
NOTE:- SEE DRAWING #210-A FOR PLATFORM
COLUMN AND PILASTER CAPS IN PLASTER.
MARBLE COLUMNS CHANGED TO MONOLITHIC - JULY 30'26 - J.T.M.
CATHEDRAL AMBRE GLASS CEILING LIGHTS DRAWN METAL SASH & FRAME
AIR CHAMBER INCLUDED IN MECHANICAL EQUIPMENT CONTRACT
HUNG CEILING
PLASTER
MARBLE
INDEX TO MATERIALS
METAL IN ELEVATION
CONCRETE IN SECTION
T.C. BLOCK
BRICK
MARBLE
REVISIONS
GENERAL REVISIONS
PLAN & SECTIONS OF SUPREME COURT ROOM
207-A
1/4"=1'0"

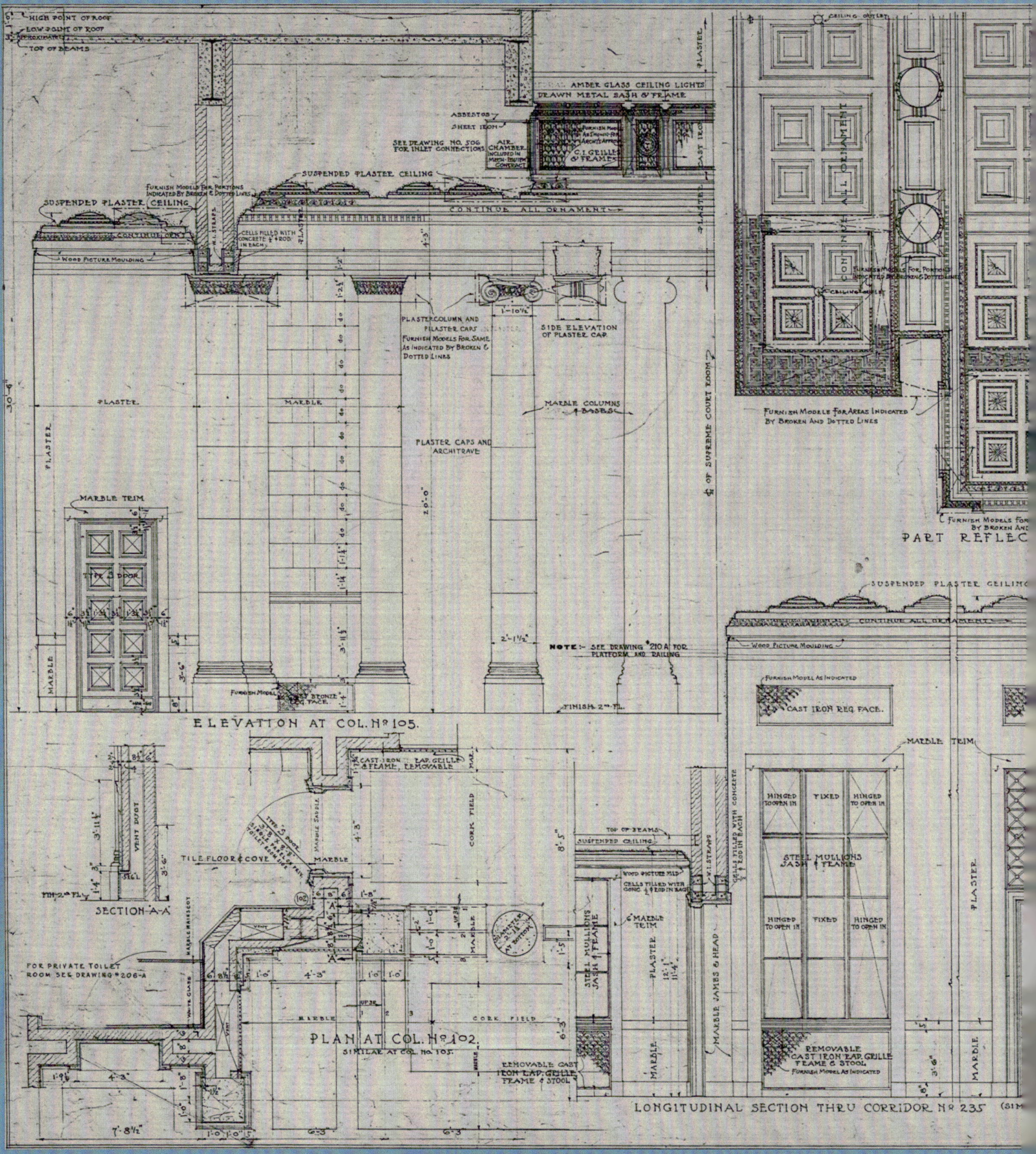
ELEVATION AT COL. No 105.
PLAN AT COL. No 102.
SIMILAR AT COL. No 105.
SECTION-A-A
LONGITUDINAL SECTION THRU CORRIDOR No 235
PART REFLEC
SUSPENDED PLASTER CEILING
CONTINUE ALL ORNAMENT
AMBER GLASS CEILING LIGHTS
DRAWN METAL SASH & FRAME
PLASTER CAPS AND ARCHITRAVE
MARBLE COLUMNS & BASES
SIDE ELEVATION OF PLASTER CAP
MARBLE TRIM
TYPE S DOOR
WOOD PICTURE MOULDING
CAST IRON REG. FACE.
STEEL MULLIONS SASH & FRAME
REMOVABLE CAST IRON LAP. GRILLE FRAME & STOOL
FOR PRIVATE TOILET ROOM SEE DRAWING # 206-A
TILE FLOOR & COVE
CORK FIELD
FINISH 2nd FL.

Fig. 52

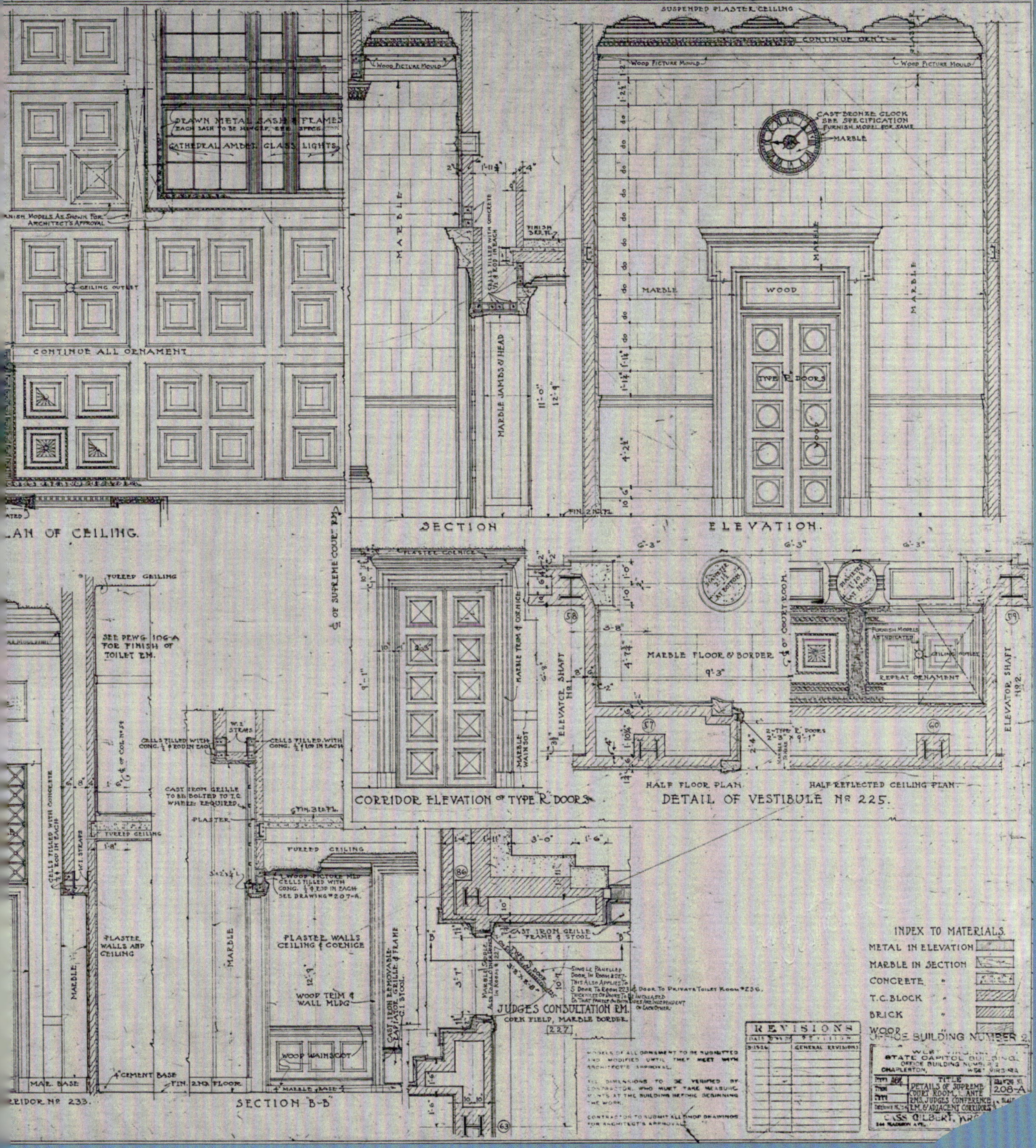

SUSPENDED PLASTER CEILING
DRAWN METAL SASH & FRAMES
CATHEDRAL AMBER GLASS LIGHTS
CEILING OUTLET
CONTINUE ALL ORNAMENT
LAN OF CEILING
SECTION
ELEVATION.
CAST BRONZE CLOCK SEE SPECIFICATION FURNISH MODEL FOR SAME
MARBLE
WOOD
TYPE "E" DOORS
MARBLE JAMBS & HEAD
CORRIDOR ELEVATION OF TYPE "R" DOORS
DETAIL OF VESTIBULE Nº 225.
MARBLE FLOOR & BORDER
HALF FLOOR PLAN.
HALF REFLECTED CEILING PLAN.
ELEVATOR SHAFT
REPEAT ORNAMENT
SEE DWG 106-A FOR FINISH OF TOILET RM.
PLASTER WALLS AND CEILING
PLASTER WALLS CEILING & CORNICE
WOOD TRIM & WALL MLDG
WOOD WAINSCOT
SECTION B-B
JUDGES CONSULTATION RM.
CORK FIELD, MARBLE BORDER.
227
INDEX TO MATERIALS.
METAL IN ELEVATION
MARBLE IN SECTION
CONCRETE
T.C. BLOCK
BRICK
WOOD
REVISIONS
OFFICE BUILDING NUMBER 2
WEST VIRGINIA STATE CAPITOL BUILDING
CHARLESTON, W. VA.
DETAILS OF SUPREME COURT ROOM ANTE RM. JUDGES CONFERENCE RM. & ADJACENT CORRIDORS
208-A
CASS GILBERT, ARCHITECT

room—a veritable temple of Justice, with all the other equipment now at our disposal, [is] unsurpassed, if not unequalled, by any other in the country." He agreed with Gilbert on the power of architecture: "Its influence in molding the artistic and aesthetic tastes and character of the old and young is great.... We hope we may perform our duties influenced and guided by the wisdom and philosophy of the great sages and statesmen whose words so appropriately adorn the frieze above and surrounding the walls that so beautifully enclose us."[52]

At the same time, Bonner Hill was expressing his dissatisfaction. In February 1928, Gilbert wrote to him: "I have noticed in several of your recent letters your statements that criticisms are being leveled at the building, that the condition of the building is making a bad impression on the visiting public." Gilbert emphasized: "While I expect unsolicited and unjustified criticisms I am not disturbed by them. The building is a fine example of good construction and a credit to the Contractors, the Governor, the Capitol Commission and myself, and has received unsolicited compliments." Gilbert asked Hill: "I would inquire whether you are conveying such unfavorable comments indirectly or whether they are expressions of your own judgment in the matter. What you ought to do is discourage such criticism since it is not justified."[53] Gilbert also wrote to Governor Gore, enclosing a copy of his letter to Hill, and questioning whether "Mr. Hill, through petty cheese-paring and unjust fault-finding concerning the only public work in the country that has cost less than the appropriation without sacrifice of quality, is trying to make trouble for the Governor, the Capitol Commission, the Architect, and all concerned, by attempting to discredit the work; or has he a mistaken idea that he is in some sense the responsible personage in charge of it and that he is protecting the interest of the State?" When he asked Gore: "Where do the occasional newspaper criticisms come from?" he seemed to suggest that Hill was responsible.

Hill responded with criticisms concerning the acoustics in the Supreme Court chamber, the height of the stacks in the Supreme Court library, and cracked wood doors. Hill concluded: "I note what you say about discouraging criticism against the building, and wish to say that it is hard to stop it under the present conditions which I am not sure you wish to know all about. I am of the opinion that these things mentioned will be a menace in getting an appropriation to complete the capitol project."[54] It is not clear whom Hill was intimidating, Gilbert as architect or Gore as governor, but he seems to be threatening that he has some kind of power over future developments.

Hill was unable to stop the construction of the Main Building, but his machinations may have played a role in delaying its financing by the Legislature. Ground was not broken until some months after Black Tuesday and the beginning of the Great Depression.

Fig. 53. Supreme Court of Appeals chamber, West Virginia Capitol. Photograph taken 2012, after the restoration of the cork floor. Photograph by Thorney Lieberman.

***Intercepted Message***

August 12, 1929.

Dear Bill:

You had better keep after Cass Gilbert. If you leave him alone he's liable to fool around until the democrats get in.

Yours,

George

Gov. William G. Conley,
Charleston, W. Va.


# [C]harleston Gazette

*"The State Newspaper"*

[Charle]ston, West Virginia, Sunday Morning, August 11, 1929.


[...]ds

DID YOU KNOW A GOOD STORY FOR THE GAZE-AT-IT?

# THE GAZE-AT-IT

THE MAN WE[...] STARTE[D]

CHARLESTON, WEST VA. SUNDAY, AUGUST 11, 1929

## GOVERNOR UPSET

HE WANTS THE PLANS

GOVERNOR CONLEY IS SAID TO BE TERRIBLY UPSET OVER THE DELAY IN THE CAPITOL PLANS, AS HE IS ANXIOUS TO FINISH THE BUILDING DURING HIS ADMINISTRATION.

### OVER LAZINESS OF CASS GILBERT

GOVERNOR CONLEY IS SAID TO BE EXTREMELY ANNOYED. HE HAS DISCOVERED THAT THE CAPITOL PLANS ARE UNFINISHED AND THAT THE ARCHITECT, CASS GILBERT, IS OFF HAVING A GOOD TIME AT HIS SUMMER VILLA IN EUROPE AS IF HE HAD NOTHING ELSE TO DO.

GAZE-AT-IT PHOTO OF CASS GILBERT AT HIS VILLA IN EUROPE BEING INTERVIEWED BY OUR CORRESPONDENT

### PLANS TO BE FINISHED

GILBERT SAYS

WHEN TOLD BY A GAZE-AT-IT REPORTER HOW MUCH THE GOV. WAS ANNOYED, MR. GILBERT SHED TEARS, SAID HE WAS AWFUL SORRY AND THAT HE WOULD SAIL FOR NEW YORK AND FINISH DRAWING UP THE PLANS.

CHAPTER SIX

# The Second Design Phase

I am myself entirely satisfied with the [new] design both from the standpoint of the arrangement of the plan and exterior appearance of the building. In short, I believe it will make a very handsome and satisfactory structure and one in which the State will take just pride. It will, I am sure, provide a building of very convenient arrangement and of beautiful and impressive proportions.

Cass Gilbert, writing to Governor Howard Gore, April 10, 1928

Fig. 54. Cartoon from the *Charleston Gazette*, August 11, 1929.

THE DELAY IN FINISHING DRAWINGS AND STARTING CONSTRUCtion on the Main Building was, as usual, due to the lack of an appropriation and revenue stream. Governor Gore urged the 1927 Legislature to appropriate $5 million and establish a related revenue stream spread over four or five years.[1] Contracts for construction could then be advertised by the beginning of 1928.

For a "certain and definite" revenue stream, Gore recommended that "the most practical method would be by direct levy [tax], this being a source of revenue concerning which there can be no doubt, and being presented in the form of authorization it becomes contractual in character, and offers a secure basis for contract both to the state and to the contractor." He proposed levying a tax on property, the assessed value of which, in 1926, was $2,130,255,951. The current levy was ten cents per hundred dollars; to raise $5 million, Gore proposed a five-cent increase for five years.

A useful review of the current financial situation was included in Gore's message to the Legislature. All available funds, including the insurance settlement from the old Capitol and the sale of the old site and other properties, had been expended or were committed to the completion of the East Wing. Gore summarized: "The cost of the present capitol grounds and office building number one represent approximately the proceeds received by the state from insurance and the sale of the old capitol grounds and buildings, ... the cost of office building number two, now under construction, about represents the additional investment over and above funds derived from insurance and the sale of the old capitol property." A new appropriation and revenue stream were essential for the Main Building.

To help the Legislature decide how to proceed, in late May 1927 Cecil B. Highland, Chair of the Senate Finance Committee, asked the opinion of "substantial citizens."[2]

Gentlemen:

Knowing that you have a genuine interest in every subject in which the state is involved, I respectfully solicit from you a full expression of your opinion in the matter of the construction of a capitol building for the state.

The cost of a building which will be at all creditable to the state, and which will suffice for its needs, will amount to something like five or six million dollars, and it would probably be economical to expend the higher amount in order to get the best possible construction, as we should build for at least a century.

In order to economize in the construction, it is necessary to have the money available at the time the contract is let, so that the construction company can push the work, as it will require a vast amount of equipment to raise the building, and if the equipment shall be compelled to lie idle until means for making payment are devised, the loss from such idleness will be necessarily thrown upon the public, as the contractor will be compelled to realize something from the equipment.

We think that possibly five hundred thousand dollars on the cost of construction can be saved if funds are available and some strong construction company, able to push the work, can be induced to take the contract and rush the building to completion in the shortest practicable time.

It is apparent that there are but two ways of raising the money: First, by levying direct and indirect taxes, which in the course of five years would raise a fund sufficient to construct a suitable building. This would delay the beginning of the work approximately four years, as the final

## THE FINANCIAL STATUS AS OF JUNE 1, 1927, FROM GOVERNOR GORE'S MESSAGE TO THE LEGISLATURE

*Statement of Cash Receipts into the State Treasury on Account of Insurance and the Sale of Old Capitol Grounds and Buildings*

| | |
|---|---|
| Insurance, old building and contents | $ 533,455.23 |
| Sale of old capitol site | 1,301,000.00 |
| Sale of two strips of land through old site to City of Charleston | 250,000.00 |
| Sale of Capitol Annex property | 500,000.00 |
| Interest on deferred payments | 37,040.84 |
| Sale and rent of houses on new site | 102,775.07 |
| Sale of [old] Mansion, Temporary Capitol and Board of Control Building | 350,000.00 |
| Sale of old Mansion (building) | 250.00 |
| Total | $3,074,521.14 |

*Expenditures for New Capitol and Site*

| | |
|---|---|
| New capitol site, including buildings thereon | $2,006,773.94 |
| Payments on contracts for Building No. 1 | 1,148,014.57 |
| Payments on contracts for Building No. 2 | 658,991.90 |
| Payments to Cass Gilbert, Architect fees, including supervision | 143,000.00 |
| All other payments | 69,908.45 |
| Total | $4,017,688.86 |
| Balance June 1, 1927, in appropriation for construction of second unit new capitol (Building No. 2) | $ 643,791.57 |

The above balance of $643,791.57 will be required for the completion of Office Building No. 2 and equipping the Supreme Court Library and grading of grounds.

*Appropriations Made by Legislature for New Capitol*

| | |
|---|---|
| Appropriation by 1921 Legislature | $2,250,000.00 |
| Appropriation by 1923 Legislature | 500,000.00 |
| Appropriation by 1925 Legislature | 968,000.00 |
| Appropriation by 1927 Legislature | 90,000.00[3] |
| Appropriation by Legislature, proceeds sale of Capitol Annex property | 501,256.59 |
| Appropriation by Legislature, proceeds sale of site occupied by [old] Governor's Mansion, Temporary Capitol and Board of Control Building | 352,223.84 |
| Total appropriated by Legislature | $4,661,480.43 |
| Amount of above raised by taxation | $1,586,959.29 |
| Amount of above derived from sales of property and insurance hereinbefore itemized | $3,074,521.14 |
| Total | $4,661,480.43 |

annual levy could accrue during the progress of the work, and the work should be completed by about one year from the date of commencement. Second, by issuing bonds, which can be authorized at the extra session, June 6, and the matter voted upon at the same election at which the proposal for issuing thirty-five million dollars road bonds will come to a vote. This method can make the funds available early in the year 1929, and the structure could be completed about the end of that year, or early in 1930. The bonds, if made payable within twenty-five or thirty years, could be met, interest and sinking fund, probably out of indirect taxes, and in no event would a direct levy exceeding one or two cents on the hundred dollars be necessary to take care of any amount not met by indirect taxes. This would be so trivial that the taxpayer could not make it a basis of complaint.

As chairman of the senate finance committee, I am endeavoring to get an expression from as many prominent citizens as possible that will be helpful to the Legislature in taking some intelligent action on this important matter, and at the same time adopt a plan that will meet the judgment of substantial citizens like yourself, and I, therefore, ask you to write me fully giving me your opinion as to the amount that should be spent on a capitol building, and the manner in which it should be raised.

I would like the privilege of making all legitimate uses of the information which you may furnish me, but will treat in confidence any matter with respect to which you may indicate a desire that it shall be so treated.

Highland's published summary of responses was instructive. He listed names and addresses and noted whether each individual preferred bonds, a tax, or a combination. In many cases he quoted the letters. Most wanted to start construction as soon as possible, and many favored bonds, with a tax as the first alternative.

G. R. Claypool of the Guyan Valley Grocery Co. in Logan, for example, wrote: "West Virginia is a rich state and it is a disgrace to her citizens not to provide a suitable building to house her employees and safely keep her records." J. W. Robinson of the State Schools for Colored, Deaf, and Blind encouraged the Commission: "I do not think that six million would be too much to spend for such a building."

Many emphasized that West Virginia needed a Capitol in which its citizens could take pride. The Follansbee City Manager wrote: "Should be more beautiful than any other in the Union at any cost." Another noted: "Should erect a building that would be a credit to the State." In urging that "the building should be completed according to the original plans prepared by Mr. Gilbert, or substantially in accordance therewith, so that the State Capitol, when completed, may be a source of pride to the people of West Virginia," Charles L. Estep, a Logan attorney, added: "I do not believe that our posterity should have occasion to look back at our efforts to construct a State Capitol, and justly say that we were a generation of materialists without any aesthetic tastes." A Charleston citizen wrote: "The whole capitol area should be put in first class shape so that the many visitors to West Virginia will appreciate what West Virginia really is.... Six or seven million dollars for this project would not be too much." C. W. Dillon, a Fayetteville attorney and former tax commissioner of West Virginia, wrote: "I was not aware that the completion of the Capitol would cost so much as $6,000,000.00, but my view is West Virginia cannot afford to economize in this respect and should complete the

Capitol and have public buildings commensurate with West Virginia's present and future progress." S. F. Glasscock, a Morgantown attorney, stated: "It will be 'Our Capitol' as West Virginia is 'Our State,' and I hope we will always be able to truthfully say that we are proud of both of them."

C. W. Osenton of Fayetteville, a Democratic National Committeeman, feared the completion of the Capitol could be used for political gain: "The people must be given to understand and believe that in the construction of a new Capitol it is not to be a one man affair and that it will not be used as a stepping stone by any person or persons to obtain advancement or political preference."

One respondent identified companies that should be taxed: "Why not lay a direct levy against the public utilities who are depleting the State's minerals and resources. For a good many years these concerns have profited and paid very little in return to the State." Another wanted to limit total expenditure to "approximately three and a half to four million dollars," funded in part by "increasing the tax rate under the Gross Sales Tax law, applied to the production of natural gas in West Virginia."

Dr. J. E. Ewing of Glenville wrote: "Money for our Capitol should be raised by the most indirect way possible. In my judgment, flotation of bonds would be best. Might take a shot at raising the required amount by increasing the rate on certain commodities." He continued: "I would like to see the oil and gas folks pay a big bunch of this money, and you fellows should make 'em do it. They never have paid anything like they should—very damn little compared to the great privileges they have enjoyed."

A property tax increase like the one proposed by Governor Gore eventually passed, but not until early 1929, after he had left office.[4] In the meantime, other possibilities were being considered. A newspaper article of October 1, 1927, for example, headlined, "Committee Sets Means to Raise Capitol Funds; Increase in Insurance and Public Utilities Taxation Is Decided on as Means to Raise Money." A November 22, 1927, article was headed: "Corporation Tax Approved to Get Funds for Capitol; Commission Reaches Agreement on Plan to Authorize Levy of One Per Cent on Corporations Until $5,000,000 is Obtained for Completion of Third Unit."[5] Despite such headlines, no special session was called and no one percent levy enacted; the only action the 1927 Legislature took was to appropriate and fund $110,000 to complete the working plans and specifications.[6] The drawings made by Gilbert and his studio during the second half of 1927 indicate that the Main Building was still to have a dome. The commissioners' commitment to the domed National Capitol model was unwavering; later, when Gilbert looked back on this period, he recalled "the more or less informal discussions in the conferences of the State Capitol Commission, especially that of December 12, 1927, in which several members of the Commission were very anxious that there should be no material change from the original design."[7]

At the December 12 meeting, Gilbert and his patrons confronted how to proceed in the face of curtailed funding.[8] The architect opened the meeting by asserting that a structure's "principal claim to beauty lies in its proportions, not its adornment." He then identified how visually satisfying proportions can be demonstrated, adding that even "ornamentation" must not be "disproportionate." "Inferior or unsuitable" materials must be avoided, but a "restrained or quiet use of material" can be "accented at focal points" by finer materials or a "splendid mural painting." Near the end, he commented on the role a capitol can play for all the state's citizens: "There the rich and poor alike may find the history of the state and the ideals of its government set forth in an orderly and appropriate way in noble inscriptions, beautiful mural paintings and sculpture and in the fine proportions and good taste of the whole design." Such statements seem intended to help his patrons make peace with an appropriation that was smaller than either he or they would like: if fine proportions can trump both ornamentation and the extensive use of fine materials, then West Virginia could have a great building even with a restricted budget.

Four months later, on April 10, 1928, Gilbert informed Governor Gore that he had finished a design for the Main Building that was closely related to the original but within the Legislature's $5 million limit.[9] He urged the governor to approve this proposal so that his office could prepare finished drawings and specifications and a contract could be let in late summer or early fall. Gilbert reassured Gore that he had followed the main proportions of the original design while making "certain reductions in its dimensions which will not affect its appearance and which will materially reduce its cost." Always the salesman, Gilbert praised the changes he had been forced to make. The new interior plan, for example, "provides better accommodations for the Legislature … and also better and more convenient accommodations for the business offices of the Governor and for the principal State officials assigned to this building." Savings came from reducing the size from 544 by 138 feet to 506 by 106 feet. Remembering the importance of the dome to his patrons, Gilbert emphasized that it was still the same size and that the reduction in the building's size would increase its "apparent majesty."[10] He assured Gore that the result would be "a very handsome and satisfactory structure and one in which the State will take just pride." Furthermore, "it will, I am sure, provide a building of very convenient arrangement and of beautiful and impressive proportions." His goal had always been to combine functionality with beauty expressed through proportions. "All these matters are closely related to somewhat abstruse questions of proportion which it is not necessary for me to go into in this letter," he wrote.

Gilbert told Gore he was always worried about cost and could not guarantee the reductions would meet the $5 million limit; he could not "express a final opinion until we have definite bids." To offer bidders flexibility, he intended to allow alternative proposals for the interior finish. If the bids were too high, certain elements could be eliminated; if the bids were lower than the authorization, more elaborate finish could be substituted as possible. The terraces surrounding the base of the building could be deferred, for example, although this was an item that the architect wanted to include. The porticoes at the west and east ends of the Main Building, with their columned porches and sculpted heads, were "not absolutely essential" and could be eliminated.

The "better and more convenient" offices for the governor were the result of moving them from the legislative to the ground floor. Perhaps worrying that Gore might not approve of what could be interpreted as a reduction in prestige, Gilbert emphasized that the change gained both "space and accessibility." The new location had another advantage, for it was nearer to the governor's mansion.[11]

Gore's April 17, 1928 reply to Gilbert's letter brought discouraging news. Unfortunately, "the legislature did not appropriate any money for building the main capitol unit. They simply authorized the preparation of the plans. I rather doubt whether we will be able to offer this building for contract this year," a delay that would mean that no action could be taken on the Main Building during Gore's tenure.[12] In his closing, the governor emphasized the cordial relationship he enjoyed with Gilbert: "You have been most kind, thoughtful and helpful, and for this I am deeply grateful." On May 12, Gilbert wrote Gore to ask if the Act of 1927 allowed him to proceed with final drawings.[13] If these preliminaries could be completed before he left for a European business trip on June 22, his office could continue work while he was away: "While the working drawings are largely matters of routine, they do take a great deal of time and detailed technical working out on the part of the experts in this organization." He explained his urgency: "With an organization of this kind it is necessary for me to undertake new and important works and to carry on others under way." He added, "I really do have to program the various operations in the office a little ahead of time so that we shall not get into a condition where one operation interferes with or delays another." He closed by complimenting Gore: "You have always been most sympathetic and helpful in carrying on the Capitol work and in expressing your approval of our successful endeavors to keep the cost within the funds available." Although Gilbert made a trip to Charleston June 7 to 9 hoping to move the project forward, the lack of a revenue stream meant that there was no point in proceeding with drawings and specifications.

As Gore had anticipated, there was no possibility for action on the project until November 1928, when William G. Conley—whose house had once stood on the Duffy Street Site—became governor-elect. To consolidate support for the Main Building as he prepared to leave office, Gore wrote to Gilbert on December 31 inviting him to Charleston; on his January 5 to 7 visit, the architect showed the reduced plans to the governor and the Commission.[14] Gore also wrote an inspiring letter to Gilbert stating that the "general plan" should be followed and that he had confidence in the architect's "judgment as to what a building of this character should represent."[15] He emphasized the importance of maintaining the dome: "In making changes in the building please understand that under no circumstances should the general scheme of the building be such as will not be in keeping with the work already done and with the general plan of the work." He trusted Gilbert's taste: "Whether it would cost $5,000,000 or more or less, it is my desire that the plans proposed be an expression of your judgment as to what a building of this character should represent when everything of an unnecessary nature not essential to its beauty or usefulness has been eliminated."

Soon after Conley was sworn in, he jump-started the Capitol project. Although he did not mention the Main Building in his inaugural address, he must have been working with a cooperative Legislature because only four days after his March 4, 1929, inauguration, he wired the architect: "Bill to raise revenue for building third unit State Capitol approved yesterday. Stop. Suggest you get plans completed necessary to commence work at earliest possible date." Conley forgot one important detail and the following day sent another telegram: "Overlooked yesterday ... the act authorizing third unit State Capitol limits the cost thereof to five million dollars."[16] Gilbert replied that the plans shown the Commission on January 5 "could be 'completed for occupancy' within the proposed appropriation ... ; it would, however, require careful management and close economy and this cost would not include furniture, mural decorations, elaborate interior finish or the terraces and development of the grounds, but it would provide a handsome, useful building ready for occupancy." Gilbert's warning that the appropriation would not be sufficient to pay for furniture should have raised a red flag to Gore, because the elegant building that was on the drawing boards could hardly be occupied without this essential component. Gilbert added: "If the bids for construction when received exceed that amount, modifications to reduce the cost can be made ... I will use my very best endeavors to comply with the requirements in this respect, and I am proceeding accordingly."

The Legislature was serious about the $5 million limit. An amendment to the appropriation bill urging "stiff jail terms" for the Commission "if it should disregard the limitation" was defeated, but the bill that passed made "the appropriation ... null and void if more than five millions are spent in completing the capitol."[17]

"All of the major problems of design and most of the minor details relating to the Capitol were settled" before Gilbert left on a ten-week trip to Europe in late June, but the final plans and specifications were still unfinished in August, when the Sunday *Charleston Gazette* published the headline "GOVERNOR UPSET OVER LAZINESS OF CASS GILBERT."[18] A drawing showing a man in overalls having a tantrum and shouting "GIMME THE PLANS. GIMME THE PLANS!" is captioned "Governor Conley is said to be terribly upset over the delay in plans, as he is anxious to finish the building during his administration" (see fig. 54). The column to the right mentions the governor's frustration at having discovered "the capitol plans are unfinished and ... the architect ... is off having a good time at his summer villa in Europe as if he had nothing else to do." A second drawing, labeled "Cass Gilbert At His Villa In Europe Being Interviewed By Our Correspondent" shows the architect lolling in a hammock and telling the reporter he "didn't think they were ever going to finish the building." "When told ... how much the Gov. was annoyed, Mr. Gilbert shed tears, said he was awful sorry, and that he would sail for New York and finish drawing up the plans." The next day, the *Charleston Gazette* followed up with a letter to Governor Conley from "George": "Dear Bill. You had better keep after Cass Gilbert. If you leave him alone he's liable to fool around until the democrats get in."

On September 13, after Gilbert's return, he wrote Virgil Highland, editor of the *Clarksburg Telegram* and a former member of the Commission, to thank him for an editorial written in response to a critical article published in the *Wheeling Intelligencer*. Gilbert praised Highland for correctly noting that "the two units of the Capitol so far erected have been finished with exemplary promptness and at a cost well within the estimated cost and appropriation."[19] Responding to the remarks made about his European trip, Gilbert emphasized that from the beginning he had informed the commissioners of his need for breaks from "working as hard as I do" and that, although one of the commissioners had pointed out that "West Virginia is a good place for a vacation," he needed to go to Europe to study "ancient architecture." He pointed out that "college presidents and professors, teachers and scientists, and most of the large business men" count on taking such breaks, otherwise "we cannot physically or mentally survive under the modern intensive pressure and very large demands that are made upon us." While in Europe, Gilbert had studied French domes "with a special view to solving certain details in the design of the dome for the West Virginia Capitol." He reassured the editor that "the talk of my having a 'villa' in Europe is quite silly. I have no 'villa' or other residence there." He added that while "the drawings are nearing completion," the previous lack of progress should be blamed on the fact that "appropriations were not available and authority was not granted until Governor Conley had entered upon his term of office at which time he took it up with very gratifying promptness."

He stressed the scale of the job: "It is perhaps difficult for the non-professional to realize the immense amount of detail that must be coordinated and correlated in a modern building and it all has to be worked out even to the exact locations of piping, wiring, conduits, electric outlets and every other detail before a contract can be let, and even then it will be found that some modifications will be necessary as the work proceeds." In constructing an office building, "much of this can be standardized, and questions of proportion are rarely involved, but in a public building of the magnitude and importance of the State Capitol every detail of proportion as well as structure and usage has to be very carefully adjusted." Progress was slowed by the limited funds available: "The effort to keep within the appropriation ... adds very greatly to the difficulty of rapid development of the plans and specifications ... and, in the disturbed state of the labor market and the present high cost of materials, we are never certain how the bids will run when the drawings and specifications are sent out for contractors' proposals." He continued, "This adds to and does not lessen any of the architect's anxieties."

At this point, Gilbert began to vent his frustration at how slowly the West Virginia project was proceeding, noting that the commissioners had originally "expected to carry out the whole project involving what was estimated to be about nine and a half millions with the greatest possible promptitude. It thought that the whole thing could be done in about 2½ years ... [but] discussions in the State as to the location and appropriations caused long delays and ... the work has had to be carried on with long intermissions." The delays had been expensive for him: "The architect's overhead expenses on such an operation are very large and if the work can be carried through with great promptness it is in his interest to do so.... My expense in handling this work has been greatly increased by these delays and the longer the work lasts the more it costs me in salaries, rent, overhead, etc." It is "for this reason, if for no other, I am very anxious to progress the work." He concluded: "I am in no sense responsible for the delay, and I welcome Governor Conley's urgent demand for prompt action. I must however have sufficient time to execute his orders on this great work—not only promptly, but faithfully and promptly."

On September 13, the same day of his long letter to Highland, Gilbert wrote to Governor Conley and enclosed a copy of the letter to Highland. The architect reassured the governor that he was "pressing every part of it as fast as possible."[20] He enclosed a copy of a letter he had written four years earlier pointing out the special concessions made for West Virginia after the Commission had assured him "that the work would be progressed rapidly and completed in a relatively short time and that the overhead expenses would not be as large as where a work extends over a number of years."[21] He must have been frustrated that he was being criticized for delays that were both costly to him and not his responsibility.

By October 4, however, the end was in sight and Gilbert invited Conley and the commissioners to New York during the week of October 14, at which time he would "illustrate by practical examples ... the various materials and the type and character of the interior."[22] He added that when he was building the Minnesota Capitol, the "entire Commission made a similar trip from St. Paul to look over important public buildings in Boston, New York, Washington and other cities with great advantage to the work." On October 10, Conley wrote he was glad the plans were nearly complete, for "there has been considerable criticism regarding the delay." He and the commissioners declined Gilbert's invitation, however, and on October 14 Conley asked the architect to meet with them in Charleston on October 30.

Gilbert's deadline to complete the project was apparently October 14, 1929, the date found on a number of drawings. A combined section and interior elevation from this group offers evidence about the Capitol's design and construction that will surprise the casual visitor. As soaring as the interior dome may seem when viewed from below (see gallery 1, 3), what one sees when looking up is actually an arched ceiling suspended below the exterior dome, which is further elevated to create the dramatic profile that came to be so beloved by West Virginians. Such a drawing exposes but cannot fully explain the complex engineering needed to erect and stabilize this part of the Capitol; the Gunvald Aus Company is listed as engineering consultants on these plans. Their offices were

Fig. 55. Cass Gilbert (concept), "½ Section Thru & of Dome Looking South" and "½ Section Thru & of Dome and Portico Looking East," October 14, 1929. The Doric vestibule (see gallery 9) is to the lower right.

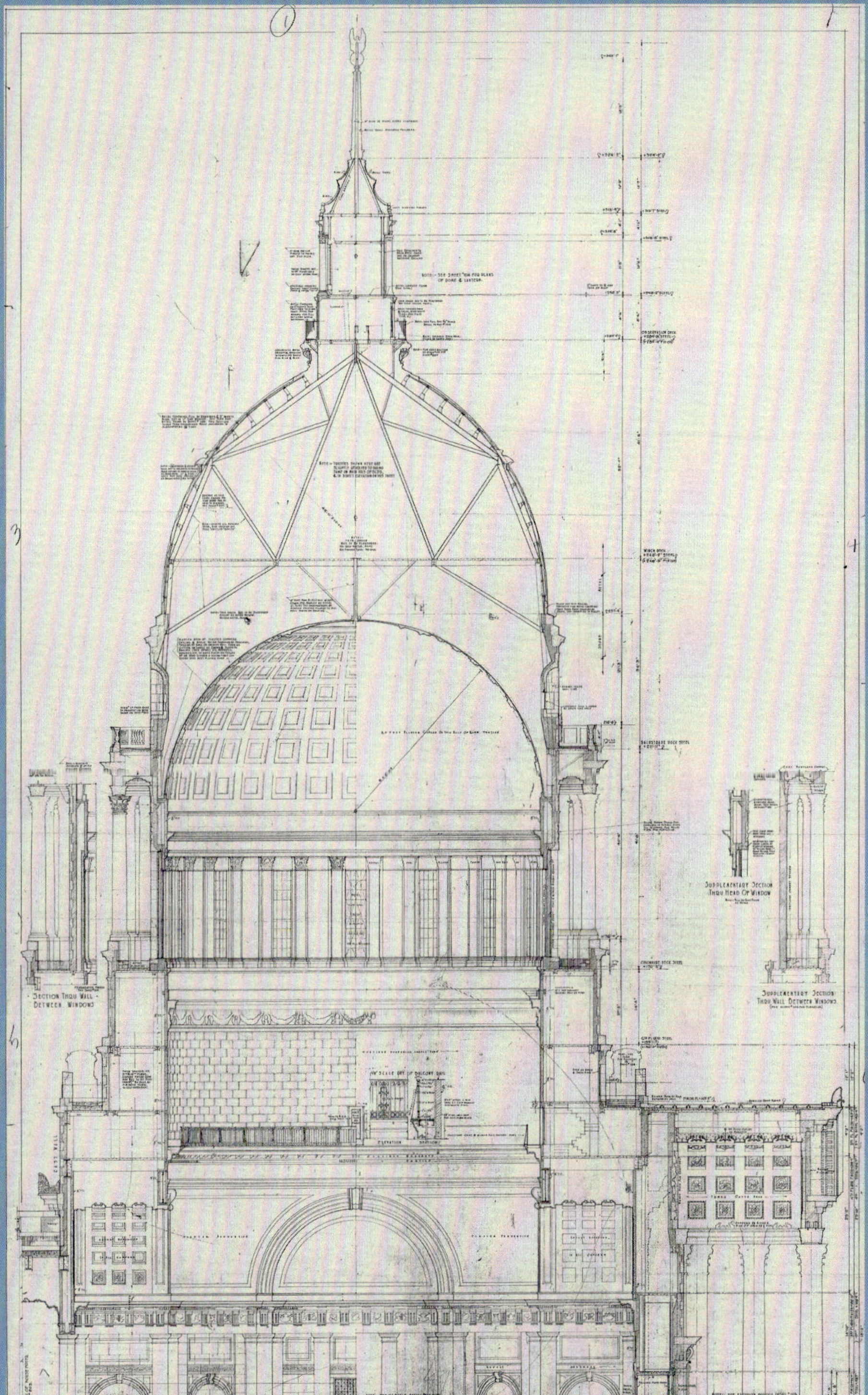

Section Thru Wall Between Windows
Supplementary Section Thru Head Of Window
Supplementary Section Thru Wall Between Windows
Indication of Materials
½ Section Thru ℄ Of Dome
Looking South
½ Section Thru ℄ Of Dome
℄ Portico Looking East
Scale = ¼" = 1'-0"

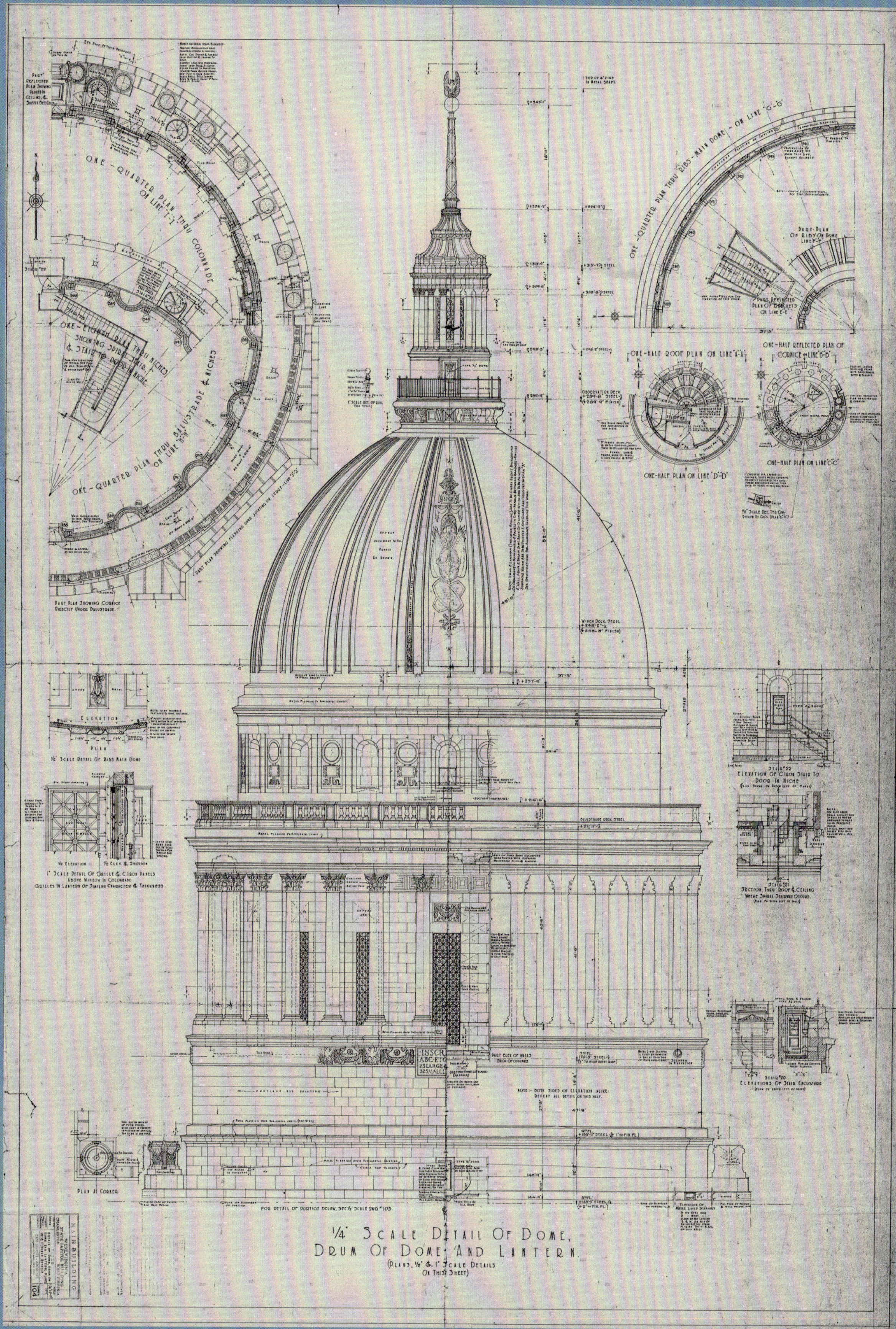

One-Quarter Plan Thru Colonnade On Line 1-1
One-Quarter Plan Thru Balustrade & Niches
One-Quarter Plan Thru Ribs - Main Dome - On Line 'O'-'O'
One-Half Roof Plan On Line 'A'-'A'
One-Half Reflected Plan Of Cornice - Line 'C'-'C'
One-Half Plan On Line 'D'-'D'
One-Half Plan On Line 'C'-'C'
Elevation
Plan At Corner
1/4" Scale Detail Of Dome,
Drum Of Dome And Lantern.
(Plans, 1/2" & 1" Scale Details On This Sheet)

at 244 Madison Avenue, in the same building as Gilbert's. Gunvald Aus assisted Gilbert with the engineering of the Woolworth Building and that of many other projects.[23]

An undated drawing that is almost certainly from this period is the first indication we have of a new plan for decorating the exterior of the dome. Until an appropriation and revenue stream had been established, Gilbert could not be sure a dome would be possible, and there had been little reason to determine a final design and materials. But it had also been clear from the beginning that if the West Virginia Capitol could have a dome, Gilbert wanted it to be unlike that of any other capitol. Drawings made in 1922 show a dome decorated with a wreath and feather/palm motif (see fig. 31); no other state capitol has this kind of decoration. Some are plain, while others have vertical ribs, a few combine such ribs with horizontal demarcations, a small number have elaborately decorated windows, and some are relatively plain but completely gilded. The most highly decorated state capitol dome before West Virginia's is, in fact, that of Gilbert's Minnesota Capitol, which has two rows of windows with decorative awnings (see fig. 13).

What materials Cass Gilbert hoped to use for the dome in the 1922 drawing and how he planned to demarcate the wreath and feather/palm motif are not documented. In 1929, with a guaranteed appropriation of $5 million, Gilbert was evidently determined to provide West Virginia with a distinctive dome despite budgetary limitations. His solution was to cover the dome's outer surface with lead, a relatively soft material that could be manipulated to form elaborate raised motifs. Highlighting these with gold leaf could provide West Virginia with the eye-catching dome that had been his goal since the beginning of the design process. Perhaps the flexibility of lead inspired him to change from the simple wreath and feather motif toward a more complex design, or perhaps his reading about the restoration of the dome of Les Invalides, the seventeenth-century military hospital in Paris (see fig. 73), encouraged him to search for a material in which similar effects might be possible.[24]

Before Gilbert could justify his design, he needed to be sure that the cost of the gold leaf to cover it would not be prohibitive. On October 24, he received a response from Mack, Jenney & Tyler, Decorators, estimating the cost at $30,000: "The metal work of the dome, lantern, etc., is to be carefully cleaned down with an acid solution, and two coats of lead, oil and turpentine with some varnish are to be applied. All parts shown in yellow on your drawing are to be sized and covered with xx 22½ karat gold leaf."[25]

On October 28, 1929, the Fuller Company, which had constructed the West Wing, wrote Gilbert saying they understood plans for the West Virginia Capitol would be presented "next week" and inquiring when they would be open for bidding. The timing was ironic, for October 28 was Black Monday, which ushered in the Great Depression.

Gilbert wired Conley to announce that he would arrive on the morning of October 29 and needed an hour with him to "explain the drawings, bid forms, and

Fig. 56. Cass Gilbert (concept), "¼ Scale Detail of Dome, Drum of Dome and Lantern," undated but almost certainly October 1929.

alternates proposed" before meeting with the Commission.[26] This strategy suggests that the state's chief executive controlled which designs would be presented the next day. Gilbert probably also wanted to clarify what he had eliminated in order to meet the $5 million budget. A memo dated October 29 listed the items not included in the plans and specifications: "1. Power and heating plant and connection from the main unit to the power house . . . ; 2. Lighting fixtures; 3. Furniture, including special furniture, typical furniture, file cases and incidental shelving; 4. Special mural decorations, such as allegorical and historical pictures. Note—Suitable space will be left, but no decoration is included thereon; 5. General mural decoration, being the ornamental painting in main corridors, rotunda, and special rooms; 6. Sculpture and war memorials; 7. Masonry terraces surrounding the building; 8. Landscape treatment of the grounds and planting; 9. Roadways, sidewalks, curbing; and 10. Special lighting of the grounds and exterior of the building."[27] Now, in addition to no furniture, the Main Building was going to lack lighting fixtures as well. There would no landscaping, no sidewalk, and no curbs. Whether the governor and commissioners had expected that the "power and heating plant" would be included in the $5 million project is uncertain.

It is not clear which plans were shown at the October 30 meeting, but approval was delayed because the governor and commissioners wanted "local experts" to review the design and specifications; perhaps they hoped to preempt what Gilbert later described as "possible controversy" by asking for the input of legislators and local architects.

At this point, the *Charleston Gazette* published a cartoon "quoting" Cass Gilbert: "The story about the plans being delayed because I was loafing at my villa in France is all a mistake. I was studying French domes to get inspiration before finishing this one."[28] A humorous drawing shows the commissioners scrutinizing Gilbert's plans (see fig. 57).

When Gilbert next came to Charleston, on December 11, it was for a Commission meeting dedicated to "reaching final agreement and approval." Once again, however, approval was delayed. Members of the Commission apparently made suggestions about "practical matters," one of which must have been the location or organization of the Governor's suite, for a letter of December 20 referred to the "rearrangement" of that area.

At last, on January 13, 1930, Rockart carried the final plans to Charleston. In a letter written that day, Gilbert reassured Conley: "Some of the suggestions . . . made by the local experts . . . called into consultation had already been adopted in our own checking, and some of them we have adopted as there was no reasonable objection to them and it would save time and possible controversy to do so."[29] Gilbert considered the design process complete and told the governor: "You can advertise for bids immediately."

Although Gilbert lamented to Conley, "The appropriation of $5,000,000.00 was made by the legislature without consulting me," he understood it was his job to fulfill their requirements. He had prepared "alternative proposals so that if

Fig. 57. Cartoon from the *Charleston Gazette*, November 3, 1929.

[bids] should run too high we can adopt the alternatives and still get a very good building." He clarified, apparently in reference to suggestions made by the "local experts," that "the addition of a number of toilet rooms and of the heating plant and other items will of course tend to increase the cost and on that subject I am frankly anxious."[30] He added, "There are some things I would like to add such as interior decoration, marble work, etc., the stone balustrades and terraces around the buildings and other items, but the appropriation is not sufficient and they are not strictly necessary to make the building habitable."

A stamp dated January 15, 1930, on the back of some plans indicates the approval of the Capitol Building Commission "per Bonner Hill for estimating use only."[31] On January 16, Governor Conley's "Notice to Contractors" announced that sealed bids would be received on March 5, 1930: "If bidders wish individual sets of drawings and specifications for their own use in preparing their bid, they may obtain such individual sets upon application in writing to Cass Gilbert, Architect, upon payment of the actual cost of blueprinting same." Payment was required: "A certified check for $200.00 is to accompany request for individual sets, which check will be returned upon return of said drawings and specifications."[32] Firms bidding on general construction were required to attach a certified check for $40,000 "drawn on some solvent banking institution and made payable to the Capitol Building Commission"; US or West Virginia bonds were also acceptable. Bids in the categories identified as heating and ventilation, plumbing and gas fitting, electrical work, and elevators required checks or bonds for $4,000. The checks or bonds would be returned after contracts had been awarded. Imperial Danby White Vermont Marble was specified for "floor borders, base, pilaster, etc. in the corridors, vestibules, Rotunda, etc.," but bidders could propose alternative marbles for these areas.[33]

By February 1, Gilbert's office had sent out more than fifty sets of drawings for general construction and more than twenty for mechanical equipment.[34] Gilbert wrote Conley that the "very high-class contractors" on the list demonstrated "there is a lively interest in the project" and such competition would lead to lower bids. The Depression was having its effect.

The bids were indeed competitive. The fourteen bids for general construction ranged from $3,287,000—the low bid, from the George A. Fuller Company of New York, which won them the job—to the high bid of $3,980,000 from the Hill Company of Oak Hill, the only West Virginia firm to bid on general construction.[35] Meyers Brothers of Charleston, who bid both on heating and ventilating and on plumbing, was the only West Virginia firm to bid in these categories; for heating and ventilating, theirs was the highest of thirteen bids, for plumbing it was competitive but not the lowest.[36] The bids were examined on March 5 and 6, with Governor Conley and eight commissioners in attendance and John Rockart and Samuel McGuire as the architect's representatives.

Gilbert was happy with the bids and wired John Rockart on March 8: "Please tell Governor Conley I am much gratified by the very favorable bids which are much lower than expected." Gilbert explained: "I ascribe low bids to the careful preparation of drawings and specifications. Our careful consideration of the design with view to economy and the earnest effort to comply with the limit of cost fixed by the Legislature." The economy was also a factor: "Bidders anticipated a dull building market and close competition.... It is a good market for them to buy in and the state gets the benefit."[37] He added: "No objection to publication of the three first sentences of this telegram as an expression of my views if governor approves."

The state signed contracts with the Fuller Company and the other main providers on March 26, 1930; by May the Fuller Company provided a "List of subcontractors, materials, etc.... approved to date."[38] Once again, as for the West Wing, the shell was going to be provided by Wheeling Structural Steel Co. Other West Virginia subcontractors included Abbott Construction Co. of Wheeling for general excavation, Blue Ribbon Paint Co. of Wheeling for structural steel paint, West Virginia Rail Co. of Huntington for reinforcing bars, Basis Products Co. of Kanawha for "green bag" cement ("security" cement was to be provided by a firm in Hagerstown, Maryland, and "magnolia" cement by a firm from Birmingham, Alabama), as well as Standard Brick and Supply Co. of Charleston, Morgan Lumber Co. of Charleston, Dr. R. Isaac Stone Contractor of Charleston, and Kanawha Planing Mill Company of Charleston.

On April 8, 1930, Gilbert appointed Harry H. Woodhouse as superintendent of construction: "You are to devote your entire time during working hours to this building. Your duties will consist of the daily supervision of the work and inspection, making usual daily reports for every working day and the correspondence incidental to the work." Anticipating problems with Bonner Hill, his instructions to Woodhouse were explicit: "You are not authorized to make or permit any changes in the drawings or specifications without written orders of myself or my authorized representative, no matter by whom they may be given."[39] Despite the distraction of working with Hill, Woodhouse fulfilled these obligations, and his reports re-create the day-by-day progress of the construction of the Capitol's Main Building.

No. 21 Taken 8-30-30
West Virginia State Capitol
Main Building
Cass Gilbert, Architect
GEORGE A. FULLER COMPANY. - BUILDERS

CHAPTER SEVEN

# Completing the "Mountaineers' Monument"

The capitol building is the West Virginia mountaineers' monument to the modern government of a freedom-loving people.

Reporter Frank Lowe, *Charleston Gazette*, November 1931

Fig. 58. The Main Building under construction, August 30, 1930. Taken from the roof of the West Wing. The railroad sidings allowed movement of heavy materials; the crane visible to the left also moved along these rails. Note the piles of steel girders awaiting erection. More construction photos are available online at *http://www.wvculture.org/history/wvmemory/*.

THE DOMED STRUCTURE THAT WAS TO BECOME THE SYMBOLIC and visual focal point of the Capitol complex was first visualized in June 1922 (see fig. 33), but the need for office space and problems with financing delayed the beginning of its construction until March 1930. Even as excavation began on the Main Building, however, decisions remained. The Fuller Company, needing the work, submitted a bid that was lower than anticipated, leaving money for enhancements, just as Gilbert had hoped when he prepared the specifications. Although his proposal that the exterior stone be upgraded from "Select Variegated Indiana limestone" to "Select Indiana Buff limestone," at an additional cost of $125,000, was accepted by the commissioners on May 16, at the same meeting they deferred a decision on his recommendation that "Imperial Danby marble" be added to the legislative chambers and foyers.[1] They did not approve this upgrade until November 14, when they voted six to four to spend $287,016 on additional marble. The *Keyser Mineral News* published a report suggesting that Governor Conley voted against this increase and quoted the malevolent Bonner Hill: "The fee of Cass Gilbert . . . , who made the recommendation that [the marble] be installed, was $17,220," a figure based on the 6 percent fee the architect received on all construction costs. Gilbert was alerted that Hill's statement was being repeated locally and nationally when he received clippings from the *Charleston Mail* and *Baltimore Sun*. He immediately wrote to Governor Conley to deny the insinuation "that my recommendation was made in order to increase my fee."[2]

Hill continued to make difficulties. On April 25, he urged the governor to ask Gilbert for a "drawing or plan of the figures he intends to have carved on the pediments or gables of the North and South porticoes of the building," despite the fact that such information would not be needed for many months, if at all. Hill also urged the governor to require the architect to submit "all inscriptions and lettering except the name Cass Gilbert, Architect, either carved or painted, exterior or interior . . . for your approval."[3] Perhaps Hill feared that with a grand signature Gilbert might try to transfer the honor of the State Capitol from West Virginia to himself or Hill may have been trying, as usual, to raise suspicion about the architect's motives in general. When Conley questioned Gilbert, the architect replied that decisions about inscriptions would come later, but said, "If you have any particular inscriptions which you would like to have considered I would be glad to know them and see if they can be adjusted to the panels or other spaces on which they are to be placed." The architect agreed that political implications should be avoided: "It must be borne in mind that the inscriptions should consist of a statement which is beyond controversy."[4] As for the sculptures, Gilbert reported that the architect usually selected a sculptor and provided "free-hand sketches."

The foundations were complete by November 5, 1930, when the cornerstone ceremony was held with the architect in attendance. As construction continued, Gilbert was being honored nationally. In 1930, for example, a jury of architects charged with selecting the "Masterpieces" erected in America since 1900, included Gilbert's Woolworth Building and Detroit Public Library. In January 1931 at the

Fig. 59. The western arm of the Main Building under construction, November 15, 1930. In the foreground left we see the steel structure for the connecting corridor leading to the West Wing.

Fig. 60. The eastern arm of the Main Building under construction, November 15, 1930. In the foreground right we see the steel structure of the connecting corridor to the East Wing. Note the boxcars on the siding to the left.

Hotel Astor in New York, the Society of Arts and Sciences awarded Gilbert a gold medal. In his acceptance speech, reported nationally in the *New York Times*, Gilbert summarized: "Architecture records with unerring accuracy the history and character of each period of civilization or each lapse into barbarism." He continued: "My plea is for beauty and sincerity, for the solution of our own problems in the spirit of our own age illuminated by the light of the past. To carry on, to shape new thoughts, new hopes and new desires in new forms of beauty as we can, but to disregard nothing of the past that may guide us in doing so."[5] The news of these awards and Gilbert's stirring words about "new forms of beauty" must have justified the pride West Virginians were feeling as they watched their grand Capitol rise in Charleston.

Construction on the Main Building proceeded quickly given its massive scale and the complex engineering required to span the open rotunda and raise the interior and exterior domes. By August 30 (see fig. 58), the steel structure of the section in the distance was already finished and the stone curtain wall was being attached, while none of the steel structure for the arm near the photographer had been erected. While such a process would at first seem counterintuitive—why not complete the steel structure before moving on to the curtain wall?—the procedure being used here allowed the Fuller Company to hire fewer workers. Steel workers were moved to another section once the previous one had been completed. In addition, fewer pieces of heavy machinery were required; the cranes that transported heavy materials, for example, could be moved to another area when their work on the previous one was finished. The continuation of the procedure is evident in two photographs taken on November 15 from different viewpoints (see figs. 59, 60). While the steel structure for one arm was still being erected, the stone sheathing of the other was virtually finished and even the cornice and balustrade were in place. Between these two arms the structure of the drum awaited the superstructure needed for the dome.

The dome was the most complex aspect of the construction; its status on February 16 and May 15, 1931, is shown in figures 61 and 62; for the completed Capitol from the same viewpoint, see figure 63. By February, the steel structure for the drum and the lower part of the exterior dome had been erected; by May, the freestanding columns ringing the drum were in place but their tops were covered with scaffolding, perhaps because their Corinthian capitals were being carved in place. In February, the columns for the North Portico were only partially erected; by May, they were finished and the pediment they supported was in place.

More decisions were required as construction proceeded. Gilbert considered incorporating representations of indigenous West Virginia animals into the cornices of the legislative areas and asked the firm of John Donnelly, Architectural Sculptors to research which were suitable.[6] On January 26, 1931, they replied that for "pioneer times" the beaver, bison, elk, panther, porcupine, and timber wolf would be appropriate. For the "present time," the firm listed the black bear, fox, hare, horned owl, opossum, rabbit, raccoon, ruffed grouse, squirrel, turkey,

Fig. 61, 62. The Main Building under construction, February 16 and May 15, 1931. The residents of the houses and apartment buildings along Washington Avenue, seen at the bottom of both photos, had ringside seats for the duration of the construction.

Fig. 62

Fig. 63. The West Virginia Capitol, as seen in an undated postcard. The limitations of the printing process meant that the details of the dome are not visible. Note the street next to the East Wing, which provided parking.

turkey vulture, and Virginia deer. Gilbert noted on this response that on January 27 he told John Donnelly Jr. to use the beaver and bison. What happened next is uncertain, but by March, five "different features"—none with a beaver or a bison—had been designed for the friezes of the legislative floor. The motifs chosen were traditional ones, based on Classical precedents (see fig. 81). On March 13, the New York Drafting Annex of the Vermont Marble Company sent drawings of these for Gilbert's approval; once accepted, the designs were carved in marble for the rotunda and replicated in plaster for the House and Senate foyers (see galleries 3–5).[7]

In May, even though the building was far from finished (see fig. 62), the Board of Public Works ordered office furniture. An unidentified newspaper clipping reports that for economic reasons "West Virginia will abandon, for the time being, at least, Cass Gilbert's dream of furnishing the final unit of the state capitol in a manner in keeping with the magnificence of the structure." The article states that the "hand carved furnishings, with elaborate scrolls, and large desks and chairs" designed by Gilbert were not going to be ordered. In this case the public was misled, for the furniture Gilbert designed for the most important state offices was not eliminated from the order. The contractor for furniture was George P. Reinhard and Company of New York, "Manufacturers, Importers and Dealers in Period Furniture."[8] Desks for the Senate and House of Delegates, to be made of West Virginia black walnut, were subcontracted to the Bentley-Gerwig Company of Parkersburg.

In July, an order was placed with the General Bronze Corporation for the four "candelabras" for the entrances under the porticoes. In August, the New York Art Iron Works Corporation estimated that four sets of fireplace equipment designed by Gilbert for the governor's reception room, his office, and the Senate and House reception rooms, each with andirons, fire sets, and screens, would cost $735; one set is illustrated in figure 85. By September 15, after the columns in the governor's reception room were in place, the size of rugs could be determined; a special twenty-by-eighteen-foot rug was already being woven for his office. Lighting fixtures and bulbs were being delivered by the Black & Boyd Manufacturing Co. By early November, the Reinhard Company was ready to deliver furnishings valued at $47,500.[9]

As construction continued during the second half of 1931, Bonner Hill complained in a number of letters to Gilbert—with copies to Governor Conley—about the work of the Fuller Company and their subcontractors.[10] The painters were "not using drop cloths as you specify," for example, and "there is a very poor fit around the door casings and the four inch concrete base mold." Hill suggested he was not the only one who was dissatisfied, noting that every day "some person complains to me about the mixed colored stone scattered throughout the exterior of the building." Two doors "have very bad knots and knot-holes and should be rejected." Radiators "have been smeared with paint," and "the painter putting on the gold leaf is not properly cleaning the window grilles in the dome before painting them."

For the governor and architect to receive these and similar complaints almost daily must have been irritating. Hill complained that in "a number of cases the state, in my opinion, is not getting the kind of work and material for which it is paying," suggesting his criticisms were motivated by a desire to save the state money. He noticed, for example, that "the stone carving on the dome of the Main Capitol Building is being finished very rough instead of smooth like that nearer the ground on this building," and when he asked, he found that "when your Mr. Rockart and Mr. Donnally [*sic*], the contractor for this work, were here, Mr. Donnally suggested to Mr. Rockart that this work be finished with a rough surface in order to bring out the desired shadow or effect and Mr. Rockart agreed to the suggestion." Hill wanted the state to be reimbursed: "This rough finish is much easier made than the smooth finish and I do not understand why the State should not get a credit for the difference in time and cost it would take to do this work. Will you please write to some of us, stating the amount of credit the State is to receive for this change in the work?"

On September 8, Hill wrote: "With the rush in which this building is being completed I cannot see how you can expect a first class piece of work and it is my opinion that it does not take an expert to see that the little things which it takes to make a good building are not being properly done here," adding, "Please do not completely ignore this letter but send some person here who knows ornamental buildings and will look this one over from basement to top of dome before it is too late." Cass Gilbert noted on many of Hill's letters that he had replied directly to the governor. On one, he scrawled in frustration: "Hill does not know what he is talking about."

As the Capitol neared completion, Gilbert was contemplating how the grounds should be landscaped. In September, he produced a plan that formalized the natural hill to the north with diagonal ramps leading up to an overlook with what would have been a spectacular view of his Capitol against the backdrop of the Kanawha River and the hills beyond. Nearer the Capitol were cascading fountains and an oval pool. The plan denies the urban setting of the Capitol with a bridge to the upper park hiding the railroad tracks and rows of trees masking parking lots.[11] This visionary proposal had no chance of acceptance, not only because of the economic situation, but also because it would have required the acquisition of a great deal of expensive property, including the houses and apartment buildings seen in the foreground of figure 61. Gilbert surely knew that it was impractical, but perhaps he hoped that at least some aspects might be accepted; finally, in 1946, his circular fountain and courtyard walkways were finished. Completing his design in this area eliminated the awkward, off-center parking lot near the East Building, which had been in place since the 1920s (see fig. 63).

By early November 1931, the interior was nearly finished. The first documented public tour, which seems to have been limited to a group of teachers attending a Charleston conference, included reporter Frank Lowe of the *Charleston Gazette,* who documented the visit in a long article on November 8 with five headlines;

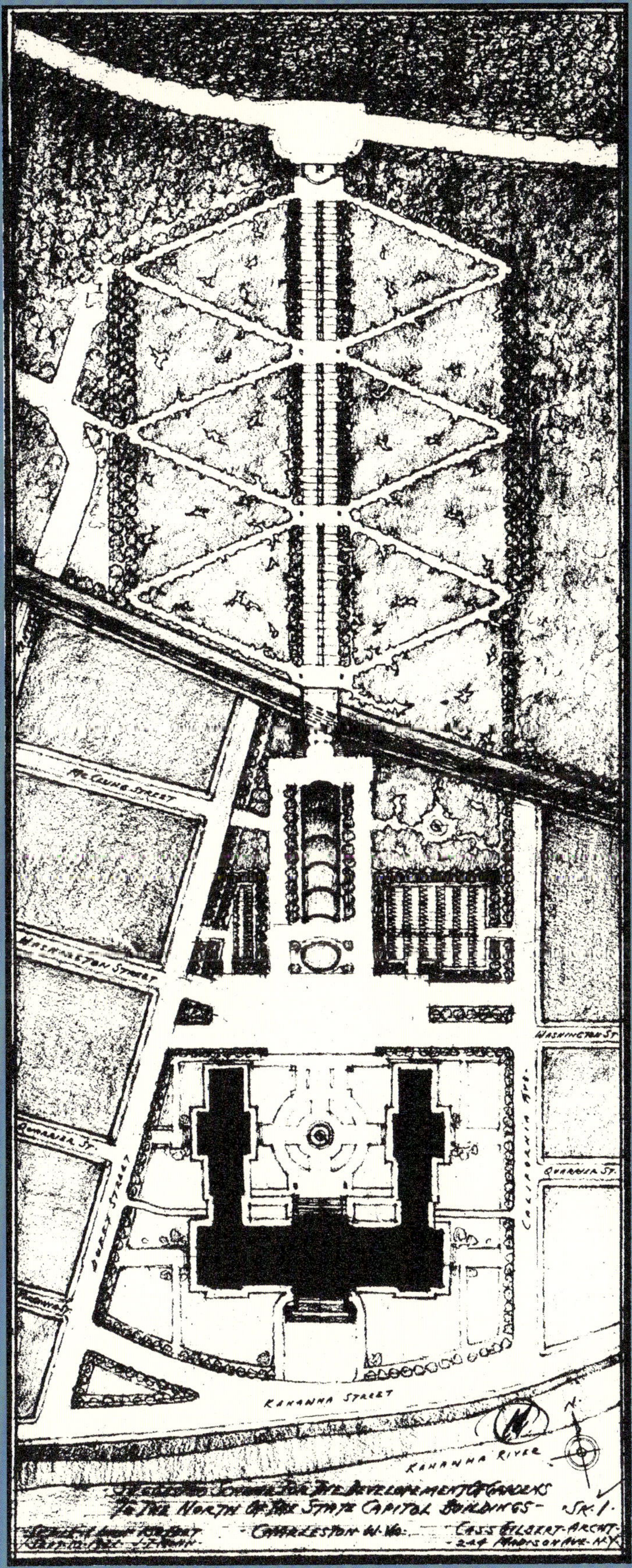


Fig. 64. Cass Gilbert (concept), Landscaping proposal for the West Virginia State Capitol, September 10, 1931.

Fig. 65. The interior dome, c. 1950.
Gilbert Family Collection.

"State's Capitol, Greek in Style, Combines Building and Setting" filled the top of the page.[12] Smaller headlines on the left announced: "Rises From Panorama of Hills as Monument of Liberty-Loving People to Government and Art; Old Idea of Perfection as Employed by Greeks in Architecture Evident; Accuracy and Delicacy Mark New Structure which Displays Feeling of Luxury and Dramatic Climax." Headlines to the right read: "Most Striking Is Quiet Dignity of Edifice; Conventional, but Suggests Freedom, Imagination; Success Due to 'Owner's' Vision and Money, Practical and Artistic Ability of Architect, Execution of Idea by Builder after Creation; Trip through Building Reveals Marvels." Above a photo of the Capitol, its dome still unfinished, was the caption: "West Virginia's Costly New Capitol."

The unifying theme of Lowe's article was the Greek character of the Capitol, which he based on both the architecture and the relationship he perceived between the ancient Greeks and his fellow West Virginians: "The capitol building is the West Virginia mountaineers' monument to the modern government of a freedom-loving people just as the Parthenon was the Greek mountaineers' temple to Athena, goddess of wisdom and counsel." He continued: "As the West Virginia mountaineer's independent spirit is akin to that of the ancient nature-worshipping Greeks, so is the spirit of old Greece suggested by the feeling of luxury and dramatic climax in the architectural form of the state's new capitol." Lowe related the Capitol's beauty to Greek ideals: "The old idea of perfection, of art and beauty which the Greeks employed in their marvelous architecture, is evident in the new capitol.... Accuracy and delicacy mark the new structure just as these two qualities influenced the ancient Grecian architectural masterpieces which are still beautiful in their ruins." Cass Gilbert's creativity in designing this new monument "suggests the imagination of the Greek artist who loved beauty for its own sake."

"An architectural success," Lowe argued, required the cooperation of architect, builder, and an owner with "vision and money." After identifying the "owner" as the Capitol Building Commission, who "wisely allowed the architect virtual free reign in carrying out his design," Lowe broadened his definition of ownership: "The utmost credit must be given to the West Virginia people who ... by the sweat of their brow [furnished] the necessary millions of dollars required for the realization of their vision." Lowe praised the Fuller Company for their sympathetic execution of the architect's design. While he generally avoided specifics about cost, the bronze doors aroused his "mercenary streak." When he asked the price, he learned they cost $50,000.

Lowe returned to his emphasis on the importance of West Virginians when he wrote about entering the rotunda: "It is but natural that the people should demand the opportunity to enjoy their state capitol themselves and take at least a small part in its achievement so this public space, the rotunda, is dedicated to the people." He added: "Virtually it is a show-place for the public, and its arches, columns, balustrades and glistening white marble make it an impressive one." (see fig. 65 and gallery 3, 4). Lowe cited the simplicity of style: "There is neither sham or flamboyance in structure or embellishment of the building, or as our guide, H. G. Plimpton, general superintendent of construction [for the Fuller Company], aptly put it: 'there is nothing ginger-bread or Christmas tinsel about this building!'"

Plimpton took his visitors to the top of the dome, "an unusual honor since but few are allowed to mount the innumerable steps to go inside the great dome." When they paused at the base of the drum, Lowe praised the view and made another comparison with Greece and the Greeks: "The panorama which unfolds before our eye is a scene that even Greece with its clear atmosphere, lovely mountains and blue sea cannot surpass." He suggests that "the vari-colored hills of West Virginia silhouetted against a sunny sky on a late fall afternoon; . . . the twining, lazy river, flowing peacefully like a thin silver ribbon below us; . . . the valley spreading snugly at the foot of the low hills" inspired the architect "to favor the Greek plan of enhancing the beauty of their temples by placing them in natural settings."

When Lowe admired the carved decoration, Plimpton described the process by which drawings were transformed into three-dimensional versions, most likely in plaster, to be followed by the stone carvers. After the sculptures were completed, he told Lowe that the models were, in Plimpton's words, "turned over to Miss Agnes Huston and her high school art class for use in modeling."[13] Lowe raised the issue of cost again when they had climbed to the base of the lantern: "behold!—we see the gold on the dome at close range—$23,000 worth!" Plimpton corrected him, pointing out that the "process of applying it" had been more expensive than the material.[14]

Governor Conley sent Gilbert a copy of Lowe's article, which the architect praised as "obviously intended to be a very fair minded and reasonable description" that would "create a just and favorable impression." He clarified, however, that Lowe was "mistaken in describing the building as 'Greek' in style. I think what he intended to say is that it is Classic in style. It is, in fact, what might be more correctly termed Renaissance, and the architectural forms are Roman rather than Greek."[15]

Gilbert also took issue with a published comment from Hill, who had told Lowe that "the main unit of the $10,000,000 capitol would be ready for occupancy January 1, 1932." Hill's suggestion that the unit "ready for occupancy" cost $10 million troubled Gilbert, who clarified: "The gross cost of these three buildings, as shown by our books including architect's and engineer's fees, furniture, carpets, curtains, draperies, interior decoration, lighting fixtures, amounts to $7,243,596.00. In other words, over $2,750,000.00 less than the $10,000,000.00 stated in this article for apparently the single central unit."[16] Mindful of how often he had written to West Virginia's governors about Hill's allegations, Gilbert sarcastically added: "I am sure the reporter must have misunderstood Mr. Hill, for he would not have intentionally given a wrong impression."

A November 30 editorial in the *Charleston Daily Mail* provided a correction to Lowe's article by noting the architect's figure of $7,243,596 and emphasizing that "there does not seem to be any basis whatever for the statement which seems to be current in some quarters that the total cost of the capitol will be $10,000,000. Not a breath of scandal has attached to [this] building." The editorial continued: "The entire project has been well, efficiently and economically managed. The people have got the worth of their money.... West Virginians have in their capitol one of the finest buildings in the country and the finest in the state," adding, "No state, however wealthy, has a finer one and few so fine, when one considers the beauty of the classic style, so admirably suited for public buildings, where are combined solidity with grace and where proportion counts more than ornament."

Another appreciation of the still-incomplete building was penned by Frederick J. Wiley of Wiley & Paris, the New York firm of decorative painters subcontracted by the Fuller Company. Wiley, planning to give this to a "newspaper man," sent a copy to Gilbert first, saying he hoped the architect would approve; in a penciled addition to Wiley's letter Gilbert noted that he did.[17] Wiley wrote that Gilbert had composed "a symphony in stone, elaborating his architectural theme much as a musician develops his musical score." He continued the metaphor: "The use of the Doric order for the columns in the Entrance Hall [see gallery 9] strikes the dominant C Major Note of the entire decorative scheme of the interior." He compared musical harmony to the optimistic quality of the Capitol, stating that the building represented "The C Major of this life—mostly free from sharps and flats." Such prose seems stilted today, but it bears comparison to the eclectic and philosophical manner in which Gilbert approached architectural design.

On December 6, Gilbert toured the completed Capitol. It was Sunday, and he clarified to a reporter that he would not inspect the building until Monday: "My visit to the capitol Sunday was not 'business' but in the nature of 'interest.' I believe in Sunday observance and therefore would not make a business visit on that day. However, I was much pleased with what I saw Sunday, and today I will make an inspection of the building. That will be the business part of my visit here."[18] In reporting Gilbert's conclusion that the new Capitol was "very fine," the *Charleston Daily Mail* noted that his assessment "was not expressed boastfully, for he attributed the success of the project to the three governors who have held office since he first took the job nearly eleven years ago and to the members of the capitol commission." Gilbert complimented Governors Morgan, Gore, and Conley, saying they had all assisted him "in every way possible," and "as a result of their cooperation West Virginia has a very fine capitol." Fearing the usual criticism about cost, Gilbert quoted the popular epigram: "The recollection of 'quality' lasts long after the price is forgotten."

There was one aspect of the cost that Gilbert could not forget, however, and he told the *Charleston Daily Mail* reporter that the West Virginia Capitol had been a "costly job" for him. In accepting the commission more than ten years earlier, he had been assured "the building was desired as soon as possible." He had replied that it could be completed in two-and-a-half to three years, but while "we had to wait for authorizations and for appropriations," he had had to "pay overhead costs and maintain his capitol building staff." These remarks, the reporter reassured readers, "were not made in complaint. On the contrary, Mr. Gilbert appears to be quite pleased with the entire project and expressed keen appreciation for the interests of the people of the state."

While Gilbert was in Charleston, he received a telegram from a representative of the Fuller Company: "Would appreciate your taking up with Governor and Commission while in Charleston an early acceptance of building. Conditions warrant this." Fuller could not pay their subcontractors without this acceptance: "This is tying up at this time considerable money for these subcontractors who I know will appreciate the checks before Christmas."[19]

In January 1932, a staff member in Gilbert's office summarized the firm's "profit" on the West Virginia project. While Gilbert had been paid $410,514.88, deducted from this were "Costs to date" of $304,554.83—apparently the expenses Gilbert had incurred for salaries, office rent, and utilities in connection with the project—and $13,245 for "PaJR," probably a reference to salary for John Rockart. The resulting "profit" was $92,715.05. When divided by eleven years, this came out to $8,427.88 per year. When Gilbert was given these calculations, he noted "Hold this for later action."[20]

The commissioners inspected the Main Building on January 26, 1932, and were photographed standing in front of it with Gilbert, Rockart, and Hill. Although the commissioners agreed to pay the Fuller Company the balance due, they held back $100,000 and refused to accept the building until Commissioners Payne and Keatley could guarantee certain mechanical and structural problems were resolved. On February 10, in a vote of four to three, the building was conditionally accepted "in so far as concerns the contract of the George A. Fuller Company," and the Commission declared that "said Main Capitol Building be immediately opened for occupancy by the various state officials."

A letter from Hill to Conley may represent the former's final attempt to create problems for the architect and contractor.[21] He again argued for discounts on the final price because of changes from specifications. He cited the use of bolts rather than rivets on some steel beams, lumber that was not tongued and grooved in making forms, and stone that did not seem to be of the specified quality. For the last problem, he suggested $20,000 be deducted from the Fuller Company's payment. Gilbert's response listed which of Hill's criticisms should be ignored, what corrections had been or were being made, and why the state was not entitled to credit for specific problems.[22] At some points the architect seemed to be restraining his temper. While the Fuller Company had not used tongued and grooved lumber, for instance, Gilbert emphasized that "the State is, in fact, more concerned with results than with methods of procedure, and with substantial performance than with technicalities." When Hill complained, "Pointing of tile roof or floor around dome came out in places and I fear it will not stay there in freezing weather," Gilbert replied: "Mr. Hill is obviously not informed concerning expansion and contraction in buildings and in roofs." To Hill's comment that "Magnet tests show the large lighting figures in house and senate are not all made of bronze as specified," Gilbert noted that chromium-plated steel had been substituted to provide "more substantial and rigid construction." Gilbert agreed that heating and ventilation were still substandard,

Fig. 66. Cass Gilbert with the Capitol Building Commission, January 26, 1932. Left to right: M. Z. White, Gohen C. Arnold, C. W. Dillon, Charles K. Payne, J. William Cummins, George A. Laughlin, Daisy M. Peadro, W. G. Distler, Cass Gilbert, W. Black, Governor William G. Conley, Commission Secretary Bonner H. Hill, Edwin M. Keatley, and J. R. Rockart (Gilbert's assistant). The body language seems revealing: Bonner Hill stands behind and close to Governor Conley, while John Rockart, also in the back row, seems to have stepped away from Hill.

No. 184 Taken 1-26-32
West Virginia State Capitol
Main Building
Cass Gilbert, Architect
GEORGE A. FULLER COMPANY · BUILDERS

pointing out that the Dunham System had been "adopted contrary to our recommendations. See my letter to you of August 13, 1930. I am endeavoring to impress upon the Dunham Company their responsibility in connection therewith." Gilbert's ability to reference a letter written more than a year earlier illustrates his meticulous business practices and the importance of his recordkeeping.

On June 17, three days before the dedication and less than a week before Gilbert's departure for Europe, he sent the governor recommendations for completing the Capitol that included sculpture, mural painting, terraces, and landscape work. Enclosed were illustrations of the "Development of the State Capitol Grounds."[23] The architect emphasized that a Capitol "should evidence the substantial character and civilization of the State, because (if for no other reason) it inspires confidence in the State on the part of both its own people and all who visit it." He confirmed that "lavish expenditure and extravagance" were not appropriate because "the expenditure of a people's money is a public trust, and unwise extravagance is just the reverse of the impression that should be conveyed." He reassured Conley that "the State of West Virginia has followed a wise middle course in erecting a group of monumental buildings of adequate character but without extravagance or lavish expenditure." He urged completion of the stone carving on the East and West Wings that had been postponed, and also of the sculpture in the pediments of the Main Building.

In support of "mural decoration of idealistic and historic character," he pointed out that the narratives and allegories in the Minnesota Capitol had led to "the growth of State pride. The building is visited annually by many thousands, school children and citizens, who learn there of the history of the State and of the ideals on which it is founded," adding, "There has never been a criticism of it or a complaint of extravagance." If the architect could select the artists, this would avoid the "well known fact that when such projects are under consideration the public authorities in charge are assailed by adroit and obscure political intrigue and beguiling personal solicitation and pressure to place the work in the hands of attractive but incompetent people."

He urged that additional property be acquired for practical and aesthetic reasons: "If this property is acquired by the State, it might not be developed at the present time but it would prevent the selfish private interests from utilizing the property for their own advantage and from defacing the locality around the Capitol with high buildings, apartment houses, garages, or other structures for objectionable usage." If the state did not acquire this property, it should pass an ordinance preventing high buildings near the Capitol.

The terraces surrounding the buildings should be added, "for without them the group of buildings would be like a picture without a frame"; to judge the truth of this comment, compare the West Virginia Capitol with Gilbert's other designs in which terraces were completed (see figs. 13, 20). The architect should be consulted on matters of "paths, roadways, lighting, planting, etc." in order to avoid the "general lack of order and dignity" that can result without that guidance. He estimated the cost of "terraces, bushes, vines, etc.; carving of the exterior stone work of the east and west wings; construction of the river wall; sculpture in the pediments [of the] Main Building; and the mural decorations in the interior of the Main Building" at $1,350,000, "of which a considerable portion would be for the river wall." Gilbert urged the state "to undertake this work at an early date as market conditions at the present time are very favorable, costs being at a minimum. Letting for contracts for this work would help in relieving the unemployment situation."

The fact that the Capitol lacked certain details did not affect the jubilant public celebrations accompanying its dedication on June 20, 1932. "Come and See Your Capitol Dedication," headlined a special supplement to the June 19 *Charleston Daily Mail* that addressed construction, appearance, and preservation.[24] "Your Capitol," not "The Capitol": one word clarified that this structure was intended for everyone. The article headed "West Virginia Proud of Imposing Capitol: Built of Limestone and Decorated Inside with Marble, It Stands as Mark of Progress" concluded that the new Capitol "is unsurpassed by any state building in the country, for its architectural grandeur and quality of materials." The many postcards of the completed structure that circulated in the 1930s indicate the pride West Virginians felt for their new Capitol. Supplement articles reviewed the history of the project ("Seven Years Used to Build the Capitol," and "City Map Changed by Capitol Plans") and put the building's design into a broader architectural context ("National Capitol and Most State Capitols Have Big Domes," illustrated with a photograph of the United States Capitol).

The supplement reviewed the state's history: "West Virginians Can Be Proud of History Made by Pioneers"; "Early Settlers Showed Fortitude in Overcoming Obstacles of Woods and in Fighting the Indians; Came From Sturdy Stock"; "When West Virginia Became Part of the Union of States"; and "Legislative, Political History of West Virginia Since 1863." Articles referred to the state's earlier capitals and capitols: "Wheeling Twice Was the Capital of the State" and "Many Records Lost With Temporary Capitol."

Advertising highlighted firms that had worked on the project and local, regional, and even national companies with a local presence, including Sears Roebuck, Montgomery Ward, and RCA Victor. The Kanawha Valley Bank and the Charleston National Bank were among local firms represented in full-page advertisements. The Kresge Stores' advertisement urged that "West Virginians, who take pride in their state, should, by all means, arrange to attend the dedication ceremonies.... Kresge stores throughout the state, but particularly those located in Charleston, are undeniably proud of West Virginia's new state building." The ad continued: This is "a capitol building that will stand for many years portraying the progressive spirit of a truly progressive state, a magnificent structure that will become increasingly more beautiful as the years roll by."[25] Ads for H. D. Baker Co. (a local furniture store), Standard Brick & Supply Co., and West Va. Sand & Gravel Co., among others, included a photograph of the Capitol, visually relating the firm to the building to be dedicated the next day.

Fig. 67. The West Virginia State Capitol, as seen in a postcard mailed from Smithers, WV, in 1938.

Fig. 68. Rotunda, The West Virginia State Capitol, as seen in an undated period postcard.

Fig. 69. "Aerial View Kanawha River and Charleston, W. Va.," as seen in a postcard mailed from Dunbar, WV, in 1945. This view demonstrates how the Capitol was nestled in the trees in a largely residential area of Charleston. "Linen" postcards such as this one were crudely printed and the colors were often exaggerated, as in the red roofs scattered throughout this landscape.

Cass Gilbert's portrait appeared next to a review of his accomplishments, titled "State Capitol Building Designed by Renowned Architect." He was quoted extensively in "Supervision for Capitol Needed to Preserve Its Beauty." Gilbert also wrote a brief description of the Capitol for the dedication program.

On June 20, when West Virginia Day and the Dedication of the Capitol were celebrated simultaneously, 15,000 spectators gathered for the festivities, which began with a parade. "America," played by the 201st Regiment band, opened the program. The first address was by Anna Jarvis, founder of Mother's Day and a West Virginia native, who had distinguished herself and her state by ensuring that a day honoring mothers was nationally recognized. In her presentation, titled "In the Name of West Virginia's Motherhood," she stated: "I would offer [the Capitol] as the true home of West Virginia—a building in which every mother and the son of every mother has an even right in its usefulness, its ownership and its duty—a building in which every citizen [is] equal."[26]

In his dedication address, Colonel Guy D. Goff, US Senator from 1925 to 1931, spoke glowingly of his state's "natural resources ... agriculture, horticulture, stock raising, timber and lumber" and her industries, including "china, pottery, and chemicals." He recognized the economic situation and pointed out that it was not limited to West Virginia: "We are passing through a period of depression, distrust and destruction, but we must not forget that it is world-wide."[27]

Governor Conley accepted the Capitol Building on behalf of the people of the State:

> We are met here today, on the seventieth birthday of West Virginia, to dedicate these magnificent buildings, representative of the hopes and aspirations of the people of this State.
>
> Look about you and behold the beauty of the setting and the buildings, the consummated dream of the architect, Cass Gilbert. Only a great architect could conceive such buildings; only great builders could carry out the plans and accomplish such undertakings; only master mechanics of the highest training and ability could perform the work we have here.
>
> The hope of the State and the Nation is in the people, and the public buildings, to a great extent, represent their ideals and character which you see symbolized here.[28]

Conley emphasized the state's historic role at the time of the Civil War: "West Virginia helped to hold the common heritage of the nation" and, because of West Virginians' contribution "to the maintenance and perpetuity of the Union, President Lincoln and the Congress ... gave another state to the Union and added another star to our flag." The governor related the new Capitol to those West Virginians gathered to celebrate its completion: "These buildings blend the beauty of the Ideal with the rugged strength symbolical of the sturdy pioneer stock.... These pillars and columns are emblematic of the characteristics of our people—honesty, integrity and industry—and are also indicative of the high ideals and hopes and ambitions of our citizens." The "simple dignity" of the building "speaks well for the sturdy and enduring qualities that have been handed down to us by an ancestry of which all of us may well be proud." Conley noted Cass Gilbert's "admonition to us all" in the inscription below the dome: "Let us burn deep into our souls today the inscription above, 'GET UNDERSTANDING.'" The official dedication ended after the band played "West Virginia Hills," but the festivities continued that evening with a public gathering in the governor's reception room offered "by the board of Public Works and the Capitol Building Commission."

In addition to the program, an extensive "Official Souvenir Program and Directory" published jointly by the West Virginia Departments of Health and Public Welfare, was also available for purchase.[29] Proceeds from its sale were "for the benefit of underprivileged children of West Virginia."[30] Its "Capitol History" was laudatory: "[The Capitol] is declared by nationally known architectural authorities to be one of the most beautiful public buildings in the United States" and "its pure classic lines and stately columns of limestone silhouette the building like a gigantic cameo against the rich green background of towering hills."

An article on "The Main Unit" enumerated the costs and ending with the proud statement: "The amount authorized by the Legislature to be expended in erecting the Main Capitol Unit was $5,000,000.00" and "the amount actually expended was ... $37,722.00 less than [that] amount." One of the advertisements in the brochure touted the West Virginia company that had supplied the Vitrolite, a modern opaque glass wall covering, used in the Capitol's restrooms.

Cass Gilbert did not attend the ceremony, but his absence was not a slight to the state. In January, months before the date had been set, Gilbert was invited to receive an honorary degree at Princeton University's June 21 commencement.[31] The June 20 date was only selected in March, after the West Virginia Commissioners had accepted the Capitol and given their permission for it to be occupied. Gilbert's office was represented on June 21 by his son and John Rockart.

The West Virginia Capitol was rededicated fifty years later, on June 20, 1982. As in 1932, the program opened with "America" and closed with "West Virginia Hills." Governor Jay Rockefeller praised the Capitol and its architect and there was a nineteen-gun salute. Blessings were offered by a Presbyterian minister (the invocation), a Baptist preacher (a prayer), and a rabbi (the benediction), and at 3 P.M. an enormous cake in the shape of the Capitol was cut and served.[32]

Although Gilbert was unable to attend in 1932, his engagement with West Virginia was not over. He continued to hope that some of the "unfinished" elements would be completed under his direction, and he also became concerned with negotiating the final payment he presumed he was due. The November 8 election of a Democrat, Herman Kump, as incoming governor probably alerted him to the need to contact Governor Conley about these unresolved issues. On November 25, Gilbert's office prepared a document updating the financial situation with new totals for travel expenses, superintendents' salaries, and steel inspections.[33] To these sums, Gilbert added others in pencil, including "interest on delayed overdue payments" and a per diem charge of $10,000 for "time occupied in traveling and personal attendance at Charleston of say $100 to $200 per day." The total was $117,748.66.

The next day Gilbert wrote to Conley, who was less than five months from the end of his term. Because the buildings of the "State Capitol Group ... have been occupied for some time and as the Legislature will presently assemble in the Main Building, I take this opportunity to express personal appreciation of the courteous attitude of the Governors, the Commissioners, and the representatives of the State with whom I have come in contact during the long period that has elapsed since I first met the Capitol Commission in April 1921."[34] Gilbert hoped "the State will find satisfaction in this group of buildings" despite the fact that landscaping, terraces, mural decorations, and sculpture remained incomplete. But the point of his letter was "to bring to your attention several matters to which I ask your consideration." He reviewed the history of the project, pointing out that it was originally estimated to cost $9.5 million. Gilbert's source was probably a 1922 article provided by his clipping service that had reported that the cost of the building, with land, was expected to be $9.5 million (*Clarksburg Telegram*; July 17, 1922). While the commissioners had assured him they wanted the project completed quickly, "the whole operation has ... consumed, up to the present time, *eleven years and six months*, in other words, *nine years longer than it was originally intended*" (Gilbert's emphases). These delays had "added very materially to the architect's expense in carrying on the operation, while at the same time the fee derived from the operation is based on an amount of money over $2,000,000.00 less than originally contemplated." Such "reductions in cost have not lessened, in fact they have increased my labor and expense."

When his contract was drafted, Gilbert had accepted a number of "conditions that were at variance with the usual terms of my professional practice and of the practice established by the American Institute of Architects." The one concession he had not accepted was traveling expenses: "the Commission agreed to leave this question to be brought up later on, stating that it would be dealt with in fairness and equity." In addition, he had received "no compensation for work done in connection with the proposed boiler plant" and "no pay for the preliminary studies done on a number of different sites." He concluded: "Relying upon the sense of justice of the Commission, and upon what was stated at the time of the making of the contract as 'a gentleman's agreement between gentlemen,' I venture to lay these questions before you as a matter of equity and to ask your consideration of them in principle." Gilbert continued: "If you approve in principle, we can then discuss the details of such settlement as may seem equitable. May I add, in conclusion, that I have endeavored in every possible way to protect the interests of the State and to honorably discharge the duties of my professional service." He closed with "Requesting your careful consideration on the foregoing, I remain, Faithfully yours, [signed] Cass Gilbert." The architect's tact only partially masks his unhappiness with the failure of West Virginia to pay him what he felt he was due. Gilbert hoped the issue would be resolved at the November 28 Commission meeting, but the governor, to whom his letter was addressed, was not present and no action was taken.

In preparation for the first meeting of the Legislature in their new quarters, Conley asked Gilbert about the national reception of the new building. The architect responded with a list of advertisements from contractors and "material manufacturers" that had illustrated the West Virginia Capitol and a list of newspapers in sixteen states and the District of Columbia that had published stories about the Capitol.[35]

What appears to be the final report of the Capitol Building Commission was included with Governor Conley's "Message to the 1933 Legislature." The Commission's report, dated December 31, 1932, provides a brief history, impressive statistics (the finished Capitol had more than 333 office rooms, for example, and 444,000 cubic feet of limestone), as well as the total cost and the sources of revenue.[36] The report states that Gilbert was still owed $4,499.55, much less than the $117,748.66 determined by the architect. Appropriations had totaled $9,825,290.03; the cost, including outstanding bills ($27,086.31), was $9,556,639.97. This included, of course, the cost of the site.

The budget constraints Governor Conley faced were clarified as the first Legislative session in the new Capitol was convened in January 1933. Light coming through the chamber skylights proved distracting and Gore asked Gilbert for a solution. The Reinhard Company estimated that shades would cost $555, to which Conley replied: "Under all the circumstances, we do not feel justified in approving such a contract and the same is herewith returned." The "circumstances" may refer not only to the ongoing Depression but also to a specific problem with state revenue; apparently certain tax laws had been found illegal by the courts, reducing the tax revenues expected by the state.[37]

In February 1933, Cass Gilbert again raised the issue of payments due him in a letter to Governor Conley, enclosing a copy of the November 26 letter discussed previously.[38] He emphasized that he would not be asking for the governor's consideration of this issue "if the amount of additional and unnecessary expense to which I have been put were not a very considerable one ... but, as it is frankly of such an amount as to be serious to me, I feel that I must take it up with you." He pointed out to Conley that after he had reviewed the "length of service that I had furnished and the cost of it to the office" at the November 1932 Commission meeting, the commissioners had led him to think that he "might reasonably bring such matters to your attention." At this point, he proposed a Commission subcommittee to "look into the matter." As it would be impractical for him to bring the complete records to Charleston, Gilbert offered to pay traveling expenses for the committee to come to New York to examine his books and see the drawings and other materials. As an alternative, his secretary could "have a statement drawn off from the books." Gilbert must have felt a sense of urgency, for Conley's term as governor would soon end.

Although the Capitol had been declared ready for occupancy on February 10, 1932, a year later the architect still found the final payment offered by the state unsatisfactory: "The balance available at the present time [probably the figure of $4,499.55 listed in the final Commission report] is insufficient to meet the regular payment now due me. I would therefore be willing to consider a deferred payment if the matter can be agreed upon." He concluded, "I do not ask that anything be done that is not in the public interest and with the full knowledge of the Legislature, but I do feel that I have a reasonable and equitable claim which would come under the head of adjusted compensation for services rendered." No response is documented, and given the governor's inability "under all the circumstances" to buy shades costing $555 for the legislative chambers, it is perhaps not surprising that no action was taken. Gilbert's reluctance to accept the "balance available" as his final payment may explain why he continued his efforts to "finish" the Capitol late in 1933.

Gilbert made his last visit to Charleston on December 18, 1933, accompanied, as he was so often, by John Rockart. They arrived at 8:30 A.M. and left that evening at 10:30 P.M. The vice-president of the Fuller Company, W. G. Distler, offered to accompany them, but the architect apparently did not feel this was necessary. Gilbert hoped the new governor, Herman Kump, would ask him to complete the landscaping and construct the terraces and the wall along the Kanawha River.[39]

Rockart documented that although he had written to Bonner Hill as early as July asking for a meeting with Kump, he had received no response. When Hill wired on December 9 suggesting that they "get in touch with the Governor regarding the terracing, landscaping, etc.," Gilbert telephoned Governor Kump and read him a letter he was sending.[40] No transcript of this call seems to survive, but the governor's response must have convinced Gilbert he needed to visit Charleston sooner rather than later. The tone of the transcript dictated ten days after they returned is perhaps colored by an exchange among Gilbert, Rockart, and Houston Young after they met with the governor: "Mr. Gilbert expressed his favorable impression of the Governor. Mr. Young on the contrary stated that the Governor was an ex-Judge and ever since taking office he had encouraged criticism of past Republican officers and officials, and that there had been remarks of criticism made of the Capitol buildings." Young suggested that "the Governor was endeavoring to discredit previous Republican administrations and went out of his way to do it." Always aware of his need to be apolitical, Gilbert added the following in pencil to Rockart's transcript: "We were not informed of such matters & did not comment on Mr. Young's statement."

During their visit, Gilbert and Rockart spent an hour with Governor Kump. Rockart's transcript suggests that the governor was hoping he could void certain areas of Gilbert's contract: "In respect to terraces, landscaping, decorations, sculpture, paintings, etc., Mr. Gilbert referred the Governor to his contract, which provides that his services ~~would~~ [crossed off in transcript] include all such work on the site or sites to be selected, including all portions of land within the street curbs." Gilbert had brought "a copy of that portion of the contract and offered to show it to the governor. The governor stated that they had a copy of the contract and that he had referred it to the attorney general for a report." Rockart added in parentheses, "This indicated to me that the Governor for the moment questions the legality of that portion of the contract, and for that reason had referred to the Attorney General."

Another disagreement is documented but not explained in the transcript: "The Governor again brought up the response Mr. Gilbert had made to his telephone call inquiring as to whether Mr. Gilbert had received any other telephone message. He questioned Mr. Gilbert's sincerity in responding thereto." Rockart noted that Gilbert had written to the governor on December 9. The architect then said that "he had contemplated this visit for some time; that he was on the point of telephoning the Governor for an appointment, and, when the Governor asked him if he had received a 'telephone' message from anyone he answered 'No,' but he then received the telegram from Mr. Hill; that it was not his intention to evade the question and, since the Governor had brought it up again, he wanted to assure him that there was no intention of evading the question; that he was very busy at the time the Governor asked him the question and, in any case, his letter of December 9th to the Governor explained the whole situation." Although the context is not clear, Kump's antagonism to and suspicion of Gilbert seem palpable in this exchange.

The rest of the meeting was straightforward. Almost at the beginning, the governor "stated that under the C.W.A. [Civil Works Administration] he had proposed to do some work by employing the unemployed in the State in some landscape work around the Capitol buildings, but opposition thereto had developed to such an extent that he had decided to do nothing." Gilbert responded: "One of the objects of our visit ... was our desire to assist in any way possible to find work for the unemployed to the end that we would be willing to furnish such information, drawings, etc. as would be needed." The governor then stated that "the matter was closed and that he would not make any further effort to proceed with the work at present." The governor then inquired about drawings and specifications for the terraces and landscape work; Gilbert replied that although no working drawings or specifications had been made, in June 1932 he had sent Governor Conley some sketches for the "proposed development of the grounds."[41]

Gilbert reviewed the reasons behind his request to Governor Conley for "an adjustment of further payment." When Kump reported that he had heard "the work contemplated" would cost about $1.5 million, Gilbert replied he had previously estimated $1,350,000, an amount that included not only the terraces and landscaping but also the construction of the river wall, which would be expensive, and the paintings and sculpture. Gilbert understood that the work could not be undertaken at the time but that he was "prepared to furnish the necessary drawings and specifications, and render all the services as contemplated in the contract."

After about an hour, Kump dismissed them: "The Governor then stated he regretted that his time was very much absorbed in the affairs of the State, that when he was elected he had not realized how difficult the governor's problems were, but that he was very glad to meet Mr. Gilbert as a distinguished citizen and architect, and for that reason he was very glad to receive him and give him this time for a discussion of the subject."[42]

During this fourteen-hour visit to Charleston, Gilbert and Rockart also inspected the Capitol. Before leaving, they met with former commissioner Payne, who headed the local Civil Works Administration. Payne had told Governor Kump he could arrange "to provide government funds to employ the unemployed in any constructive work, provided the State would appropriate the money to take care of the relief of the unemployed." He had suggested to the governor that he "take the matter up with Mr. Gilbert." The architect agreed he "would be willing to furnish any drawings and specifications that were needed and, in view of the economic situation, would not demand payment therefor at present but would be willing to wait until the State could afford to pay for such services." Although Payne promised to see Kump about this possibility, there is no evidence that such a meeting took place.

The change in administration, from the Republican governors who had been so supportive of Cass Gilbert over the years—Ephraim F. Morgan, Howard M. Gore, William G. Conley—to the Democratic administration of Herman G. Kump profoundly changed Gilbert's relationship with the West Virginia Capitol. On February 19, 1934, Kump wrote to Gilbert: "The fact is that there are a number of things about the capitol building that are entirely unsatisfactory and seem to me to require attention." Kump's comment seems deliberately insulting and, because no problems were specified, to demand a reply. The architect's response, written February 28, seems to be his final communication on the West Virginia State Capitol.[43] Gilbert revealed once again his sense of responsibility toward the creation that he and his West Virginia patrons had labored so long and intensely to bring into being. Although the financial considerations seem not to have been resolved in his favor, Gilbert demonstrated his willingness to do all he could to guarantee that his work was satisfactory:

> If you will kindly send me a list of the items in the State Capitol Building which you understand to be "unsatisfactory," I will give them immediate attention and endeavor to make them satisfactory in so far as it may be possible to do so. We know in this office that we have rendered conscientious service to the State of West Virginia, and we believe that you have, in the State Capitol group, buildings of unusually good quality and as well equipped and substantial in character as it was practicable to obtain within the appropriations available. In a group of buildings so extensive as this, and especially in the main unit where the foundation conditions were extremely difficult, it would be surprising if there were not some minor items which might need attention. If such should be the case, we would be grateful if you would, either personally or through your representative, let us know what they are so that we may take appropriate action toward their betterment.
>
> May I ask the favor of an early reply,
> Very truly yours,
> [signed] Cass Gilbert
> Architect

There is no record that Kump responded to Gilbert's offer or any indication of which details were, in his opinion, "entirely unsatisfactory." Now, more than eighty years after the building's dedication, most would judge West Virginia's Capitol to be entirely satisfactory, an inspiring monument to the idea and ideals of American democracy.

CHAPTER EIGHT

# Symbols of Democracy: "The Best Evidences of the … Culture and Civilization of a State"

The hope of the State and the Nation is in the people, and the public buildings, to a great extent, represent their ideals and character which you see symbolized here.

Governor William Conley, at the dedication of the West Virginia Capitol, 1932

Fig. 70. The dome, lantern, and spire. Photograph by Thorney Lieberman.

THE WEST VIRGINIA CAPITOL IS IMPOSING AND ELEGANT, a handsome tribute to the state and American democracy.[1] Although unique in certain details, the Capitol does not differ greatly in design and symbolism from many earlier and contemporary seats of state government. It follows the tradition of emulating the National Capitol, and adheres to the practice of referring to the state's attributes in its decorative details. The Capitol complex conveys ideals of American democracy and makes specific references to West Virginia. This is a building with which West Virginians identify and of which they are proud. The ongoing relationship between the people of West Virginia and their Capitol is a reminder of Winston Churchill's remark: "We shape our buildings; thereafter they shape us."

Symbolism is addressed here by discussing the overall effect of the design, encompassing the Capitol's architectural elements, scale, and materials, and by considering how some decorative motifs refer to West Virginia and allude to the more general concepts of power and democracy.

When Gilbert was commissioned to design the West Virginia Capitol, the idea that Greco-Roman architecture best expressed the ideals of American democracy had been firmly established. Americans have long been fascinated with Greek and Roman antiquity; until relatively recently, many schools required students to study Latin and ancient culture. Furthermore, travel abroad and visual accessibility through photography and art allowed increased familiarity with both the ancient world and its revival during the Italian Renaissance. Greek and Roman temples, imperial basilicas, homes and businesses in Pompeii, and the classically inspired monuments of Florence, Venice, and Rome have long intrigued Americans. As we examine the cultures of ancient Greece and Rome and of Renaissance Italy as symbolic of our own, however, we should not compare too closely. The Athenian and Florentine "democracies" were not representative, and imperial Rome, whose buildings were often emulated in American monumental architecture, was anything but a democracy. But these are not the important issues. The perception is what matters: for Gilbert and his contemporaries, democracy and law giving were represented by Greco-Roman architectural and decorative motifs: columns, pediments, domes, garlands, and fasces, as well as military and mythological narratives and heroes. The fact that so many governmental buildings in America are based on Classical prototypes bespeaks the significance of this historical perception. West Virginia's Capitol fits well within this tradition.

The terms Greek, Roman, Greco-Roman, and Renaissance, when used to describe architectural forms and details, are often arbitrary and overlapping. The Classical elements that were applied to governmental and other public and private buildings were intended to associate America with Greco-Roman culture. Many elements of Greek architecture, from Doric and Ionic columns to sculpted pediments and coffered ceilings, were incorporated into ancient Roman architecture. Centuries later the architects of the Italian Renaissance "rediscovered" and reinterpreted antiquity. The use of antique forms continued in Baroque, Neoclassical, and other later architectural styles. Gilbert, delighting in ancient precedent, incorporated elements from antiquity and the Renaissance in his designs for contemporary, functional structures. The public buildings he created between the 1890s and his death in 1934 are among the many examples of how antique motifs can be combined to create grand structures that express the power and majesty of our democracy.

As one approaches, enters, and explores the West Virginia Capitol, the sense of grandeur is tempered by the recognition of familiar images. While size and elegance impress, details delight. The architecture symbolizes governmental power and democracy by design and association, intended or not, with historic buildings, from the Athenian Parthenon and the Pantheon in Rome to Charles Bulfinch's Massachusetts State House and the United States Capitol. On the exterior of the West Virginia Capitol, columns and pediments refer to Greek architecture, while wide steps leading to bronze entry doors echo those of their Roman predecessors. Inside, the vastness of the rotunda and the soaring dome above, with its rows of coffers diminishing in size, create an effect of simple majesty reminiscent of that conveyed by the Pantheon in Rome. To either side of the grand rotunda, marble halls direct our attention to legislative chambers impressive in materials and decor. The power and solemnity of the complex are deeply indebted to the inspiration of its ancient sources.

The West Virginia Capitol is open to anyone, whether elected official, employee, citizen, or visitor. We can freely wander, observe, experience; in the democratic spirit, the building and governmental sessions are in great part available to all. While we may not be fully aware of the complexity and pervasiveness of the symbolism surrounding us, we cannot help but be impressed. We may not recognize Zeus or the sugar maple, magnolias or fasces, and we may not connect the dome with its European precedents or bronze doors with ancient Rome, but we are affected by the combination of architecture and sculpture. In fact, the incorporation of sculpture into architecture is itself an ancient convention. As in his earlier Minnesota State Capitol and Woolworth Building, then, Gilbert invoked the past as he shaped the present and looked to the future.

The thirty-fifth state admitted to the Union, West Virginia was established by secession when residents of the inland area of Virginia opposed the Confederate supporters of the eastern and coastal regions. The Virginia Capitol (1785–89) had been designed by another renowned architect, Thomas Jefferson, and while the columns and pediment of Gilbert's portico echo those of Jefferson's Virginia Capitol, the overall effect of the Capitol in Charleston is transformed by the high dome, which creates visual drama and establishes a relationship with the National Capitol in Washington. Perhaps Gilbert's patrons chose this design in part because they wanted their Capitol to surpass the one that had been their state's original seat of government. Choosing the National Capitol as a model may also have been intended to suggest the state's alliance with the Union that led to the establishment of West Virginia.

Many American public buildings, including the West Virginia Capitol, parallel those of the monumental buildings of ancient Rome. Material and size became increasingly significant as the Roman Empire developed, from the time of Augustus and the Julio-Claudian emperors to the Flavians and beyond. The Pantheon and

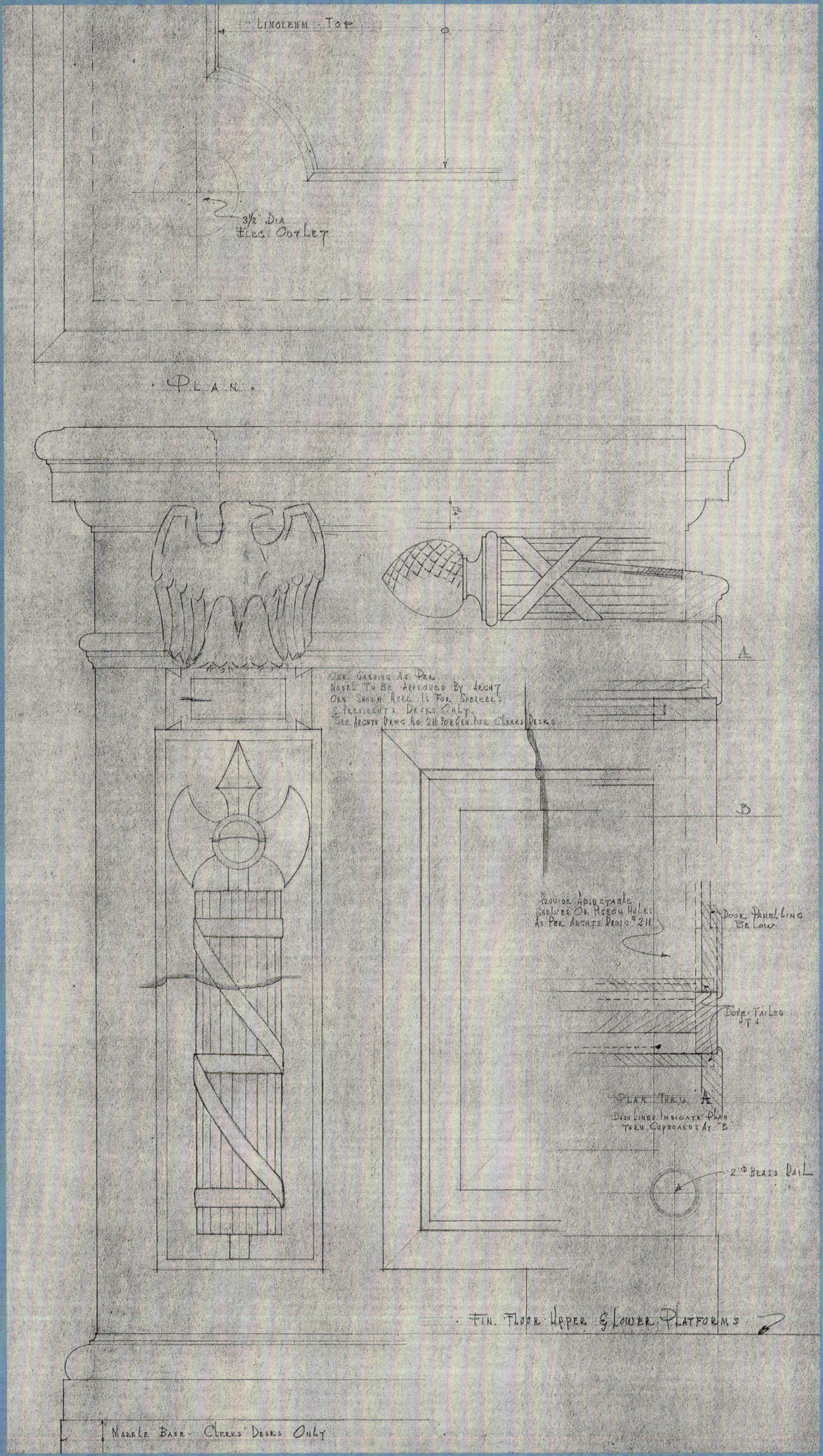


Fig. 71. Drawing for the rostra for the House and Senate chambers, dated February 9, 1931, detail. There are no axes on the completed rostra, and the bindings on the fasces are of the more common crossed design (see fig. 83).

## THE PROBLEMATIC FASCES

One particularly problematic symbol, the bundled rods known as fasces, appears throughout the Capitol: on the frieze below the drum on the exterior and the balcony railing inside the dome, for example, and even on the slender, tapered shaft that raises the eagle high above the lantern (see figs. 70, 75, and gallery 1). The fasces and eagle combination is similar to that used on the ceremonial mace, the symbol of authority used in the United States House of Representatives. Fasces are also seen in the legislative chambers, where they appear both with and without eagles (see figs. 71, 83). When the Capitol was designed, fasces and eagles were common symbols of American democracy and power. While the eagle is still a prominent emblem of our country, the fasces became problematic when their meaning was transformed.

The original fasces, ancient in origin, were composed of bundles of birch branches bound together. While a single branch is easily bent, a bound group is neither bendable nor breakable. Carried in processions by ancient Roman lictors, civil servants who served as bodyguards for officials, fasces symbolized authority and expressed the idea of strength through unity. To indicate military might during the ancient period, a single- or double-headed ax was embedded in the fasces. Because of their symbolism of unity and power, fasces continued to be used; sculpted and painted versions, with and without axes, appear in many American contexts, including the West Virginia Capitol.

The current interpretation of fasces, unfortunately, is affected by its association with fascism. Once a motif is adopted by a totalitarian regime, it often becomes suspect and undesirable.[2] Today people may be shocked at the appearance of an emblem now associated with Mussolini, who derived the name Fascism and its symbol from this powerful ancient Roman motif. But at the time of the design and construction of the West Virginia Capitol, fasces still had positive connotations. For Cass Gilbert, his West Virginia patrons, and Americans in general, the fasces expressed the unification of equal individuals into the larger and more powerful democratic whole. The importance of the fasces as an American symbol is evident in its appearance on the reverse of the Mercury dime next to the motto *e pluribus unum* (from the many, one); both fasces and motto stress the concept of unity as the country's ideal. Fasces also decorate the base of Thomas Crawford's statue of *Freedom* atop the dome of the United States Capitol and the president's chair in Daniel Chester French's seated figure of Abraham Lincoln at the Lincoln Memorial in Washington. Gilbert used this symbol in the mural decoration for the Minnesota State Capitol, and later in his career, as at West Virginia, he incorporated it into his Supreme Court building, where a Roman centurion holding a fasces is depicted on a frieze.

Fig. 72. United States "Mercury" dime, with fasces and olive branch, minted between 1916 and 1945. Photograph by Brandon Bigheart.

Domitian's Palace in Rome, for instance, were among the structures that were adorned with marble of various colors and origins. The incorporation of exotic materials from the corners of the empire, in combination with the scale of these imperial buildings, overtly expressed the extent of Roman power and wealth. Similarly, in the West Virginia Capitol, the incorporation of different and sometimes exotic materials on floors, walls, columns, and lamps can be understood as an expression of the state's prosperity and importance.[3] Boyd B. Stutler, who published an enlightening article on the Capitol in 1932, was impressed with Gilbert's selection of materials: "The resources of six nations on two continents were drawn upon to supply the material that went into the building and finish of the main unit ... Tennessee, France, the Slavish kingdoms and Italy furnished special marble for finish of detail, and also from Italy came more than sixty-five thousand square feet of travertine." America was the source for much of the marble: "The exterior is constructed of Indiana limestone ... while the interior finish is principally in Imperial Danby white marble from Vermont. More than one hundred and fifty freight cars were required to transport this marble from the Vermont quarries to the building."[4] The symbolic importance of fine materials witnessed in ancient Rome is seen in Charleston, although cost and issues of maintenance also played a role. Gilbert clarified his ideas: "Marble was chosen after careful consideration by the Commission in order to save up-keep. It has been proved that marble is cheaper in the long run, as the saving in up-keep of painting and cleaning over a not long period of time will pay for the extra cost of marble over plaster."[5] While the use of marble is symbolic, then, practical considerations were also important and indicative of Gilbert's integration of practicality with tradition.

Even as Modernism became increasingly prevalent in America in the 1920s, Classicism continued to be Gilbert's preference, as seen in his comments on the West Virginia Capitol: "The building is classic in style, and in fact what might be correctly termed as Renaissance and the architectural forms are Roman with the single exception of the Doric vestibule at the ground floor on the river side of the building." He emphasized that Rome was a more important source than Greece: "The porticoes and colonnades of the exterior are distinctly Roman, the main porticoes being of the Roman Corinthian order, which was, of course, indirectly derived from the Greek precedent and the other porticoes or colonnades are of a modified Roman Doric type." This is also true of the dome: "The exterior of the dome closely follows the Roman precedent, although I know of no dome as high in proportion among Roman examples. The bell of the dome, which is of metal, was studied from certain Renaissance domes in Europe."[6] While Gilbert emphasized the Roman origin of specific details, his identification of the style as "Renaissance" is probably a reference to the signature motif of the complex, the great raised dome. In addition, he related his complex to earlier American architecture: "In designing the interior as well as the exterior I have endeavored to give it a noble and distinguished simplicity; to keep it closely within the lines of the great tradition and precedent which were characteristic of the early public buildings of America, lines

## THE DOME: TO GILD, OR NOT TO GILD?

The treatment of the dome's exterior decoration has changed over the years. At the time of its construction, debate ensued when West Virginians realized that Gilbert wanted to highlight the dome's motifs with gold leaf. In response to the outcry, Gilbert clarified that a metal dome with gilded decoration was economical: "If we had built the dome of stone, as in the Arkansas Capitol, or of marble as in the Minnesota Capitol or the Rhode Island Capitol, it would have cost five or ten times as much money." He also noted the precedent of other notable buildings with gilded domes, such as the Library of Congress and the Capitols of Massachusetts and New Jersey.[7]

The motifs on the dome were originally gilded by the Mack, Jenney & Tyler Company in 1931. As is evident in extensive correspondence, however, there were problems with the gold, which began to flake off. Fifteen years later, the gilding was removed and both decoration and background were covered with gold paint, rendering the motifs difficult to discern. In 1961, the motifs were again highlighted when they were painted bright yellow against a blue background, but once more there were problems with deterioration, and more blue and gold paint was applied during the 1970s. Gold leaf was applied to both motifs and background, obscuring the motifs, between 1988 and 1991, and yet again there were problems, since the adhesive did not set as it should have. Eventually, an architectural preservation firm was consulted, and in 2004 work was begun on repairs and regilding. The issue of how to treat the dome's external decoration was eventually decided by popular opinion when West Virginia citizens were asked to vote by computer or telephone. The options were either to follow Gilbert's design or to gild the entire dome, obscuring the military and patriotic motifs. The majority favored following the original plan, which explains the dome's breathtaking appearance today and reconfirms Gilbert's vision.[8]

... largely influenced by Washington, Jefferson and their associates and by architects like Thornton, Bulfinch, and Mills, who were leaders in their profession in the early days of the Republic." He elaborated: "Simplicity and good proportion are finer characteristics of architecture than ornamentation, and it has been my endeavor that in the rotunda and the principal corridors, and the rooms of the House and Senate especially, there should be an air of simplicity, amplitude and dignity, and I believe this has been achieved."[9]

The imposing dome of the Capitol commands attention from near and far. In Gilbert's words: "The Main Building is crowned by a dome of majestic proportion, rising to a considerable height, and is a conspicuous and notable feature of the landscape from every point of view." He emphasized the national symbolism of the dome: "The dome has become by habit and use as much a feature of the American State Capitol as the steeple is a feature of the American village church."[10] And in Stutler's words at the time of the Capitol's dedication: "With a towering dome, reminiscent of that surmounting the Capitol at Washington ... the graceful lines of the structure greet the eyes of the travelers who enter Charleston from the East, and [they are] the last sight of the capital city to those whose faces are turned [back] toward the East [as they leave the city, traveling West]."[11] The total height is 292 feet, approximately four and a half feet taller than the National Capitol.[12] The emphasis on this statistic in Stutler's writings demonstrated his pride in his state's Capitol, the dome of which is both reminiscent of and, at least in height, grander than that of the nation's Capitol.

In its general outline, the dome Gilbert created is not exceptional: it sits atop a high drum and is surmounted by a soaring spire with an eagle on a sphere. Although there is no one source for the Charleston drum and dome, their proportions and evenly spaced Corinthian columns are similar to those of the United States Capitol, which in turn were inspired by those of Christopher Wren's St. Paul's Cathedral in London (1669–97). That Gilbert refers to the Charleston Capitol as "Renaissance" in style is perhaps attributable to Wren's work being traditionally classified as "English Renaissance" or "Late Renaissance."

It is not the form, then, that distinguishes West Virginia's dome; it is the brilliant effect of its gilded patterns that makes it like no other in America (see fig. 70). Each of the dome's sixteen vertical panels display patterns of military and political symbols that are highlighted by gold leaf against a dark background. No other state capitol offers such a wealth of symbolism.

The immediate source for Gilbert's paneled, gilded decoration is drawn from the French Renaissance and specifically from the Église du Dôme des Invalides, King Louis XIV's private chapel for the national military hospital, L'Hôtel National des Invalides, in Paris.[13] This chapel, commonly referred to as Les Invalides and perhaps best known as Napoleon's burial place, was designed by Louis XIV's favorite architect, Jules Hardouin-Mansart, and completed in 1708. The decoration Mansart devised for his dome incorporated antique military and other motifs arranged as if suspended from a vertical ribbon or sash, imagery that seems appropriate, given the

Fig. 73. *Église du Dôme des Invalides*, the chapel of L'Hôtel National des Invalides, Paris, by Jules Hardouin-Mansart, designed 1680. Photograph by Benh.

## DECIPHERING THE MOTIFS OF THE DOME PANELS

The decorative grouping of motifs in each of the sixteen main panels is identical (see fig. 74). At the top of each an eagle with outstretched wings, a Roman motif, is perched upon a wreath. Below each eagle is a Roman military standard;[14] in the blueprint this standard carried the letters SPQR, the abbreviation for the motto of ancient Rome, "Senatus Populusque Romanus" (The Senate and the People of Rome). The standard today, however, is decorated with a shield, a rosette in the center, and an ax and club crossed behind it.[15]

Below, the prominent awning of the dormer window is decorated with a head in the Classical style; a dormer placed on a sloping roof, as here, is known as a lucarne. Running vertically from below the lucarne is what seems to be a ribbon or sash, with objects suspended from it as in earlier versions by Palladio, Mansart, and others. Below the window a large oval shield is framed by a pair of unfurled American flags; their supporting staffs are topped with spear points. The three staffs to each side suggest multiple flags. On the left, the staffs are accompanied by an ax; on the right, by the profile head of an eagle.

In front of the large oval shield, which is decorated with an ancient Roman symmetrical vine pattern known as a rinceau, is a second shield. This unusually shaped object, scalloped across the top, is known from antiquity as a peltoid shield. In the center is a female apotropaic head, and, to both left and right, the shield terminates in fierce eagle heads.[16] The intentionally terrifying appearance of the female, perhaps Medusa, recalls the use of such apotropaic heads in antiquity; when the head of Medusa was placed on the exterior of early Greek temples or on the shield of Athena or those of warriors, it was intended to repel the enemy and ward off evil. The overlapped shields flanked by American flags form the largest motif in each panel and, because of their placement on the curve of the dome below the window, they are the most prominent motif of the decoration.

Beneath this decorative ensemble two overlapping shields are placed diagonally, each decorated with palmettes. The shield in full view features a rosette between the palmettes. Such decorative motifs are not uncommon on shields held by Roman warriors on the Column of Trajan and elsewhere. Below each shield hangs a horizontal quiver full of arrows. This motif is easily visible from afar, and its repeated shape suggests a right-to-left movement around the base of the massive dome. The motifs end with a tassel flanked by stylized ribbons.

Between the wider panels are narrow ones derived from the ribs that form part of the structural system of many European domes. These narrow areas are decorated with slender fasces that lead the eye up toward the one that supports the eagle high above. Below each fasces is a cascade of what seem to be lotus blossoms resembling those in the same position on the Invalides dome. Each cascade ends in a rosette.

The overlapping of motifs and the manner in which several are diagonally crossed in Gilbert's cascade of arms are similar to the treatment of arms and armor on Mansart's designs for the Invalides dome. Some motifs are found in both Paris and Charleston: the eagle with wings spread at the top, the peltoid shield, the pairs of furled flags, the standard designed with "SPQR," and the quivers with arrows. While both architects used lucarne windows, Mansart's are decorated with helmets rather than the heads used by Gilbert. Gilbert's design is more formal and symmetrical than Mansart's more irregular compositions.

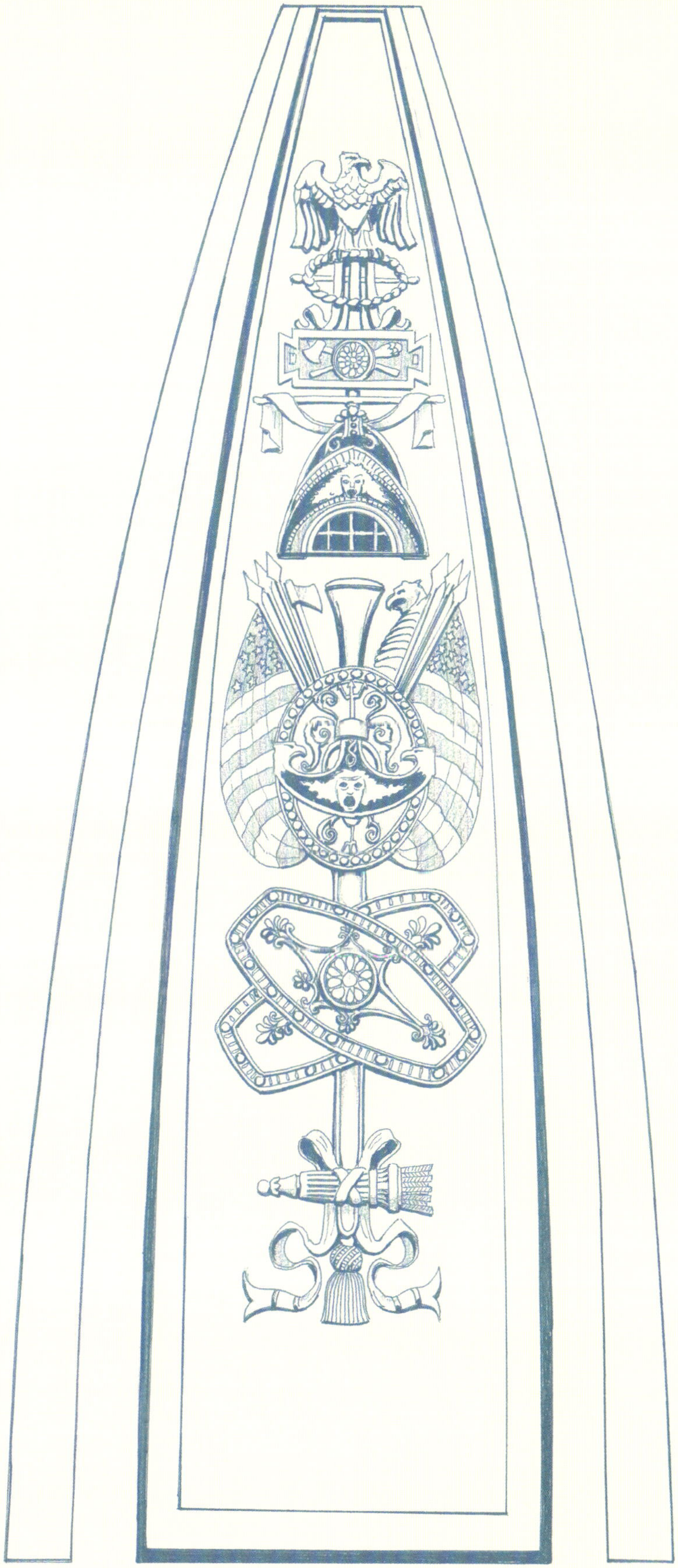

Fig. 74. The decorative motifs of the West Virginia Capitol dome. Drawing by Raymond Agius.

military functions of the building. While Mansart used three different designs for the panels, Gilbert repeated one pattern sixteen times.

Ancient Romans displayed confiscated shields, helmets, armor, spears, and other military spoils like those found on the Invalides dome to announce the submission of a defeated enemy; representation of such displays became popular in the post-ancient world. An influential Renaissance example is found at Palladio's Loggia del Capitaniato in Vicenza, where piles of military trophies are represented in the larger reliefs and groups of such implements seem to be suspended vertically in the narrow reliefs between the windows.[17] Such motifs continued to be popular into the early twentieth century, and were used by Gilbert at his Minnesota State Capitol.[18]

The motifs embedded in the patterns of the West Virginia dome are rich with references to American democracy as well as to Roman traditions and military power. The details of this decoration have puzzled observers for decades, however. In 2005, as the dome's restoration was celebrated, an article titled "Mystery of the Dome" appeared in the *Charleston Gazette*.[19] Referring to the decorative details, "long obscured because they were either painted or gilded," the author pointed out that even after more than seventy years, the meaning of Gilbert's symbols had not been elucidated. The architect's meticulous recordkeeping is well known, but on this subject, it seems, he was silent. A blueprint clarifies his original intent for the decoration (see fig. 56) but offers no explanation of the specific meaning for each motif or for their combination. Furthermore, the motifs as executed differ slightly from those represented on the blueprint. Gilbert was methodical; surely there were reasons for his original choices and subsequent modifications, but until evidence surfaces to explain these decisions, one can do no more than analyze the final result.

Despite the complexity of these decorative motifs, or perhaps because of it, an overall effect of splendor and decoration is what first strikes the visitor to Charleston. The motifs of the panels, outlined with broad frames in gold, are less important than the richness of design they project. The combination of horizontal, vertical, and diagonal forms in each panel, the contrasts between simplicity and complexity, the manner in which the wide central motif under the windows emphasizes the dome's curvature, and the directional rotation suggested by the quivers all testify to Gilbert's brilliant sense of design. The symbolism is merely the icing on this particular cupcake.

Gilbert's ability to combine potent symbols into a decorative whole is especially impressive. In so doing, he gave West Virginia a unique dome, one that is extraordinarily rich in symbolism and allusion, distinct among American state capitols, and, despite its elaborate appearance, relatively inexpensive.

The sculpted frieze under the dome's colonnade is also Classical in theme. Fasces and eagles with spread wings grouped with rosettes and garlands encircle the drum. The garlands, which Gilbert often referred to as "festoons," predominate from a distance and echo the dome's curving silhouette. They are bound with a crossed pattern, repeating the design of the binding of the fasces. The combination of eagle and garland suggests the union of peace with fecundity, a proposal confirmed by the use of the same two motifs on the reliefs of the Altar of Peace in

Fig. 75. Decorative corner element based on the ancient tripod, with lions' heads on the terrace below the drum; garlands, fasces, and eagles below the colonnade.

Fig. 76. Garlands, fasces, eagles, and the inscription below the colonnade of the drum; palmette and rinceaux decoration on the south pediment.

Rome (the Ara Pacis, built for Emperor Augustus and dedicated in 9 BCE). The theme of peace achieved through vigilance or war is not a new one, but whether Gilbert was referring to military triumph and peace in the wake of World War I is uncertain. His combination of American and ancient Roman symbols could also be a nod to the roots of Western heritage in antiquity, but perhaps it is no more than the imposition of a decorative pattern pleasing to the eye. Without a statement from the artist it is difficult to determine if a particular motif or combination of motifs is primarily symbolic or decorative.

Cass Gilbert's ideal that architecture and sculpture should be inspirational is found not only in symbols but also in the framed Biblical quotations above the north and south entrances. On the south is "Happy is the man that findeth wisdom and the man that getteth understanding" (Proverbs 3:13) and on the north "Wisdom is the principal thing; therefore get wisdom: and with all thy getting get understanding" (Proverbs 4:7). Chosen by Gilbert, these maxims emphasize the importance of knowledge for the individual and for the state.[20]

Marking the corners of the square terrace below the drum are massive decorative elements (see fig. 75). Fierce lions' heads, mouths open revealing large teeth, stare from under palmettes and between prominent, fruited garlands. In form they are based on the large ancient vessels identified as "tripods," which served practical, religious, and honorific functions, often as trophies for athletic competitions. The palmettes, although of different proportion, echo the acroteria and other palmettes bordering the pediments.

Second in prominence to the towering dome are the south and north porticoes, which connect visually with the dome through their repetitive Corinthian columns and, like the dome, are impressive even from afar. The porticoes are Classical, with both Greek and Roman elements; the entrances, with their grand stairways and massive bronze doors, bespeak power, democracy, and Classical heritage. The main entrances of a number of state capitols—Virginia, Tennessee, Kansas, Utah, and Wisconsin among them—are dominated by similar Greco-Roman pediments and columns. In West Virginia, the octostyle colonnades that mark the south and north entrances are especially forceful because, as at the National Capitol, they are echoed above by identical Corinthian columns encircling the drum.[21]

The ultimate models for the columns and pediments that mark the entrances of so many American public buildings are ancient Greek temples, the most ideally proportioned of which has long been recognized as the fifth-century BCE Parthenon in Athens. The Parthenon was designed using the earliest of the Greek orders, the Doric. Gilbert's use of the more elaborate Corinthian order combined with simple, unfluted columns is based on the most famous of all Roman temples, the Pantheon, a print of which hung in his Minnesota studio (see fig. 18). While the relationship between the entrance porticoes of the Pantheon and the Charleston Capitol is clear, a close look at the Corinthian capitals on the West Virginia building shows that eagles with open wings are incorporated into the design, adding an American reference to the ancient model.

The pediments of West Virginia's two entrances and the Pantheon are similar in their lack of sculpted decoration, but we know from Gilbert's writings and drawings (see fig. 32), from the bronze plaque marking the completion of the East Wing, and from Stutler's 1932 appreciation that sculpted figures were intended. The physical evidence supports this, for the blocks installed in the pediments during construction are deep enough that figural sculpture could later be carved in situ; those in the north pediment are even varied in depth. The drawing for the complex (see fig. 32), which shows a centralized seated female flanked by other figures, suggests that at least one of the themes would have been allegorical, most likely with references to governmental virtues.[22]

On all three buildings, a giant order of Doric pilasters between the windows enhances the Classical appearance (see fig. 99). The pilasters echo the columns of the porticoes and match in design and proportion those of the porches. They also add a vertical emphasis within the broad horizontal buildings of the complex. Carved garlands with rosettes between the pilasters (see fig. 99), like those below the drum, are derived from Roman decorative motifs and especially those on the Augustan Altar of Peace in Rome.[23]

The grand staircases leading to the porticoes, also based on Roman models, create a sense of anticipation as one ascends toward the people's rotunda and the foyers leading to the centers of legislative power on the main floor.[24] The rows of coffers decorated with rosettes in the ceilings under each portico are Classical in inspiration, as are the double door frames, marble and bronze, which display garlands, palmettes, and floral designs. Also Roman in inspiration are the sets of bronze entry doors, reminiscent of those of the Pantheon. Because these are pocket doors, however, they are only visible when the Capitol is closed. Their restrained decoration is directly relevant to West Virginia, as seen in the leaves of native trees—elm, oak, maple, beech, and hickory—within clusters shaped as rosettes. Bronze grillwork over the doors is based on designs adapted from windows in ancient Roman bath complexes, and the bronze lamps are inspired by ancient lamp bases in design and solidity.

In a complex of such extent, additional entrances are required. The discreet driveway that passes under the south staircase leads to three sets of bronze doors opening into the Doric vestibule.[25] Above the left and right doors, on both exterior and interior, are bronze reliefs featuring bulls and boars. On each relief, the animals are placed in profile; the pairs of boars face a disk decorated with corn; the bulls flank a plain one. Although these animals could well refer to West Virginia's rich agricultural traditions, the manner in which they are represented gives pause.[26] Each wears a wide belt and has a decorative braid hanging from behind its ear; the braid, an ancient sacrificial fillet, indicated animals destined for sacrifice. The precedent for these bulls and boars is more closely associated with imperial Rome than with ancient Greece, although similar sacrifices were held in both cultures: during the Roman *suovetaurilia* ritual, a belted and braided boar, bull, and ram were sacrificed to Mars, the god of war, to bless and purify the land.[27] Gilbert's visual inspiration for the bulls and boars in Charleston were marble reliefs portraying sacrificial boars, bulls, and rams

Fig. 77. Corinthian capital with eagle, portico of the West Virginia Capitol. Photograph by Edward Crim.

Fig. 78. Drawings of the bull and the boar in the bronze reliefs above the doors of the Doric vestibule. Drawings by Raymond Agius.

from the period of Emperor Trajan. These impressive large-scale reliefs, discovered in 1872 shortly before Gilbert's first trip to Europe, were displayed amid the ruins of the Roman Forum.[28] The archaeological excitement surrounding their recovery and interpretation and their prominent display in the forum guarantee the architect would have known them. When he was commissioned to create a new Capitol for a state with a strong agricultural heritage, Gilbert must have been reminded of these impressive ancient representations.

The materials and decoration of the Doric vestibule (see gallery 9) are based on those of ancient Greek temples. The bronze door frames feature a Greek key motif and the proportions of the fluted Doric columns are based on fifth-century BCE Greek precedents. The railings are of an appropriately Classical design, and the extensive use of marble contributes to the effect of richness.

The courtyard entrances of the Office Buildings and the east and west entrances to the Main Building are marked by porches with unfluted Doric columns; in the keystones below are sculpted heads of Greco-Roman divinities and heroes (see figs. 79 and 45). Each entrance features three divinities or heroes. A memo from Gilbert's office provided a short description of each figure but no explanation for his particular choices or groupings.[29] The divinities and heroes, identified below by both their Greek and Roman names, are listed from left to right in each grouping.

The heads over the east entrance of the Main Building represent Hermes/Mercury, Hephaestos/Vulcan, and Athena/Minerva. Hermes, the messenger god, is connected with commerce, while Hephaestos is the metalsmith, architect, and engineer (the "celestial artist" in Gilbert's description), and Athena symbolizes wisdom and the arts. Their relevance to a state capitol seems clear: commerce and economic strength, architecture and workmanship, and meticulous planning are all required for the construction of such a complex. On the Main Building's west entrance, the heads are those of Hestia/Vesta, Poseidon/Neptune, and Demeter/Ceres, divinities that respectively reference home and family life, seas and rivers, and agriculture (see fig. 79). Perhaps they were selected to recall the state's grassroots strength and economy.

The heads above the entrance to the West Office Building (see fig. 45) are Herakles/Hercules, representing strength and the overcoming of obstacles, accompanied by Zeus/Jupiter, "guardian of political order and peace" and king of the gods, and Fortuna, an allegorical Roman divinity "believed to guide the destinies of man." The strength, power, and fortune inherent in these divinities are essential to a well-run state. At the East Office Building the heads represent Hera/Juno (whose consort, Zeus, appears on the West Building and who was at times equivalent in power), followed by Prometheus, whom Gilbert describes as "friend of mankind ... who taught them civilization and the arts," and Perseus, whose myths involve strength and rescue. Perhaps this trio simply illustrates power and culture.

A visual pattern is also evident in the sculpted deities and heroes, for in each group of three the central head is of a heavily bearded male, while the figures to left and right are either females or beardless males. Such symmetry is, of course, characteristic of Gilbert's approach to design and decoration.

Fig. 79. The west entrance of the Main Building, with sculpted heads of Hestia/Vesta, Poseidon/Neptune, and Demeter/Ceres, photograph dated June 11, 1931. West Virginia State Archives Memory Project CL10-0036.

Fig. 80. Lamps in the lower rotunda, c. 1950. This historic photograph shows the lamps with the bronze eagles that originally surmounted each globe; these were subsequently removed but there are plans to replace them. Gilbert Family Collection.

The use of mythological figures to convey broad ideas about life, human behavior, and culture dates to antiquity. That the heads at the Charleston Capitol were chosen for their symbolic import is supported by the absence of some of the best-known gods and heroes: Aphrodite/Venus, goddess of love and beauty, is not represented, nor is Dionysus/Bacchus, god of wine with connections to irrational and ecstatic behavior—figures less appropriate for an American state capitol.

The integration of sculpture with architecture seen here, which is characteristic of the ancient Greek and Roman styles, was revived during later periods and became an important part of the Beaux-Arts style that influenced Gilbert. In ancient Greece, sculpture was architectural or placed in sanctuaries; Roman sculpture appeared in public, private, and religious settings. While the practice of decorating the keystones of arches with sculpted heads as seen at Charleston was not common in either Greece or Rome, it was popularized during the Renaissance by Palladio, who incorporated it in various buildings illustrated in his *Four Books on Architecture*. Later examples are found at the Palace of Versailles, for example, and in Rome at the Classically inspired Palazzo della Giustizia (completed 1911). Gilbert would certainly have seen (and probably sketched) this motif during his many European sojourns, as suggested by his use of it in several buildings.[30]

The heads over the four ground floor entrances in the Capitol are certainly prominent, and while some divinities are easily recognizable, most notably Hermes and Athena, thanks to their headgear, the identity of others is clarified only through Gilbert's memo. The overall effect, however, even to those not familiar with Greco-Roman mythology, is that of watchfulness and protection. To visitors with an understanding of mythology, and to the architect, these divinities suggest attributes of both the state and its Capitol.

While the exterior of the complex is rich with Classical references, the grand interior appears refined and restrained, despite the abundance of decorative motifs, many of which symbolize the state. The rotunda below the dome is most dramatic when one enters through the south or north doors and approaches the soaring arches that lead into the central space (see gallery 2). Stutler described the rotunda: "The interior is painted a sky blue, and from the center is suspended a gigantic chandelier weighing almost a ton, composed almost entirely out of beveled crystal."[31] This chandelier—impressive in size, weight, number of faceted crystals, and brilliant light effects—was made in Czechoslovakia and recalls old-world European elegance.[32] In shape it echoes the dome and matches the arches, unifying the commodious space. The chandelier appears larger today than it did in 1932, when it hung much higher (see figs. 68, where it is too high to be visible, and gallery 3). Lowering it has made both chandelier and the elaborate chain from which it is suspended more prominent. This sparkling sphere draws the attention of visitors as they ascend the grand exterior staircases.[33]

The floor of the rotunda on the main level is Italian travertine; the walls are of white Vermont marble. The white marble balustrade is echoed in the wrought iron railing encircling the drum, which is decorated with bronze fasces with axes. On the floor below, simple square piers create a circular colonnade, and the bases of the bronze lamps are patterned after examples discovered at Pompeii. Each is topped with a glass sphere that was originally surmounted by a bronze eagle.[34] Extensive use of white marble in both upper and lower areas of the rotunda adds to the effect of restraint and simplicity.

Although Gilbert's ultimate plan did not separate the three branches of government into individual buildings as he had at first envisioned, the complex as completed emphasizes the symbolic primacy of the largest and most democratic branch, the Legislature.[35] Located in the most desired spaces of the Capitol, on either side of the grand rotunda on the main floor, are the chambers of the Senate and House of Delegates. Their location, scale, fine materials, large vestibules, and decor speak of their functional and symbolic importance.

The marble-lined foyers anticipate the importance of the work performed in the legislative chambers (see gallery 5). Gilbert's training in the Beaux-Arts educational system at MIT included reconstructing ancient exteriors and interiors in drawings; the coffered ceilings of the foyers and the columns *in antis* that frame the chamber entrances reveal Gilbert's recreation of how the interiors of ancient Greek and Roman temples might have appeared. The Roman Doric marble columns, Vermont white marble walls, and travertine and marble inlaid floors are somber in their simplicity. Uniting the foyers with the rotunda are forty elegant lamps with black-and-gold Belgian marble pedestals and translucent Italian alabaster bowls.[36]

The metopes that alternate with triglyphs in the friezes are carved in marble in the rotunda and reproduced in plaster in the foyers; their style is based on ancient Greek models. Their symbolism refers to West Virginia's heritage and to life in the Mountain State: art and education, agriculture and industry, mining, Native American origins, peace, religion, justice, and patriotism. Some metopes are fairly obvious in their subject matter: justice with her scales, for instance, and a peace pipe and tomahawk represent the Native Americans who lived in the area that became West Virginia. The bull's head combined with ears of corn symbolizes agriculture, and pickaxes, shown with a shield, refer to mining and industry. A book with an owl, recalling Greek symbolism of the owl and Athena, goddess of wisdom, suggests the arts and education. Attributes of West Virginia are thus integrated within an ancient Greek architectural and sculptural context.

The beautiful stylized rosettes set in the coffers of the foyer ceilings and the arches of the chambers are thought to be symbolic as well. Those in the legislative arches are said to be representative of trees native to West Virginia: white pine cones appear with pine needles and gooseberry leaves, white oak leaves with acorns, and cucumber magnolia blossoms with leaves. The foyer coffers are said to depict the sugar maple, red oak, and magnolia.[37]

Each legislative chamber is graced with an identical crystal chandelier of similar brilliance to the rotunda's but more traditional in design. Bronze light fixtures

Fig. 81 (opposite). Drawings of the five designs used for the metopes of the friezes of the rotunda and legislative foyers. The motifs are drawn from West Virginia history and from antiquity. From top to bottom, they reference justice (blind, with scales and a sword), wisdom (Athena with the book and owl), agriculture (the ox and corn), and West Virginia's Native Americans (the peace pipe and tomahawk). The sequence concludes with mining and industry (the pickaxes behind the shield). Drawings by Raymond Agius.

Fig. 82. Drawing of one of the rosettes that decorate the coffers in the legislative foyers and chambers. There are many different patterns of rosettes in the coffers in the various parts of the Capitol. Drawing by Raymond Agius.

in the shape of torches on the walls are based on fasces and thus allude to unity and strength. The black walnut rostra feature the Greek key motif, rosettes, and carved fasces, some beneath eagles (see fig. 83). A clock and a seal are behind each rostrum; "Montani Semper Liberi" (Mountaineers are always free) decorates the seal of the House chamber, while in the Senate a new seal has recently replaced the original. Public galleries on three sides of each chamber are enclosed within broad arches framed with rows of decorated coffers. The arched Diocletian windows with bronze grilles in the galleries are reminiscent of those in Roman baths.

There are differences between the two legislative chambers (see gallery 6, 7). The Senate's domed skylight, for example, contrasts with the flat rectangular skylight of the House. The legislators' desks differ in number (one hundred in the House, thirty-four in the Senate), allowing the senators' desks to be larger. Two rows of wooden, carved coffers grace the arched openings into the Senate galleries, while a single row of plaster coffers is found in the House.

The area dedicated to the judicial branch, on the third floor of the East Wing, is distinctive.[38] Practical reasons dictate a smaller area; there are only five judges, and thus fewer requirements for space and staff. When one approaches the Supreme Court of Appeals, there is little indication of its importance; there is no grand foyer, the hallway is relatively narrow, and the materials are modest. Wood rather than bronze surrounds the elevators, and while some areas of the walls are lined with marble, others are of painted plaster. The chamber itself, however, is impressive in design, materials, and decor (see fig. 53). The ceiling decoration is Classical: a Greek key pattern surrounds the skylight and separates the coffers into groups of four; each coffer is decorated with a sun with sixteen rays, another motif from antiquity. Symbolism reflects the nature of the court: bronze reliefs of the scale and balance and the book of law are placed in the recessed sides of the rectangular, stained-glass skylight. Quotations chosen by Gilbert decorate the frieze: "The true foundation of republican government is the equal right of every citizen in his person and property and in their management" (Thomas Jefferson, *Notes on the State of Virginia*) and "Firmness in the right as God gives us to see the right" (Abraham Lincoln, Second Inaugural Address).[39] These are inspirational messages from two great lawyers with important connections to the state. Jefferson, whose father Peter Jefferson helped to survey western Virginia for the 1751 Fry-Jefferson map, served as governor of Virginia before the division that led to the establishment of West Virginia, while it was Lincoln who, after much internal debate, proclaimed West Virginia's statehood.

Monolithic unfluted Ionic columns of Danby Vermont white marble with black Belgian marble bases line three sides of the chamber; the walls are of the same Vermont marble, while dark green Vermont marble forms the steps that lead to the rostrum. The restrained Classical elegance establishes the somber importance of the court. While in some Supreme Court chambers a low bar divides the justices from the public, the absence of such a barrier here, it is said, was intended to emphasize that nothing stands between the people and the highest state court.

Fig. 83. Fasces and eagles on the rostrum of the Senate (see also fig. 71). Photograph by Thorney Lieberman.

It has long been recognized that Gilbert modeled the chamber for the United States Supreme Court in Washington on the courtroom he had designed for West Virginia's highest court: the two chambers are nearly identical, with rows of impressive columns on three sides.[40] Where West Virginia's chamber has inscriptions, the higher chamber in Washington allows for a sculpted frieze.[41] In both courts, the justices enter simultaneously from behind curtains, a ritual apparently invented by Gilbert.[42]

Gilbert based his design for the two main areas dedicated to the executive branch, the governor's reception room and office (see gallery 8, figs. 84–85), on domestic and public interiors of the Colonial period.[43] The intimate scale and predominance of wood in these rooms signal spaces that are distinct from the rest of the Capitol, although the Classical traditions seen throughout the rest of the complex are not completely dismissed; note, for example, the triglyphs and metopes of the Doric frieze in the reception room. Gilbert identified the style of the rooms: "The interior of the Governor's reception room, forming part of the Governor's suite, is of so-called Colonial or Georgian type of architecture, furnished with appropriate carpets, draperies, and furniture."[44] The nearby governor's mansion is also Colonial, creating a stylistic unification that is surely intentional. The location of the governor's suite on the ground floor at the west end of the Main Building, at the nearest point to the mansion, also connects these areas of executive power. The interrelated style of the mansion and the governor's suite in the Capitol can be understood as a reference to West Virginia's origin in the Old Dominion and is an indication of Gilbert's sensitivity to regional American styles.

Gilbert described the governor's private office as having "American walnut paneled walls with walnut furniture and harmonizing carpet and draperies. An ornamental plaster ceiling completes in a satisfactory manner the furnishings of these two rooms."[45] While the reception room was painted white, a typical Colonial practice used to disguise the fact that the paneling and details were made from mismatched woods, the more exclusive and intimate space of the private office is paneled in choice hardwood with matching furniture.

Portraits of West Virginia's governors hang in the ground floor corridor that leads from the lower rotunda toward the reception room, as Gilbert recommended: "corridor no. 6 would be an appropriate place for the portraits of the governors as it is the corridor which connects the reception room, the governor's office and the office of the board of public works."[46] Portraits of past governors also hang in the reception room.

The paintings in quite a different mode that decorate the ceilings of the first-floor corridors of the East and West Wings demonstrate the often unnoticed distinction in style between the Wings and the Main Building. The paintings in the wings depict winged female figures carrying branches or sheaves of wheat against a neutral ground. Similar figures found in ancient frescoes in the ruins of Pompeii inspired paintings at the Library of Congress and the United States Capitol.[47] The shades of tan and brown that predominate in the figures and the accompanying stenciling match the rather

Fig. 84. Governor's reception room, c. 1950. In less than two decades, the décor of the reception room had been changed. Gilbert Family Collection, Gift to the WVSA. For a view of the reception room as originally furnished, see Damron, p. 81. For a view of the room today, see gallery 8.

dark Tennessee marble on the walls below; this is in contrast to the white marble corridors that connect these hallways with those of the Main Building. This rather startling distinction is probably the result of changing tastes between the early 1920s and 1931. Another distinction is found in the coffer decorations of the entrance halls of the wings. They are more highly decorated than the coffers of the rotunda, legislative foyers, and House and Senate chambers in the Main Building; in addition, the designs in the wings are emphasized with varied colors of paint. Depicting shells, lively dolphins, cornucopias, and a variety of elaborate floral motifs, they are closer to the observer because of the lower ceiling height. These motifs are less geometric than the large rosettes that decorate the coffers in the Main Building, which are so stylized that it is difficult to identify the various flowers they are said to represent.

Despite the wealth of symbolism in the complex, from the dome with its references to Roman military power and American democracy to the decorative coffers depicting native trees, the Capitol is incomplete. Gilbert addressed the missing elements: "There are certain things which should be done to complete the Main Building and the grounds. The sculpture in the pediments ... are essential to the completion of the exterior design. Mural decorations of an adequate character should embellish the rotunda and the House and Senate."[48] A drawing of the rotunda reveals murals on the walls and sculptures planned for the niches.

In 1932, Stutler reacted to the unfinished nature of the capitol: "When accepted by the Capitol Commission and dedicated to the use of the State forever, the building seems completed to the casual observer, and yet it is unfinished." He elaborated: "There are niches to be filled with statues of the great of West Virginia and of the nation, and walls that may some day bear great mural paintings illustrating the history, art, culture, industry and commerce of the Mountain State. That work will be carried on for generations."[49] His comments suggest that the incompleteness did not require immediate attention. This project could span time, the missing elements could be added, and the Capitol could continue to be enhanced. In 1931, in the midst of praise for the new building, a writer for the *Charleston Daily Mail* addressed the issue of decoration: "West Virginians have in their capitol one of the finest buildings in the country. No state, however wealthy, has a finer one and few one so fine, when one considers the beauty of the classic style, so admirably suited for public buildings ... where proportion counts more than ornament," adding: "Not that ornament does not have its place, but ornament in restraint and in good taste wears longer than an excess of it."[50]

The Capitol's architectural sculpture that is complete—including the mythological heads, the fasces and eagles, and West Virginia's native trees—is symbolic but not representative of state history. While pedimental sculptures and some murals would probably have contributed allegory, others could have narrated specific events.

The topic of mural paintings is especially interesting. When Gilbert presented an award to painter Edwin Blashfield nearly two years after the Capitol's dedication, he noted: "When the great Exposition in Chicago in 1893 occurred, Burnham and his associate architects made mural painting a notable feature of the great Fair,

Fig. 85. Governor's private office, c. 1950. For a view of the Governor's office in 1932, see Damron, p. 81. The andirons and fireplace set seen here were designed by Cass Gilbert. Gilbert Family Collection.

and a remarkable group of American artists rose to the occasion."[51] Subsequently, mural painting by major artists became enormously popular. In the case of West Virginia's Capitol, correspondence allows us to glean information about the intended painted references to the state's history, the process of choosing painters, and the socio-economic issues of the time. For instance, on January 6, 1922, Cass Gilbert wrote to Commissioner Keatley: "I am delighted to know that you like the Detroit Public Library [designed by Gilbert]. I wish you could see Blashfield's beautiful pictures which are yet to be placed in the grand stairway. They are approaching completion and will be a superb addition to the work." Referring to his hopes for West Virginia, he added: "We must see to it that in the new Capitol there will be some fine examples of mural decoration and sculpture."[52]

In his 1934 presentation to Blashfield, Gilbert announced: "Blashfield, LaFarge, Simmons, Kenyon Cox ... joined in making a splendid series of mural decorations and gave fresh impetus to this noble art. Public appreciation and approval were instant and outspoken. Iowa, Wisconsin, and, later Missouri and Nebraska followed, until no new public building in the Middle West was regarded as complete unless it were adorned with splendid mural paintings." He concluded: "The movement continued in the Eastern States, and the Capitol of Harrisburg provided new splendors of mural painting in historic subjects by Edwin Abbey, and that genius among women painters Violet Oakley."[53] Gilbert insisted on quality: "There is nothing so valueless as poor art, and nothing so ephemeral as passing fashions in art. Therefore, what is to be done should be done by competent and serious artists of proved ability and in accordance with the highest standards of established good taste."[54] A number of artists interested in producing murals for the West Virginia Capitol came forward, as did their patrons. William de Leftwich Dodge, for example, wrote Gilbert on May 26, 1930: "Could you not find it possible to let me do a mural decoration in the West Virginia State Capitol you are building. Being a Virginian I feel very interested and would be proud to have something down there."[55] The request was followed by a long list of his works, including the dome of the administration building for the 1893 World's Fair in Chicago.

Mrs. Homer Wilson of Charleston wrote to Gilbert on June 4, 1930: "I was in to see Governor Conley this morning and he suggested that I write you in regard to mural decoration to be used in the new Capitol Building in Charleston ... I see by a resolution unanimously adopted by the Capitol Building Commission, that they expect to use state's material as much as possible, so would think they would be most willing to use their local talent." She made a specific recommendation: "I represent Joseph Hugo of this city and would say that his work is excellent. He has lived fifteen years in Paris and studied at École Des Beaux Arts under Bonnat. He has painted extensively in Pittsburgh PA and was teacher for five years in Carnegie School of Technology ... I would think [him] better than most ... and also cheaper, since he lives in the city of Charleston."[56] On June 6, Gilbert responded to Mrs. Wilson: "Your letter of June 4 is at hand. Replying thereto I would say that there is no provision for mural decoration in the State Capitol at Charleston at the

Fig. 86. Cass Gilbert/Studio, Rendering of the rotunda of the West Virginia Capitol as published in *The American Architect* in 1929. This drawing suggests how the rotunda might have looked with the addition of mural and sculptural decoration.

ALL OF THE TIME INSCRIPTION TO BE PLACED

present time. Your letter will be placed on file and given careful consideration if the matter comes up later on."[57]

From the offices of Cram and Ferguson came another letter, not involving local talent: "Mr. Smeraldi of Los Angeles has asked me for a letter of introduction to you and I am really very glad to give it. I have seen Smeraldi's work in Los Angeles and it really is most admirable."[58] Smeraldi himself had already composed a letter on July 17, 1931, to Mr. Rockart: "Mr. L. E. Lamb of NY . . . wrote me that he had the occasion of a talk with you about the decoration of the West Virginia State Capitol, which interested me very much. I could give you reference from every leading architect in New York City, and I could refer you to a long list of buildings decorated by me all over the United States and out of it. I would appreciate it if you could give me an opportunity on the decoration of the Capitol."[59]

Historical and allegorical depictions are not a part of the Capitol, and representation of the state's complex and sometimes controversial history is missing. The absence of both murals and pedimental sculpture reflects the state's economic situation in the early 1930s, which, although the scale and elegance of the Capitol suggest otherwise, was becoming more dire. By the time the Main Building was completed, approximately one in four workers in the United States was unemployed and a severe drought in West Virginia in 1931 further weakened the state's economic condition.[60] Today, aesthetic and financial debate continues with regard to the addition of murals and sculpture, further indication of the vital relationship between West Virginians and their Capitol.[61]

While Gilbert hoped that the West Virginia Capitol would include sculpture and mural decoration, by calling these elements "additions" he indicated his understanding that they would not be completed when the building was finished in 1932. Had they been included, the state's symbolism would have been even more overt. Pedimental sculpture would have added allegory and changed the appearance of the building's exterior, rendering it more ornate. Mural paintings in the rotunda and legislative chambers would have created a vastly different decorative effect while adding specific historical and cultural symbolism. More sculpture in the round, placed within the still empty niches, could have highlighted specific individuals important to West Virginia history.[62]

Even without the planned "additions" of sculpture and murals, Cass Gilbert's West Virginia Capitol expresses its meaning and purpose architecturally and symbolically. The Classical style and the foundation of the design in the National Capitol model communicate the democratic content, while specific references to West Virginia in the decoration honor the state's heritage and richness. In an article composed three years before the dedication, Gilbert wrote that a state capitol is "an inspiration toward patriotism and good citizenship, it encourages just pride in the state and is an education to on-coming generations to see these things, imponderable elements of life and character, set before the people for their enjoyment and betterment." The importance of symbolism for the West Virginia Capitol is evident in Gilbert's words that a state Capitol is "a symbol of the civilization, culture and ideals of our country."[63]

## SCULPTURE ON THE GROUNDS AT THE TIME OF THE DEDICATION

It is common for state capitol grounds to become repositories for war memorials and commemorations for noted individuals connected with the state's history, and the West Virginia Capitol is no exception. At Charleston, the oldest sculpture is a bronze statue of the Confederate general Thomas J. "Stonewall" Jackson, which was dedicated at the previous Capitol in 1910 and moved to the new grounds in 1926, while the complex was still under construction. The inscription indicates that this figure was "Erected as a Memorial to the Confederate Soldiers" by the "Charleston Chapter No. 151 United Daughters of the Confederacy," who had petitioned the Senate and House of Delegates for permission to erect it in honor of West Virginians who fought in the Confederate army. Permission was granted in 1905 and the figure was commissioned from sculptor Moses Ezekiel, who had it cast in Italy.[64]

In contrast to this Confederate commemoration, *A Mountaineer* is dedicated to "the hallowed memories of the brave men and devoted women who saved West Virginia to the Union." This bronze figure honors the Home Guards, who began to fight on the Union side in 1861, two years before West Virginia was recognized as a state. Sculpted by Henry Kirke Bush-Brown, it was placed at the previous Capitol in 1912 and later moved to the new grounds.[65]

One proposed monument was never erected on the new Capitol grounds. On April 24, 1922, the Lions Club of Charleston resolved that the "stone pillars and arches forming the main entrance" of the old Capitol be moved to the grounds of the new Capitol as "the best and most appropriate way of preserving this treasured and splendid piece of architecture for the people of the state of West Virginia. This relic of early days so appealing in sentiment and tradition will not only be well preserved in this way but will prove not an uninteresting piece of architecture for the new Capitol grounds." This proved to be impossible because, as the reply to their resolution reveals, "all the material on the Capitol grounds, including the arch forming the main entrance, has been sold to the Allen Construction Company."[66]

*The Union Soldier* (Union Soldiers and Sailors Monument) by Roy H. Stewart was dedicated on Memorial Day, 1930, after the 1927 Legislature established the Soldiers and Sailors Memorial Commission.[67] Cass Gilbert was unsuccessful in his attempt to prevent this sculpture from being placed on the grounds, even though he argued "it did not have artistic lines and was not in keeping with his grand design."[68] The monument is dedicated "to the 32,000 soldiers, sailors and marines, contributed by West Virginia to the Union—1861 to 1865."[69]

*West Virginia State Capitol and Kanawha Boulevard, Charleston, W. Va.* 2B-H779

# CHAPTER NINE

# Cass Gilbert's West Virginia Capitol in Context

We are the trustees of a great tradition, let us preserve and develop it.

Cass Gilbert, responding to a letter from William E. Harmon, April 2, 1923

Fig. 87. "West Virginia State Capitol and Kanawha Boulevard," as seen in a postcard mailed from Poca, WV, in 1947.

THE CITY ON THE KANAWHA IS SMALL, THE HILLS ROLLING—green in the warm months, brilliantly colored in the fall, white in winter. Commanding the landscape along the river in every season is the glittering dome that crowns Cass Gilbert's West Virginia State Capitol. Our study of this building and its architect, which began with the intrigue surrounding Gilbert's appointment, has followed the project through to its completion. In conclusion, it is useful to reflect upon some of the issues raised throughout: how and why is the West Virginia Capitol both traditional and exceptional in the history of American state capitol design? Does this timeless example of Classicism also reflect the broader history of the period? How does it fit within the trajectory of Gilbert's work? Does it respond to the challenge of Modernism? A comparison with four other state capitols designed and built in approximately the same time period addresses this last issue and clarifies the place the West Virginia complex holds in the continuum of architectural history.

At the time of his appointment in 1921, when he was sixty years old, Cass Gilbert anticipated the position the West Virginia Capitol would hold in the chronology of his works: "I want to make this capitol building the crowning work of my life. It is the type of building to which I have devoted the past 25 years of my life, and I feel that the opportunity is now presented to me for a splendid architectural monument." The West Virginia Capitol, however, was quickly overshadowed by his US Supreme Court Building. Julia Finch Gilbert noted that after her husband received this new commission, "all of his thoughts and most of his time were occupied with perfecting the design he had conceived for the Supreme Court Building."[1] Nevertheless, Gilbert's determination and organization allowed him to continue to give attention to other major commissions, among them the West Virginia Capitol, the Federal Courthouse on Foley Square (1929–36), and the American Embassy in Ottawa (1928–32).

Both the US Supreme Court Building and the West Virginia State Capitol express the enduring values of Classicism in design and symbolism. But while the Supreme Court Building is based on ancient temple designs, the model for the West Virginia Capitol is an American "classic": the National Capitol. The decorative scheme Gilbert devised for its dome, however, has no American parallel. For this most prominent and glorious element, Gilbert combined ancient Roman military motifs with symbols of American democracy, surmounted the dome with the fasces—expressing strength in unity—and topped the whole with the American eagle, wings outspread. While the aesthetic and decorative impact of West Virginia's dome is self-evident, it is also possible that there might be a historical rationale. Gilbert was a notable patriot, and perhaps his choices can be related to the poignancy of this particular moment in our history: he chose these particular military and patriotic motifs for the dome shortly after America had played a leading role in suppressing threats to democracy in Europe. Indeed, the Capitol as a whole might be considered an appropriate response to the traumas of the second decade of the twentieth century, for its calm monumentality can be interpreted as reassuring and its stability suggests the enduring nature of traditional values.

The simplicity and restraint of the West Virginia complex is especially evident when it is compared to his Minnesota Capitol (see figs. 1, 13). At Charleston Gilbert chose to leave behind much of the Beaux-Arts elaboration he preferred when he designed the earlier capitol. This was recognized as early as 1934, when a critic wrote that Gilbert's first capitol represented "the exuberance of his vigorous youth, as contrasted with the mature strength and dignity shown by his later design for the West Virginia Capitol."[2] Maturity of the architect may certainly play a role in the explanation, as may the response to World War I.

Other historical factors might also help to explain the distinctive appearance of the West Virginia Capitol. Given the period, financial impacts must be considered. Our examination of the project's financing demonstrated the role partisan politics, fueled by the local news media, played in delaying the project and requiring its redesign. Some restraint in design was most likely a result of these criticisms. In the later phases of the project, the unstable global economy must also have played a role in restricting elaboration. Despite political standoffs and economic difficulties, however, West Virginia's Capitol is magnificent: gold leaf, marble, bronze, richly appointed chambers, and elaborate coffers with rosettes abound. Only the absence of details—murals, sculpture in the pediments, decorative motifs between the windows of the wings, and terraces with balustrades framing the base of the building—speak to the economic distress that was pervasive by the time the complex was dedicated.

Modernism must also be examined in discussing the style of Gilbert's West Virginia Capitol, which was identified by Hitchcock and Seale as "the requiem for American Renaissance capitols" because it was the last example in a long and vigorous tradition in state capitol design.[3] Already in 1927, an article in the *Architect's Journal* criticized Gilbert's reliance on traditional motifs: "With rapid changes taking place in the forms of design one might have expected to see Mr. Gilbert carried forward in an endeavour to outshine the daring designs of younger architects now rising. But this was not so. . . . He still prefers to rely on the established form of pilasters, columns, and entablatures . . . while another designer might feel himself impelled to try something extraordinary."[4] The opinion that only by eliminating the Classical could an architect of the period attempt to be "extraordinary" must not affect our assessment of how the West Virginia Capitol fits into the continuum of architectural development. Despite Gilbert's stated lack of interest in the modernist movement, the simplicity with which he interpreted Classical forms in all three buildings of the West Virginia complex parallels certain qualities found in the architecture of Frank Lloyd Wright and International style architects. Had the program of murals and pedimental sculptures that Gilbert envisioned been realized, the overall effect of the West Virginia Capitol would, of course, have been different, but it still would have been distinct from the Beaux-Arts enthusiasm demonstrated in his Minnesota Capitol. Certain decorative elements in Charleston have a notable simplicity: the unfluted columns of the porticoes and porches, the square columns of the ground floor rotunda colonnade, and the bold geometric forms of the staircase railings in the Doric vestibule. The manner in which the details of the sculpted heads of the entrance arches are distanced from Classical idealism as they approach the bolder geometricized forms of the Art Deco style suggests Gilbert's willingness to accept certain aspects of Modernism; the same style seems to have pervaded the designs for the metopes of the rotunda (see fig. 81). The simplicity of these forms sets Cass Gilbert's final capitol apart from his earlier and more elaborate structures, including the Minnesota Capitol, the US Custom House, and the Essex County Courthouse, even though it remains firmly ensconced within the Greco-Roman tradition. Another influence may also be at work, for at least one West Virginia commissioner stated his preference that the Capitol be based on "a simple design with proper proportion" and that it should impress through "simplicity rather than ornament."[5] These words, echoing Gilbert's ideas, indicate that the architect was not the sole voice advocating simplicity and good proportion.

Another connection between Gilbert and Modernism can be made through his use of new materials at West Virginia, including Vitrolite in some restrooms, compressed cork floors for the Supreme Court chamber and conference rooms, and copper-coated lead to seal the exterior of the dome. All of these exemplify his interest in new structural and material developments.[6] Gilbert's use of these innovative materials is consistent with his early practice; the Woolworth Building was praised for Gilbert's incorporation of new technology into the structure.

Among the modernists whose styles challenged Gilbert's traditionalism were Frank Lloyd Wright, Walter Burley Griffin and Marion Mahony Griffin, Paul Cret (whose Folger Shakespeare Library in Washington of 1929–32 signaled his move from the Beaux-Arts toward the modern), William Van Alen of Chrysler Building fame, and Raymond Hood, whose journey from Gothic to Art Deco can be seen in his Chicago Tribune Tower (1924, in partnership with John Mead Howells) and Rockefeller Center (1932–37). European masters including Eliel Saarinen, Mies van der Rohe, Walter Gropius, and Le Corbusier influenced American architecture, some after emigrating for political, economic, or religious reasons.[7] One new modernist development was the emergence of highly personal styles. Over time this self-assertion, hand in hand with continued technological innovation, would give us buildings such as Richard Meier's Getty Museum, Rem Koolhaas's Seattle Public Library, and Frank Gehry's Guggenheim Museum and New York residential skyscraper on Spruce Street (completed 2011), which has been interpreted as enhancing, not diminishing, its neighbor, Gilbert's Woolworth Building.

The modernist aesthetic that affected the appearance and construction of many types of buildings—residential, ecclesiastical, purely functional, and public, including state capitols—was not to be ignored. West Virginia's new Capitol can be compared with contemporary capitols being designed and erected in Nebraska, Louisiana, North Dakota, and Oregon that exemplify the emergence of modern public architecture (see figs. 88–91). They illustrate the changing context in which Gilbert was working at the close of his career; while he personally chose to adhere to the Classical tradition, the architects of these capitols moved away from the eclecticism that had characterized American architecture since its inception.

Bertram Goodhue's Nebraska Capitol, for example, is vastly different from Gilbert's complex; as Hitchcock and Seale summarize: "Long before the West Virginia Capitol was finished, the architectural symbols of American democracy had cast off their heavy Renaissance cloak and begun to try new costumes. The first monument of the new era of capitol building sprang up on the agricultural plains of Nebraska." Nebraska's 350-foot tower, visible for up to 40 miles, dominates its prairie landscape in a way that no traditional dome could have done. In Goodhue's departure from the National Capitol model, he simultaneously harked back to the Gothic and turned to contemporary European models. While Goodhue's building at first glance seems far removed from other state capitols, it provides a transition between the Classical domed capitol type and the three examples that can be termed "skyscraper capitols." Rather than being designed to provide extensive office space, the primary purpose of Goodhue's slender tower was to create visual impact by establishing a distinctive silhouette for the complex. Its summit is crowned with an octagonal lantern and vestigial dome, which in turn is surmounted by a sculpture of *The Sower*.[8]

Goodhue continued the Beaux-Arts tradition in his concept of the "harmony of the arts," in which architectural-artistic collaboration resulted in an elaborate unity of symbolic representation. Goodhue worked with an iconographer who selected themes and coordinated the artists who produced sculptures, paintings, and mosaics. The artistic and iconographic complexity of the Nebraska Capitol kept alive the Beaux-Arts decorative tradition despite the lack of specifically Classical elements. The themes, far from pertaining only to state history and democratic ideals, embrace humanity and history. Two predominate: the history of law (represented mainly on the exterior) and the relationship of civilization to the natural world, with specific reference to Nebraska (most of which is represented inside). This symbolism encompasses centuries of history as it pertains to the state and the world.

When Gilbert was beginning work on the West Virginia complex, then, Goodhue was designing a capitol that was both traditional and innovative, particularly in a design created specifically for its plains topography. Like Gilbert, Goodhue planned the inclusion of other arts and themes that would enhance the meaning of the building. Unlike Gilbert, and with the guidance of a collaborating iconographer, Goodhue created a Capitol that was both distinctly Nebraskan and worldly, with its history of law: Lee Lawrie's sculpted figures of lawgivers, from Hammurabi to Akhenaten and Julius Caesar to Napoleon, connect Nebraska to the works of great men throughout history. The Nebraska Capitol thus recognizes the intellectual development of mankind as well as the people of its own state.[9]

Nebraska's Capitol announced the trend away from the National Capitol model, with its dramatic but expensive and space-consuming dome, toward the efficient

Fig. 88. Nebraska State Capitol, 1920–32, by Bertram Goodhue, as seen in an undated period postcard. The text on the reverse reads: "The Capitol of Nebraska, designed by the late Bertram Goodhue, is one of the most dignified and imposing public buildings that have been erected in this country. It is gravely simple; its style is essentially its own; it perfectly fulfills its purposes, and it symbolizes to Nebraskans and to succeeding generations the people's idea of government, of statehood."

skyscraper. Concerns more practical than symbolic were emerging: functionality and space utilization are better served by designs that do not leave vast open areas, no matter how inspiring and potentially useful for large gatherings.[10]

In 1928, as the West Virginia and Nebraska Capitols were under way, Governor Huey Long was advocating a new State House for Louisiana. Dedicated in March 1932, Louisiana's Capitol is a 450-foot-tall skyscraper. The windows announcing the practical function of the symbolic tower's interior space, however, produce an effect different from the verticality that de-emphasized the windows at the Nebraska Capitol. Sculptures, friezes, and murals represent the state's history, flora, and fauna. While the overall design asserts Modernism, then, traditional iconography connects this Capitol to its predecessors.

Another skyscraper capitol, that of North Dakota, resembles a commercial building even more closely because the rather heavy proportions of its tower signal an overtly functional structure rather than one that might be considered primarily ornamental or symbolic. This Capitol, with its nineteen-story tower, was erected between 1931 and 1934 despite the financial straits of the Depression. Because the economic situation led to modification of the intended exterior decoration, it has an even more commercial appearance than originally planned.[11] The lack of symmetry also signifies the departure of this building's design from those of Classical or Beaux-Arts style as well as from that of Goodhue's Nebraska Capitol.

One further contemporary capitol should be mentioned, although it cannot be included among the group of skyscraper capitols just discussed. Oregon's State Capitol, like so many others, is reminiscent of the National Capitol in its design, with a raised central element and broad flanking wings. Rather than the traditional dome, however, the exterior focal point is a cylindrical drum that supports a colossal gilded sculpture, *The Pioneer*. On the interior, however, the large dome that is encased in the exterior drum defines a rotunda that includes murals and sculpture. The impact of Modernism is evident in the unremittingly Art Deco style of architectural forms and decorative motifs.[12]

The three skyscraper capitols, while not negating all traditional architectural elements, stand apart from the popular National Capitol model—still followed by Oregon despite its overt Art Deco nature—as they look to the future.[13] Gilbert, who had chosen not to explore such alternatives, remained rooted in the tradition and styles that had served him and his country so well. In contrast to the now outdated Modernism of the four contemporary capitols, the Classicism of Cass Gilbert's West Virginia complex is timeless. While various styles have changed and will continue to change the architectural face of the United States, Classical forms will surely continue to exert their authority and to represent the country; the buildings represented on the currency and coinage that we use every day are almost exclusively Classical in style. Gilbert excelled in designing public buildings that, rather than forging into new realms of design, are resplendent with memories of grand architecture and cultures, as well as steadfast in their message of moral authority.

Fig. 89. Louisiana State Capitol, 1930–32, by Weiss, Dreyfous & Seiferth of New Orleans, as seen in a period postcard. The text on the back identifies it as "the tallest building in the south." The Louisiana Capitol was constructed by the George A. Fuller Company, contractors for the West Wing and Main Building of the West Virginia complex.

Fig. 90. North Dakota State Capitol, 1931–34, by Chicago-based John A. Holabird and John W. Root (with Joseph Bell DeRemer and W. F. Kurke, both of North Dakota, as associates), as seen in a period postcard. The text on the reverse describes the Capitol as "of latest architectural design."

Fig. 91. Oregon State Capitol, 1936–38, by Francis Keally, in conjunction with the New York firm of Trowbridge and Livingston, as seen in a period postcard.

Fig. 92. West Virginia State Capitol, as seen in a period postcard. This ideal rendering shows the impressive north façade from a distance but without the houses and apartment buildings along Washington Street that would have blocked such a view.

On the first page of the *Charleston Gazette* on June 19, 1932, a commentary expressed the heightened emotions expected on dedication day: "To get the thing of charm and beauty that is the state capitol of today is worth the years of waiting. For we say without fear of contradiction that there is no finer, no lovelier state capitol ... than that which belongs to West Virginia today." The *Gazette* urged every citizen to "feel a swell of pride as he looks at that impressive and noble, yet simple, structure ... It is our capitol. Make yourself acquainted with its beauties. Sense the genius that has made it harmonious while apparently different in every corner." Visit the interior and "go to the supreme court chamber and know the dignity that architecture can build into a room. Above all get the whole feeling of spacious beauty that is so evident throughout the capitol. Use it; it is yours. That is what it was built for."

Interest in the Capitol's well-being continues. West Virginians voted to return the dome's decoration to Gilbert's original concept, for instance, a decision that illustrates both public engagement and dedication to historical tradition. His complex serves West Virginia's populace well and, in turn, it fosters pride.

The architect's own words provide a fitting closing. He was writing in 1923 in response to a letter from William E. Harmon, a philanthropist who was using the pseudonym Jedediah Tingle. Harmon had praised Gilbert for his achievement in the Woolworth Building and had enclosed a gift of five dollars to honor Gilbert's professional success. The architect returned the money, which he considered "a souvenir more valuable than the books you suggest it would purchase." Gilbert urged Tingle to:

> Give [the money] to some young writer, painter, sculptor, musician or architect who may need it and thus let it serve its purpose twice. There are young men and women in the art schools and in the music schools, or who are writing for the newspapers and magazines to whom a word of encouragement will go very far. Let one of them have it, especially if it goes with a word of appreciation for some serious, earnest, sensible thing they may have done or said. Such an act may influence for good a lifetime of effort yet to come. Select such a one who is not radical in his tendencies, who is content to build on the foundation of our civilization and not [one who] in a spirit of restless ... criticism is attempting to destroy it. We are the trustees of a great tradition, let us preserve and develop it. I do not believe that progress is made by destruction, and if those who write with the facility obviously yours will encourage the young to build up not tear down, we may hope for sane progress and renewal of beauty in life and in art in this good old world which we have inherited from our forefathers.[14]

CODA

# Appreciating the West Virginia State Capitol

THE WEST VIRGINIA CAPITOL CAN BE APPRECIATED IN MANY ways. Foremost, of course, we admire the impression of strength and elegance it makes as a building. The hills of the Mountain State complement the dome, while the flowing Kanawha emphasizes the Capitol's breadth. When the river is calm, a reflection enhances the building's symmetry and balance.

The Capitol was intended to convey to a nation founded on democracy that West Virginia is the equal of other states, even those of greater size and wealth, larger populations, and longer histories. Its completion during the Great Depression demonstrated the determination of West Virginians to have the Capitol envisioned in 1921; not even an international economic crisis could prevent the fulfillment of this plan. We appreciate the Capitol even more when we are reminded that circumstances could so easily have derailed its construction.

The Capitol Building Commission's choice of Cass Gilbert as architect was almost certainly based on the desire for the new West Virginia Capitol to follow the National Capitol model, as had so many others. Gilbert gave them something more; by decorating the dome with patriotic and other motifs highlighted in gold, he created a Capitol that is distinctive, unlike that of any other state.

Creating a public building is a political act. West Virginia's Capitol came into being only after scuffles between Democrats and Republicans and skirmishes that engaged the executive and legislative branches. Democracy is difficult, but the Capitol's completion illuminates the process and confirms the success of the American way.

Studying the Capitol brings us into contact with West Virginia's governors, legislators, newspaper editors, and members of the public. Contemporary documents re-create the experiences of those who planned the Capitol as they recount the selection of architect and site and record the design process, legislative debates, financial solutions, and the progress of construction.

The Capitol also connects us with the trajectory of world history. References to ancient Greece remind us of the traditional sources of democracy, while motifs and materials inspired by the grand structures of ancient Rome suggest the dignity of American government. Gilbert's building brings to Charleston the art and architecture of the ancient Greeks and Romans, Renaissance masters, and later periods: as we explore the Capitol, we confront the impact of the Parthenon and the Pantheon as well as the domes of the Cathedral of Florence, St. Peter's Basilica in Rome, St. Paul's Cathedral in London, and the Hôtel National des Invalides in Paris.

Studying the Capitol and its history encourages an appreciation for Cass Gilbert, who with the Commission created a monument that would draw national attention and bring respect to West Virginia. Reading his telegrams, letters, and diaries illuminates the creativity, professionalism, and sound business practices of one of the giants of American architecture.

While the fashion for Modernism led scholars to neglect the Capitol for decades, the respect of the state's governors, legislators, and citizens for the building seems seldom to have waned. As Gilbert recognized, Classicism endures; it is a style that civilization returns to often for designs, motifs, and inspiration.

The West Virginia Capitol demonstrates how a public building can express the power, unity, and stability of a state. On a more personal level, its refined details, magnificent materials, and carefully controlled proportions convey a traditional vision of harmony and beauty to visitor and citizen alike.

Fig. 93. View of the West Virginia Capitol at night. Photograph by O. Palsson.

EPILOGUE

# The Capitol Complex after 1932

*Chad N. Proudfoot*

Fig. 94. The Capitol with parking around the U-shaped plaza; fountain based on design by Cass Gilbert; photograph c. 1950. Gilbert Family Collection.

As someone who has loved and admired the West Virginia State Capitol for many years, I view it as an honor to have been invited to prepare this summary of the architectural development of and sculptural additions to the complex made in the years since Cass Gilbert created his masterpiece on Kanawha Boulevard.

The Capitol and its grounds were always meant to be a living place, and Cass Gilbert recognized this. Some changes and additions he probably would have approved. Others, no doubt, he would have seen as slights.

The years following the Capitol's 1932 dedication saw changing trends in society and government as well as architecture. You have read about the Capitol's completion during the Great Depression, which was followed by the Second World War, when resources were devoted to fighting the Axis and not to domestic building concerns. As West Virginia emerged from the war with the rest of the nation, its government was much larger than when the Capitol opened its doors, and postwar technological advances were rapidly changing society. One development that had immediate effects on the Capitol was the increasing availability of automobiles.

The first major changes at the Capitol in the postwar boom, then, were those that enabled everyone to have easier personal access to West Virginia's seat of government. In 1946 parking was made available along the loop running inside the U shape created by the Capitol and its wings from Washington Street. Also, at this time, the installation of the circular fountain and walkways designed by Gilbert (see fig. 64) began the landscaping of the site, which had been his long-term intention.

The growth of state government required additional space for agencies and offices, and once laborers and materials became available in the late 1940s the Legislature provided funds for more office space. The Capitol Building Commission, which had hired Cass Gilbert and supervised the construction of the main buildings, had passed into history once its original mandate had been completed. Thus, a new State Office Building Commission was created to oversee the erection of a new office building.

By this time, Cass Gilbert had died, but the admiration West Virginians felt for him had not diminished. His architectural firm was again retained by the state, and in 1945 Cass Gilbert Jr. was commissioned to design the first addition to the Capitol complex. Known as the New State Office Building, State Office Building 3, or the Motor Vehicles Building (for its primary first-floor occupant), this eight-story structure was built across Washington Street near the end of the West Wing of the Capitol. The new building was planned not to compete with the design of the Capitol, but to complement it. Opening in 1951, the Motor Vehicles Building has as its most decorative element terra cotta reliefs over the main doors. In one relief, the *Spirit of West Virginia*—represented as a standing female figure—is surrounded by six scenes representing the state's agricultural and industrial heritage. The second relief shows a winged wheel—a reference to the Department of Motor Vehicles—superimposed on a map of the state; Charleston is marked by a miniature representation of Cass Gilbert's Capitol.

Fig. 95. "State Office Building Number Three," by Cass Gilbert Jr., 1949–51, as seen in a postcard mailed from Charleston in 1956. The caption on the back states: "The building is of concrete-encased steel finished with granite and limestone and provides 200,000 square feet of air conditioned office space, 275 rooms." It does not name the architect.

Fig. 96. The Capitol complex, as seen in a period postcard, c. 1960. The dark brown building in the upper right is Building Number 2, a parking garage designed by Cass Gilbert Jr. It opened in 1953 and was demolished fifty years later. The lighter brown building below it is Building Number Four, which opened in 1954.

At the same time, Cass Gilbert Jr. was also commissioned to design and construct the Capitol's first parking structure. Located at the corner of Washington Street and California Avenue, this garage, which became known as Building 2, was said to be one of the first continuous-pour concrete structures in the state. It opened in 1953.

The completion of these structures marked the end of the two Cass Gilbert eras of the Capitol. After the parking garage, there would be no further buildings designed by Cass Gilbert Jr. Also at this point, philosophies of design were changing, and the subsequent buildings in the complex would be designed primarily for function, with little thought given to how they could visually complement the surrounding structures or landscape.

In 1954, Building 4, across Washington Street from the California Avenue parking garage, was completed. It was designed by C. E. Silling and Associates of Charleston. This new six-story building represented a departure from the aesthetic qualities of the existing buildings in its scale and lack of ornamentation. Its location—across California Avenue to the east—meant that it had little effect on the overall appearance of the campus.

By 1971, however, the campus was radically transformed. In 1968, the State Building Commission—the body that had replaced the State Office Building Commission—issued state revenue bonds to finance the construction of two office towers, Buildings 5 and 6, designed by the local firm of Zando, Martin & Milstead (ZMM) and completed in 1971. These new buildings, connected by a small meeting facility, are located northeast of Building 3 and form an L shape along Piedmont Road and California Avenue. Each is topped by a two-story mechanical space for heating and air conditioning units. The small two-floor connector between the two towers is known as Building 7. The layout of the new buildings created a small courtyard space between their entrances and Washington Street where a modern fountain was installed. Metered parking was also added with the new construction. It is hard to imagine that these two austere office towers would have been in line with the ideals of the same man who designed the Woolworth Building and the United States Supreme Court Building.

The most notable change in the area close to Cass Gilbert's Capitol and the Governor's Mansion was the construction in the mid-1970s of what was originally known as the State Science & Cultural Center, now known simply as The Culture Center. Completed in 1976 by C. E. Silling and Associates of Charleston, this bold structure was completed west of the Capitol between Washington and Greenbrier Streets and the Governor's Mansion following a bond issue by the State Building Commission. The aim of this building was to physically join the state agencies working with cultural programming while joining them administratively as well. A project of then-Governor Arch A. Moore Jr.—the five-story rectangular building in which no offices have windows is sometimes jokingly referred to as Arch's Bunker—it houses the State Archives, State Historic Preservation Office, State Museum, and Library Commission, as well as a large theatre. The first three of these agencies were joined on July 1, 1977 (under the administration of Governor John D. "Jay" Rockefeller, IV), to form the Department of Culture and History (now the Division of Culture and History within the Department of Education and the Arts). While the architecture makes no reference to its immediate surroundings, the decision to locate these historical and cultural entities immediately adjacent to the Capitol is a benefit to all visitors to the complex.

The completion of the Culture Center marked another turning point in the history of the Capitol complex, as there have been no other large-scale office building projects since it opened in 1976. Also, in that year, the Legislature began to take more action regarding changes to the Capitol complex and its future. Without affecting the authority of any existing agencies, the 1976 Legislature re-created the Capitol Building Commission as an independent agency to review and give approval before any substantial physical changes could be undertaken. The commissioners consisted of an architect, an engineer, a member with knowledge of history, and two citizen members. However, with no upcoming major physical alterations and no power to enforce its decisions, the Commission was never seen as a major force to be reckoned with by agencies at the complex.

The 1970s and 1980s were periods of declining fiscal stability in West Virginia, and these economic difficulties took their toll on the Capitol buildings. Maintenance was deferred or poorly funded, and the buildings began to deteriorate. Some long-term problems may also stem from the piecemeal method used by the Legislature to determine which agency was responsible for maintenance at the Capitol. In the period since the Main Building's completion in 1932, several entities—including the State Office Building Commission, Board of Control, Board of Public Works, State Building Commission, and finally the General Services Division—have been entrusted with authority over some or all of the buildings.

In 1986 the Capitol Building Commission was accidentally abolished when a technical error in that year's sunset law renewal legislation passed without being corrected. Through the end of the 1980s, only two major projects were completed at the complex. First, in 1989, Washington Street was closed to vehicular traffic from Greenbrier Street to California Avenue, and the road and surrounding sidewalks were converted to brick pathways, creating a pedestrian campus. The second major undertaking was the first Capitol dome re-gilding project, at a cost of $472,282. Cass Gilbert's original specifications were not followed and gold leaf was applied to the entire dome; as a result, the decorative elements were lost in a sea of gold.

In 1990, the Capitol Building Commission was re-created, this time with the Commissioner of Culture and History as the statutory chairman, replacing the designated historian member. The authority of the Commission remained the same (and, to date, it has not changed): to approve all physical changes occurring at the Capitol complex. However, since the Commission lacked authority to enforce its decisions, agencies often bypassed its approval or ignored its recommendations, and some presumed that it met only to approve the removal of trees at the complex. Even the *Handbook for the Division of Purchasing* contained a separate section for changes at the Capitol complex that quoted from the Capitol Building Commission law but removed the Commission's name and inserted "General Services Division" as the agency required to approve such changes. After two reports by the Legislative Auditor's office in 1998 and 2002, the Capitol Building Commission began to take a more proactive approach to its function, and agencies began to take it more seriously.

The first decade of the twenty-first century saw a state with greater fiscal stability and responsibility. As a result, more attention was paid to the Cass Gilbert landmark and its surrounding structures—but not without some major setbacks. In 2003, for example, the demolition of the California Avenue Parking Garage (in direct violation of state law requiring approval by the Capitol Building Commission) by the Department of Administration caused a great deal of controversy. This led the Capitol Building Commission to attempt to promulgate a legislative rule giving it authority to issue "stop work" orders when its approval had not been given for projects. However, since the Secretary of Administration was required to approve all proposed Capitol Building Commission rules, and since most violations occurred from within the Department of Administration's General Services Division, this proposed rule never made it further than the Secretary's desk. In 2006, a proposed Capitol Building Commission Act to expand the powers of the Commission was introduced in the Legislature (HB 4725 and SB 639), but it was not taken up by either chamber.

Nevertheless, the mid-2000s have seen much more attention and funding dedicated to the preservation of the Capitol complex. Starting shortly after Governor Manchin's 2005 inauguration, new leadership was brought to the General Services Division, and the agency began to focus on the proper maintenance of the campus, especially Cass Gilbert's Capitol building. The major achievement during the last few years has been the structural repair and regilding of the dome at a cost of more the $4 million. The cleaning of the dome preparatory to the gilding was accomplished with an environmentally safe chemical stripper and the state's citizens voted to follow Gilbert's original scheme, with the motifs set off in gold against a neutral ground. It was no small accomplishment that the project was completed ahead of schedule and within budget.

Although the dome project has been the most visible sign of progress at the Capitol, several other major projects have been completed. Roof repairs stopped plaster from falling in the House of Delegates chamber, for instance, and electrical wiring was upgraded and made safer. The entire exterior of the Main Building was cleaned and restored to its former brilliance. The chandeliers in the rotunda and legislative chambers were rewired, stabilized, and refurbished. The fountains around the building were repaired and the problematic fountain in front of Buildings 5, 6, and 7 (known to some as Cleopatra's Barge because of its unusual shape) was removed, giving way to more green space.

This is by no means an exhaustive list of the changes to the complex after 1932, but it's a good representation of the work that has been done and continues to be undertaken. In addition to the construction of needed office space and the upkeep of Cass Gilbert's original structures, one more aspect of the never static Capitol complex must be mentioned: the post-1932 sculpture that has been added to the grounds. Perhaps the best-known work, and the most prominent because of its location directly in front of the south portico, on the river side, is *Abraham Lincoln Walks at Midnight*. The Charleston version is based on a statue created by sculptor Fred Torrey that was exhibited at the New York World's Fair in 1939–40. Torrey's inspiration was Vachel Lindsay's 1914 poem of the same name, which imagines that the spirit of Lincoln was wandering sleepless in the early twentieth century because of the troubled state of the world. Charleston's larger-than-life-size bronze figure—created by Bernie Wiepper, a local artist, after Torrey's model—was dedicated in 1974.

A bust of Booker T. Washington, a West Virginian noted for his dedication to education, is located near the West Office Building. The text below the bust relates Washington's accomplishments. Created by Bill Hopen in 1985, this bust replaced the one originally located near Washington's home after that monument had been vandalized. The West Virginia Veterans Memorial, designed by Charleston artist Joe Mullins and erected in the 1990s in conjunction with the architectural firm of ZMM, honors West Virginians who died defending the nation during the twentieth century. Four figures in niches—a World War I doughboy, a World War II sailor, an aviator from the Korean War, and a Marine from the Vietnam Conflict—represent four major twentieth-century conflicts and four branches of military service. They stand in niches facing a reflecting pool. Names of the more than ten thousand men and women who died in these conflicts are etched in the polished black granite walls of the interior. Mullins's figure of a female servicewoman was added in 2010; this is the only statue of a female figure on the grounds. *Fallen Partner*, erected in 1990 and dedicated to law enforcement officers who have been killed while on duty, is also by Bill Hopen; the Fallen Firefighter Memorial, created by James E. Lykins and added in 1994, honors those who have died in the line of duty, and a memorial to West Virginia's coal miners by Burl Jones, added in 2003, commemorates the state's mining history.

In the courtyard a replica of the Liberty Bell given by the American government in 1950 recognizes the state's role in raising money to support participation in the Korean War. And finally, to emphasize Charleston's central role as the capital of the state, the Zero Mile Marker in front of the Capitol is the starting point for all highway measurements in West Virginia.

Times and tastes have changed since the death of Cass Gilbert Sr. in 1934. In spite of all the additions, his Capitol remains the state's grandest landmark, of which millions of West Virginians are infinitely proud. I am honored to have served for seven years on the Capitol Building Commission, which is dedicated to preserving and protecting the gem that Mr. Gilbert built for a grateful state. If he were here today, I think he would be pleased to see how many of us honor and care for his creation and would appreciate the continued use of his splendid monument by the people of West Virginia.

# ACKNOWLEDGMENTS

WE COULD NOT HAVE COMPLETED this book without the help and support of many individuals and institutions. First, we thank Senator Brooks F. McCabe Jr., who conceived of the book in 2002 and has been a strong advocate in the West Virginia Legislature; Gerald E. Lang, former provost at West Virginia University, who embraced the project and advanced it with research funding; Kay Goodwin, cabinet secretary for the Department of Education and the Arts, who approved start-up funds; Randall Reid-Smith, commissioner, Division of Culture and History, who enthusiastically supported the project and assisted in funding publication costs; Myers Trust Funds, which helped support research and author expenses. Carrie Mullen, director of the West Virginia University Press, has been most supportive, as have been the members of her staff, including Hilary Attfield, Floann Downey, Abby Freeland, Nathan Holmes, and Than Saffel. We gratefully acknowledge Robert Wiser, whose thoughtful design of each page demonstrates both his appreciation of the West Virginia Capitol and his understanding of the significance of its historic context. He successfully showcased the historic postcards, construction photographs, and Cass Gilbert drawings that we selected to compliment the narrative of the Capitol's creation. The several contemporary photographers who provided stunning images of today's Capitol are listed in the Credits on page 298. We want to offer a special thank you to Jenny Bowman for her meticulous work as proofreader. We also acknowledge the readers, Barbara Christen and Barbara Rasmussen, both of whom made many useful and supportive suggestions. We give special thanks to Bernard Schultz and Mary Louise Soldo Schultz of West Virginia University, who wrote "Cass Gilbert and the Classical Tradition of Architecture." In addition, Bernard Schultz guided this project from its inception, and opened the opportunity for us to take on this book. Also at West Virginia University, Vicki Grim oversaw a variety of budgetary matters relating to this publication. Chad Proudfoot provided a helpful epilogue bringing the history of the buildings of the Capitol complex up to date.

We thank our family—Katherine Wilkins Bienkowski and Frank Bienkowski, Rebecca Wilkins, Chris Colborn, and Sofia Colborn—for their patience and support throughout. We give special thanks to Rebecca for detailed and insightful proofreading.

We owe much to our Charleston friends, Carol and Wayne Eich, who have been extraordinarily helpful, from fact-finding to careful proofreading. Carol's perseverance and humor buoyed us throughout the final months of writing.

We thank Ann Pierce for her many thoughtful and helpful comments and corrections, as well as for her encouragement as she patiently read and reread our chapters. Braxton Hinchey perused our work in its early state and helped us move forward during the initial phases. We are grateful to Christine Dvonch, who offered helpful comments as she read our manuscript.

Everyone with whom we worked at the West Virginia State Archives, the New-York Historical Society, and the Library of Congress was patient and helpful as we requested file after file of Cass Gilbert documents. West Virginia State Archivist Debra Basham and her obliging staff labored long hours with us. Susan Kriete and Miranda Schwartz, reference librarians at the New-York Historical Society, were of great help as we worked with the society's extensive Cass Gilbert collection. The Library of Congress and the Archives at the National Museum of American History shared their wealth of materials. Martin Aurand, head of the Arts Library and Special Collections at Carnegie-Mellon University, assisted us in acquiring reproductions we needed.

Mary Cronin and the late Leonora Southwick at the Madison Public Library in New Hampshire tirelessly ordered interlibrary loan materials for us, as did the interlibrary loan staffs at the Boynton Beach and Delray Beach Public Libraries in Florida. Francis Luca, chief librarian at the Wolfsonian Library of Florida International University, guided us through that institution's fine collection of materials.

We thank Mary Ann Long, West Virginia Capitol Complex tour guide, who helped with our detailed and often strange questions; Rory L. Perry II, clerk of court, Supreme Court of Appeals, West Virginia, for his willingness to answer questions and guide us through the court chambers; and Robert P. Krause, state architect and engineer, who led us through the Capitol and into the dome on our first visit. Jim Wallace, author of a 2012 survey of West Virginia's capitals and Capitols, provided useful information and promptly answered our queries.

Raymond D. Agius enhanced our book with renderings that convey the complexity of the Capitol's decorative motifs; Jane Whitehead was a helpful resource as we pondered ancient sources for the dome's motifs; and Gary Woolson was generous in sharing his knowledge of and documents about Cass Gilbert with us and the Gilbert family.

Additional thanks go to Nancy Hadley, manager, Archives and Records, The American Institute of Architects; the Cass Gilbert Society, especially Cindy Stephani, vice president; guides at the Minnesota State Capitol; and Mary Holmes of Silver Lake, New Hampshire, for her kind support and the baking that kept us nourished.

Finally, we are grateful to our many friends who asked about Cass Gilbert and the West Virginia Capitol and heard more than they probably ever wanted to know.

Surely, there is more to discover about this building's design and construction, more questions raised, more to be answered. The story of Charleston's Capitol and its architect and patrons will continue to evolve. This is a project of broad scope and complexity. Some sources may not yet be available, and we may have overlooked others in the extensive archives; any omissions or mistakes are, of course, ours alone.

Through our work on this project we feel that we have come to know Cass Gilbert not only as an architect but also as a person. It is a pleasure to know his great-granddaughter, Jeannette Gilbert Allyson of Durham, New Hampshire, and to learn more of Cass Gilbert and his family through her. We are grateful to her and her family for sharing a newly found collection of photographs of the West Virginia Capitol, several of which are published here for the first time. The family has generously agreed to donate these materials to the West Virginia State Archives.

Lastly, we have to note that construction in all its phases on a project this size is fraught with the possibility of danger. In the building of the Capitol, one man, Robert Cox, a stonemason, lost his life.

This is the story of a building, its architect, and the many others who made the West Virginia State Capitol a reality, but it is also the story of real people and their aspirations. Thank you, Cass Gilbert and the people of West Virginia.

# NOTES

Prologue
CASS GILBERT AND THE CLASSICAL TRADITION OF ARCHITECTURE

1 The opening quotation by Thomas Jefferson is from a letter of September 6, 1785, written to James Madison; *Papers of Thomas Jefferson*, vol. 8, 535. Cass Gilbert's quote is from a letter of March 2, 1929, to Elihu Root, Gilbert Papers, 214, box 1, folder 3, Library of Congress (hereafter LC).

2 Vitruvius's *De architectura* is often known in English as *Ten Books of Architecture*. See Vitruvius, *Ten Books on Architecture*, trans. Morgan. On Palladio, see Andrea Palladio, *Four Books on Architecture*. Also see James Ackerman, *Palladio*. Andrea di Pietro della Gondola was given the name Palladio as a reference to Pallas Athena, ancient goddess of wisdom.

3 Cass Gilbert, quoted in Damron, *West Virginia Capitol*, 21–22.

4 On Thomas Jefferson and the Virginia State Capitol, see Fletcher, "An American Vision of Harmony," and Kostof, *History of Architecture*, 617–26. On Thornton and his design for the National Capitol, see Frary, *They Built the Capitol*; also see Scott, *Temple of Liberty*, 5–6. For Jefferson's comment on Thornton's design, see Peterson, *Jefferson and the New Nation*, 449. On Mills, see Bryan, *Robert Mills*. On the influence of Palladio, see Hind and Murray, *Palladio and His Legacy*, 142–65.

5 Palladio, *Four Books on Architecture*, 81. (The somewhat dated translations from Vitruvius and Palladio used here are those that were available to English-speaking Beaux-Arts architects and probably known to Cass Gilbert.)

6 Scott, *Temple of Liberty*, 10.

7 See *Columbian Magazine*, Philadelphia, 1788, iii-iv, for a discussion of the iconography of this print. The two cracked columns represent the two states that, at the time of this print, had not yet ratified the Constitution, North Carolina and Rhode Island. See also *Temple of Liberty: Building the Capitol for a New Nation*, loc.gov/exhibit/us.capitol/so.htlm, and Nichols, *Jefferson's Architectural Drawings*, 4–10, for a discussion of how Classical temples came to symbolize the values of the young United States.

8 See Wilson, "Pennsylvania Ratifying Convention."

9 Gilbert, "Greatest Element," 144.

10 Gilbert to Gore, March 2, 1927; N-YHS, box 516, folder 8.

11 Gilbert, "Greatest Element," 141.

12 For a discussion of harmonic proportions in music see the entries on "Harmony," "Pythagoras," and "Theory, theorists," in *Grove Music Online* at www.oxfordmusiconline.com. Plato referenced the relationship between proportions and the universe when he wrote in the *Timeaus*: "the body of the cosmos was harmonized by proportions and brought into existence" (Plato, *Timaeus*, trans. Burry, 61). The theory that the universe is governed by mathematical laws of proportion and geometry came to be known as the Ptolemaic world system, and the widespread belief in this structured universe continued through the Renaissance. The idea that the ideal proportions expressed in nature could play a role in creating a work of art or architecture contributed to a universal definition of beauty. See Wittkower, *Architectural Principles*, 101–54, for a detailed discussion of harmonic proportions and architecture. Polykleitos had created visual harmony by establishing a set of ideal proportions that governed every part of his sculpted figure. A later commentator, Galen, cited Polykleitos's accomplishment when he wrote, "Beauty ... arises ... in the commensurability [proportion] of the parts, such as that of finger to finger, ... and of the forearm to the upper arm, and, in fact, of everything to everything else, just as it is written in the *Canon* of Polykleitos. For having taught us in that work all the proportions of the body, Polykleitos supported his treatise with a work; that is, he made a statue according to the tenets of his treatise, and called the statue, like the work, the 'Canon'" (Galen, *de Placitis et Platonis*, V, quoted in Pollitt, *Art of Ancient Greece*, 76).

13 Vitruvius, *Ten Books on Architecture*, 72.

14 Vitruvius, *Ten Books on Architecture*, 72–73.

15 See Kemp, *da Vinci*, 114–19, for a discussion of Leonardo's understanding of proportions and the microcosmic-macrocosmic analogy.

16 Wittkower, *Architectural Principles*, 11, and see Kruft, *Architectural Theory*, 57–58.

17 Palladio, *Four Books on Architecture*, 1, and see Kruft, *Architectural Theory*, 89.

18 Damron, *West Virginia Capitol*, 22.

19 Gilbert to V. H. Crocker, February 2, 1927, LC, Cass Gilbert Papers, 214, box 12, folder 1. Also see Blodgett, "Conservative at Bay."

20 Gilbert to the editor of *Personality*, November 4, 1927, LC, Cass Gilbert Papers, 214, box 12, folder 1.

21 Vitruvius, 5.

22 Gilbert to Gore, March 12, 1927, Gilbert Papers, LC.

23 Gilbert, "Greatest Element," 144.

Chapter One
WEST VIRGINIA NEEDS A CAPITOL: SELECTING THE ARCHITECT

1 On the complex history of West Virginia's capital cities and Capitols, see Stutler, "Capitals and Capitols"; Damron, *West Virginia Capitol*; Cohen and Andre, *Capitols of West Virginia*; and Wallace, *House of State*. Cohen and Andre offer many illustrations of the earlier Capitols. Wallace provides an up-to-date discussion of the social and political issues pertaining to the choice of capital city, as well as a review of the various Capitol buildings.

2 On the 1870 decision to move the capital to Charleston, see Stutler, "Capitals and Capitols," 708. In 1867, an eight-page pamphlet was published titled "The Capitol: A Plea for Its Location at Charleston: to the Legislature of West Virginia." On the 1869–70 Charleston Capitol, see Riddel, *Historical Atlas of West Virginia*, 116. Its cornerstone was laid on November 3, 1869. On October 27, 1869, a reporter for the *West Virginia Journal* referred to the rivalry among West Virginia's cities: "At this rate it will not be long until West Virginia's temporary Capital [*sic*] building will reach its spire heavenward, to catch the golden beauties of Kanawha's morning dawn, and will say to the troubled waters of Clarksburg, Parkersburg, and other rival places, 'peace, be still.'" (Quoted in Cohen and Andre, *Capitols of West Virginia*, 4). Hauck stated that West Virginia's Second Capitol was designed by "competent architects from Cincinnati," one of whom was named Garcelon (Hauck, *American Capitols*, 272).

3 The architect was Joseph S. Fairfax. For his works in West Virginia, see Chambers, *Buildings of West Virginia*, 621.

4 The vote was Charleston 41,243, Clarksburg 29,942, and Martinsburg 8,046. Riddel, *Historical Atlas of West Virginia*, 116. Thanks to Barbara Rasmussen, professor of history at West Virginia University, who pointed out to us that there is a long-held belief that the black population in the Kanawha Valley was encouraged to vote, which helped Charleston win.

The fascinating story of how two young lawyers, John E. Kenna (later US senator) and Romeo H. Freer (later West Virginia attorney general), traveled with John Robinson's Circus to speak in favor of Charleston is well known; see Cohen and Andre, *Capitols of West Virginia*, 15. For more details, see "Speaking Tour with Circus: How Senator Kenna and Another Began Political Life in West Virginia," *New York Times*, December 28, 1902. Despite the popular vote for Charleston as the state's "permanent" capital, legislators continued to raise the issue of the location of the capital as late as March 31, 1923, when Houston Young reassured Cass Gilbert that "the Capitol site will not be moved to Parkersburg." (The transcript for this meeting is preserved at N-YHS, box 519, folder 10).

The architects of the Fourth Capitol were C. C. Kemple, A. Peoples, and S. M. Howard; Chambers, *Buildings of West Virginia*, lists no works by Kemple or Peoples in West Virginia; for works by Howard, see 629. The *New York Times* reported on March 22, 1885, that representatives of the West Virginia Board of Public Works were inspecting the new Capitol on March 21 preparatory to the May 1 arrival of the State Archives. For more on the 1885 Capitol, see Cohen and Andre, 17–27.

For the Annex, see Cohen and Andre, 55–58. J. S. Darst, West Virginia state auditor, proposed that the state erect a skyscraper capitol by adding floors to the Annex building; he suggested that the foundation was strong enough to support eight to ten additional stories. This information is from an undated, unidentified clipping reproduced by Cohen and Andre, 60.

5 The *New York Times* reported that the chief of police and several others were "in the Tax Commissioner's office pitching records out of the windows. As they started down a ladder there was a roar and a cloud of smoke as part of the roof fell." For further information on the fire, including eyewitness accounts and photographs, see Cohen and Andre, *Capitols of West Virginia*, and Wallace, *House of State*. The *New York Times* article on January 4, 1921, is headlined,"FIRE RUINS CAPITOL OF WEST VIRGINIA: Only the Shell is Left of Handsome Brick Building in Charleston." It was presumed that a blanket insurance policy on West Virginia state buildings would cover the complete loss; the *New York Times* reported that the policy covered up to $6 million; the amount received was $533,455.23. "Report of Special Senate Committee," 1.

6 Quoted in Damron, *West Virginia Capitol*, 6.

7 For the renewed debate over the location of the capital city, see Wallace, *House of State*, 25–27.

8 For the letter from Josias Pennington and the reply from Governor Cornwell, see *Correspondence: Capitol Commission* (hereafter *CCC*), 904. Governor Cornwell's response is dated January 24, 1921.

For the decision to remain in Charleston, see "State of West Virginia Capitol Building Commission: Report to the House of Delegates," 5–6 (hereafter referred to as *Report to House of Delegates)*. In the meantime, a "Memorial from the Rotary Club of the City of Bluefield" reported, "It was the sense of the club that the capital of the state of West Virginia should remain at Charleston, and all efforts to locate the same elsewhere be disregarded." (*Journal of the Senate . . . 1921*, January 20, 1921, 67–68). Senate Joint Resolution No. 13 also supported Charleston, but some of its wording was problematic and it was not passed; see *Journal of the Senate . . . 1921*, January 24, 1921, 101–4. One passage suggested that moving the capital away from Charleston "would be a great economic waste involving the expenditure of large sums of money and result, if not in actual corruption, at least in charges of corruption, bribery, bad faith and injustice." On March 30, 1921, the Senate's Committee on Public Buildings and Humane Institutions reported that bills that proposed moving the capital to Buckhannon, Elkins, and Clarksburg had not passed (*Journal of the Senate . . . 1921*, March 30, 1921, 78).

For other statistical information on the Charleston of 1924, see David, "Charleston Today." The information about churches is listed under "Religious Activities" on page 46, but there is no reference to synagogues in the city or to any religion other than Christianity. For a discussion of the active Jewish community in Charleston, which dates back to c. 1854, see Preisler, *Jewish West Virginia*, 29–52. By 1920, Kanawha was by far the largest county in West Virginia, with a population of 119,650. See *West Virginia Legislative Handbook* (1925), 281.

The contractor for the "Pasteboard Capitol," which took forty-two days to construct, was David Dick of Charleston, who in a letter of May 26, 1921, presented his formal application "for the position of Supervising Architect and Superintendent of Construction of the proposed West Virginia Capitol Building" (*CCC*, 422).

The members of the first Commission are not documented if, indeed, they were ever named. A second Capitol Building Commission was established during the Extraordinary Session of the 1921 Legislature under section 24-j of the general appropriation bill. It assumed the duties of the first and had seven members led by the governor as ex officio chair. Membership was to be drawn from the Senate and House, but the appointments awaited the change in administration. The membership of building commissions varied from state to state; Minnesota's Board of State Capitol Commissioners, with whom Cass Gilbert had worked earlier, was composed not of politicians but of seven civilians led by Channing Seabury, a wholesale grocer.

On the complex history of the general appropriation bill and attempts to modify it, see *Journal of the Senate . . . 1921*, May 2, 1921, 8–19. These pages also include a summary of the debate among senators as to how large a site in Charleston would be needed for the new Capitol. One proposal urged,"Upon a site of not less than ten acres, and at an elevation of not less than thirty feet above the surface of the present Capitol ground," while another asked for "a site of not less than five hundred feet frontage and of like depth." These deliberations seem to have been irrelevant, and the site was still undecided when Cass Gilbert was selected in July 1921. Another amendment that did not pass stated, "All contracts authorized herein shall be submitted to the legislature for its approval at a special session called for that purpose by the Governor."

9 Morgan, E. F., inaugural address, West Virginia Division of Culture and History, *http://www.wvculture.org/history/morgania.html* (consulted March 1, 2010). He explains that these deficiencies were "accounted for in part because the Act of the Legislature of the Extraordinary Session 1919, providing a special privilege tax on the transportation of oil and gas through pipe lines, has been held to be constitutional only in part, and is still in litigation. No revenue has been collected thereunder." It is, therefore, not clear how precarious the state's finances actually were at this time. Morgan, a Republican, may have been trying to criticize the administration of Governor Cornwell, the Democrat he was replacing; prior to Cornwell, West Virginia had had Republican governors continuously since 1897.

David Alan Corbin reported that both Cornwell and Morgan were indebted to and influenced by those who controlled West Virginia's coal industry, pointing out, "It was quickly revealed that the coal companies had paid $750,000 to secure [Morgan's] election. . . . Several

UMWA locals demanded the recall of Morgan, others advocated a statewide movement to impeach him." *Life, Work, and Rebellion*, 212.

10 The maximum price information is from "Report to House of Delegates," 4. It was reported by Governor Howard Gore in 1927 that the insurance on the old building provided $533,455.23 and the sale of the property netted $1,301,000, for a total of $1,834,455.23, but this is somewhat misleading; see chapter 6, "The Second Design Phase." N-YHS, box 516, folder 8. For the figures affecting the construction of the new Capitol as of June 1, 1927, see chapter 6, page 147.

The *New York Times* report on the blanket policy is dated January 4, 1921.

The suggestion that the state would receive $3 million from the sale of the Old Capitol site is found in the *Clarksburg Telegram*, July 17, 1922; the paper reported that the total cost of the new building, with land, was expected to be $9.5 million, with $6.5 million raised by taxation and $3 million from the sale of the old property (N-YHS, box 683).

More accurate numbers can now be determined, however. The December 31, 1932, report of the Capitol Building Commission, published as part of the "Appendix to the Biennial Message of Wm. G. Conley, Governor to the Legislature of 1933," reveals that the "$6.5 million plus" figure would have totaled $8,584,455.23: $6,500,000 plus the sale of the old site ($1,551,000, including "a strip of land through temporary Capitol site for street purposes") and $533,455.23 for the insurance on the old buildings and contents. Added to this could be "sale and rent of houses on new site" of $104,586.52, for a grand total of $8,689,041.75. The cost of the new site, including "Sundry expenditures" and "Grading grounds Office Buildings nos. One and Two," was $2,111,825.43. If this amount is subtracted from the grand total given above, it is clear that the formula of "6.5 million plus" established by the 1921 Legislature would have yielded a budget of $6,577,216.32 for the design and construction of the new Capitol, excluding land. This figure became irrelevant with later developments and the budget of $5 million for the construction of the Main Building established by the 1927 Legislature.

According to the *West Virginia Legislative Manual* (1929), 295, the 1921 Legislative Session appropriated $750,000 for 1922 and $1.5 million for 1923. These figures may be misleading, for they may include rent for temporary office space paid during this period; the *Manual* combines these expenses under the heading "New Buildings and Rent." The costs for rent while the three components of the new Capitol, the East and West Wings and the Main Building, were under construction must have been substantial. The figures under "New Buildings and Rent" are: 1922: $750,000; 1923: $1,500,000; 1924: $250,000; 1925: $250,000; 1926: $522,500; 1927: $502,500; 1928: $160,000; 1929: $35,000; 1930: $7,000; 1931: $7,000. The figures for 1929, 1930, and 1931 are probably for rent and have nothing to do with the financing and construction of the third component, the Main Building.

Actual construction time was five years: West Wing, fifteen months; East Wing, eighteen months; Main Building, twenty-seven months. Problems with legislative-controlled financing delayed the construction of many state capitols, including Minnesota's. See the discussion in Thompson, *Minnesota's State Capitol*.

11 Governor's introduction, "Report to House of Delegates." The following list of members of the Commission is derived from Cohen and Andre, *Capitols of West Virginia*, 61: Gohen C. Arnold (1921–32), Harry P. Camden (1922–25), J. William Cummins (1929–32), C. W. Dillon (1929–32), Herbert Fitzpatrick (1921–32), Virgil L. Highland (1922–23), Boyd Jarrell (1929–32), Edwin M. Keatley (1921–32), George A. Laughlin (1923–32), William A. MacCorkle (1925–30), William McKell (1921–22), Charles K. Payne (1930–32), Mrs. J. T. (Daisy M.) Peadro (1926–32), Fred M. Staunton (1921–26), N. Price Whitaker (1921–22), M. Z. White (1929–32), and Houston G. Young (1921–23). Under Governor William G. Conley the membership was increased to eleven (including the governor). William Alexander MacCorkle had served as West Virginia's governor from 1893 to 1897. Daisy M. Peadro, from Parkersburg, was the only woman to serve on the Commission.

The commissioners were compensated for their expenses. Receipts for Gohen Arnold dated April 27, 1922, totaled $777.89. Arnold's expenses included thirteen trips from Buckhannon to Charleston; eight direct and five via Parkersburg, and meals en route ($208). A room for two nights cost $4, and a room for three nights, with meals, totaled $30. *CCC*, 305–7.

12 Young volunteered as secretary until 1922, when he was replaced by Bonner Hill, a salaried employee. Hill resigned from his position as City Manager of Charleston to take the position, which when construction began included serving as the state's representative on site. In 1923 his salary was $5,000 a year ("Report to House of Delegates," 10). A letter to the architect from Houston Young written October 6, 1922, stated, "The detail of the Capitol Commission matters is becoming so burdensome that I am gradually getting away from it. At a meeting of the Commission held some days ago, I was instructed to notify you that most of the correspondence from now on will be between yourself and Mr. Bonner H. Hill, Agent of the Commission." (*CCC*, 80). Eventually Hill was appointed secretary.

It was Commissioner Edwin M. Keatley who told Gilbert he had been mentioned in the meeting. Keatley was writing in response to Gilbert's June 15 letter of interest, which the architect sent to each commissioner (N-YHS, box 503, folder 7).

13 *CCC*, 533–34, April 7, 1921. Gilbert continued, "Both the Montana and Wisconsin instances were due, I think, to local political differences in which I had no part and involved no criticism of myself either in a personal or a professional way."

The history of Gilbert's role in the Montana State Capitol competition is problematic. The summary in Hitchcock and Seale, *Temples of Democracy*, is inconsistent with materials in the Cass Gilbert collection at N-YHS, which would not have been available to the authors at the time they were researching this topic. While Hitchcock and Seale reported that in the Montana competition Gilbert placed second in the first round, *Architectural Record* for 1899, #11, 138 (preserved in the Gilbert collection at N-YHS) illustrates Gilbert's design as "First Premiated Design." Hitchcock and Seale state that Gilbert came in second in the second round as well, but Gilbert reported that he did not participate in that round at Montana. The published history of the Montana State Capitol makes no mention of a competition, reporting only that the Commission "advertised for bids" and "fifty-nine architects submitted drawings." There is no list of the fifty-nine architects and no mention of Cass Gilbert (Lambert, Burnham, and Near, *Montana's State Capitol*, 7).

For the troubled history of the Wisconsin competition, undertaken after the previous capitol was damaged by fire in 1904, see the accurate summary in Hitchcock and Seale, 240–41. Correspondence and other materials relative to the Wisconsin project are preserved at the N-YHS, boxes 526–27. Of special interest is W. S. Eames's evaluation of various proposals and the announcement by O. H. Ingram, president of the Capitol Improvement Commission, that the winning design was by Cass Gilbert; both are published in the *Journal of the Senate* [for the State of Wisconsin] for January 31, 1905, 201–10, and preserved in an extract at N-YHS, box 527, folder 7. The N-YHS Gilbert collection also preserves a tattered copy of the front page of the *Milwaukee Free Press* for February 1, 1905, with an elevation of Gilbert's winning design. Across the top, in large script, someone has written: "Hurrah for us. Oh, but the other fellows are sore. Yours, W. H. S."

Gilbert's role in completing the Arkansas State Capitol (1899–1915) is well documented. He was hired in 1907 after George Mann, the original architect, was dismissed. Mann's engineering and construction skills were questioned, and there were allegations of bribery. Gilbert's most important task was to complete the complex; his redesign of the dome followed the governor's suggestion that it be based on that of the Mississippi State Capitol, which, ironically, had been designed by Mann. For a history of the scandals and Gilbert's subsequent involvement written by the man who was governor from 1909 to 1913, see Donaghey, *Building a State Capitol*. Gilbert was appointed in 1909, but before accepting this appointment he consulted with Mann and "secured a letter from him, addressed to the Commission, which stated that he (Mr. Mann) believed Mr. Gilbert to be competent in every respect to perform the duties required and recommended that he be employed by the Commission" (236).

14 Gilbert was invited to participate in the competition for the Utah State Capitol in 1911, but did not enter, nor did other prominent architects, in part because of the manner in which the competition had been designed; the highly publicized problems with the Utah competition may also explain why West Virginia's Commission sought professional help in deciding how to proceed in hiring an architect. The broad history of architectural competitions in America remains to be written, as do the stories of many of the individual commissions. See N-YHS, box 189, folder 3, for Cass Gilbert's letter of invitation from the Committee on Competition of the Utah Association of Architects of September 1, 1911; for the response of the office of Geo. B. Post & Sons of September 20, 1911, a copy of which was, interestingly, sent to Gilbert; and "MEMORANDUM from the *Herald-Republican*, Salt Lake City, Utah, Friday, Sept. 1, 1911, Relative to the new Utah State Capitol Competition."

In 1922, after winning the commission for the West Virginia complex, Cass Gilbert entered the competition for the Tennessee Capitol Annex and War Memorial. His diary records that he worked on this project on January 5, 17, 18, 19 ("Worked on Nashville competition. I designed the niches and stairways approaching Capitol" [accompanied by a small drawing]), and again on January 20, 21, 24, 27 ("The boys are working on the competition for Nashville, Tenn"). On January 28, he wrote, "Finished competition drawings for Memorial and Capitol Annex, Nashville Tenn. And sent them to Prof. Laird at Phil on 2 P.M. train by Johnston." On February 28 he reported in his diary that "McKim Mead and White have now the Nashville competition. I'm glad of it. I don't want the burden of it. I went into the competition half-heartedly. I had to drive myself to work on it." For Gilbert's involvement with Nebraska and Japan and the question of his engagement with the new Cuban Capitol, see chapter 2.

15 N-YHS, box 524, folder 3.

16 For the editorial in the *Intelligencer*, see N-YHS, box 524, folder 3. The two reports and the published volume of correspondence are: "State of West Virginia Capitol Building Commission: Report to House of Delegates"; "Report of Special Senate Committee"; and *CCC*. The documentation provided in *CCC* is helpful, but the thousands of entries are in no order, some are repeated, and there are many typographical errors. We suspect that the lack of organization was intended to blur the historical trail that a careful chronological sequence might have exposed.

The "Report to the House of Delegates" stated that Cass Gilbert would be in Charleston on January 22, 1923, to meet with members of the House and to show them "such plans as are available."

In January 1923, the commissioners reported they had entered into only two contracts. One was with the engineer making borings to determine the strata, a process estimated to cost $3,300. The other was with Cass Gilbert, whom they describe as "one of America's greatest architects" and the designer of the much-admired Minnesota State Capitol and of the world's tallest structure, the Woolworth Building in New York City. The architect's fee would be based on 6 percent of the cost of the building and the development of the grounds; given that the price of the building in 1922 was estimated to be no more than $6,500,000 plus approximately $2,500,000 from the sale of the old site and the unknown amount to be received from the insurance on the old Capitol, Cass Gilbert's fee could have been $500,000, perhaps more. This alone helps to explain why the Commission was being questioned by the Legislature at the beginning of 1923.

17 For Pennington's letter and the governor's reply, see *CCC*, 904. A reply to one of the February inquiries explained: "It has not yet been definitely determined where the power to build a new Capitol will be lodged" (*CCC*, 756; February 5, 1921). The reply to Litchfield and Rogers, February 2, 1921, is in *CCC*, 756. Sill, Buckler & Fenhagen of Baltimore wrote on January 20 (*CCC*, 856; a letter of recommendation for this group was sent on January 24, *CCC*, 811, and they wrote again on May 16, 1921, *CCC*, 857); Litchfield & Rogers of New York wrote on February 2 (*CCC*, 755–56 and again on April 19, 1921, *CCC*, 756); Dennison & Hirons of New York wrote on February 4, 9, and 21 (*CCC*, 417–20); and Henry C. Pelton of New York on February 21 (*CCC*, 835).

Egerton Swartwout pointed out that in addition to his work on the Missouri State Capitol, which he "won in a national-wide competition," he was "one of ten invited in the recent competition for the Nebraska State Capitol, and was in the finals of the competition for the State Capitol Building at Sacramento." (*CCC*, 882). Tracy & Swartwout's design for the Nebraska State Capitol Competition followed the National Capitol model and featured a massive dome. Egerton Swartwout, incidentally, prepared Cass Gilbert's biography for the *Dictionary of American Biography*.

For the letter from the United Spanish War Veterans, see *CCC*, 757 (June 8, 1921). Halls to honor veterans were common in earlier state capitols; at the dedication of Cass Gilbert's Minnesota State Capitol, for instance, the flags of Minnesota's military units were paraded by surviving veterans and installed in showcases in the rotunda.

The letter from the Limestone Quarrymen's Association is published in *CCC*, 710 (June 24, 1921). Controversies over building materials and demands that local stone be used for state capitols were common and had been a problem for Gilbert when designing the Minnesota Capitol; see Thompson, *Minnesota's State Capitol*, 30–33, 35–38, 40–41.

18 The cashier was named Hubert Echols; see *CCC*, 807–8 (June 13, 1922). The engineers at the Brooklyn firm of A. Stanley Miller, Inc., reported "[We] believe it to be marble.... It is rather dark for interior marble but still it should make a very good exterior building material." They cautioned the cashier: "Do you realize the equipment required to properly cut these blocks out of the quarries and load them on the cars ready for the marble mills? It requires rather expensive machinery to cut these blocks out of the hills requiring channelers and also steam power." Echols sent the sample and report to Governor Morgan, stating "It would certainly be a send off to the state, as well as our county, if we could get them to build out of this marble." That Echols's sample came from Pocahontas County is suggested by a letter from J. A. Sydenstricker, a cashier at the First National Bank of Marlinton, who also encouraged the use of this local stone (78, July 20, 1922). That there was a concerted effort to convince the Commission to use this Pocahontas marble is evident in another letter written to the Commission from Andrew Price of Marlinton on July 20, 1922 (153). A letter to Gilbert from the West Virginia State Geologist dated July 28, 1922, however, reported that the only West Virginia stone that might be usable was a

deposit of sandstone near Kingwood (N-YHS, box 519, folder 10). This did not, however, stop discussion of this topic. The issue of using West Virginia stone was still alive in November 1922, when K. T. Crawley, a manager in the Agricultural and Industrial Department of the Chesapeake and Ohio Railway Company, showed Cass Gilbert a sample of marble from Marlinton (Crawley to Bonner Hill, *CCC*, 95). Gilbert rejected this stone for the exterior because he wanted the building to be white, but told Crawley "some of this marble might be used on the interior work."

In March 1923, Houston Young called on Gilbert in New York and reported that a recent article in the *Wheeling Register* about "Pocahontas marble from West Virginia" was probably "written with a view to impressing the Commission." (Transcript dated March 31, 1923, N-YHS, box 519, folder 10). Young complained that the stone was "very dark material and not all suitable for the building," but Gilbert answered that "it might possibly be used in the interior."

19 For Egan & Reese's letter, see N-YHS, box 503, folder 7. The firm of Egan & Reese does not appear in the later documentation. No works by architects named Egan or Reese are found in Chambers, *Buildings of West Virginia*.

For Herbert S. Kyle's letter, see N-YHS, box 503, folder 7. It is uncertain what "legislative committee" Kyle is referring to, since the Capitol Building Commission created by the Extraordinary Session of the Legislature of 1921 had yet to be named. The letter concludes: "I have laid as much of our position before you as, in good faith, I feel that I can. I have admired your work, and would like to consider an association with you. The time is nearly ripe and I would like to hear from you at once." Kyle & Wilkins is not documented in later discussions. No works by Kyle & Wilkins are recorded in Chambers, but the W. G. Wilkins Company is included in a list of Huntington architects and architectural firms published in 1914–15; see Chambers, *Buildings of West Virginia*, 244.

A letter from A. F. Wysong, of Wysong & Jones, (*CCC*, 919, May 13, 1921) states that after the Capitol burned he "immediately wired to whom I considered one of the best architectural designers in the United States and asked if he would associate with me on the plans for a new capitol, to which he has agreed, and I would appreciate an opportunity to be heard in company with him before your commission." Although Wysong did not identify his partner, a later document identifies him as Henry Hornbostel (A. F. M. Lange to Francis A. Kane, October 7, 1921, N-YHS, box 503, folder 7). For Hornbostel, who had won the competitions to design the campuses for both the University of Pittsburgh and Carnegie Institute of Technology in Pittsburgh, see Kidney, *Henry Hornbostel*. Wysong appeared before the Commission on July 7, but no mention was made at that time of an association with Hornbostel. For works by Wysong in West Virginia, see Chambers. Sidney F. Heckert Jr. of Pittsburgh stated that an association between his firm and that of George B. Post & Sons of New York might be possible: "We desire to bring to the attention of your Commission our name and that of George B. Post & Sons of New York, associated, for consideration." (*CCC*, 622; June 29, 1921).

For the reply to Cass Gilbert, dated May 18, 1921, see N-YHS, box 503, folder 7. The letter from Senator Elkins was in response to a letter from Gilbert dated May 5, 1921. Gilbert had given this letter to Senator Knute Nelson of Minnesota, asking his old friend to deliver it personally to Senator Elkins.

On May 19, John Rockart wrote to Gilbert to inform him that he had heard from "Mr. Paris, of Paris & Wiley," who had "received a letter from his brother in West Virginia, to the effect that he had seen Senator Elkins and that the Senator had told him that the selection of an architect for a proposed new building was in the hands of the Governor, and that it is proposed to give the commission to a native of West Virginia." N-YHS, box 516, folder 5.

20 Gilbert's letter to Morgan is published in *CCC*, 534; the reply, 535.

21 Quoted in Blodgett, "Conservative," 630. The letter is preserved in the Cass Gilbert collection at the Library of Congress, box 10. A contractor's bond was drawn up by a lawyer between the contractor and a surety company to guarantee that the contractor will complete a job to satisfaction; it would also cover unpaid suppliers or subcontractors, as well as other problems. For Gilbert's attitudes about Roosevelt, see Blodgett. Blodgett's conclusion that Gilbert "accepted the West Virginia commission while scarcely lifting a finger to win it" suggests he did not have access to the N-YHS archives (630).

22 The information on the June 3 meeting is found in "Report of Special Senate Committee," Appendix B: State of West Virginia, Capitol Building Commission, Minutes, June 3, 1921 (N-YHS, box 516, folder 6). Commissioner Staunton had been proactive on this issue, for a letter reveals that on June 2, 1921, he had been sent several issues of the *Architectural Review* that reported on the Nebraska State Capitol competition. The writer encouraged Staunton to contact the AIA for their "Competition Code" and the *Architectural Record* and *Architectural Forum* for information on this issue. He also listed where Staunton might find information of interest in the *Journal of the American Institute of Architects*. *CCC*, 308–9, June 2, 1921. The replies from the Commission and the commissioner are published in *CCC*, 498 and 499.

23 New York firms applying included Litchfield & Rogers (*CCC*, 755–56; February 2, 1921, April 19, 1921, and May 25, 1921); Dennison & Hirons (417–20; February 2, 4, and 21, 1921); Herts & Robertson (644–46; June 1, 1921); Henry C. Pelton (835; February 21, 1921); Tracy & Swartwout (882; April 4, 1912); Cass Gilbert (533–34; April 4, 1921); George Hunt Ingram (711; April 5, 1921); Alfred C. Bossom (319 and 331–33; before April 9, 1921); James Riely Gordon (605; April 16, 1921); Warren & Clark (899–900; April 16, 1921); Walker & Gillette (899; June 9, 1921); and Cross & Cross (410; June 27, 1921). Crow, Lewis & Wick of New York probably also applied; Luther W. Lewis of this firm appeared before the Commission on June 26, 1921; 747–48; see also the recommendation for them, 749–50.

Sometime before April 9, 1921, Alfred C. Bossom sent a book illustrating his work (*CCC*, 319). A letter of June 30 listing some of his works, a prize he had received, and his references also document a visit his representative had made to Charleston. Bossom was sent a telegram inviting him to meet with the commissioners, but a reply from his office dated July 1 reported that he was in Texas and a representative of the firm would meet with them (331–32, July 1, 1922). There is no record this meeting took place.

Cross & Cross wrote on June 27, 1921, requesting an opportunity to make a presentation; a telegram of July 5 said they would be heard on July 7, but apparently they did not appear that day, for J. W. Cross made a presentation on July 13. Dennison & Hirons of New York City reported that they already had an office in Charleston, where they were responsible for the design of the Renaissance Tower (Kanawha Banking and Trust Company); see Chambers, *Buildings of West Virginia*, 62. Walker & Gillette thought that there was going to be a competition; their letter asked that they be supplied with the rules.

James Riely Gordon's letter is especially interesting:

> I am pleased to learn that you contemplate the erection of an appropriate, modern capitol for West Virginia, and as I have specialized in this particular field of architecture for many years, with several capitols and nearly seventy court houses standing to my credit, I sincerely hope that you will not consider me

presumptuous in assuring you that the many complicated, scientific and highly technical problems involved, can be mastered before starting, and that such a structure can be erected within a given sum, without the usual extras or excessive cost over[runs] ... which misfortune, political opponents and opposition newspapers invariably criticize so successfully.

I have devoted a great deal of time during this period to the careful survey, experiment and successful correction of the fatal defects in acoustics, lines of vision, ventilation and light diffusion so frequently found in architecturally beautiful buildings.

Through these successful experiments I have developed many modern transitions in the antiquated capitols of yesterday, which I have gradually incorporated in a perfected amphitheatre chamber.

As I have hitherto successfully collaborated in these matters with state officials and gentlemen of the bench and bar, I would be pleased to visit Charleston at your convenience, to submit some of these examples to you and your friends, in the hope that they might shed such new light upon these important subjects, as would materially lighten the burden of your responsibilities in the planning of so important a structure.

Please understand that you incur no obligation whatsoever, that I ask no favor beyond that of a patient hearing and that I stand strictly on my merits.

Gordon, who was originally from San Antonio, designed the Arizona Territorial Capitol (1899–1900) and submitted a competition design for the Mississippi State Capitol. He designed many Texan courthouses. The grandeur that architects envisioned for public buildings during this period is encapsulated in his design for a 1,000-foot-high courthouse crowned with a 192-foot statue of Justice; see Fenske, *Skyscraper*, 61–62.

The Washington firms included Clarence L. Harding (*CCC*, 623–24, 622–23, May 31 and June 23, 1921); Milburn, Heiser & Co. (806, June 30, 1921); and George Oakley Totten Jr. (886–89, May 6 and June 11, 1921) Harding reported that he had designed several buildings in West Virginia, including some in Charleston, adding that a number of his West Virginia friends had been urging him to "go for it." (623–24). Milburn, Heiser & Co. reported that they "rebuilt the Florida State House, remodeled the South Carolina State House, made plans to rebuild the North Carolina State House, and were awarded Second Prize in competition for the Kentucky State Capitol." Totten reported that on "two occasions I have given serious study to state house planning," probably a reference to past competition entries, and that he had provided Commissioner Arnold with a design for a state capitol to show the Commission.

Pittsburgh firms asking for consideration were Sidney F. Heckert (*CCC*, 622, June 29, 1921); Kennedy & Ellington (657); and William H. King Jr. (721, June 14, 1921).

The West Virginia firms were Richard M. Bates Jr. (*CCC*, 320, May 12, 1921), Robert L. & Sidney L. Day (420, June 18,1921), David Dick & Son (422, May 26, 1921), and Wysong & Jones (919, May 13, 1921). Works by Richard M. Bates are listed in Chambers. Robert L. Day is included in a list of architects in Huntington in 1914–15; see Chambers, 244.

The Dick firm presented a formal application "for the position of Supervising Architect and Superintendent of Construction," suggesting that "before the selection of the general architect the associate architect or superintendent should be named so that a general understanding may be had and that you might get the full benefit of both." David Dick's letter also proposed that the architect's fee be divided, and that "while there is no general rule for the division in W. Va., I would say two-thirds to the general and one-third to the associate architect." Dick's letter was sent to the commissioners, with a copy to Houston Young.

The letter from A. F. Wysong of Wysong & Jones locates the firm in Charleston, West Virginia, but a later reference states that Wysong is from Princeton, West Virginia ("Report of Special Senate Committee," 16, N-YHS, box 516, folder 6). Wysong was the architect of the Wyoming County Courthouse and Jail, built in 1916; in the nomination form for the National Register designation he is listed as a "West Virginia State Architect." He was also a member of the West Virginia State Legislature. Wysong was the secretary of the board that registered architects in West Virginia, established in 1921 (N-YHS, box 503, folder 8). For works by A. F. Wysong and the various firms with which he was associated, consult the index in Chambers.

Baltimore firms were Josias Pennington (*CCC*, 904, January 12, 1921) and Sill, Buckler & Fenhagen (856–57, January 20 and May 16, 1921; a letter of recommendation for the latter group was sent on January 24 [*CCC*, 811]). When G. Corner Fenhagen returned from a long trip to the West on July 9, 1921, he wrote to Commissioner Staunton to ask about the possibility of entering the competition (*CCC*, 472); when Staunton replied that Cass Gilbert had been selected, Fenhagen wrote, "In selecting Mr. Gilbert the Commission have assured the success of the new building" (473).

Others were Benton & Benton of Richmond (*CCC*, 321, June 7, 1921); Paul A. Davis 3rd of Philadelphia (*CCC*, 421; May 14, 1921) F. G. & J. A. Dempwolf of York, Pennsylvania (no letter, but a reply to one of their references is dated June 27, 1921; *CCC*, 763); Garber & Woodward of Cincinnati (*CCC*, 497; June 3, 1921); and Mills & Millspaugh of Columbus (*CCC*, 804, June 39, 1921). Paul Davis was going to be in Charleston on May 19 and asked for an appointment with the governor. Garber & Woodward later provided letters of recommendation (*CCC*, 500–502; both June 24, 1921), one of which mentions that they had worked with Cass Gilbert on the construction of the Union Central Building of Cincinnati. Frederick W. Garber returned home on June 23 after visiting Charleston, where he had called on four commissioners and presented the firm's credentials. In mid-July, when a preference for Cass Gilbert was widely suspected, a Garber supporter sent a witty wire to Secretary Young: "Garber thinks you still love Gilbert. Do not love Gilbert less but love Garber more." The writer was W. G. Brown of the Consulting Company in Cincinnati (*CCC*, 376). The telegram is undated, but what seems to be the reply is dated July 19, 1921. Young replied that "it was a real pleasure ... to meet Mr. Garber," but added that, "it seemed best to give the contract to one of the better known architects" (376).

Wilbur T. Mills of Mills and Millspaugh wired on June 30 to request an interview and was informed by a telegram of July 1 that he should come on July 2. When Mills responded that this was impossible, a wire of July 5 told him to come on July 7 but no presentation is documented (*CCC*, 804–5).

24 For Keatley's letter, see N-YHS, box 503, folder 7. Cass Gilbert's June 15 letter has not been located; it may survive in the "Letter Books" in the Cass Gilbert collection at the N-YHS, but some of these are water damaged and difficult to consult. Keatley reported to Gilbert that he had "been urging upon the Commission the advisability of employing an architect before proceeding with the selection of the site, there being several sites under consideration, but at this time no decision has been reached and no meeting has, at present, been called by the Governor, in whose hands the matter rests, as Chairman."

For Staunton's letter, see N-YHS, box 503, folder 7. On June 22, Gilbert, who had returned to New York, replied to Staunton's June 17 letter:

"I should be very much pleased to meet the members of the Capitol Commission and would be glad to go to Charleston for that purpose if a time were appointed when I could see them. It would be understood, of course, that such a preliminary conference would involve no obligation or expense on the part of the Commission" (*CCC*, 529). Secretary Young's reply pointed out: "It has not yet been determined when the Capitol Commission will meet again, but your telegram will be placed before the Commission for its consideration" (587).

25 For Gilbert's telegram, see N-YHS, box 516, folder 5. The wire to the Commission is documented as well (*CCC*, 587). That Fenner came to West Virginia by invitation is unlikely, as no documentation suggests that the Commission had invited any architects to visit Charleston by this date. McKim, Mead & White were among the firms invited to make a presentation on July 7.

Gilbert added that he would be willing to use West Virginia engineers or architects "if desired." Elkins replied, "Your telegram of the 18th inst., was duly received, and I immediately took up with the West Virginia State Capitol Commission the matter of extending to you an invitation." Elkins apparently communicated with at least one of the commissioners, for Commissioner Arnold wrote him that Gilbert "has been most seriously considered by a number of the members of the Commission and [I] assure you ample opportunity will be given him to present his plans." Elkins forwarded this reply to Gilbert (N-YHS, box 503, folder 7).

26 Kellogg (*CCC*, 532); Nelson (531, telegram, June 20, 1921); Preus (530, telegram June 20, 1921); Moore (531, telegram June 20, 1921); Donaghey (529, telegram, June 19, 1921); McAdoo (575–76, June 22, 1921).

Gilbert asked Senator Kellogg if he would present his letter of recommendation to West Virginia Senator Howard Sutherland and request that Sutherland forward it to Governor Morgan. In his cover letter of May 24, Senator Sutherland noted that Senator Kellogg's endorsement should entitle Cass Gilbert "to serious consideration in connection with the work of rebuilding the Capitol." (*CCC*, 883). The dates of the telegrams suggest that Gilbert asked his referees to write or telegram on or before June 20; Knute Nelson's wired reply stated "WILL WIRE WEST VIRGINIA CAPITOL COMMISSION AS YOU SUGGEST." (N-YHS, box 503, folder 7). The date of May 23, 1921, given for Kellogg's recommendation is probably one of the many typographical errors found in *CCC*.

27 One or more of the commissioners may have suggested that letters of recommendation in support of firms would be appropriate; in any case, a number of such letters are documented. Letters supporting Arnold W. Brunner are documented from the Pennsylvania Superintendent of Instruction (*CCC*, 376, June 16, 1921), Ambrose Swasey (882, June 13, 1921), and from Mr. Highland of the National Republican Committee (376, June 16, 1921), who reported that Brunner was also recommended by William R. Wilcox, former chairman of the Republican National Committee. Such endorsements suggest the importance of political affiliation when appointing architects for public projects.

Herts & Robertson were recommended by "Mr. Mellon" (probably Andrew Mellon, secretary of the Treasury) and also by James J. Davis, secretary of labor, among others (421, 625–27). Herts & Robertson's letter of June 1, 1921, to Commissioner Staunton includes a list of projects they had prepared "following your suggestion." (*CCC*, 644). The list is repeated verbatim in the letters of their referees, indicating that they had forwarded it to them and asked for its inclusion. One letter emphasizes that this firm had been chosen to design Victory Hall, "probably the most important undertaking of an architectural character as yet proposed by the people of New York, involving an expense of upwards of twenty millions." They were apparently selected because this complex would contain several large auditoriums and Herts & Robertson "had never failed in the question of acoustics in the vast number of auditoriums they had built," a recommendation that was especially important because of the "several debating chambers" needed in a state house. Because certain passages are identical in the recommendation letters for Herts & Robertson, the firm seems to have provided referees with a model to follow.

Documented letters support Brunner, but there are none for Bacon, Carrère & Hastings (who did not receive the invitation until August), Pope, or the Post firm.

On June 27, Albert B. White of the IRS office in Parkersburg wrote to Commissioner Staunton and, presuming that the architect for the new Capitol would be "one of experience in the line of Capitol designing, and a non-resident," recommended Theodore T. Sansbury of Parkersburg (misspelled as Stansbury in *CCC*) as an appropriate associate for the job (*CCC*, 913–14). This letter is dated the same day as Sansbury's visit to Cass Gilbert in New York City.

28 *CCC*, 497, 500–502. One of Garber & Woodward's references pointed out that some years before they had been "associated with Mr. Cass Gilbert of New York, in connection with the construction of the Union Central Building" in Cincinnati. Garber & Woodward may have been hoping for another collaboration.

29 The June 23 letter is found in *CCC*, 654. The letter from Commissioner Arnold to Senator Elkins is preserved at N-YHS, box 503, folder 7. That Gilbert was aware of activities behind the scenes is apparent in the fact that a copy of this letter from a commissioner to a US senator is found in the Cass Gilbert archives.

The supervising architect of the Treasury Department with whom they met is not named, but it may be relevant that Cass Gilbert had designed the Treasury Annex in Washington, DC, in 1917–18, when W. G. McAdoo was secretary of the Treasury. Gilbert had often worked with Laird, as is indicated in penciled comments on a letter written by Laird to Gilbert asking the architect to serve as a juror for the competition for All Souls' Church, Washington (N-YHS, box 585, folder 2). Gilbert was acquainted with Laird as early as 1905; see Fenske, *Skyscraper*, 116.

The quotation in the text is from the "Report to House of Delegates," 13. Laird's expense account for the trip, with expenses totaling $44.25 and his professional fee of $300, is preserved (*CCC*, 746–47). The train fare from Washington to Charleston was $14.98, plus $3.89 for an upper berth.

Warren P. Laird was the second head of the University of Pennsylvania's Department of Architecture. He succeeded Theophilus Parsons Chandler Jr., who had founded the department. Chandler and Laird followed the curriculum of the École des Beaux-Arts in Paris. That Laird had developed a specialty in advising on such architectural issues indicates the vigorous level of activity in the design and construction of public buildings during this period.

For the letter from the Pittsburgh AIA, which at this time encompassed West Virginia, see *CCC*, 300–302; June 25, 1921. The letter stated that there were two methods for selecting an architect, direct selection and selection through competition in design, and added, "The selection of an architect through competition in design should be followed only if it is deemed absolutely impossible to reach a choice by direct selection." Direct selection "places an owner in proper position to acquire accurate advice immediately concerning the many phases of any building problem and especially in the consideration of sites." Selecting a site was, of course, a pressing need for the West Virginia Governor and Capitol Building Commission.

The history of the competitions that had been held for various state capitols reveals that, in addition to being "slow and costly," competitions were often inconclusive, as was the case with the first competition held for the Minnesota Capitol.

The West Virginia chapter of the AIA was created in December 1922. It had sixteen members, but by 1938 the effects of the Depression had reduced its membership to seven. Chambers, *Buildings of West Virginia*, 42–43.

30 The transcript of the call is preserved at N-YHS, box 519, folder 9. Thirty-one trips are documented in Cass Gilbert's weekly appointment calendars between 1921 and 1932 (N-YHS, box 607), but the calendars are not complete and even more trips may have been made. Gilbert made what seems to have been the final trip in December 1933, accompanied by John Rockart, the assistant who had worked in his office since 1889. Although Rockart worked almost exclusively for Gilbert, the *New York Times* headline for his obituary read: "John Rockart Dies, Noted Architect" (October 14, 1951). In January 1930, Rockart and Samuel A. McGuire brought the final drawings and specifications to Charleston for approval by the Capitol Building Commission. In a letter to the governor dated January 13, 1930, Gilbert wrote:

> Mr. Rockart has been associated with me for so many years that he is thoroughly familiar with all the questions that might arise and can speak with authority. He was my assistant at the time I built the Minnesota State Capitol and later in rebuilding the Arkansas Capitol and you can rely absolutely on what he says and upon his judgment. Mr. McGuire is our chief mechanical engineer and a very able and competent man in his department. (N-YHS, box 516, folder 10)

The 1933 trip is documented in a letter dated December 16, 1933 (N-YHS, box 516, folder 1). Because Gilbert missed the dedication ceremonies in 1932, this was perhaps his first and only opportunity to see the Capitol completely finished.

Additional trips to Charleston by members of Gilbert's office, including Cass Junior and John Rockart, are also documented. In 1922, one could leave New York at 3:40 P.M. and arrive in Charleston at 12:30 P.M. the next day (N-YHS, box 8, folder 14; in 2009, the Amtrak "Cardinal Route" from New York to Chicago traveled the same route, passing through Philadelphia, Baltimore, Washington, Charleston, Cincinnati, and Indianapolis). A document dated November 25, 1932, that seems to represent a final calculation of fees owed the architect lists "Traveling expenses paid from the signing of the contract to date" as $13,012.24.

31 *CCC*, 657–58. Even though Young suggested that the appointment of an architect might be imminent, he added, "It has not yet been determined whether or not selection will be made direct or by a limited competition."

32 For the June 30 *Daily Mail*, see N-YHS, box 683. The newspaper clippings in Gilbert's scrapbook are in poor condition and some of the dates are illegible; in addition, some articles are no longer complete. For the July 1 morning *Daily Mail*, see box 683. For the afternoon July 1 *Daily Mail*, see box 683.

33 The typescript was dictated by Gilbert and the typed copy corrected by him in pencil, as was his common practice; it includes some references to the telephone conversation as well. The transcript of the telephone conversation was made by R. D. Read and includes one penciled comment by Gilbert (both are in N-YHS, box 519, folder 9). It is perhaps ironic that in 1922, when he was president of the State of West Virginia Board of Examination and Registration of Architects, Sansbury had to sign Cass Gilbert's 1922 certification (box 504, folder 1). For Sansbury's works, consult the index in Chambers, *Buildings of West Virginia*, 650; Chambers identifies him as Theodore T. Sansbury Jr.

34 Luther H. Lewis of Crow, Lewis & Wick of New York City appeared before the Commission on June 29 and asked to present, but no presentation is documented. Whether other firms appeared at the meetings with Laird is not documented.

35 Ferriss, *Power in Buildings*, 7–8. The architect Egerton Swartwout also commented on Gilbert's ability to convince his clients of his viewpoint; see Fenske, *Skyscraper*, 74. Fenske summarized: "As Gilbert's skills with speculative real estate development, salesmanship, and drawings as tools of persuasion show, he had thoroughly mastered a range of market-inspired methods for securing architectural commissions" (75).

36 The telegram to Commissioner N. Price Whittaker notifying him of the July 7 meeting is documented (*CCC*, 913), but the transcription has July 17 as the date; this is clearly an error. For the wire to architectural firms, see 845. *CCC* documents that this telegram was sent to John Russell Pope and Geo. B. Post & Sons on July 5. Post & Sons responded the same day that a member of the firm would leave on the first train and arrive in Charleston at 11:40 A.M. on the 7th (845).

37 When Brunner and Gilbert were classmates at MIT in 1878–79, the former won first prize in a competition in which Gilbert's rendering of a Pompeii reconstruction received second place. See Blodgett, *Cass Gilbert: The Early Years*, 21. Writing in *Architecture* in December 1934, Matlack Price dismissed Brunner as an architect who "never reached anything but mediocrity" (quoted in Hartman and Cigliano, *Pencil Points Reader*, 2004, 381). For the telegrams to Carrère & Hastings, Pope, and the Post firm, see *CCC*, 624, 845. Although the firm of McKim, Mead & White continued under the established name, by 1921 both McKim and White were deceased.

It is not known if John Russell Pope responded to the invitation. Thomas Hastings of Carrère & Hastings did not reply until August 15, when he reported that he received the invitation only after his return from Europe (*CCC*, 624).

It is not clear whether at this point Wysong & Jones proposed to work alone or in collaboration with Henry Hornbostel; see note 19 above.

38 Why Bacon would have traveled to Charleston and only belatedly realized that he could not undertake the project is curious. His comments are documented in "Report of Capitol Building Commission," 16. Bacon wired Houston Young on July 1, 1921, that he would arrive on July 2 (*CCC*, 320). Bacon's early arrival, before he could have received the telegram of July 5, would have given him time to see the city and, perhaps, to speak with the commissioners. Perhaps discussions with commissioners made him aware that a grander edifice was planned than he had suspected. The commissioners may already have decided that they wanted a domed structure in the National Capitol model; designing such a structure would not have been difficult for an architect with Bacon's background and experience, but engineering and managing its construction might have given him pause. The reason for including his statement in the Senate report, however, is clear. These minutes, prepared for presentation to the Senate Committee in 1923, more than a year after the contract with Gilbert was signed, were intended to justify the Commission's decision; Bacon's statement supports their process because Gilbert, who had already built two monumental domed state capitols, was an architect with just such an organization in place.

39 N-YHS, box 519, folder 9.

40 *CCC*, 588. Before Gilbert's purchase, the family's home in Ridgefield had been a farmhouse, a tavern, and a stagecoach stop; later owners modified some of Cass Gilbert's additions, but his garden pavilion survives intact. It became the Keeler Tavern Museum in 1966.

41 "Report of the Special Senate Committee on Capitol Commission," 17. The telegram is also documented in *CCC*, 588. Supervising the construction meant that the architect could monitor the bidding process and thus exercise control over quality and hopefully avoid graft. Some

architects of the period had pointed out that "they began to earn a profit only during the supervisory phase of building." See Woods, *Craft to Profession*, 158.

Cass Gilbert had fought hard for the 6 percent fee, which by 1921 was the industry standard. For the Woolworth Building (completed 1913), Gilbert had received the earlier standard of 5 percent, but only after many discussions with his patron, who had tried to reduce Gilbert's fee by arguing that such a commission would bring "a fortune in the shape of fame"; see Fenske, *Skyscraper*, 181. For a discussion of the evolution of the 6 percent fee, see Woods, *Craft to Profession*, 37, 51–52, and 172, who reports that in 1866, the AIA had tried to establish a fee of 5 percent, and that in 1896 there had been an unsuccessful move to increase the fee to 6 percent. In 1908, the AIA set a minimum of 5 percent, "but in 1909, after a pep talk by Cass Gilbert, it was raised to six percent" (Saylor, "A-I-A's First Hundred Years," 60). In the early 1970s, the AIA was forced by the Justice Department to abandon a fee schedule.

42 That Gilbert was asked to pay these fees out of his own pocket may be a result of a conversation Burt Fenner of McKim, Mead & White had with the commissioners. When Fenner wrote on July 15, 1921, to congratulate Gilbert on his appointment, he indicated that during his interview he may have given the commissioners a mistaken impression about the fee structure:

> I want to tell you that if any member of the commission should say that I ever suggested a willingness to accept a fee of less than six per cent, plus engineers' fees, such a statement would be without foundation in fact.
>
> During my hearing before the Commission, I was told that the Commission would insist upon the payment of an inclusive fee to the architect, rather than a fee to the architect, plus other fees to the engineers. I expressed agreement with this general principle. After the meeting, one member of the Commission asked me a question which led me to believe that my answer might possibly have been understood to be an assent to the proposition that engineers' fees would be included in the architect's six percent. I think I set this one gentleman straight, but if anyone else got this wrong impression, and should make use of it in the negotiations with you, you will know the facts. (N-YHS, box 503, folder 7)

43 For the minutes, see "Report of Capitol Building Commission," 20–25. The text of the telegram is published in *CCC*, 588. On Gilbert's copy of the wire is typed "Ridgefield, Received 10 AM Daylight time, Saturday July 9, Answered 11.45 AM Daylight time." N-YHS, box 503, folder 8. For the phone conversation, see the transcript at N-YHS, box 516, folder 5.

44 Gilbert Papers, LC. The next day Gilbert received a telegram from architect George Pratt Ingersoll: "Hearty Congratulations on your new and great honor. We all rejoice." (N-YHS, box 503, folder 7).

45 For the *Gazette* article, see N-YHS, box 524, folder 3. In 1912, four West Virginia towns had Woolworth stores: Charleston, Huntington, Parkersburg, and Wheeling. See the list of Woolworth stores in 1912 in Fenske, *Skyscraper*, 314–18. For the *Washington Times* and *New York Times* articles, see N-YHS, box 683.

46 N-YHS, box 524, folder 3.

47 Gilbert's survey was reported in the *Charleston Daily Mail* on June 14 (N-YHS, box 683). The original contract is preserved at the WVSA; it is published in full in the "Report of Capitol Building Commission," 19–25. Gilbert's contract for the Minnesota State Capitol had stated that he would "supervise the construction, erection, finishing and furnishing entire and complete the said State Capitol building including the embellishment of the grounds constituting the site of said State Capitol." Quoted in Thompson, *Minnesota's State Capitol*, 21.

48 The Special Senate Committee estimated the cost of a competition as $40,000 with a delay of eight or nine months. "Report of Special Senate Committee," 3. The quote from the Commission is found in "Report to House of Delegates," 13.

49 A letter from West Virginia's chief auditor and accountant, E. A. Dover, to Governor Morgan dated February 24, 1925, indicated that as of that date Gilbert had been paid $95,000 and he was due another $15,000 if certification indicated drawings and specifications were one-half complete (N-YHS, box 508, folder 1).

We did not find documentation for all payments to Cass Gilbert. On July 15, 1926, Secretary Hill wrote to his office to inquire if $1,149,218.13 was the correct amount to which the 6 percent commission should be applied; if so, the architect's commission would be $68,953.09 (N-YHS, box 508, folder 1). The list of suppliers indicates that this was for Office Building 1: George A. Fuller Company ($984,416.91), Riggs Distler and Company ($29,126.86), James McCrea and Sons ($72,976.08), Otis Elevator Company ($18,235.00), Woodrum Home Outfitting Company ($1,485.00), Goshorn Hardware Company ($128.00), Abney Barnes Company ($14,907.61), Black and Boyd Manufacturing Company ($10,002.50), John Polachek Bronze and Iron Company ($1,665.00), Paris and Wiley ($8,075.00), United Fuel Gas Company ($865.78), International Time Recording Company ($2,847.00), John Donnelly and Company ($1,150), and P. J. Henly ($3,337.39).

A memo in the West Virginia State Archives dated March 15, 1929, reveals that as of that date Cass Gilbert had been paid $183,000, of which $40,000 had been paid him on January 30, 1929, for work on plans and specifications for the Main Capitol Building. Also listed is his 6 percent commission on the "total cost of Buildings No. 1 and No. 2": $146,014.88.

50 N-YHS, box 516, folder 8. Gilbert to C. G. Hequembourg, April 20, 1925.

51 N-YHS, box 524, folder 3. This article misinterprets the details of the contract as follows:

> Instead of the architect drawing but six percent of the cost of the new capitol building, as declared by Charleston propagandists, the contract states that he is to receive "6 per cent of the total cost of the development of the grounds and the construction of the capitol building and any other buildings thereon."
>
> "Development of the grounds" includes the price paid in damage and purchase of private property moved to clear the 16 acres for the capitol site. With even the most conservative estimates placing the total cost of the entire project at $12,000,000, the New York architect draws $720,000 in fees.
>
> A provision of the contract calls for the payment of $160,000 in architect fees before a tap of work is done the schedule of advance payments being: [the article then lists the advance payments stipulated in the contract].

52 N-YHS, box 504, folder 1. Other passages from the document include:

> The printed document enclosed forms the basis of all compensation for architects in all monumental buildings for the United States Government where such are executed by architects outside of the Treasury Department. It is commonly used for all banks and corporation buildings, public libraries and municipal structures. It has been repeatedly approved by the United States Treasury Department and by the courts and by the arbitrators in the settlement of claims. It formed the basis of my contracts for the St. Louis Public Library, the Detroit Public Library, the Waterbury City Hall and many other public and private buildings of all classes.
>
> I suggest that you communicate with Dr. Warren P. Laird, Professor of Architecture, University of Pennsylvania, Philadelphia, Pa., and Prof. W. A. Boring, Columbia University, New York

City, N.Y., who are experts in these matters, especially the former, who has conducted many important competitions for public work, and ascertain from them what the standard fees are for architects' services.

53 An editorial from the *Wheeling Intelligencer* on December 20, 1922, is published in *CCC*, 578–79. After reading Gilbert's contract, the writer concluded that the commissioners

> have paved the way for Mr. Gilbert to be paid a sum of the people's money entirely out of proportion to the worth of his services, a sum that is absolutely ridiculous. It is certain the members of the Capitol Building Commission would never have sanctioned such an expenditure for an architect if they were paying for it out of their own private funds. There is, of course, on the face of the contract no evidence of dishonesty, yet it is hard to believe any body of businessmen would, without some hidden reason, or under persuasion, enter into such a contract. There is no possible explanation that does not suggest the possibility of collusion.

On March 1, 1923, Gilbert wrote to Professor Laird to ask about the "standard practice in regard to the payment of architects and other expert services upon monumental buildings of the best class." Laird summarized the principles of practice recognized by the AIA:

> a proper minimum charge is 6%. (2) The architect is to be re-imbursed for the costs of the services of heating and ventilation, mechanical and electrical engineers. (3) That the owner shall pay for the services of the clerk of the works or local superintendent, and that the architect is to be re-imbursed for the costs of transportation and living expenses incurred by him and his assistants while traveling in discharge of duties connected with the work.

Laird's response is dated March 19, 1923 (N-YHS, box 504, folder 2). Laird noted that the contracts for the Carnegie Technical Schools in Pittsburgh (by Palmer & Hornbostel) and the Tennessee War Memorial in Nashville (by McKim, Mead & White) included the stipulations he listed in his response.

## Chapter Two
## "THE MOST REMARKABLE ARCHITECT OF HIS GENERATION IN AMERICA"

1 The obituary from the May 18, 1934, *London Times* is quoted in Blodgett, "Conservative," 615. Gilbert's confidence in the lasting importance of his work is implied in his statement that he intended to construct "a small building in Ridgefield [Conn.] in which to place memorabilia of our family ... works of art, the records of my office, drawings etc." Reference to this plan was followed by suggestion of an alternative: "a permanent building for the Academy [National Academy of Design] and ... sufficient space ... set aside for the Gilbert collection of memorabilia and objects of art." Although neither plan was carried out, the intent clarifies his view that his office and personal memorabilia should be kept intact in commemoration of his life and work. Gilbert Papers, LC, 1929 Diary.

2 Much information about Gilbert's projects and professional life is available in the extensive primary sources located in the Cass Gilbert Collection at the New-York Historical Society, the State Archives of West Virginia, the Library of Congress, and other locations. Also see the works of Christen and Flanders, Fenske, Heilbrun, and Irish in the bibliography. Some details of Gilbert's life and building projects, including dates, vary from source to source.

3 There are other composite representations of the works of a particular architect, but to the best of our knowledge, Gilbert's is the only drawing that compares the artist's own contemporary works with great works of the past. The most important examples known to us are Joseph Gandy's 1818 panorama of the public and private buildings executed by Sir John Soane, C. R. Cockerell's 1838 *Tribute to Sir Christopher Wren*, and Augustus Pugin's composite drawing of his own works. Pugin's was published in 1843 as the frontispiece to his *Apology for the Revival of Christian Architecture.* Many thanks to Larry Silver for his assistance with this question. The Wolfsonian in Miami Beach owns a large painting by Lloyd Morgan dated 1936 that represents buildings completed by the firm of Schultze & Weaver between 1921 and 1936, including three New York hotels (the Pierre, the Waldorf-Astoria, and the Sherry-Netherland) and, in Florida, the Miami Biltmore and the Breakers. Thanks to Amy Silverman, assistant registrar at the Wolfsonian, for her help with this object.

4 "In Memoriam: Master Architect Leaves Many Permanent Monuments to His Memory," *Archi*, June 1934, 25. *Archi's* masthead states that membership in Alpha Chi Rho, a "social undergraduate fraternity," was limited to "students of architecture, architectural engineering, landscape architecture, or the allied arts, enrolled in the departments leading to a bachelor's degree." *Archi* reported that the Grand Council of Alpha Chi Rho had sent the following letter to all chapters: "It is with sincere sorrow that I call to your attention the death of our Master Architect Cass Gilbert. In his death we have lost a friend, an adviser and an ardent supporter of Alpha Chi Rho. As a tribute to Brother Gilbert and what he has done for our Fraternity, I am asking our chapters to meet on Thursday evening, May 24, at 6 P.M., for a short memorial service. We enclose some material to be read at that service. Following the service, please drape your badges for a period of twenty-four hours." *Archi*, June 1934, 26.

5 Stern, *Life and Work*, 15.

6 Roth, "Cass Gilbert," *Dictionary of Architects and Architecture*, 1: 312.

7 Gilbert to R. C. Coleman, N-YHS, Letter book August 1920–July 1922, 166, quoted in Betts, "Sketch to Architecture," 78.

8 Blodgett, "Politics," 72, referring to a letter from Gilbert to Reginald Bloomfield, April 5, 1933, Gilbert Papers, LC.

9 The Capitol was praised in West Virginia publications following the building's dedication; see, for instance, Stutler, "West Virginia's Magnificent State Capitol." Elsewhere, the Capitol is mentioned only briefly or not at all. An important exception is an essay by Lorimer Rich ("Capitols and Legislative Buildings," *Forms and Functions*, Hamlin, ed.), in which the West Virginia Capitol is the only domed state capitol illustrated.

10 For Frank Lloyd Wright, the "1893 World's Fair disaster" held back the development of American architecture: "Came the Chicago Fair of 1893. Eclecticism won the day—there was so little to put against it—and the debacle began that has lasted to this moment [1936]." In 1933 he had written, "At the Columbian Fair, the provincials of the United States saw for the first time Architecture as co-ordination on the grand scale. Thrilled by its orchestral effects the provinces, aided by the group of eclectics responsible for the ensemble, went heavily pseudo—and imagined they went 'classic.'" In 1934, Wright crafted his definition of the modern: "Actually, the modern idea is a definite turning away from the artificial, from the extreme, from the synthetic and back to the simple, the wholesome, the natural." Pfeiffer, *Wright Collected Writings*, 3: 300, 190, 153, 170.

11 On responses to the Supreme Court Building, see Blodgett, "Politics," especially page 72 regarding "chilly opulence" and the fact that the "only positive evaluation ... in a professional journal" was by Cass Gilbert Jr. In a statement documented in 1938, Frank Lloyd Wright

condemned Cass Gilbert's Supreme Court building as a "bastard" because it continued the eclecticism and revivalism characteristic of the premodern period: "When Michelangelo piled the Pantheon upon the Parthenon and called it St. Peters, he, a painter, had committed architectural adultery.... It is an imitative anachronism that characterizes our public arts, as illustrated by our capitols, courthouses, and town halls.... In short, in this present time only the bastard survives, even as a temple for the work of the Supreme Court of the United States" (Brownwell and Wright, *Architecture and Modern Life*, 56–57).

See also Byard, "Representing American Justice," 285: "The building was a fine building, but by 1935 the live and athletic sense of duty and right Gilbert wanted to embody in the building was something relatively few felt or warmed to any more. The authority it meant to convey was easily confused with authoritarianism—a confusion to which Gilbert himself contributed in his admiration for Mussolini." It is important to note that Gilbert's dealings with Mussolini were during the early years of Mussolini's administration when international public opinion was focused on the order and optimism he brought to Italy. Gilbert wrote to Mussolini on August 11, 1932, complimenting Italy: "I have chosen a very delicate light ivory and soft yellow colored marble from the Montarrenti quarries near Siena [for the US Supreme Court].... I am most anxious Your Excellency that this room should be as dignified and beautiful as possible and that it should have the aspect of refinement and distinction of the classic examples only to be found in Italy and especially in Rome" (handwritten, noted as "first draft," Manuscript Division, LC). On this topic see Wilkins and Wilkins, "Cass Gilbert and Mussolini," in preparation.

The move toward Modernism was already demonstrated in 1930 in Sheldon Cheney's *The New World Architecture*, in which the author acknowledged that while ninety-nine out of one hundred practicing architects "profess faith still in revival or adaptation of the 'accepted' styles, or in what they call Eclecticism—appropriate 'choosing' from the past," he wanted to speak positively about a "different architecture, and particularly about the passing of the historic styles" (14). To indicate his point of view, Cheney titled one chapter "The Past and Its Slaves." Although he used both the front and back views of the Woolworth Building as illustrations (69, 71), his praise of Gilbert's building was conditional: "Here, then, is where Eclecticism came closest to an acceptable achievement, by the happy circumstances of a past style of ornament being fitted into a new type of structure and through the architect's understanding of the limits and uses of surface ornament." He continued: "But nothing that we can say or do will ever alter the fact that the reason any architect today borrows a stylistic envelope from the past is because he is not original enough to create the one truly appropriate to the new era. There is an element of dishonesty in his approach, in his thinking" (70–71). It should be no surprise that the only other work by Cass Gilbert that was used as an illustration is the US Army Supply Base in Brooklyn (117 and 300).

Already in 1918, the architect Claude Bragdon had argued against the mindless copying of earlier models: "[The architectural designer] is taught that all the best songs have been sung.... The Glory that was Greece, the Grandeur that was Rome ... the ordered restraint of Renaissance are so drummed into him during his years of training, and exercise so tyrannical a spell over his imagination that he loses the power of clear and logical thought and never becomes truly creative" (13).

12 Evidence for the renewal of Cass Gilbert's reputation abounds in the 2010 edition of the *AIA Guide to New York City*. The text reports that the US Custom House is "one of the City's most splendid Beaux Arts buildings, now re-loved by modernists searching for fresh meaning in the history of architecture" (13), while the Woolworth Building "soars; only the Seagram and CBS Buildings have the combination of articulate architecture and massing to achieve similar drama" (74). The authors also pointed out that the New York Insurance Company's pyramidal "hat" has inspired Cesar Pelli, Kevin Roche, David Childs of SOM, Helmut Jahn, and others (240). Even more recently, architectural critic Paul Goldberger, writing in the *New Yorker* about Frank Gehry's new skyscraper (8 Spruce Street, completed 2011) near the Woolworth Building, concluded, "From the east, you see [Gehry's building] against the Woolworth Building, Cass Gilbert's ode to height, from 1913, and the most lyrical skyscraper in New York. Gehry's building isn't its equal, but it is the first thing built downtown since then that actually deserves to stand beside it" (March 7, 2011, 74). The *New York Times* critic Nicolai Ouroussoff highlighted Gilbert's architectural sensibilities in his review of Gehry's building:

> The power of the design only deepens when it is looked at in relation to Gilbert's Woolworth building. A steel frame building clad in neo-Gothic terra-cotta panels, Gilbert's masterpiece is a triumphant marriage between the technological innovations that gave rise to the skyscraper and the handcrafted ethos of an earlier era. Mr. Gehry's design is about bringing that same sensibility—the focus on refined textures, the cultivation of a sense that something has been shaped by a human hand—to the digital age. (February 10, 2011)

13 Blodgett, "Conservative," 625: "He ran what was possibly the country's largest architectural practice headed by a single man." At one point, Gilbert considered adding John Rockart, George Wells, Samuel Stevens Haskell, and Thomas Holyoke as partners, but he admitted that "my temperament has always prevented me from doing so" (Gilbert to Henry Rutgers Marshall, Gilbert Papers, LC, box 7, file 1905, noted in Irish, "Gilbert in Practice," 8). Irish also noted Gilbert's words (30, n. 15): "I can never do my best work when I have to consider what an associate wants me to do or say" (Letter to Cass Gilbert Jr., June 28, 1925, N-YHS, Personal Letters).

That Gilbert was aware of the dangers of pride is found in a quotation from his *Maxims for My Office Organization*: "In conducting business (especially for the office) never forget that the greatest danger arises from cocksure pride" (Gilbert Papers, LC, box 6, file 1899). For the complete list of maxims, see Irish, "Gilbert in Practice," 1–2.

In Gilbert's personal copy of the *Architects' Journal* (65.1 [June 8, 1927]: 990) he penciled in some editorial comments on "Mr. Cass Gilbert" by F. E. Bennett, noting "not so!!" next to "He is surrounded by a number of very capable-looking assistants, five of whom he has made his partners" (797). Gilbert Papers, LC.

14 Betts, "From Sketch," 76 and n. 49; the source is a memorandum dated September 23, 1919, preserved at N-YHS. Also, in a letter of 1879 to his friend Clarence Johnston, the twenty-year-old Cass Gilbert had referred to his own "audacious egotism" (quoted in Irish, *Modern Traditionalist*, 13).

15 Julia Finch Gilbert, *Reminiscences*, 4. Julia also discussed his early speeches in schools and to groups of architects where "he found the opportunity of passing on to them his own high ideals in regard to the profession of architecture and the allied arts" (3). That the extemporaneous speeches were greatly successful "was proved by the many invitations he had to deliver talks, addresses, and—as one might say—sermons on the profession that claimed all of his attention and interest.... His speeches were so thoroughly a part of himself" (3).

16 See Fenske, *Skyscraper*, for this quotation (218) and general information about the event. Fenske reports that those invited to attend "summed up virtually all aspects of the nation's contemporary political, economic, and cultural life" (221). Gilbert's willingness to recognize those

who worked for and with him is documented by the inclusion of his assistants Theodore Johnson, John Rockart, and George Wells, and engineer Gunvald Aus at the dinner celebrating the completion of the Woolworth Building.

17 Woolworth, "Dinner Given to Cass Gilbert," 35, 38, 51. Gilbert's desire to share credit for his work is seen in his response to a letter of praise he received a decade after the completion of the Woolworth Building:

> An expression of appreciation of my work is always very gratifying indeed and gives me new encouragement to go forward, and I am happy to say that I have had many such expressions couched sometimes in prose, sometimes in rhyme, and sometimes in line or color about the Woolworth Building.... I feel that I cannot accept these complimentary expressions without an acknowledgement of the fact that the Woolworth Building represents the combination of effort of many others who were associated with me in it. First of all, no good work in architecture is possible without a good client.... I think I am justified in saying that Frank W. Woolworth deserves a large portion of the praise.... There were with me ... architectural assistants, designers, engineers and constructors who rendered most admirable and effective service and to who[m] I feel that great ... credit should be given.... It is true that I was, so to speak, the leader of the orchestra and held the baton. (Gilbert to "Jedediah Tingle," April 2, 1923, N-YHS, box 504, folder 4. Jedediah Tingle was the pseudonym used by William E. Harmon, a philanthropist who died in 1928.)

Humorous sculpted portraits of Gilbert and Woolworth, incidentally, were a permanent part of the lobby decoration along with those of structural engineer Gunvald Aus (who later worked on the West Virginia Capitol), the builder (Louis Horowitz), a real estate agent (Edward J. Hogan), and a bank president (Lewis E. Pierson, president of Irving Bank, with offices in the Woolworth building).

18 The school of architecture had been established at MIT in 1865. Gilbert's earliest architectural experience has been credited to his summer work with a carpenter in Red Wing, Minnesota, while he was still a youth. See Blodgett, *Early Years*, 7. On Gilbert's lack of interest in studying at the École, see Blodgett, *Early Years*, 29. In an account written in 1920, Gilbert said: "At this time I was an enthusiastic follower of the Gothic, and looked upon Viollet-le-Duc as its chief exponent. Hence the École des Beaux-Arts did not attract me. Richardson had broken away from the École and was doing great work in America" (Gilbert Papers, LC, box 17).

For a summary of the Beaux-Arts "system" of education and its impact on American architectural education, see White, *Paul Philippe Cret*, 21–24. The system was still being used in such schools as Carnegie Institute of Technology, Pittsburgh, in the late 1920s and the University of New Hampshire in the early 1930s.

19 For his itinerary and other information about the trip, see Larson, *Gilbert Abroad*. Until his twenty-first birthday on November 24, 1880, Gilbert had a stipend of $25 a month from his father's estate; to make the trip possible, he wrote to his friend Clarence Johnston that he would need an additional $250. $125 of this would come from his savings from a summer job and the other $125 would be a loan from his mother. Like many young students, Gilbert ran out of money near the end of his trip, and in a letter to his mother from London dated July 18, 1880, he expressed disappointment at being unable to find a job there and accepted her offer of money to pay his passage home.

20 For Gilbert's watercolors and their exhibition, see Fenske, *Skyscraper*, 334, n. 25. The critic H. Van Buren Magonigle wrote that in the period c. 1883–84, Henry Bacon and Cass Gilbert were producing travel sketches that transcended "in merit those of most of their contemporaries." (Magonigle, *Pencil Points*, January, 1934, 336).

21 His longest European trip was probably the five-month journey begun in December 1897, before the plans for the Minnesota State Capitol were finalized. The office appointment calendars preserved at the New-York Historical Society reveal that Gilbert traveled not only to Europe but also to Havana and Chichen Itza in 1932. Another example of a focused study visit was his 1913 trip to Europe, when he visited the Villa Farnesina, Villa Madama, and the Cancelleria in Rome in preparation for final design work for the Detroit Public Library; see Federman, "Detroit Public Library," 86. The 1921 letter is published in *CCC*, 523. The 1929 reference to his study of French domes is found in a September 13 letter from Gilbert to Virgil Highland, editor of the *Clarksburg Telegram* and a former member of the West Virginia Capitol Commission, preserved at the WVSA.

22 Even before he went to Europe, he wrote to his friend Clarence Johnston: "The office I wish to get into is that of George E. Street; his brilliant genius, widespread fame and scholarly manner, his endeavor after pure Gothic, and his surprising exactness of detail in all his office work have an attraction for me" (August 3, 1879, from Garrison on the Hudson, when he was working for the US Coast & Geodetic Survey to make money for his trip to Europe, quoted in Larson, *Gilbert Abroad*, 28). See his earlier letters to Clarence Johnston of June 22 and July 21, 1879. In the first of these he wrote, "There are architects in London now, such as we may never see grouped in another generation of men. Street, Seddon, Waterhouse, Norman Shaw, [and] Burges are names which will belong as well to posterity as to the present age.... My idea is to enter the office of one of these men as a student." In the July 21 letter, he ranked the architects with whom he wished to work: Street first, then Waterhouse, Shaw, and Burges (quoted in Larson, 15, 25, 27).

23 Mary N. Woods reported that by 1919 more than five hundred men had worked in the McKim, Mead & White office (*Craft to Profession*, 146). Woods includes a plan of the offices from 1891; see 124. At that time, the drafting room had twenty-nine tables, with stools for forty-six draftsmen.

For information about other architectural offices, see, for example, *Architectural Record*, July 1900, which featured the article "Geo. B. Post's Workshop, Where Our Architects Work, No. 1," with photos of the reception room and the large "draughting room." A photo captioned "Part of the Office Force" features thirty-eight men.

Gilbert's payroll records, for instance those of 1927 and 1928 (preserved in N-YHS, box 604), provide information about his office. In January 1927, forty-eight employees were working on fourteen different projects.

24 Fenske, *Skyscraper*, 83.

25 For his partnership with Taylor, see Irish, *Modern Traditionalist*, 37–56.

26 In 1907, the year before Gilbert became the president of the AIA, however, the Committee on Education presented the recommendation that "prerequisite to receiving a degree in architecture the candidate should show a reasonable proficiency in Latin." Important also is "that an adequate architectural education should consist of four categories: (1) a year of preparatory study ... ; (2) four years in a school of architecture; (3) at least one, and preferably two or three years studying advanced design in Paris, Rome, or in American ateliers; (4) at least a year of travel in Europe." This is reported by Saylor, "First Hundred Years," 114–15.

27 Frank Lloyd Wright possessed enormous talent and capacity for innovation. It is interesting, however, that he designed more residences than public buildings. Gilbert, who began his career designing homes and churches, ultimately designed many more public buildings than did Wright.

28 The publication of professional journals such as *American Architect and Building News*, *Architectural Record*, *Architectural Review*, *Brickbuilder*, and

*The Inland Architect and Builder* were important sources for the continuing education of architects. On this topic, see Woods, "Profession's Voice," *Journal of the Society of Architectural Historians*, 48 (1989): 117–38. Thanks to Martin Aurand of Carnegie Mellon University for his help with this topic.

29 Gilbert Collection, LC.

30 Cass Gilbert's Society of Arts and Sciences Gold Medal was given in honor of his design of the Woolworth Building; it was presented during a ceremony held at the Hotel Astor. The *New York Times* (January 17, 1931) reported that because of his skyscraper design, Gilbert "was hailed by many distinguished men as the prophet of a new and great movement in architecture." In Gilbert's speech, he recognized the importance of his patron, who had died in 1919, as someone "who loved beauty in architecture." While declaring that "the most beautiful skyscraper possible has not yet been built," Gilbert, who loved a learned reference, concluded "if we have met the challenge and pointed out one of the many ways in which Caliban may be exchanged for Ariel, in which ugliness may flower into beauty, we shall not have lived in vain."

31 The importance of Cass Gilbert's AIA presidency is suggested by several comments in Saylor, "First Hundred Years." During his tenure the minimum fee for architects was raised to six percent after a "pep talk" by Gilbert (60) and the debt on the AIA's home, the Octagon in Washington, DC, was wiped out (70). In December of 1909, the AIA published a "Circular of Advice Relative to Principles of Professional Practice and The Canon of Ethics" (102–3), but what role Cass Gilbert may have played in its drafting is uncertain.

At the AIA in Washington in 1900, Gilbert spoke on the future development of the Mall in Washington, DC; this impetus led to the McMillan Plan (named for its chairman, Senator James McMillan of Michigan), which, among other things, suggested that a purpose-built structure be created for the United States Supreme Court, a building that Gilbert himself was later chosen to design. See Blodgett, "Conservative," 619–29. Gilbert also helped to establish the Architectural League of New York, over which he presided in 1913–14.

32 On Gilbert's role at the National Academy of Design and the process by which his portrait, required for admission, was painted by Kenyon Cox, see Dearinger, ed., *Paintings and Sculpture in the Collection of the National Academy of Design*, 122–23.

Gilbert also served as president of the National Institute of Arts and Letters from 1926 to 1932. He was a member of the Architectural Society of Liverpool, served on national committees, published articles, and was frequently invited to give lectures.

International honors included the Grand Gold Medal for Architecture at the 1900 Paris Exhibition and medals from Leipzig (1913) and Belgium (1920), being named Chevalier of the Legion of Honor of France in 1924, and being presented at the Court of St. James in June 1925. His international reputation was further enhanced when he became an honorary member of the Royal Institute of British Architects and the Royal Architectural Institute of Canada and an honorary foreign member of the Royal Academy of Arts.

In 1921 he received the Gold Medal from the American Academy of Arts and Letters. An informal honor bestowed on him was his inclusion among the one hundred and fifty "men of genius" at the "Peacock Feast," hosted at Laurelton Hall by Louis Comfort Tiffany, on May 15, 1914. Frelinghuysen, *Tiffany and Laurelton*, 196.

In 1910, President Howard Taft appointed Gilbert to the National Commission of Fine Arts, charged with overseeing the McMillan Plan. President Wilson reappointed Gilbert to the same position and considered appointing him ambassador to Denmark or Italy. See Blodgett, "Conservative," 621. A February 6, 1924, diary entry, at the time of Woodrow Wilson's funeral, provides information about Gilbert and his view of Woodrow Wilson: "He was a shrewd politician but it remains to be seen if he was a statesman.... I have no personal cause of enmity toward him. I was well treated in his administration—I could have been appointed Minister to Denmark possibly Ambassador to Italy.... I was ... practically offered appointment as a Minister to Siam.... If the League of Nations had been approved ... I was to be the architect of the $10,000,000 League buildings at Geneva" (Gilbert Papers, LC).

33 Gilbert's assertive boldness was seen when, as a young professional, he assumed that Daniel Burnham would choose him as his partner in planning the Exposition. See Blodgett, *Early Years*, 104–5; the correspondence on the proposed partnership is preserved in the Gilbert Collection at the Minnesota Historical Society. Gilbert suggested that he be hired to replace Root and traveled to Chicago to meet with Burnham. Evidently there was friction between the two men; Gilbert was anxious to work first as an associate then quickly rise to a partnership. Burnham was unsure, not knowing Gilbert and initially disapproving the idea of eventual partnership; the negotiations proceeded, but eventually Burnham rejected the young man's application and Gilbert's only role was as a member of the Jury of Architecture. See Blodgett, *Early Years*, regarding Gilbert as a member of that jury, a "distinctly modest honor, charged with selecting examples of recent work around the country to be exhibited in photographs." William Channing Whitney was selected to design the "Minnesota Building."

34 For the fair and its influence, see Appelbaum, *World's Fair*. Gilbert met with Governor Knute Nelson in March 1893 to discuss the fact that Minnesota would soon need an architect to design its new Capitol, suggesting that even then he may have been pondering designs for the competition; see Thompson, 19–20.

35 Gilbert's concern that everything go well on this project was revealed by the delay between his winning the competition in 1895 and the laying of the cornerstone in 1898. In December 1897, he left on a five-month trip to Europe to confirm his final plans.

36 September 24, 1899, Gilbert Papers, LC, box 6, file 1899. Initially the family lived in an apartment; in 1902 they moved into a townhouse at 45 East 78th Street.

In 1886 Gilbert had informed his fiancée that he intended "to stand not only well in, but at the head of my profession" (Cass Gilbert to Julia Finch, December 16, 1886, Gilbert Papers, LC, quoted in Blodgett, *Early Years*, 80). Sharon Irish considered the irony that the Minnesota State Capitol contributed to Gilbert's declining practice in that state, which may have eased his transition to a New York–based practice. She attributed the problem in part to Gilbert's determination to use Georgian marble rather than Minnesota stone for the building; the problem arose because the stone was not local, and, even more damning, was the product of a state that had seen a number of deaths of Minnesota soldiers during the Civil War (Irish, *Modern Traditionalist*, 44).

37 Included in the Essex County Courthouse is a skylight by Louis Comfort Tiffany. We know that there was also a social connection between him and Cass Gilbert. In addition, Gilbert was among the "committee of established artists" to be trustees of the Tiffany Foundation (established 1918). Frelinghuysen, *Tiffany and Laurelton Hall*, 205.

38 See Blodgett, "Oberlin: The Great Collaboration" and *Oberlin Architecture*; Speck, "The University of Texas;" Christen, "Cass Gilbert and the Ideal of the City Beautiful;" Speck and Cleary, *University of Texas at Austin*.

39 There were Woolworth stores in Charleston and Wheeling by 1910. See Fenske, *Skyscraper* for further information on Woolworth stores across the United States (311–18). On July 14, 1921, the *Charleston Gazette* had

headlined: "CASS GILBERT, ARCHITECT OF FAME, TO PLAN NEW CAPITOL; Man Who Designed Woolworth Building Picked by Commission to Plan New Home for State Government; SELECTION OF SITE TO FOLLOW SOON; Gilbert Promises to Help Find Place for State House; First Important Step of Commission." For the *Gazette* article, see N-YHS, box 524, folder 3.

40 In comparison, the Singer Building is 612 feet tall; the Chicago Tribune Tower, 463 feet; the Chrysler Building, 1,047 feet; and the Empire State Building, 1,250 feet.

41 Marin's kaleidoscopic *Lower Manhattan (Composition Derived from Top of the Woolworth Building)* of 1922 is in the collection of the Museum of Modern Art, New York. Marin also made paintings while the building was being completed; see *Woolworth Building, No. 31* (1912), in the collection of the National Gallery of Art.

42 See Woods, "Camera's Eye."

43 Wright's comment came in a discussion of style in "In the Cause of Architecture II: What 'Styles' Mean to the Architect," *The Architectural Record*, February, 1928:

> Style is a consequence of character.
>
> The serpent has "style." Bees as well as butterflies [have style]. So has the scarab that tumbles its ball of cow-manure in the hot sun of the dusty road. The white crane, the horse, the rat, every flower, any tree—even human beings, when they are natural—have it, because they are genuine. They have *character* [Wright's emphasis]. Buildings often have it when they too are genuine, not posing as "architecture." The rear of the New York Public Library has something of this quality of style, while the front has only "styles." The Woolworth Building would have had it to a degree but for professional Gothic prejudices and predilection. The Suspension Bridge from New York to Brooklyn has it. Some aeroplanes have it and some steamships: by no means all of them. Many grain elevators, steel plants, engines have it, and occasionally an automobile. The Wainwright Building of Saint Louis by Alder and Sullivan, as a tall building, has it. There are many tall buildings, now, that are stylish to some degree but all more or less marred by "styles." (Quoted in Pfeiffer, ed., *Wright: Collected Writings*, 1:268)

Wright made two explicit references to Cass Gilbert by name: in both he grouped Gilbert with architects who worked in the "Eclectic" style Wright dismissed; see Pfeiffer, ed., *Wright: Critical Writings*, 289 and 379.

44 When the building was still under construction, the manner in which it had captured the public's interest was demonstrated in *Popular Mechanics* articles in September and October 1912 (338–39 and 491–94); the September article features a series of breathtaking photographs of the workers "taken at a greater height than any photographs of this kind ever were before." See also "The Tallest Office Building in the World: Erection of the Woolworth Building, New York," *Scientific American* 108 (March 8, 1913), which featured a view of the finished building on the cover (see Fenske, *Skyscraper*, 280–81). An entire publication was dedicated to the construction: *The Master Builders: A Record of the Construction of the World's Highest Commercial Structure* (Baltimore: Munder-Thomsen Press, 1913).

An early criticism of the Woolworth building was made by architect Claude Bragdon in 1918: "The Woolworth Building is a notable example of the complete coordination between the structural framework and its envelope, and falls short of ideal success only in the employment of an archaic and alien ornamental language used, however, let it be said, with a fine understanding of the function of ornament" (12). Despite this criticism, the Woolworth Building was so important for the history of architecture that it is the first illustration in the book.

45 Gilbert's letter to Mussolini was written in response to an article about the Mole Littoria (designed by architect Mario Palanti) published in the *New York Tribune* in 1924 (the date is not preserved, but Gilbert's rather ragged copy of the article is preserved at N-YHS, box 672, file 9). Gilbert's letter to Mussolini (October 16, 1924) is preserved at the Library of Congress. To strengthen his argument, the learned architect included a long quotation from the letter written by Belisarius to Totila in the sixth century urging him not to destroy Rome because of its great historic importance.

In 1933 Gilbert wrote to his brother Samuel: "I wish America would leave Europe to run its own affairs.... I like Mussolini's way.... He looks out for Italy! And you know there is no nonsense about him." Heilbrun, *Inventing the Skyline*, xxi. The Mole Littoria, the skyscraper version, was planned in 1924, only two years after Mussolini's march on Rome; plans were changed within a few years. (Mario Palanti, *L'Eternale, Mole Littoria*, at the Wolfsonian Library, Florida International University). A letter dated April 26, 1927, to Cass Gilbert from Henry James (representing, according to the letter head, the Regional Plan of New York and its Environs) concluded with "The American architect who has prevented Mussolini from putting up 1,100 feet of building in Rome deserves, I think, a more enduring monument than Il Duce himself" (Gilbert Papers, LC).

Cass Gilbert's support for re-erecting the fallen columns of the Parthenon is mentioned in a *New York Times* article of June 15, 1930 ("North Side of the Parthenon"), and in personal letters from 1923 to 1933 at N-YHS (Irish, "Cass Gilbert in Practice," 33, n. 42). A letter preserved in the Library of Congress reports: "I count myself fortunate indeed to be among those who join in the replacement of the stones of the Parthenon. How those grand old columns will greet the sun again as they stand with their fellows, sentinels of beauty, looking out over the blue Aegean guarding, as it were, the traditions of the greatest of the arts for all posterity" (Gilbert to John H. Finley, July 12, 1926).

46 N-YHS, box 524, folder 2. The Union Club, founded in 1836, was recognized for its Republican nature (Fenske, *Skyscraper*, 71). Gilbert's personal diaries preserved at the Library of Congress refer to this and other clubs and hotel meeting places: for instance, on January 25, 1922: "annual meeting Union Club 9 pm." In most diaries there is a list of family information and addresses of various clubs such as "Century Club, Union Club, University Club, S. Andrews Golf Club, Cosmos Club Washington DC." The earliest surviving sketches for the West Virginia Capitol were made on Union Club stationery (figs. 23, 24).

47 The telegram was sent on July 13, 1921. A similar sentiment is expressed in a letter dated April 10, 1929, regarding the attainment of the Supreme Court commission: "The meeting was very cordial and satisfactory all around—we discussed details of procedure, estimates of cost ... and the plans.... With my dearest love to you who have been my real partner in all these great enterprises for over forty years." And in a letter written from a trip abroad during the West Virginia construction years, he tenderly stated, "I miss you so much and am lonesome without you tagging around and asking where I am going and what I am going to do next when I don't know myself" (July 19, 1928, Gilbert Papers, LC).

The role Julia played in the business aspect of Cass's life was summarized by Alice Sparberg Alexiou: "Julia had made it her life's work to protect her husband, both from his own propensity for overwork, and those she deemed were trying to work him to death, or in any other ways to take advantage of him." Alexiou, *Flatiron*, 215.

48 For Cass Gilbert Jr.'s portrait at the National Academy of Design, by Henry R. Rittenberg, and a brief biography, see Dearinger, ed., *Paintings and Sculpture in the Collection of the National Academy of Design*, 472.

Several published accounts have credited Cass Gilbert Jr. with a significant role in designing and supervising the construction of the West Virginia Capitol; archival evidence puts such claims to rest.

This assertion of Cass Jr.'s involvement dates to 1974 in Hitchcock and Seale, *Temples of Democracy*. Hitchcock and Seale were writing before the Cass Gilbert Collection at the New-York Historical Society had been fully organized and much of the evidence we have been able to consult was still unavailable. Their account of the West Virginia State Capitol reads, in its entirety:

> The requiem for American Renaissance capitols was sung at Charleston, West Virginia, in 1922, when that state commissioned a Cass Gilbert Capitol from the master himself. It had been Gilbert's own better judgment to avoid the job entirely, but his son Cass, Jr., home from the army, was excited by the challenge of following in his father's footsteps. 'Between my mother and me,' [Cass Junior] later said, 'the old man finally agreed to go ahead. But he never did like it.' Completed in 1932 largely from the younger Cass Gilbert's designs and under his supervision, the West Virginia structure presented to the winding Kanawah [*sic*] River the familiar massing of the capitols of the American Renaissance. Two office wings were built first. With the immense main building between, they form a Capitol group on a scale appropriate to this mountain town.
>
> West Virginians got from Cass Gilbert exactly the Capitol they wanted. It was the very last of the American Renaissance capitols, built many years after the epoch was over. For ten years the project went steadily, if not always smoothly, forward. Getting things done had always been a special feature of the Gilbert package. (271–72)

Seale repeated the claim of Cass Jr.'s involvement in 1994 in Oxendorf and Seale's *Domes of America*: "Cass Gilbert was the architect in name, but his son ... was in fact the architect, and the building shows that the father's sensitivity to detail was passed on to the son" (103). Seale based his conclusions on a conversation with Cass Jr. in 1974.

Cass Jr. on occasion claimed he had played a more important role in his father's work than is supported by surviving documentation. In 1963, an agent of the American Electric Power Service Corporation reported: "I had a most enjoyable visit with Mr. Gilbert [Junior] on January 9 and learning that he and his father were instrumental in designing many capital [*sic*] building structures. To name a few ... United States Custom House ... , the Woolworth Building, the state capitol building in Minnesota, West Virginia.... Mr. Gilbert mentioned quite a number of other structures" (Letter preserved at the WVSA). Since Cass Jr. was born in 1894, he could not have played a role in the 1895–1905 Minnesota Capitol or the 1899–1907 Custom House in New York, and there is no mention in the archives of his participation as a teenager in the design of the 1910–13 Woolworth Building.

The documentation supporting Cass Sr. as the architect responsible for the design and supervision of the West Virginia Capitol is unequivocal. It was he who made the original presentation to the commissioners, and he ran the meeting at which the basic design was approved in June 1922. In January 1930, John Rockart and Samuel A. McGuire—not Cass Jr.—brought the final drawings and specifications for the Main Building to Charleston for approval by the Capitol Building Commission. To the best of our knowledge, only one drawing of the hundreds that survive for the West Virginia Capitol indicates the participation of Cass Jr. (see fig. 27). The voluminous correspondence from the Gilbert office that can be related to the West Virginia project is almost without exception signed by Cass Sr.; to the best of our knowledge, not a single important letter or telegram is signed by Cass Jr. While Cass Sr. made more than thirty trips to Charleston, the appointment books indicate that Cass Jr. accompanied him only three times. The transcripts of the meetings held during those visits reveal that Cass Sr. was clearly in charge of the discussion. Cass Jr. attended the dedication of the West Virginia Capitol in June 1932 as his father's representative because Cass Sr. was on his way to Princeton University to receive an honorary degree.

Notations in Cass Sr.'s diary for 1922, after the site had been selected and he was beginning to design the West Virginia Capitol, indicate that Cass and Julia Gilbert were worried about their son's work ethic and his role in the business. On January 4 he wrote: "Julia had a long talk with Cass Jr.... He seems to be in a very distressing mood. We are anxious about him." The entry for January 5 reported: "Cass Jr. came to me ... and said he understood from his mother I wanted to talk office matters with him and he would do so at any time. I am too depressed to do it tonight." After dismissing his son, however, he added, "I worked on the Tennessee competition for a time, and on the West Va. Capitol sketch plan with Rockart." On February 25, Cass Sr. wrote: "Cass Jr. lunched with me. We talked about the office. I tried to inspire him with the idea of taking responsibility and of carrying things, once undertaken, clear thru to a finish. How I need a young strong capable man to carry out my initial instructions." On June 30, Cass Sr. lamented:

> Jaw hurts—Arm hurts—tired out. Sometimes I think I cannot keep on much longer. I am successful but my business worries me by its complexities. Cass Jr is willing to work but does not seem to know how to study architecture as an art.... This worries me more than anything else as it is largely for him I keep the office going. The outlook is not good with C.M.P. [apparently an architectural firm going bankrupt] in receiver's hands and among the men of my family I seem to be the only one on whom they all lean. For this reason I must keep on—and on.

In August 1922, when Cass Sr. was unable to attend a meeting with the commissioners in Charleston, he was represented by Cass Jr. and John Rockart. The transcript reveals how much Cass Sr. was missed: "The conference dragged. There were long periods of silence when no one spoke and no one wanted to speak first. Invariably one of the Commission would break the silence." When a question was raised about cost, Cass Jr. phoned his father, who replied, "Tell the Commission that the buildings as shown by the plan could be built inside the appropriation and that he [Cass Sr.] did not contemplate a building program in excess of the appropriation." This is Cass Gilbert Sr.'s standard reply to such questions; that his son was unable to repeat what he must have heard his father voice over and over again indicates how little engaged he was with the project.

While Cass Sr. was the consummate professional, he must often have felt overwhelmed by the demands of his many projects, as is suggested in the diary entry cited above. During the years when he was designing and supervising the construction of the West Virginia Capitol, he would have welcomed assistance. But such help does not seem to have been readily available; anyone who has worked in his archives has to have been impressed by the evidence of his personal role in making not only important decisions and defusing the difficulties that arose as projects were designed and built but also the innumerable minor queries that required attention. His continuous concern and engagement is unquestionable. If Cass Jr. had played the role he claimed, there would certainly be more evidence of his participation in the documentation.

Cass Jr. suggested to Seale that his father had wanted "to avoid the [West Virginia] job entirely" and that he only accepted it upon the urging of his wife and son. This is refuted by the vigorous and enthusiastic manner in which Cass Sr. pursued this prestigious commission, as documented in chapter 1.

And why Cass Jr. would denigrate what is supposedly his own work by stating that his father "never did like it" is uncertain. Cass Sr. consistently spoke favorably of his own work in West Virginia, as we have seen; any disappointment he may have felt can probably be related to the financial difficulties that prevented the state from bringing the project to the level of completeness he had envisioned and paying him the final compensation that he felt he was owed. Cass Sr. had hoped that the West Virginia Capitol could be his "crowning work," a wish that was superseded only when he was invited to design the Supreme Court of the United States. His understanding of what he had accomplished in Charleston is evident in his comments at the time of the dedication: "I have endeavored to make this group of buildings useful, and also to give it a dignified and beautiful character without elaboration or extravagance." He concluded with his hope that his Capitol would be "preserved as among the many evidences of the dignity, importance, and civilization" of the state of West Virginia. ("Judgment of This Work in Hands of People, Says Gilbert, Architect," in the *Charleston Gazette*).

49 For further information on Cass Gilbert's conservatism, see Blodgett, "Conservative." For a study of conservatism during this period that centers around John W. Davis, the United States representative from West Virginia, solicitor general of the United States, US ambassador to the United Kingdom, and acquaintance of Cass Gilbert who ran against Calvin Coolidge in the 1924 presidential election, see Tucker, *High Tide of American Conservatism*.

50 N-YHS, box 186, folder 6. Nancy Hadley, manager of Archives and Records at the AIA, reported that Gilbert's letters to the institute about this issue gave no reason why he resigned; he wrote only: "I have some doubt of the desirability of presenting my reasons at this time. I believe that some of the officers of the Institute are aware that I have differed with the Institute in certain matters which I regard as important." Nancy Hadley, e-mail message to authors, April 12, 2011.

51 See Blodgett, "Politics," 62, and "Conservative."

52 See Irish, "'Great Gray Buildings,'" regarding this project and other strictly functional buildings designed by Gilbert, including the Fireproof Storage Warehouse in Minneapolis (1902) and the Austin, Nichols and Co. Warehouse in New York (1909). For its influence on later architects see Irish, "'Great Gray Buildings,'" 174, and Gebhard, *Guide to Art Deco in America*, 9, 52. Gebhard summarizes: "This row of immense eight-story reinforced-concrete warehouses helped to set the stage for the American Vertical skyscraper style that emerged in the mid-1920s. . . . The U.S. Army Supply Base was often invoked in the 1920s as a proto-type for the development of a new architecture as, in a sense, it turned out to be." He cites its impact on Goodhue's design for the Nebraska Capitol. Julia Finch Gilbert referred to the US Army Supply Base as "the prototype for many of our so-called modern structures, with its vertical lines surmounted by no cornice—a building of dignity, solidity, and utility" (8).

53 In 1930, the Detroit Public Library was included in a list of eighteen masterpieces of recent American architecture, as was the Woolworth Building; see Hoak and Church, *Masterpieces*. This was noted by Kirkham in *Pencil Points*, 551. Kirkham added that the Detroit Library was "considered by many to be Mr. Gilbert's finest work."

54 N-YHS, box 604. A diary entry from December 20, 1929, states: "At the present time the following works are underway or under preliminary stages or are under consideration by me as architect.: . . . The Supreme Court . . . The Capitol of the State of West Virginia, The Hudson River Bridge . . . The Kill van Kull Bridge . . . The Maumee Bridge, near Toledo Ohio . . . The Grand Island Bridge, Niagara River . . . on [all] these bridges I am consulting architect. The N.Y. County Lawyers Association Building . . . The Academy of Arts and Letters Art Gallery and Auditorium, Theological Seminary . . . Oberlin, auditorium . . . The Emigrant Savings Bank . . . probably Extension Treasury Annex Washington . . . legislative Building Ottawa Canada." Next to each building's name is its cost, written in pencil (Gilbert Papers, LC).

55 Gary Woolson provided us with a copy of a typescript headed "Competitions in which this Office has submitted drawings." The list, which includes 38 items, was typed in 1914; the last two entries, numbers 37 and 38, dated 1914 and 1916, were added by hand. Of the 38 competitions entered, Gilbert won eleven. Of the first seven, dated between 1895 and 1903, he won five.

56 N-YHS, box 186, folder 6. Later, in a transcript of a meeting dated December 18, 1919, Gilbert stated:

> [The Nebraska state engineer] had understood from Mr. Thomas R. Kimball that I had been invited and was unwilling to enter the competition. . . . I further stated that I had a pretty large program of work ahead of me and that I told Mr. Kimball so when he called upon me in November and that if a considerable portion of it went through I would not have time to enter competitions, but that if the State of Nebraska wanted my services under conditions that were normal and attractive I would be very glad to design the building for them.

57 See Solomonson, *Chicago Tribune Tower*, for a thorough discussion of this competition.

58 The New York Life Insurance Building was erected on the site previously occupied by the Madison Square Garden building, which Stanford White, for whom Gilbert worked at the beginning of his career, had designed. White's firm also had finished the New York Life Insurance Company's previous building; Gilbert installed McKim, Mead & White's director's office from the earlier, demolished New York Life building into his own. See Broderick, *Triumvirate*, 328.

59 In addition, during this period Gilbert turned to projects outside the United States, including the American Embassy in Ottawa (1928–32); see Loeffler, *Architecture of Diplomacy*, 267. Gilbert has also been connected with the design project of the National Capitol of Cuba, completed in 1929, but his role in this is very uncertain; see "Cass Gilbert Society Newsletter" (May 2010). Correspondence alluding to other potential projects in Cuba, including a hotel, give insight: "A small project, such as this hotel, handled in a satisfactory manner by an able architect would place Mr. Gilbert before the public in a very prominent way and he or his representative there would be in condition to take charge of the improvements which might later be projected" ("Report Regarding Hotel in Cuba, Dictated by Mr. Wells, November 13, 1903," N-YHS, box 54, folder 3). Earlier, in 1908, Gilbert had been involved in discussions about the design for the new Japanese Parliament building; see N-YHS, box 184, folder 13.

60 Drawings and correspondence for the Charleston library are found in the Cass Gilbert Collection at N-YHS. See Wilkins and Wilkins, "Cass Gilbert's Public Library for Charleston, West Virginia," in preparation.

61 From a letter dated June 12, 1888, as found in Kirkham, "Master of Style," 543.

62 Cochran, "Cathedral of Commerce" foreword, by S. Parker Cadman, 5–6.

63 Quoted in Betts, "Twelve Projects," 126. Lewis Mumford criticized the skyscraper as a form in the first comprehensive history of American architecture, his *Sticks and Stones: A Study of American Architecture and Civilization*, first published in 1924. In the 1955 edition of this important book, Mumford stated that his chapter "The Age of the Machine" had emphasized his "social criticism of the skyscraper as promoter of

urban congestion and disorder" (ix). In the same volume, however, Mumford praised Gilbert's Woolworth Building as one of "the most satisfactory examples of the skyscraper," while simultaneously pointing out that it suffers from "numerous defects in detail" (78).

64 Cass Gilbert, "The Financial Importance of Rapid Building," *Engineering Record* 41 (June 30, 1900), quoted in Irish, "West Street Building," 376–97.

65 Cass Gilbert to Walter E. Clark, editor of the *Charleston Daily Mail*, April 8, 1932, WVSA.

## Chapter Three
## "DUFFY STREET SITE IS SELECTED FOR STATE HOUSE"

1 The headlines announcing Gilbert's appointment are from the *Charleston Gazette*. N-YHS, box 524, folder 3.

2 The notice of the meeting is from N-YHS, box 683. A July 17, 1921, article in the *Charleston Gazette* reported that "broadcast invitations have been issued through all the newspapers of the state, and there is every confidence expressed that the meeting will be well attended." The headlines about the meeting are from N-YHS, box 683.

According to an unidentified newspaper report published the day after the meeting, the ten sites considered were:

1. The south side of the Kanawha River, opposite Duffy and Elizabeth Streets,
2. Capitol Hill at the head of Capitol Street,
3. Upper Kanawha Street, near Elizabeth and Duffy Streets,
4. Kanawha Street, from Clendenin and Broad Streets,
5. Kanawha Street, from Clendenin Street to the Elk River,
6. Columbia Boulevard near Luna Park, on the west side of Elk River,
7. Plateau near Lincoln School, on the west side of Elk,
8. Tract near Watts Street Station, across Crescent Road on the hill, on the west side,
9. Kanawha City, and
10. The old site, in the heart of downtown, with an additional block added.

The article stated that former state auditor J. S. Darst said the Old Capitol Site would "do" for the next 300 years.

According to the summary published in 1923 in the "Report of Capitol Building Commission," twenty individuals spoke in favor of five different sites (18–19). The five sites (and the number of individuals who spoke in favor of each) were:

1. The site "located on the North side of the Kanawha river and the East side of the Elk river immediately adjacent to the confluence of the two rivers" (4 individuals);
2. the South Ruffner Site (9 individuals)
3. the old Capitol Site (5 individuals)
4. the site "at the foot of Capitol Street on Capitol Hill" (1 individual)
5. the Duffy Street Site (1 individual).

Three other individuals appeared before the Commission but made "no particular suggestion as to site." For the site that was offered free, see "State of West Virginia Capitol Building Commission: Report to the House of Delegates," 6 (hereafter cited as "Report to House of Delegates").

3 N-YHS, project file 683. Over the next months, letters concerning the site were written to the Commission and editorials were published. "Report to House of Delegates," 18–19. Letters from individuals stating preferences for sites are published in *CCC*, 409, 607, 844. An article in the *Charleston Daily Mail* on June 30, 1921, reported, "West Side Location is Favored by Gen. Watts," and the *Charleston Gazette* on June 30 had an article headlined, "MAJORITY WANT CAPITOL BUILT ON OLD GROUNDS; Woman Citizen Says, in Letter to Gazette, That 98 Per Cent Are Against Change; Hints at Graft." Both: N-YHS, box 683.

4 August 4, 1921, *CCC*, 535. The July 22, 1921, *Charleston Gazette* reported, "Officials of the state government are engaged in preparing a statement of space requirements, to be offered to Mr. Gilbert for his information in preparing plans."

During the late summer and fall Gilbert wrote several additional letters urging that the information be submitted. He wrote again on September 1, 1921 (*CCC*, 592–93), and on October 4 he wrote yet again, asking when he might expect to receive the information he had requested a month earlier: "I . . . would inquire when I can expect it as I should like very much to make some careful studies of the required space preliminary to making some sketches of the proposed buildings" (*CCC*, 593–94). On October 19, he telegraphed the adjutant general that he needed the information on his space requirements within twenty-four hours, if possible (*CCC*, 594). In a letter of January 16, 1922, Gilbert requested "that a conference be held with authorized representatives of the different State Departments for an analysis of the space requirements presented by such departments. I would inquire whether the representatives of the departments noted below can meet Mr. Rockart in Charleston the latter part of this week for that purpose." (*CCC*, 544–45). A document preserved in the Gilbert Archive (N-YHS, box 516, folder 5) has three columns listing the department name, "Active Space asked for, sq. ft.," and "Active Space Occupied Dec. 1, 1921, sq. ft." Between the two columns are penciled numbers that may indicate the square footage Gilbert had decided to allot to each department. In many cases the requested numbers are two, three, or even four times larger than the 1921 figure; Gilbert's penciled-in compromise figures, if that is indeed what they are, often cut the requested numbers in half. The totals are: actual space, December 1921 = 80,297; requested space = 204,335; penciled "compromise" = 140,469.

In January 1922, Rockart went to West Virginia to assess the spatial requirements for various state offices; on February 3, Gilbert noted that one of his assistants is "scheduling space for West Va. Capitol." (*CCC*, 544–45). This apparently did not solve the question of space, for on February 27, 1922, Gilbert sent Secretary Young a "diagram" of space requirements and asked him to please talk to the state officers and convince them to reduce their requirements so that "we" will be able to "keep within the appropriation" (560–61). A later reference reveals that the reductions in space needed were made by Rockart during a visit to Charleston (transcript of June 22, 1922 meeting, N-YHS, box 519, folder 9). In February 1923, J. Mohn and Rockart from the Gilbert office traveled to Charleston to "secure the signed approval of each department head to his assignment of space in the new buildings." Such a move indicates the caution with which the Gilbert office proceeded (N-YHS, box 519, folder 10). The spreadsheet with statistics is found in the same folder. It offers slightly different figures, for it lists that the total space occupied by the departments (including the Senate and House) in December 1921 was 80,325 square feet and that these units had initially asked for a total of 205,703 square feet. Their modified requests in August 1922 asked for 140,415 square feet and the "Space assigned and approved, February 1923" totaled 154,770. In many cases, the space assigned for units was nearly doubled. The units that showed the largest proportional increases were the governor (from 1309 to 4840 square feet), the Senate and House (from 6525 to 33,000), and the banking commissioner (from 732 to 1,820 square feet).

The letter from the judges is dated July 27, 1921 (*CCC*, 880–81). The Washington State Capitol has a separate building for the state's

Supreme Court, which is interesting because Cass Gilbert apparently offered a design for this competition. See Johnston, *Audacious State Capitol.* We have not located Gilbert's competition drawings for Washington, but his description of his drawings dated December 11, 1893, is at N-YHS, box 482, folder 9. The description does not mention a dome, but one is implied by the rotunda that "gives ample moving space for the public during the session of the Legislature." Gilbert concluded:

> I would say that it has been my intention to design a building with a plan so simple that the most direct and convenient access can be had to all parts of it.... All the rooms will be ample, well arranged for the business to be done in them and comfortable for the occupants, without luxury, abundantly well lighted and thoroughly ventilated.
>
> In the exterior of the building, I have followed the Commissioner's wise instruction to the effect that the building should have "appropriate proportions and solidity of design, avoiding extreme or superfluous ornaments." Believing as I do that such a design will best express the idea of the dignity and grandeur of the great Commonwealth for which it is to be erected, and for which it will stand before posterity as a monument to the civilization and high intelligence of this generation.

5 Gilbert to Young, *CCC*, 537. By August 19, sixteen of twenty-nine departments had reported the square footage and number of offices they needed (538, 589).

6 The sketches are on a sheet of stationery from the Union Club in Manhattan—which, coincidentally, had been designed by Cass Gilbert almost two decades earlier. N-YHS, box 524, folder 1. Fig. 23 is probably the first version because it is drawn on the front side of the paper and is the more general plan; fig. 24 seems to develop the project seen in fig. 23.

There are other indications that Gilbert was thinking about Rome: the curved arcade in the first version is probably a reference to Bernini's Piazza in front of St. Peter's Basilica, and the compact silhouette of the domed structure is reminiscent of Michelangelo's original plan for the church. The statues on the bridge in the second version are inspired by the figures of *Angels of the Passion* by Bernini and his workshop that have lent their name to the Roman bridge.

7 *CCC*, 525–26. Legislative Enactment H. B. 176 was sponsored by the legislator and West Virginia architect A. F. Wysong as early as April 25, 1921 (*Journal of the Senate ... 1921*, April 25, 1921, 635). Later, Wysong was consistently critical of Gilbert's selection as project architect (see below, p. 69). For the bill, see *West Virginia Legislative Handbook 1922*, 210. Wysong was named secretary of the board to register architects (N-YHS, box 503, folder 8). A letter of October 27, 1921, told Gilbert how to apply for his West Virginia registration (*CCC*, 594). In December of 1922, sixteen West Virginia architects established the state's first branch of the American Institute of Architects; previously West Virginia architects had belonged to the Pittsburgh branch of the association.

8 For Gilbert's list of locations, see *CCC*, 536; Gilbert's letter is published in *CCC*, but the list of twenty-four locations is not, and it is not clear where the "joke" location was.

For the telegrams to the custodians of other capitols, see N-YHS, box 503, folder 7. Telegrams to the custodians of the Capitols of Pennsylvania, Rhode Island, Tennessee, Kentucky, Missouri, Arkansas, Minnesota, and Texas were sent on August 12; on August 26 he sent a similar request to the custodian of the Capitol of Connecticut. He shared these figures with the commissioners in the August 31, 1921, "General Memorandum": Kentucky 35 acres, Minnesota 16 acres, Missouri 14.75 acres, Texas 22 acres, Arkansas 46.62 acres, Pennsylvania 42 acres, Rhode Island 14 acres, and Connecticut 47 acres (*CCC*, 520).

Gilbert reported that he had received the corrections on August 19 (*CCC*, 589). At this same time, Young wrote to inform Gilbert that he had received a map of the South Ruffner Site made by Charleston engineer J. J. Venable. Houston forwarded this map, as well as an estimate of how much it would cost "to fill in the Elk River site," on August 25. See *CCC*, 539, 590.

9 August 19, 1921. *CCC*, 523.

10 *CCC*, 522, 525.

11 Both "Report" and "General Memorandum" are published in *CCC* ("Report," 553–55; "General Memorandum," 508–22). The introductory letter is *CCC*, 551–52. Gilbert also enclosed a survey of sites conducted by J. J. Venable; we have not found this map, and it is difficult to locate precisely some of the sites referred to in the documents.

12 He added, "At Hartford, Conn., and at Providence, R. I. fine views of the State Capitol buildings are obtained from the railroad tracks. The Capitol buildings at Albany, N.Y., and Harrisburg, Pa., Little Rock, Ark., Nashville, Tenn., and others are visible from the railroad trains. The Capitol at Washington is a very conspicuous and beautiful object in the landscape, and in the approach to the city by railroad from the south." *CCC*, 513.

13 *CCC*, 514. Gilbert emphasized that whatever site was chosen, a height restriction for surrounding buildings, as in Washington, New York, and elsewhere, would be needed.

14 Many clippings are preserved in a scrapbook at the N-YHS, box 503. On August 12, Gilbert hired the Romeike service to track the news about the West Virginia project. He consulted the Office of the Chief of Engineers at the War Department in Washington about the specifications required for bridges over the Kanawha and Elk Rivers. For the response of this office, see *CCC*, 559–60. Their reference is to file 126702/15. His letter recommending six sites is published in *CCC*, 553.

15 The other areas recommended are:

> 4. The "Capitol Hill" site, but for this to be viable the railroad crossings would have to be eliminated and restrictions would be necessary on the height of the surrounding buildings; Gilbert doubted if these conditions could be met.
> 14. Within Charleston, the area bounded by Edgewood Drive, Swarthmore Avenue, and Carr Street.
> 16. The area adjacent to the Kanawha River, southwest of the toll bridge.

16 N-YHS, box 503, folder 7. Kane's response to Lange (October 12), his letter to Cass Gilbert, which enclosed a copy of Lange's letter (October 12), and Gilbert's response to Kane (December 22) are preserved in the same folder. No works by Lange are listed in Chambers. Lange further identified Wysong as "President of the Society of West Virginia Architects and a member of the Board of Examiners for the registration of architects."

17 Lange was certainly mistaken in suggesting that the drawings were being prepared, as this part of the process would certainly have to await a decision on the site.

18 The request from the Commission written about their October 22 meeting is found in *CCC*, 591–92. The same letter includes some information on space requirements for the "Forest, Game and Fish office" and lists fourteen state offices that will not be housed in the new Capitol. Young's telegram is found in *CCC*, 595. Gilbert's letter about Olmsted is published in *CCC*, 915. In a letter of November 15, Olmsted stated that he could have little to say about the sites and the city plan after a visit of only twenty-four hours.

19 November 5, 1921; N-YHS, box 503, folder 7. Gilbert's appointment books indicate that he and Olmsted had a meeting in the office about the West Virginia project on November 17.

20 Information on acreage and "cubical contents" is found at N-YHS, box 519, folder 9. Of the eight capitol plots on which he had requested information, only one had fewer than fourteen acres; the approximate "cubical contents" of their structures ranged from 3.5 to 7.1 million cubic feet. "Cubical contents" is a figure calculated by multiplying the *area* of the building by its height, measured from the bottom of the *cellar* to the top of the *roof beams*. The acreage of various state capitol sites had been given to the commissioners in the "General Memorandum" of August 31, 1921 (*CCC*, 520).

What decisions were made at this time are unknown, but a memo preserved at the WVSA reveals that the final Capitol complex has 10,662,000 cubic feet plus another 793,000 cubic feet in the dome above the central rotunda.

Two other sites offered the possibility of placing the Capitol on a hill above Charleston; for Site 23 (location unclear), Gilbert proposed a single large building at an elevation of 342 feet. Site 20—"between Porter's Branch and Lick Branch"—rose to a height of 400 feet and required a viaduct across the Kanawha and elaborate approaches with ramps and flights of steps. One of the sketches for Site 20 shows seven buildings, others indicate three buildings.

The proposals for five buildings for Site 9 differ; in one the Main Building is oriented east to west, in the other the orientation is north to south.

An essay by C. C. Watts favoring a site "on the west side of Elk, on Columbus boulevard, . . . extending back to Virginia street" is published in *CCC*, 900–903. C. C. Watts admitted that he owned land in this area.

21 Drawings were also created for Site 14, which was bounded by Charleston Street, Edgewood Drive, Swarthmore Avenue, and Carr Street. A railroad crossing rendered this site difficult to build on and required elaborate approaches with ramps. Optional designs for Site 14 offered three, five, or seven buildings.

22 In a letter written on November 26, 1932, Gilbert complained to Governor Conley that he had received "no pay for the preliminary studies done on a number of different sites."

23 The letter from the Charleston Building Trades Council is found in *CCC*, 395–96. The Kanawha Valley Central Labor Union is *CCC*, 393–94. Although this resolution is undated, it indicates that the Capitol Commission had been created "nearly a year ago."

24 Gilbert's diary reveals that a meeting in Charleston originally scheduled for December 1 had to be postponed until December 15, perhaps because the office had not completed the plans. Some of the drawings have a specific date, while others are dated December 1–15, suggesting that they were all dated on the 15th when the office's work was being compiled to be taken to the meeting.

25 Gilbert to Governor Morgan, December 1, 1921, *CCC*, 555–57. The architect hoped to have at least one additional meeting with the railroad's representatives so that he could have the necessary information before meeting with the commissioners on December 15.

26 The plan of the larger building resembles that of a basilican church with a small dome at the crossing. The large chamber at the end of the long arm, to the east, was probably intended for the House, while the semicircular chambers to the north and south would most likely have been for the Senate and the Supreme Court. The columned entrance to this structure would have been on Capitol Street. The governor's reception room and office would most likely have been located in the square office building across Capitol Street; two large light wells would have illuminated the interior of this building.

A plan offered for the equally limited "McFarland Street Site" also featured two buildings; in this case the plot was so small that only Kanawha Street separated their entrances from the riverbank. The larger building has a small dome, while the second building would have been devoted almost entirely to a single large legislative chamber. Rather than presenting a functional alternative, this proposal seems designed to expose the inadequacies of this site.

27 WVSA. Jeffries's letter was published in the *Charleston Daily Mail* on December 7, 1921. Another skyscraper proposal was made by J. S. Darst, West Virginia state auditor, who proposed adding floors to the Annex (see fig. 12). This information is from an unidentified clipping reproduced by Cohen and Andre, *Capitols of West Virginia*, 60.

28 *CCC*, 404–9. Conley graduated from West Virginia University in 1893 with a degree in law and began his practice in Parsons, West Virginia. He was governor from 1929 to 1933.

29 In discussing the need for a bridge in his "General Memorandum," Cass Gilbert had reported "that railroads are located at the base of the hills on each side of the valley, that floods are of frequent occurrence, that the Federal Government requires that bridges must have at least seventy feet of clearance above low water (necessitating high bridges with long inclines except where they terminate directly at the base of the hills)" (*CCC*, 510).

In response to those who preferred the new Capitol be located outside the city limits at the South Ruffner Site, Conley pointed out, "It is peculiar, to say the least, that none of these 'forward-looking' gentlemen of great vision, who so strenuously insist that the Commission locate the Capitol in the country, never thought to locate their businesses there, never advocated that the city hall, the county courthouse, the federal court and post office building, the schools, the churches, etc, should be located somewhere in the country amid the green hills and far away from the busy marts of commerce and industry."

30 The state paid Conley $38,750 for his home. See "Report to House of Delegates," 19.

31 Later, he had dinner at the Governor's Mansion and walked up the Kanawha "at night."

In a letter of December 30, 1922, Gilbert wrote that he had made "preliminary drawings for nearly all of [the potential sites] and estimated the cost of the preparation of such sites such as grading and roadways to make them accessible." (N-YHS, box 504, folder 4.)

32 These drafts are preserved at N-YHS, box 503, folder 8; the telegram is found in box 503, folder 7.

33 "Report to House of Delegates," 26–28. A letter written by a citizen on December 15 also supported the South Ruffner Site (*CCC*, 809), as did a letter from the Charleston architect A. F. M. Lange written on December 20 (*CCC*, 744–45). Lange argued, "An environment that will enhance the beauty of the structure and a location that will make the Capitol building the crowning point of Charleston's most beautiful district; these must be the dominating points in choosing the site." It was Lange who had written the letter attacking Gilbert that was discussed in chapter 1.

34 Both telegrams are found in *CCC*, 528.

35 "Report to House of Delegates," 30–36. The chairman of the Chamber of Commerce Capitol Site Committee was R. G. Hubbard, who had been one of the prominent businessmen supporting the South Ruffner Site in the mayor's proposal of December 16, 1921.

The assumption that the city would provide the land was based on a petition offered to the Legislature and signed by 24,000 citizens in an effort to retain the capital in Charleston; the proposal to move the capital from Charleston was defeated by the Legislature by a vote of twenty-one to nine (see *Journal of the Senate . . . 1921*, 104–5); at the same time, a resolution supporting the retention of the capital in Charleston was passed by a vote of twenty to ten.

In addition, although the question seems to be moot at this point, the city officials pointed out that the property adjacent to the Old

Capitol Site had increased in value from approximately $750,000 or $1,000,000 to $1,500,000. The city officials offered to purchase both the old Governor's Mansion and the Capitol Annex, the latter for use as a city library.

36 The ballot information is found in "Report to House of Delegates," 36–38. A telegram from Houston Young, sent on December 20, 1921, at 11:26 P.M. informed Gilbert: "Capitol Commission has selected sixteen acre tract Duffy to California" (N-YHS, box 503, folder 8).

The *Charleston Gazette* article is found at N-YHS, box 683. The article was accompanied by an aerial photograph of the site with dotted lines marking the extent of the intended site. The decision to build the new Governor's Mansion in this neighborhood had been made before the fire that destroyed the former capitol; see Stutler, "Capitals and Capitols," 723.

37 The Commission later reported that early in the process they had decided that "the old site, without acquiring additional land, was entirely too small for a State House of sufficient size to take care of the work of the State of even the present without making any provision for the future. The Commission realized, however, that the people of the State attached a great sentimental value to the old site." The commissioners "felt constrained to locate the Capitol on the old site if they could acquire sufficient land without too great a financial sacrifice in doing so. The investigations of the commission showed this to be wholly impracticable." "Report to House of Delegates," 5. In 1923, the Commission suggested that their selection of the Duffy Street Site had saved approximately $1,500,000 that could then be spent on the new Capitol building. The origin of this figure is uncertain, as the total cost of the Duffy Street properties had exceeded $2 million.

The quotations starting "there would be no outlook" and "The opinion" are from "Report to House of Delegates," 37.

38 *CCC*, 540–41. A copy of the telegram is also preserved in the Gilbert archives at the N-YHS, box 503, folder 8.

39 During the voting on December 18, the South Ruffner Site received one vote on ballots 1, 2, and 3 and no votes on ballots 4, 5, and 6. In 1960, Houston Young quoted Staunton as having said, "I own most of the land in Kanawha City, and if you select that site, I will be accused of engineering it; I will never be able to live it down in my lifetime." Young's statement is cited in a March 23, 1960, press release written by Kyle McCormick, director of the West Virginia Department of Archives and History. McCormick concluded, "Thus, the best capitol site was passed up for fear the Commission would be accused of graft and scandal." Staunton's later comment was made in a conversation with John Rockart in New York on September 18, 1922. (N-YHS, box 9, folder 18.)

40 Criticism was leveled against the commissioners for selecting a site that required the removal of established homes and their residents. In 1923, they justified their choice: "While the Commission regretted to be compelled to destroy some beautiful homes, it seemed to us to be the logical location, taking into consideration all the circumstances which confronted us. Most of the homes will be removed without being destroyed." ("Report to House of Delegates," 6–7). The choice of the Duffy Street Site put certain demands upon the city. On December 21, 1921, for example, the secretary was told to inform the mayor, the City Council, and the Chamber of Commerce that the commissioners expected their cooperation in widening Lee and Washington Streets and extending Washington Street ("Report to House of Delegates," 38). On January 10, 1922, the Commission agreed to sell to the city the plots of land needed to make these changes for $250,000 ("Report to House of Delegates," 39–40).

41 *CCC*, 541–42.

42 The process of acquisition took much longer than anticipated. A letter from Secretary Young to Gilbert on March 4, 1922, stated, "We are now taking steps to acquire the new grounds and I hope to have title to same by July 1st" (*CCC*, 547). A letter from Commissioner Staunton dated August 24, 1922, stated, "We are now in the midst of condemning the property, with a strong fight being made for higher prices." If these could be purchased for the amount fixed by the Condemnation Commission, the total cost for the site would be $1,993,066.37, an amount that would be more than offset by the sale of the old downtown property, estimated at that time to be worth at least $2,500,000. The Old Capitol Site was advertised for sale on March 4, 1922 (*CCC*, 547). Bids were due on April 25, 1922 (*CCC*, 776). The sale of the Old Capitol Site brought in $1,551,000, the Capitol Annex property sold for $500,000, and the sale of the "Mansion, Temporary Capitol, and Board of Control Building" realized $350,000, for a total of $2,401,000. Governor Gore's Message to the 1927 Legislative Session, West Virginia Legislature, Journal of the House of Delegates, First Extraordinary Session, 1927, Appendix "B," 6.

For more information on the process of acquiring these properties and the moving of some houses across the Kanawha, see Wallace, *House of State* 31–32.

43 Gilbert to Commissioner Keatley, N-YHS, box 504, folder 4. Moore's *Daniel H. Burnham* was published in 1921.

44 Gilbert's letter of December 30 is found in *CCC*, 545. The arrangements for the sale of the Old Capitol Site are documented in *CCC*, 547, 298–99, and 775–76.

## Chapter Four
## THE INITIAL DESIGN PHASE: "A SIMPLE DIGNIFIED STRUCTURE OF FINE PROPORTIONS"

1 The history of the evolution of state capitol design remains unwritten, in part because of the large number of buildings—many more than fifty—and the numerous design proposals that would have to be considered. Many states had a sequence of capitol buildings because of changes in the state's capital city, political maneuvering, destruction of buildings by fire, requirements for more space, changes in taste, a desire for a more impressive symbol, or a combination of these factors. For a fascinating compendium of the changing locations for capital cities, see Daniel and Daniel, *51 Capitols of America*, 252–54. The years or even decades needed to complete capitols meant that plans were often modified and architects replaced. Accepted designs were sometimes abandoned during political and economic difficulties. A full review would also examine the competitions that were held, submissions to which sometimes numbered in the hundreds, and the role that all these submissions played in the history of state capitol design.

Most books dedicated to surveying all fifty state capitols focus on the current structures: see the bibliography for books by Thomas G. Aylesworth, Willis J. Ehlert, Richard R. Gibson, Charles T. Goodsell, Eldon Hauck, Henry-Russell Hitchcock and William Seale, Eric Oxendorf and William Seale, Jean Houston Daniel and Price Daniel, Francis Pio Ruggiero, Don Severin, Jim Stembridge, and Susan W. Thrane and Tom Patterson. Hitchcock and Seale discuss some of the earlier capitols as well. See the bibliographies of these books for further information on individual state capitols. In addition, most states offer a website with a review of their capitol's history and architecture.

2 For a summary of the history of the art and architecture of the US Capitol see Reed, *United States Capitol*. Reed includes a brief chapter on "The Influence of the United States Capitol" (36–39), but his interpretation of the extent of the influence is limited. The only capitols he

mentions are those of Minnesota, Missouri, Oklahoma, Rhode Island, Washington State, West Virginia, and Wisconsin.

Three main sources have been identified for Walter's high dome with a drum encircled by freestanding columns: St. Paul's Cathedral in London by Christopher Wren, the Pantheon in Paris by Jacques-Germain Soufflot, and St. Isaac's Cathedral in St. Petersburg, Russia, by Auguste Ricard de Montferrand. For a discussion of these influences on the US Capital see Reed, 29–31.

3 Those built before 1900 are the Capitols of California, Colorado, Georgia, Illinois, Iowa, Kansas, and Texas; the seven for which foundations were laid between 1893 and 1899 are the Capitols of Arkansas, Minnesota, Montana, New Mexico (later remodeled), Oregon (destroyed by fire in 1935), Pennsylvania, and Rhode Island. Arizona's Capitol, begun in 1899, has a low dome in the Pantheon model.

The nomenclature used by scholars to define the style of the numerous state capitols that are identified as following the "National Capitol model" has been unnecessarily complicated. Scholars have used Neo-Classical, Neo-Grec, French Renaissance, Beaux-Arts, Greek Revival, and "French and Italian Renaissance Revival" to describe buildings that, in essence, are similar in design. By emphasizing the role of the National Capitol, we hope to bring new clarity to the study of state capitol architecture from 1860 to 1930. The examples that most closely follow the National Capitol model have a row of freestanding columns decorating the drum: these are, in chronological order, California (1860–72), Texas (1881–88), Rhode Island (1895–1904), Arkansas (1899–1915), Mississippi (1901–3), Idaho (1905–12), Maine (added 1909–11), Utah (1911–16), and, of course, West Virginia.

4 For the 1898 quote, see Graves, "Introductory Address." For the 1901 quote, see Thompson, *Minnesota's State Capitol*, xiii.

5 The dates of the early twentieth-century capitols are: Mississippi (1901–3), Kentucky (1905–10), South Dakota (1905–10), Idaho (1905–12), Wisconsin (1906–17), Utah (1911–16), Missouri (1911–17), and Washington (1923–28).

6 There are differences in design and materials: the drums that support the domes vary in style and proportion, for example, and some domes are pierced with windows. Some exteriors are stone, others metal. In a letter titled "Materials to be Used" relative to his design for the Minnesota State Capitol, Gilbert wrote, "The bell of the dome would be of white marble if contract estimates will allow of such expense, otherwise of heavy cast iron either gilded or painted white, as in many of the notable domes of the world." Quoted in Thompson, *Minnesota's State Capitol*, 15. The lanterns above the domes are often distinctive in design and proportion, and the whole crowned with a figure, a flagpole, or a spire. In most cases, the portico is surmounted by a pediment that is plain or decorated with sculptural figures.

The architect of the 1901–3 Mississippi State Capitol, Theodore Link, suggested a three-hundred-foot-tall bell tower rather than a dome, but the commission demanded that he substitute a dome; this action and the architect's capitulation support the idea that the dome is a basic identifying factor in the history of state capitol design.

The tradition of using the National Capitol as a model, which was presumed to have ended with Cass Gilbert's West Virginia State Capitol, was revived at the Oklahoma State Capitol, which was constructed in 1914–17 without its intended dome. In 2002, the dome designed for it in 1914 by its architect, Solomon Layton, was added to the structure.

The National Capitol model also influenced the design of the San Francisco City Hall (1912–15). Smaller domes became a common identifying motif for county courthouses across the country.

The expense and inefficiency of a dome were used by defenders of North Dakota's skyscraper capitol when they pointed out that Cass Gilbert's Minnesota Capitol, completed in 1905 for $3.25 million, offered only 29 percent of its interior space for use. Nebraska's and Louisiana's Capitols were more space efficient but had cost $11 million and $4 million respectively—$1.10 per cubic foot. The latter utilized 70 percent of its interior. North Dakota's statehouse, completed in 1934 for slightly under its $2 million limit, was 80 percent usable, and cost only forty-six cents per cubic foot; see Remele, *North Dakota State Capitol*, 51. In contrast, West Virginia's Capitol complex cost about seventy-five cents per cubic foot. A comparison of the North Dakota and West Virginia Capitols (see figs. 90 and frontispiece) suggests that economy is not the most important consideration.

7 "Revised General Summary, Showing possible changes & omissions to reduce costs," N-YHS, box 519, folder 10.

8 Only six state capitols (including West Virginia) were designed after 1920; three are tall buildings and are often referred to as skyscrapers (see figs. 88–90). The three "skyscraper" capitols are those of Nebraska, Louisiana, and North Dakota; Nebraska's Capitol, the earliest, was begun in 1922 based on a winning competition design submitted in 1920; the Capitol of Louisiana was built in 1930–32; that of North Dakota was designed in 1931 and constructed 1932–34. Oregon's Capitol has a prominent interior dome but on the exterior its curved shape is disguised within a cylindrical drum; it was designed in 1936, after the state's second capitol was destroyed by fire, and constructed in 1936–38. For the four state capitols in the Art Deco style, see Capitman, Kinerk, and Wilhelm, *Rediscovering Art Deco*, 38–40. The exceptions to the move toward Modernism were the Capitols of West Virginia and Delaware; the latter was designed in the Georgian Revival style in 1933 as a reference to the state's colonial origins.

9 Architectural historian Henry-Russell Hitchcock states in *Modern Architecture: Romanticism and Reintegration* that it was "impossible to find any building reflecting a truly new aesthetic until 1922" (157). A year-by-year graph plotting the number of Art Deco style buildings reveals that the style was in its infancy in 1921 and 1922, with only three buildings the first year and seven the second. The trend reached its first peak in 1930, with 194 buildings. This was followed by a decline due to the Depression and a second peak in 1936, with 241 buildings. See Capitman, Kinerk, and Wilhelm, *Rediscovering Art Deco*, 7.

10 1922, Diary, LC. Gilbert often noted in his diary who was with him as he evolved a design, documenting the input of his associates. The "Tennessee competition" is the Tennessee War Memorial Auditorium, which included offices for a number of state agencies. (Gilbert's diary entry calls it the "Memorial & Capitol Annex.") His diary reveals that he had worked on his competition entry on January 17 ("It goes slow"), January 18, January 19 ("I designed the niches and stairways approaching Capitol," accompanied by a small drawing), and January 20, 21, and 24. On January 27, after attending the annual dinner of the Mayflower Society at the Hotel Pennsylvania, he stopped "at the office for 25 mins. The boys are working on the competition for Nashville, Tenn." The drawings were finished the next day and sent "to Prof. Laird at Phila on 2 P.M. train by Johnston." On February 18, Gilbert wrote "McKim Mead and White have now the Nashville competition. I'm glad of it. I didn't want the burden of it. I went into the competition half-heartedly. I had to drive myself to work on it. I am glad to [illegible]."

11 1922, Diary, LC. Frederick G. Stickel was the head of Gilbert's drafting room and in 1925 was one of seven individuals listed on Cass Gilbert's letterhead. See Irish, "Cass Gilbert in Practice," 12. For more on Stickel, who entered Gilbert's office in 1900 and worked there until at least 1934, see Betts, "Sketch to Architecture," and Fenske, "Cass Gilbert's Skyscrapers."

12 The sketch drawn in the diary on April 23 is in Chambers (*Buildings of*

*West Virginia*, 75), who asserts that it was a refinement of the April 20 plan. He states that the April 23 sketch became Gilbert's "guiding design principle throughout the project," but it seems clear that the April 20 plan, with its three building complex around a courtyard, was ultimately more important.

13 No photograph of Gilbert's Madison Avenue office from this period is known to us, but a c. 1911 photograph of his office on East 24th Street, while construction of the Woolworth Building was under way, reveals the size and extent of office space required by an architect working on a major project; see Fenske, *Skyscraper*, 127.

The *Wheeling Register* announced on June 19, 1922, that the commissioners were going to New York to view the plans because "Mr. Gilbert advised the commission that it is 'impossible' for him to bring the plans to Charleston." The article informed the public that "The expenses of the members are paid by the state" (N-YHS, box 683). Governor Morgan and the commissioners stayed at the Waldorf-Astoria Hotel (*CCC*, 898).

14 Transcript preserved at N-YHS, box 519, folder 9.

15 Until 1893, when West Virginia's first executive mansion was purchased, the state's governors had been forced to find their own accommodations. Governor A. B. Fleming recommended the purchase of an official residence in 1893, and that same year a large wooden residence on Capitol Street was bought for the governor's use. For photographs of this house and more history, see Cohen and Andre, *Capitols of West Virginia*, 100–101.

The site for the mansion had been selected at the Commission meeting on July 7, 1921. Cohen and Andre report that the site for the new mansion involved the purchase of three lots, each with a house on it; the total cost was $64,270. "Included in the sales tax legislation for a new Capitol building was an appropriation of $100,000 for an Executive Mansion. Final cost figures approached $200,000" (100). According to the *West Virginia Legislative Handbook*, 1929, 295, the legislative appropriations for the new mansion between 1922 and 1926 totaled $240,000, but this figure may have included the furnishings.

On August 17, 1922, Gilbert wrote to Commissioner Staunton:

> I want to say that I hope that an arrangement can be made, as you suggested, for me to design the Governor's house.
>
> It is not for the financial result, for that would at best be a small consideration—but because I would like very much to make the building in harmony with the Capitol and a suitable and dignified residence for the head of the State, both within and without. If it were necessary to associate to a local architect, while I do not find such associations helpful, I am willing to arrange it that way if you wish.
>
> I am writing to you in this personal way because it was you that spoke to me about it. (N-YHS, box 511, folder 1)

16 Commissioner Staunton brought the news on June 20 that Bonner Hill, former city manager of Charleston, had been appointed the Commission's "agent" in buying the lots for the site. Robert Damron summarized Hill's experience and why he was chosen by the commissioners: "Hill had overseen the construction of Charleston's City Hall, serving as the general contractor by proxy and saving the city thousands of dollars during the project; he was chosen by the commission for his expert knowledge of construction and administration." (*West Virginia Capitol*, 60). Damon omitted much of Hill's earlier history, however. Hill was Kanawha county sheriff during the infamous Paint Creek–Cabin Creek mine war of 1912 and he was on the "Bull Moose Special" armored train when the Holly Grove miners' settlement was attacked. He was questioned about his role in this attack by the US Senate Subcommittee of the Committee on Education and Labor on September 8, 1913; the transcript is available on the website of the West Virginia Archives & History Center. Hill managed to evade answering most of the subcommittee's questions and, if we believe his testimony, he played no significant role in the "Bull Moose Special" attack.

Other reports provide a different picture of Hill's activities during this period. The *Labor Argus* of January 30, 1913, reported:

> When Bonner Hill was a candidate for Sheriff of Kanawha County we knew he would prove but another tool of the coal barons by the fact that his campaign was financed and supported by the coal operators, and while we fully expected him to use his official power in the interest of his masters we did not expect him to stoop so low as to personally gather up scabs and strikebreakers to go to Paint Creek and Cabin Creek to take the places of the striking miners who were fighting for their rights in the face of every opposition. . . . When the sheriff of our county prostitutes his high office and descends to the level of a common scab hunter and herder, it is time for the people of the county to file their protest. (Quoted in Steel, ed., *Court-Martial of Mother Jones*, 229–30)

On February 13, the *Labor Argus* editorialized:

> The brutal and cold-blooded attempt of Sheriff Hill and his hirelings and thugs to murder the sleeping miners in their tents at Holly Grove last Friday night precipitated a condition that culminated in a civil war in which scores of men lost their lives. . . . Never before in the history of the nation has a public official so prostituted himself to the interest or resorted to such cold-blooded and brutal tactics as the high sheriff of Kanawha County attempted last Friday night. . . .
>
> We learned from a reliable source that Bonner Hill gave the order to the machine gun operator to open fire on the tents. There are a score of more witnesses who will testify that the first shots came from the train and that the train was running with the lights off. (Quoted in Steel, 235–36)

Bonner Hill's exact role in these events has never been certain and it is not clear how his previous history can be related to the role he played in the completion of the West Virginia Capitol complex, but the fact that successive West Virginia governors ignored the difficulties Hill created for Cass Gilbert and his supervisors suggest he must have had a certain political and personal power.

On October 6, 1922, Houston Young wrote Gilbert to inform him that Bonner Hill would gradually be taking on a larger role:

> The detail of the Capitol Commission matters is becoming so burdensome that I am gradually getting away from it.
>
> At a meeting of the Commission held some days ago, I was instructed to notify you that most of the correspondence from now on will be between yourself and Mr. Bonner H. Hill, Agent of the Commission.
>
> This does not mean that I will not keep in touch with what is going on, however. You may still write me at any time you desire, but most of your correspondence will be with Mr. Hill. (*CCC*, 573–74)

Hill signed his letters "Agent" until at least June of 1923, but he eventually took on the title of secretary. Hill micromanaged the construction process to the frustration of the architect and his superintendents on site.

17 The transcript, dictated by Cass Jr., is found at N-YHS, box 519, folder 9. The meeting included lunch. Cass Sr. documented how he used drawings in a 1905 letter to Warren Laird: "I make for [clients] as many sketches as necessary to meet their views, trying one design after

another." Quoted in Fenske, *Skyscraper*, 126. Paul Starrett described one of Gilbert's sketches, completed in twenty minutes, while in a meeting with a client, as a "wonderful performance" (Starrett, *Changing the Skyline*, 272). That Gilbert made quick sketches at the June 22 meeting is suggested by the following exchange: "[Commissioner Camden] asked if it might be possible to lengthen the Capitol building. Mr. Gilbert showed what would happen if the building were lengthened and the office buildings joined to the Capitol as wings."

18 Even with these reductions, Gilbert thought that the group of buildings he wanted to show his patrons were "about twice as large as a great many other capitols" and were sufficient for the state's needs. For information on the space they requested and how it was, in most cases, reduced by John Rockart, see chapter 3, note 4.

19 The transcript records that Gilbert had also "tried out a large office building but found it to be quite unsatisfactory as it made an unbalanced plan and a tall building would compete with any dome and two tall buildings would be unbalanced."

20 The renderings were drawn by Hugh Ferriss, Chesley Bonestell, and F. G. Stickel. Naming these delineators in the transcript was probably intended to document which drawings were shown, as there was no reason why the governor or commissioners would have been interested in the identity of these draftsmen. The transcript indicates that the rendering by Stickel was an elevation; that by Ferriss was probably the night scene discussed below.

Hugh Ferriss, who worked for several years in Cass Gilbert's office (c. 1912–15), became one of the great architectural draftsmen of the twentieth century; for a review of some of his later works see Ferriss, *Power in Buildings*, which includes only buildings designed after 1929. After Ferriss was self-employed, Gilbert often hired him to make renderings of buildings he had designed (see figs. 36, 37). Ferriss apparently had to hurry to finish his drawing before June 22, for he wrote to Gilbert on June 24:

> I think it might prove desirable to give a little more time to the West Virginia Capitol drawing which I made for you this week, especially if you plan having any photographs or reproductions made from it; I was somewhat rushed toward the last, and do not know that the values throughout the building, or the indication in the foreground, are sufficiently convincing. I also wish to reconsider it in the light of any opinions you have formed of it. Please advise me of your wishes regarding this.

In case Gilbert thought it was fine as is, Ferriss added, "The enclosed bill is brought to your attention on condition that, having looked over the drawing again, it is still acceptable" (N-YHS, box 504, folder 1).

In *Power in Buildings*, published in 1953, many years after his work for Cass Gilbert, Ferriss discussed the evolution of designs in the Gilbert studio. He lamented that engineers were not at that time more integrated into the initial design process: "The engineers were not full-fledged partners contributing to the design from its inception; rather, they seemed to be regarded as tough but necessary accomplices to call in at the last moment to hold up the architecture" (7).

21 Gilbert was praised for his ability to visualize the appearance of his projects from several viewpoints prior to construction. Writing about the design for the Woolworth Building, the distinguished early twentieth-century architectural critic Montgomery Schuyler stated, "There is no point of view from which it 'comes in wrong,' which means there is no point of view from which the designer had not been beforehand with the observer" (Woolworth & Co., *Woolworth Building*, 606).

Gilbert was probably aware that some recent domed capitols that had seemed handsome on the drawing board proved cumbersome when completed; one possible example would be McKim, Mead & White's Rhode Island Capitol. A comparison between Gilbert's elevation drawing for the Minnesota State Capitol and a photograph of the finished structure demonstrates how different the proportions are when seen in an elevation or from the ground; the two views appear in Irish, *Modern Traditionalist*, 39. The differences are less evident when the building is seen from afar.

22 Some of the drawings of National Capitol type shown to the patrons in June may have been damaged and discarded because they were handled while revised drawings were being prepared, although the extent of the Gilbert archives suggests that nothing was ever thrown away. It should also be noted that some of the drawings in the West Virginia section of the Cass Gilbert archive at N-YHS are inaccessible because they could only be unrolled during the course of an expensive, prepaid conservation process.

23 For comparison, the completed Main Building measures 558 by 120 feet; the height of the dome is 292 feet. Gilbert contrasted his plans with those of other capitols; on one plan he compares his 430-foot-long structure with McKim, Mead & White's 330-foot-long Rhode Island Capitol (N-YHS, box 524). In his plan the Senate and House Chambers were to be seventy by seventy feet, with seating for a minimum of 150 in the Senate gallery and at least 600 in that of the House. The galleries in both chambers of the finished Capitol are identical in size, seating approximately 200 people.

24 The governor also asked that his offices not be placed "in the rear of the building unless it was absolutely necessary."

25 An estimate of "cubage" made on June 21, 1922, in preparation for the meeting lists the two office buildings at 1,650,000 cubic feet each and the capitol at 5,900,000, for a total of 9,200,000.

26 Bonner Hill proposed that a model be made; on July 28, 1922, John Donnelly & Co. Inc., Architectural Sculptors, estimated that a model would cost $4,600. The Commission did not approve this expenditure (N-YHS, box 504, folder 1).

27 *CCC*, 550–51.

28 MacCorkle, a Democrat, was governor from 1893 to 1897; in 1925, he became a member of the State Capitol Commission, serving until his death in 1930.

29 Also on July 10, Gilbert had a conference with the French architect Ernest Hèbrard at the University Club, at which he sketched plans for the Wisconsin, Minnesota, West Virginia, and another, unidentified capitol. The sketch is preserved at the Library of Congress, Prints and Photographs Division (call # ADE11-Gilbert, no. 84 recto; reproduction # LC-USZ62-96431).

30 John Rockart prepared the transcript of the July 17–18 meeting. Rockart started working with Gilbert in 1891 and continued in the office until after Cass Sr.'s death in 1934. Rockart's transcript (N-YHS, box 519, folder 9) reveals that Mrs. Gilbert accompanied Mr. Gilbert on this trip to Charleston, after which they went on to vacation at the Greenbrier. Only four commissioners were present; also in attendance were Secretary Young and the governor. Bonner Hill did not attend, perhaps because at this time he was not yet secretary.

31 The requested changes were: (1) the Senate be located on the Duffy Street end of the Main Building; (2) the Supreme Court be located in the office building along California Street; (3) the offices of the governor, secretary of state, and attorney general be in the Main Building, with that of the governor on the riverfront adjacent to the Senate, that of the secretary of state on the riverfront adjacent to the House, and that of the attorney general across the corridor from the office of the secretary of state.

32 The final costs per square foot (excluding the architect's fee of 6 percent) were:

| | |
|---|---|
| Building #1 [East Building] (1924–25) | 71 cents |
| Building #2 [West Building] (1926–27) | 77 cents |
| Main Building (1930–31) | 65 cents |

Adding 6 percent (the architect's fee) brings these to:

| | |
|---|---|
| Building #1 (1924–25) | 75.26 cents |
| Building #2 (1926–27) | 81.62 cents |
| Main Building (1930–31) | 68.9 cents |

The average cost per cubic feet for all three buildings was 75.26 cents. The reduction in price per square foot from the East and West Buildings to the Main Building is surely due to the low bid made by the Fuller Company because of their desire to find work during the Depression. The cubic footage, including the passages, tunnels, and power house, exceeded the 8,000,000 by more than 50 percent:

| | |
|---|---|
| Office Building #1 (1924–25) | 1,797,000 |
| Office Building #2 (1926–27) | 1,965,000 |
| Capitol Building (exclusive of dome) | 6,900,000 |
| Dome above Capitol Building | 793,000 |
| Passages between Capitol Building and Buildings #1 and #2 | 131,000 |
| Power House | 900,000 |
| Tunnel between Buildings #1 and #2 | 37,960 |
| Tunnel between Building #2 and Power House | 64,000 |
| Total | 12,637,960 |

33 The July 17 headline is from N-YHS, project box 683. Much of the article is devoted to the difficulties that the Commission was having in buying the properties on the site for prices that were "reasonable, equitable and fair." The July 19 headline is from N-YHS, project box 683.

34 N-YHS, oversize 683.

35 On August 7, 1922, Cass Gilbert responded to a telegram from Houston Young requesting a meeting with the Commission in Charleston on August 11. Gilbert replied, "Will come to Charleston to submit sketch plans for final approval. Important this action taken to expedite progress." The meeting was delayed until August 14, however, and Cass Gilbert was unable to attend; the revised plans were presented by Cass Jr. and John Rockart. The office appointment books list the dates of this trip as August 12–15, including travel. On August 8, 1922, telegrams were sent to the Commissioners: "Architect desires meeting Commission Monday, August fourteenth; submit final plans. Can you be present?" (*CCC*, 656). Three commissioners attended, plus the governor and Bonner Hill. The transcript was prepared by Cass Jr. (N-YHS, box 8, folder 14). He and Rockart left New York on the 3:40 train on the 12th and arrived at Charleston at 12:30 on the 13th; they went directly to the Edgewood Country Club, where they played golf all afternoon with Houston Young. The reason for Cass Sr.'s absence is not clear from the documentation, but on August 19 he left for Europe with his daughter Julia Post on the SS *Homeric*; he sailed back on September 25 on the new SS *City of Paris*. His absence must have been keenly felt, for he would certainly have kept the meeting moving smoothly. According to the transcript, "The conference dragged. There were long periods of silence when no one spoke and no one wanted to speak first. Invariably one of the Commission would break the silence."

36 On August 13, Cass Jr. had met with a West Virginia ex-governor who stated that "he hoped we would build a very beautiful building, ... the finest of its type." (The ex-governor is not identified in the transcript.) Cass Jr. replied that his father's "object was, of course, to build inside the appropriation, and that there was quite sufficient money to build a really fine Capitol. However, there might be some difficulty getting interior decoration within the appropriation." Cass Jr. added "that we had two elements fixed, the price and the size, and that the material would have to fit those two elements. We would, therefore, put the money into a handsome exterior and leave the interior finish very plain."

37 The acceptance of these drawings also meant that payments were due to the architect. A letter from Houston Young written August 28, 1922, included two checks, each for $5,000; the letter indicates that the total had been paid Gilbert as of this point was $25,000 (N-YHS, box 504, folder 1).

38 NYHS, project box 683. The *Charleston Daily Mail* featured two renderings, the river façade and the court side, but all other publications known to us show only the river façade.

39 John Rockart transcribed this conversation; N-YHS, box 9, folder 18.

40 The Brooklyn Museum Curator was William H. Goodyear and the artist was Wilford S. Conrow, who had painted a mural of George Washington in Charleston; Gilbert's reply is preserved at N-YHS, box 511, file 1 (November 29, 1922). The N-YHS archives also contain several letters from representatives of the Moravian Tiles and Mosaics Company, inquiring if "tiling or colored clay work will be used in the new West Virginia Capitol." (N-YHS, box 504, folder 1, October 19, 1922).

41 *CCC*, 506–7. Young's letter is dated December 12, 1922; Gilbert's December 16, 1922. These letters also discussed the development of the riverfront and raising the grade of Kanawha Street.

## Chapter Five
## THE WEST AND EAST WINGS: POLITICS, MONEY, PROGRESS

1 The history of the financing of Gilbert's Minnesota Capitol exemplifies the possible difficulties; see Thompson, *Minnesota's State Capitol*, 23–27, 57–58, 62–73. The Minnesota Legislature at one point questioned the Commission and audited its books (68–71). One conclusion of this process was a commendation, for the report to the Legislature found that "the architect Mr. Cass Gilbert has performed his duties in every detail with the utmost fidelity, honesty, ability and skill, and that the state has received full value for the money it has expended on said capitol, and that the building promises to be an object of pride and satisfaction to the State of Minnesota" (Minnesota Legislature, House Committee on Public Accounts and Expenditures, "Investigation of Capitol Commission," 5).

2 The letter to Julia is from the Manuscript Division, LC.

3 Herschel Coombs Ogden (1869–1943) played a prominent role in West Virginia politics as a result of his ownership of and influence on the editorial policies of the *Wheeling Daily News*, the *Wheeling Intelligencer*, and a number of other West Virginia newspapers. Ogden was a reformer and a supporter of education. When he was inducted into the Wheeling Hall of Fame in 1982, he was described as an entrepreneur who "took a firm stand for good government and the welfare of the ordinary man." Wheeling Hall of Fame 2000 Induction booklet, accessed February 25, 2012, *http://www.wvgenweb.org/ohio/hof.htm*. He was a tireless promoter of Wheeling and was often suspicious of the administration that was governing the state from Charleston.

4 The content of this meeting is summarized in a letter of December 30, 1922, from Gilbert to Houston Young, N-YHS, box 504, folder 4. Gilbert had just received the clipping from the December 21 *Wheeling Intelligencer* titled "Cause for Indignation" (N-YHS, box 524, folder 3) and Laughlin brought with him a critical article from the *Wheeling Daily News* of December 27 (N-YHS, box 524, folder 3). Gilbert reported that Laughlin, who had called on him previously, was "very friendly and cordial" and that he invited the architect to call on him in Wheeling.

5 Young's letter, dated January 4, 1923, is preserved at N-YHS, box 504, folder 4, but we have not located a copy of the published article.

6 As reported in an article of January 5 in the *Parkersburg Sentinel*, N-YHS, box 683. The final paragraph is tattered and missing a number of words: "Business men who have analyzed the situation since the exposure of [missing] by Representative [missing] in The News says that [missing] Commission could hardly [missing] ignorant of the architect [missing] cost of doing business."

7 N-YHS, box 683. Criticism of the 6 percent fee must have continued, for on March 1, 1923, Gilbert wrote to a number of prominent architectural firms to inquire about their fee schedules; the replies uniformly supported the 6 percent figure. Replies were received from Henry Bacon; Arnold W. Brunner; Carrère & Hastings; Paul Philippe Cret; Cross & Cross; Delano & Aldrich; Bertram Grosvenor Goodhue; McKim, Mead & White; Charles A. Platt; John Russell Pope; George B. Post & Sons; Rankin, Kellogg & Crane; Edgerton Swartwout; Trowbridge & Livingston; York & Sawyer; and Zantzinger, Borie & Medary, as well as from the AIA and University of Pennsylvania professor Warren Powers Laird (N-YHS, box 504, folder 2).

8 This figure may have been provided by Gilbert. When the Gilbert office was preparing the drawings for the Woolworth Building, admittedly a more complex job, he employed twenty to twenty-five assistants; see Fenske, *Skyscraper*, 176.

9 N-YHS, box 504, folder 3.

10 The two reports and the published volume of correspondence are "State of West Virginia Capitol Building Commission: Report to the House of Delegates," "Report of the Special Senate Committee on Capitol Commission," and *CCC*.

11 The transcripts for the January 21–26 visit, made by Cass Gilbert Jr., are preserved at N-YHS, box 519, folder 10. A perspective study (drawn December 12, 1922) looking up at the dome from below marked "taken not used" is found at N-YHS, box 524, folder 1. A more finished perspective view of the complete Kanawha façade dated December '22 is also marked "taken not used" (N-YHS, box 4, roll A). Another drawing dated December 19, 1922, illustrates the layout and elevations for the three buildings (N-YHS, box 516, folder 5).

12 Gilbert to Morgan, May 23, 1923, N-YHS, box 516, folder 6. Gilbert was accompanied by John Rockart and Cass Gilbert Jr., both of whom left New York for Charleston on March 13 (Gilbert to Hill, May 23, 1923, N-YHS, box 516, folder 6).

13 N-YHS, box 516, folder 6, dated May 27, 1923. The capitols were Minnesota, Arkansas, Kentucky (on which he was unable to obtain definite information), Rhode Island (full cost not determined), Nebraska (under construction), Pennsylvania, Iowa, Wisconsin, and Missouri. He emphasized that such a comparative study should also include "the nature of the soil," "the location with reference to transportation," "the era in which main contracts were let," "the labor conditions (union, nonunion, prison labor . . . )," and it would be useful to know if any or all of these factors were included or omitted from the cost. It is not clear if such information proved effective in defusing criticism of the project.

14 It is also not clear what forces suggested moving the capital to Parkersburg. The transcript for this meeting is preserved at N-YHS, box 519, folder 10.

15 Clipping from the *Charleston Gazette*, April 7, 1923, preserved at N-YHS, box 683 and letter from Houston Young dated April 30, 1923 (N-YHS, box 504, folder 4). Young reported that the resolution was defeated despite the fact that Zimmerman "is supposed to be the majority leader in the House of Delegates."

16 Hill to Gilbert, May 17, 1923, N-YHS, box 504, folder 4: "I suppose you know that the West Virginia legislature has failed in its attempt to pass the Budget Bill which contains the appropriation for the construction of the new Capitol Buildings" (Gilbert to Hill, May 23, 1923, N-YHS, box 516, folder 6).

The reference to bidding is based on an inaccurate criticism leveled against Gilbert in the *Charleston Gazette* on May 20, 1923: "There is a feeling over the state that [the Commission] made a mistake in making a hard and fast contract with Mr. Cass Gilbert, allowing him to purchase materials and make plans for a capitol on a basis of expenditure that the people feel is too extravagant. The people of my county criticize the contract with Mr. Gilbert, by which he is to pass on all materials and really be the purchasing agent" (N-YHS, box 516, folder 6).

Gilbert's offer to come is found in a letter from Gilbert to Morgan, May 23, 1923, N-YHS, box 516, folder 6.

17 N-YHS, box 516, folder 6.

18 N-YHS, box 504, folder 4.

19 N-YHS, box 516, folder 6. Gilbert continued: "If we had the money to let all the contracts now at a time when bricklayers are getting in this market from $14.00 to $16.00 a day, and plasterers from $15.00 to $20.00 a day, and other trades in proportion and clamoring for more, we would be paying too much for the building and could not keep within any reasonable figure."

20 A memo dated May 31, 1923, indicates that Gilbert was calculating the cost of the carved decoration. Having sculptors make the models was the smallest part of the budget, probably because the motifs he was considering were part of the relatively standard repertoire of Classical decoration used by many architects of the period:

| | |
|---|---|
| Limestone carving, Building No. 1 and 2 | $ 47,220.00 |
| Marble carving, Building No. 1 and 2 | $ 63,750.00 |
| Models, Building No. 1 and 2 | $ 1,500.00 |
| Limestone carving, Capitol | $128,556.00 |
| Marble carving, Capitol | $168,580.00 |
| Models, Building Capitol | $ 2.900.00 |
| Limestone carving, Dome | $ 82,850.00 |
| Marble carving, Dome | $112,520.00 |
| Models, Dome | $ 3,200.00 |

(N-YHS, box 519, folder 10).

21 N-YHS, box 519, folder 10. These figures were somewhat deceptive, for he noted at the bottom: "*In view of the fact that present prices of materials and labor are unusually high, this estimate is priced as of 1922."

22 The transcript of the Charleston meeting of June 6–9, 1923, dictated by Cass Gilbert, is preserved at N-YHS, box 519, folder 10. The letter to Julia is from the Manuscript Division, LC. Gilbert's energy in his early sixties is demonstrated in this trip: he left Charleston about 8:30 on the evening of June 9. He arrived in Cincinnati at about 5:30 A.M. on June 10 and wrote to Julia on Hotel Sinton stationery after he breakfasted. He was waiting to catch the 9 A.M. train for Chicago, which would arrive there at 5:35 P.M., in time to catch the 6:30 P.M. train for Minneapolis, the last leg of this long trip. He informed Julia that the weather was perfect—"clear, cool, and most comfortable for travelling"—after the heat he had recently experienced in New York, Washington, and the first day in Charleston. He also wrote that his "Union Central Life building still towers above everything in Cincinnati and holds its own. I am proud of it. This is the first time I have seen it for nearly ten years."

23 The transcript is preserved at N-YHS, box 519, folder 10.

24 Gilbert received a copy of the *Telegraph* editorial from his clipping service. It is typical of the care with which he negotiated his commissions that he responded to this favorable publication, writing to the author, Mr. McLaughlin, on June 16: "Unworthy as I may be of the high praise conveyed by this article, I wish to thank you and the 'Telegraph' for it most heartily. If the State of West Virginia will provide the

means and the people will have a little patience with my limitations, I will do all I can to justify the compliments you have so generously accorded to me."

25 Byrne was a lawyer, fishing enthusiast, and author of a series of articles published in book form in 1940 as *Tale of the Elk*.

26 "Mr. Lighter" is clearly an error, as there was no delegate during that session named Lighter. Gilbert may have misheard or misremembered the name of the delegate from Harrison County, Edgar E. Righter. Another possibility is that the stenographer typing the transcript failed to correctly read Gilbert's handwriting. Thanks to Debra Basham of the WVSA for her help with this problem.

27 N-YHS, box 519, folder 10. Young's conversation also included information about other Charleston projects: "Library: He asked if we had heard anything about the Library for Charleston. I told him we had not. He stated he expected it would come to the office too. Governor's Mansion: He stated that they were endeavoring to arrange to have Mr. Gilbert plan the Governor's Mansion. While it will be comparatively a small operation they want Mr. Gilbert to do it. He stated that as soon as the matter had been finally passed Mr. Hill would notify the office accordingly." Bonner Hill wrote Gilbert on June 15 and enclosed a copy of the bill that had been passed, "the result of a compromise between the two factions, and I expect it is the best that could be had under the circumstances" (N-YHS, box 504, folder 3).

Enrolled Bill H. B. No. 371. Sec. 32-b, which passed on June 14, 1923, appropriated $250,000 from the Treasury: "The governor shall secure new plans and specifications for a capitol building and one or two office buildings and power plant as part of and in connection therewith, to be erected on the Kanawha street capitol site lately secured by the state in the city of Charleston, the total cost of which capitol building, office building or buildings and power plant, including architects' fees for plans and specifications and superintendence of construction, complete and ready for occupancy, shall not exceed five million dollars" (N-YHS, box 516, folder 6). The governor is only authorized at this time, however, to "let to contract" the office building or buildings and the power plant, the complete cost of which was not to exceed $2,500,000.

28 Morgan to Gilbert, June 15, 1923, N-YHS, box 504, folder 4. Gilbert's penciled comments on the governor's letter indicate he had filed these plans with Hill on June 8. He added, in pencil, that he "would want to revise and cheapen Boiler House before asking bids." The formal reply he sent to the governor on July 16, however, refers to the plans and states that "it may be necessary to modify them, especially the power house, before asking for proposals" (Hill to Gilbert, June 15, 1923, N-YHS, box 504, folder 3).

Some of the funds needed for construction would have to come from the sale of state property. On June 20, Young explained: "The Governor ... has several right embarrassing things to work out before we can start on our program. One of the most embarrassing is the sale of the land here. We cannot deliver this land until after the office buildings have been completed, and at the same time we must have the proceeds from this land in order to complete the office buildings." He concluded, "You will, therefore, see that it is going to be a slow process." Young suggested that perhaps Gilbert could "cut down the two office buildings about fifteen feet and not have to make entirely new plans" (N-YHS, box 504, folder 4). Bonner Hill's letter of June 15 had pointed out that the sale of the state's property is "mentioned in the bill" (N-YHS, box 504, folder 4).

29 In the meantime, Gilbert requested sample borings of the site. On July 28, 1922, he pointed out that the map acquired by the state "does not permit sufficient number of borings"; he needed a map of "vacant property where permission can be obtained to locate additional borings" (*CCC*, 126). On August 4, Young replied that the state hoped to have possession of the property "in a very short while," and that "there would be no trouble in making these borings in any location you should choose" (*CCC*, 125–26). Young also reported that the commissioners are "anxious to know what you have decided in regard to the retaining wall along the river bank."

30 November 22, 1923, N-YHS, box 504, folder 4.

31 "A Moving Monument" transcript, 11.

32 Transcript of Martens's visits to Cass Gilbert in New York, July 11 and 12, 1923, N-YHS, box 519, folder 10. Martens's letter of August 24, 1923, is preserved at N-YHS, box 504, folder 4. Although Martens reported that he had been appointed by the Board of Control, a 1960s interview with him included in "A Moving Monument" reveals that Governor Morgan called him directly to offer him the commission. "I had no idea that I was being considered since I was a young architect just getting started in my practice."

Martens reported that after the meeting, Cass Gilbert "dictated a letter to Mrs. Morgan, ... stating that he felt the planning of the mansion had been placed in capable hands." No letter to Mrs. Morgan survives, but a July 13 letter to the governor mentions her frequently and is probably the one to which Martens is referring; Gilbert stated that Martens "has told me of his conversations with Mrs. Morgan and her many admirable and helpful suggestions about the plan, and bearing these in mind I have made a few suggestions in conference with Mr. Martens which I am hoping will meet the views of Mrs. Morgan and yourself."

After citing other governors' mansions built in brick with white trim, Gilbert outlined his arguments against the use of stone for the mansion: "I am afraid if we use limestone or marble we might get the effect of seeming to try to imitate the Capitol in doing it on such a minute scale as to make it lack in dignity, and I would very much rather see the money which stone would cost put into the comfort and quality of the building."

The New York architect complimented Martens as "a very attractive and agreeable gentleman" and sent his "compliments and regards to Mrs. Morgan."

One of Cass Gilbert Jr.'s roles in office business is suggested by Martens's August 24 correspondence, expressing gratitude "for the kind treatment afforded me while in New York, especially the pleasant hours spent at the Yale Club with Mr. Gilbert Jr."

The *Charleston Gazette* article is at N-YHS, box 683. The Morgans moved into the mansion on March 4, 1925, just one week before the end of his term as governor.

For an in-depth discussion of both this and the earlier mansion, see Wallace, *West Virginia State Capitol*, 57–63.

33 December 1, 1923, N-YHS, box 504, folder 4. Gilbert penciled on the letter: "Send copy of Gov Morgan."

34 The Fuller Company had erected the Flatiron Building in New York City, and had hoped to win the contract to erect Gilbert's Woolworth Building, but that contract was awarded to the Thompson-Starrett Company. The efficiency of these two firms enabled them to complete large projects quickly; Fenske summarized that they "had imposed a new level of modern rationalization, efficiency, and financial control over the entire construction process" (Fenske, *Skyscraper*, 167). On the Fuller Company and Gilbert's relationship with Harry S. Black, George Fuller's son-in-law, who took over the company after Fuller's death in 1901, see Alexiou, *Flatiron*, and Fenske, *Skyscraper*, 171–72.

The contact was an example of the "single-contract system," with which the contractor established a fixed price, provided a date when construction would be completed, and employed all the subcontractors.

The system had been pioneered by the Fuller Company in 1886–89. See Fenske, *Skyscraper*, 168–74.

The details of the accepted bid for Building 1, with cubical contents of 1,650,000 cubic feet, are:

| | |
|---|---|
| General Construction | $ 980,000 |
| Heating | $ 62,000 |
| Plumbing | $ 35,000 |
| Electrical Work | $ 21,000 |
| Elevators | $ 22,000 |
| Total | $1,120,000 |

The estimated approximate price per cubic foot was sixty-eight cents. Automatic leveling devices for the elevators would probably add another $5,000.

In 1937, the Fuller Company privately published *George A. Fuller Company: General Contractors, 1882–1937, A Book Illustrating Recent Works of this Organization*. The title page indicates that in 1937 the firm had offices in New York, Boston, Washington, Philadelphia, Chicago, Los Angeles, Montreal, and Toronto. They built two state capitols, West Virginia and Louisiana, and added the new, larger dome to Bulfinch's Maine Capitol. The firm also erected Cass Gilbert's Canadian Embassy in Ottawa. Their pride in the West Virginia State Capitol is evident in the frontispiece: "The Golden Dome of the West Virginia State Capitol against the Evening Sky."

35 Although Gilbert suggested he would consider a West Virginian for this position, the first superintendent he hired was Charles G. Hequembourg, who apparently had no connection with the state. We know little about Hequembourg other than that he was an 1897 graduate of Cornell University. He arrived in Charleston on January 8, 1924. A document from November 25, 1932, reveals that the total salaries that Cass Gilbert's office paid to superintendents from 1922 through March 1932, was $34,914.27.

36 The spades used for the 1924 and 1930 groundbreakings are exhibited at the West Virginia State Museum. Gilbert provided the copper box to be placed in the cornerstone, which Hill acknowledged in a letter to the architect dated February 28, 1924. The final cost per cubic foot, excluding the architect's fee, was seventy-one cents. That the steel was made in Wheeling is recorded in "A Moving Monument" transcript, 11.

37 In plans at the WVSA, the garlands have been crossed out. In the elevation drawings at the WVSA, the profile heads are surrounded by stars and framed by what seem to be fasces. A transcript preserved at the N-YHS, however, states that on May 7, at John Donnelly & Company's modeling shop, Gilbert "inspected the models of the panel on the stair pavilions about the level of the third story and directed that the Medusa head should be much larger and the torches smaller and gave detailed instructions to the modeler." The transcript includes two small drawings marked "change this [drawing] to this [drawing]." Gilbert also corrected the "festoon" that was to be placed below the windows: "I directed them changed to be of more Classic form, *not* [Gilbert's emphasis] the late Renaissance."

Drawings reveal that wrought iron gates were planned for the arched courtyard entrances into the East and West Wings. Whether these would have been designed and executed by the premier American wrought iron artist Samuel Yellin, who was in contact with Gilbert about the West Virginia project, is uncertain.

38 The transcript of the meetings on April 13 and 14 was prepared by C. G. Hequembourg, N-YHS, box 506, folder 8. Mr. McGuire arrived at noon on April 13 and inspected the mechanical equipment in the presence of representatives of the contractors that afternoon. Cass Gilbert arrived at 7 A.M. on April 14, conducted his inspection until 10:30, held meetings with the governor and commissioners in the morning and afternoon with a break for lunch, and departed at 7:30 the same day for New York. Among the specific complaints was one about the lunette panels over the east entrance doors, which were "not satisfactory to Mr. Gilbert. Mr. Hequembourg was instructed to return the models to J. Donnelly & Company who will later receive instructions from Mr. Gilbert." Cass Gilbert was also "not pleased with the lanterns in east entrance. He has this matter under advisement."

The state's treasurer, W. S. Johnson, refused to move into his new office because he thought its vault was not secure; why he had not played a role in defining his needs more specifically is unknown. Gilbert protested that Johnson's requirements would be costly, but the Commission asked him to provide the treasurer with acceptably secure quarters in Office Building 2 ("A Moving Monument," 11). Ultimately a specialist in building banks provided plans that were apparently satisfactory to the treasurer. In his office in the East Wing, the inner surfaces were lined with three layers of half-inch steel and the twelve-by-seventeen-by-ten-foot vault was enclosed in eighteen-inch-thick walls reinforced with Wheeling steel. Inside the vault were forty separate safes with double combination locks. The solid steel door was fifteen inches thick.

Governor Conley's Appendix to his "Biennial Message to the Legislature of 1933" lists the cost of various aspects of Office Building 1 (preserved at N-YHS, box 524, folder 3). The elevators were $29,126.86, for example, and electric fixtures cost $10,002.50. Decorative painting in the vestibule and halls cost $8,075. Electric clocks were $2,894, but this figure may have included special equipment, as the subcontractor was the International Time Recording Company. Cass Gilbert's 6 percent commission totaled $68,953.09.

On July 15, 1925, the West Wing was struck by lightning, which damaged the balustrade at one corner and threw one piece of stone to the ground. This is documented in a photograph that Superintendent Hequembourg sent to Gilbert (N-YHS, box 506, folder 8).

39 N-YHS, box 506, folder 8. This copy of the article was sent to Gilbert by Hequembourg, who offered in the attached letter to discuss the matter with Gilbert by telephone.

40 N-YHS, box 524, folder 4.

41 N-YHS, box 506, folder 8.

42 N-YHS, box 506, folder 8.

43 For more information on Bonner Hill and Young's letter of October 6, 1922, see chapter 4, n. 16.

44 N-YHS, box 516, folder 7.

45 N-YHS, box 516, folder 8.

46 Gilbert was notified of the early June appropriation in a letter from R. D. Read, June 10, 1925. He received the letter while staying at Claridge's Hotel in London on June 20 and posted his reply on June 23 (N-YHS, box 507, folder 3). While the cost could not exceed $1,400,000, it seems that the Legislature only authorized $1,300,000 for the construction. Governor Conley's Appendix to his "Biennial Message to the Legislature of 1933" indicated that the 1925 Legislature appropriated $968,000 for the Capitol (N-YHS, box 524, folder 3).

47 Both of Hequembourg's letters are at N-YHS, box 506, folder 8. Gilbert's response to this discouraging news was a note that he had in mind to ask Hequembourg "to act as Supt. on another operation if the capitol work does not go ahead."

48 Gilbert's trip is documented in his appointment books.

The James Baird Company was established by James Baird in 1925. Baird, who had been a famous University of Michigan quarterback, started work at the George A. Fuller Company in 1899; he supervised the Fuller Company's construction of the Flatiron Building in New York City and the Lincoln Memorial in Washington; by 1922, he was the firm's president. The Baird Company may have offered the low bid for the East

Wing because it was interested in establishing itself as a company engaged in large public building projects. Gilbert may have wanted to avoid hiring the Fuller Company for Office Building 2 because of his disastrous experience with Harry Black, president of the Fuller Company, on the failed Floranada project (Alexiou, *Flatiron*, 246–48).

The information about works by the Baird Company is from N-YHS, box 507, folder 5. Other works listed include a garage, a Methodist home for the aged, a warehouse, and a private residence that was expected to cost approximately $140,000.

The letter from Cass Gilbert informing the Baird Company that they had won the commission is dated July 19, 1926 (N-YHS, box 523, folder 1; copy at WVSA). Their original bid of $1,151,000.00 "based upon the use of steel windows of the Campbell type approved by the Architect" was revised by a number of changes and omissions down to $1,090,016. The following changes were stipulated:

- omit the tunnel between Buildings 1 and 2 (saving $17,000);
- use reinforced concrete throughout, rather than combination terracotta and concrete arches (saving $4,700);
- substitute monolithic marble columns in the Supreme Court chamber (saving $4,500);
- omit the carving of exterior stone work, excepting the three carved key blocks over the main entrance (saving $33,784);
- reduce the decorations in the Supreme Court chamber (saving $10,000).

Another modification that would not change the price was the substitution of Northern Ivory marble in the Supreme Court room, entrance lobby, and in niches, passageways, and rooms as listed.

49 The information on the fire at the Pasteboard Capitol is from the *New York Times*, March 3, 1927. The Pasteboard Capitol and the adjoining brick building that housed the Attorney General's offices burned to the ground on March 2, 1927, in a fire that moved so rapidly that employees, escaping from the second story by ladders, left behind their purses. Five cars parked nearby were destroyed and the fire ignited three homes that were saved by firemen. Fortunately, many state offices had already moved into the West Wing, completed in 1925; the most important tenants still in the Pasteboard Capitol were the Road and Public Services Commissions and the State Workmen's Compensation Department. For a discussion of the fire and views of the destruction, see Cohen and Andre, *Capitols of West Virginia*, 52–54.

The new East Wing was 1,965,000 cubic feet; the West Wing was 1,797,000. The cost per cubic foot of the East Wing was seventy-seven cents—six cents per cubic foot more than the West Wing.

In August 1927, some of the final details of the interior were being arranged. On August 8, Cass Gilbert commissioned a bronze memorial tablet for Building 2 from the John Palacheck Bronze & Iron Company for $495 (N-YHS, box 523, folder 1). On August 18, he commissioned Paris & Wiley (51 West 29th St., New York City) to decorate the Supreme Court room, the entrance lobby, and the main floor corridor; their fee of $27,750 included scaffolding, velour curtains for the Supreme Court chamber, and the stipulation that "all material and workmanship throughout shall be of best quality" (N-YHS, box 523, folder 1).

50 The telegram is at N-YHS, box 516, folder 8. The cost of sending this wire was $8.43; the number of wires preserved in the archives reveals that such communications must have been a major expense for the Gilbert office.

The letters are preserved at N-YHS, box 508, folder 2. The serious accusations Hill leveled against Hequembourg included arriving late for work, having a "love affair," securing "Walton the place of watchman with the James Baird Company in order that he might supply [Hequembourg] with moonshine whiskey," and getting drunk with "the Raymond Pile Company's Superintendent ... the Saturday night Mr. Martin was in Washington."

Gilbert surreptitiously kept a copy of Hill's letter. Hequembourg reported that Hill saw Hequembourg's November 8 letter to Gilbert, but not the following postscript:

> Mr. Hill stated to me that he has resented the treatment he has received from Mr. Gilbert, Mr. Rockart, and myself.... I am now sure that if Mr. Hill is kept in touch with things and if I pay more attention to him and take him into my confidence *to a certain extent* [Hequembourg's emphasis] and make him feel that he is part of the building work—that he will cooperate with all of us and that everything will be all right. Mr. Hill has been ignored and he has been thinking it over and over for so long that he had about determined that he did not care what happened—(He told me so). Now, he seems pleased and I feel that if I manage to keep him in good spirits that he may develop as a friend. I shall do my best in this matter and shall not give him cause for any more complaints.

51 In June 1925, Gilbert had been contacted by the justices of the West Virginia Supreme Court of Appeals in connection with the design of their chamber and quarters in the East Wing. The two parties had been in contact since July 1921, almost immediately after Gilbert had been appointed architect, when they wrote to recommend that the Supreme Court be housed in a separate building, a "Temple of Justice." By March 1923, they had approved the preliminary plans for their area in the East Wing. As these plans were being finalized in 1925, they suggested a number of "fundamental changes in the floor plan of the offices." The reply from Cass Gilbert's office assured them that their suggestions would "be given careful consideration."

The letter from the justices to Gilbert asking for movable chairs is dated April 25, 1927. Some of the responses to their requests for information about the arrangements used in other courtrooms had included rough plans of their chambers, with the locations of benches indicated. The chambers of the Supreme Courts of Ohio, Delaware, Virginia, New Jersey, and Massachusetts had moveable chairs or benches, while those of Kentucky, Pennsylvania, and Minnesota had fixed seats. Rhode Island had chairs fastened together in rows that were movable to facilitate cleaning.

Somewhat earlier, on April 4, 1927, the clerk of the Supreme Court of Appeals had written to both the Capitol Commission and to Cass Gilbert about a problem with the organization of their offices, and asking about the possibility of either moving one door or adding another. The Supreme Court seems to have been the only governmental unit allowed to micromanage the design of their new quarters. John Rockart, responding on behalf of Gilbert, wrote to Governor Gore that although this would involve additional expense, in part because of the marble work in the corridor, such an expense "would be justified on the premise that it would be well to satisfy the reasonable demands of the tenants in the building" (Letter dated April 5, 1927).

Thanks to Rory L. Perry II, Clerk of Court, for providing us with photocopies of these letters and documents.

52 N-YHS.

53 N-YHS, box 516, folder 8; Gilbert to Gore, February 4, 1928; Gilbert to Hill, February 4, 1928; Hill to Gilbert, April 10, 1928.

54 Hill to Gilbert, April 10, 1928. In May 1927, when Bonner Hill was running for the Republican nomination for state auditor, Superintendent Hequembourg sent Hill's campaign brochure to the architect, who annotated it. One testimonial reports that Hill's service as "Superintendent in the construction of the new Capitol ... was of the best," Gilbert wrote in the margin: "He was *not* [Gilbert's emphasis] Supt. of Construction."

## Chapter Six
## THE SECOND DESIGN PHASE

1 N-YHS, box 516, folder 8.

2 The results were considered important enough to be published as *Abstract of Letters Received from Taxpayers of West Virginia Expressing Their Opinion Relating to Financing and Completion of the State Capitol Building*. The rest of the title page states: "These letters were received in reply to a letter mailed out by Hon. Cecil B. Highland, Senator from the Second Senatorial District and Chairman of the Senate Finance Committee." There is no additional publication data. The sample letter quoted here was addressed to "Sheet Metal Specialty Co., Follansbee, W. Va." One respondent refers to "yours of 28th of May," providing a date for at least one of Highland's letters.

3 Governor Conley's Appendix to his "Biennial Message to the Legislature of 1933" indicates that the 1927 Legislature appropriated $240,000 for the Capitol, N-YHS, box 524, folder 3.

4 According to Damron, the Legislature passed the levy on March 2, 1929. The Commission then borrowed approximately $2,000,000 to "ensure the speedy completion and furnishing of the crowning unit of the complex. This loan to the state was paid in full and the Capitol Building Fund was dissolved at the end of the fiscal year of 1934" (Damron, *West Virginia Capitol*, 16).

5 "Committee Sets Means" is found at N-YHS, box 509, folder 3. "Corporation Tax" is at N-YHS, box 524, folder 3.

6 "Capitol Building Commission, " a WVSA document dated March 15, 1929. On March 15, 1929, this $110,000 was still in the State Treasury, along with $8,559.76, which was the "balance of appropriations made for Capitol Building No. 2." The total appropriated by the 1927 Legislature is listed as $240,000 in Governor Conley's Appendix to his "Biennial Message to the Legislature of 1933" (N-YHS, box 524, folder 3).

7 Gilbert to Gore, April 10, 1928, N-YHS, box 516, folder 8.

8 Gilbert's "Memorandum Relative to a State Capitol" was prepared for this meeting. It is dated December 11, 1927, and must have been typed in the morning or early afternoon, just before he and John Rockart left for Charleston. The notation at the top reads "File West Va. Cap." (N-YHS, box 516, folder 8).

9 N-YHS, box 516, folder 8.

10 While the cubic feet were reduced from 7,927,500 to 5,918,000, the new plan would still fulfill current demands for office space and provide additional space to be finished later as needed. "The building is susceptible of additional office space by the construction of an upper story above the central portion of each main section as shown by dotted lines on the cross section. (Drawing SK33.) This space would be surplus space and is not required at the present time and can be added at a later time without in any way marring the appearance of the building or causing any inconvenience to the occupants."

11 In an attempt to keep the governor's office on the legislative floor, Gilbert told Gore that he had explored the option of placing it on the north side of the rotunda by eliminating the courtyard portico and exterior staircase; he had rejected this possibility not only because it would be less convenient for the governor but also because it would add cost. Gilbert was still exploring this possibility in June, however, as is indicated on a rough plan drawn June 11 (N-YHS, conservation box 4, roll B). Calculations on this plan indicate that the purpose seems to be to save cubage; at eighty-five cents per cubic foot, the cost of this revised plan, with the architect's 6 percent, was $5,213,744.45.

12 Gilbert to Gore, April 10, 1928, and Gore to Gilbert, April 17, 1928, N-YHS, box 516, folder 8.

13 N-YHS, box 516, folder 8. Letter dated May 12, 1928.

14 Gore to Gilbert, December 31, 1928, WVSA.

15 Gore to Gilbert, January 8, 1929, WVSA.

16 The telegrams and other information mentioned here are preserved in a letter from Gilbert to Conley dated March 11, 1929, N-YHS, box 516, folder 9. In a later message to the Legislature, Governor Conley reported that the $5 million the Legislature appropriated for the construction "is being raised by a special tax of five cents on the one hundred dollars valuation of all assessable property within the state, covering a period of five years beginning with the year 1929 and ending with the year 1933" (Damron, *West Virginia Capitol*, 14–16).

17 "EVENTS AS SEEN AT STATE CAPITAL," editorial from the *Parkersburg Sentinel*, December 3, 1930, N-YHS, box 524, folder 3. The quotation is from the later editorial, not from the 1929 proposed amendment.

18 Gilbert to Conley, September 13, 1929, WVSA. "Governor Upset" is preserved at N-YHS, box 524, folder 3. In April, Cass Gilbert and Governor Conley had been corresponding about the color and quality of the furnishings for his private office. Gilbert had provided a blueprint showing drapery suggestions and samples of red damask drapery and a red carpet, although for the latter the architect stated that he would prefer "a lighter brown or buff shade." The estimate for the carpet was $562. WVSA, Gilbert to Conley, April 26, 1929.

19 Gilbert sent Governor Conley a copy of his letter to Highland; the letter is preserved at the WVSA.

20 Gilbert to Conley, September 13, 1929, WVSA.

21 Gilbert to "My dear Mr. Hequembourg," April 20, 1925, N-YHS, box 506, folder 8.

22 Gilbert to Conley, October 4, 1929, WVSA.

23 Aus played such an important role in that project that he was one of those memorialized in caricatured portraits in the building's lobby. For Aus's role at the Woolworth Building, see Fenske, *Skyscraper*.

24 Two clippings from 1928 and 1929 at N-YHS, box 524, folder 4 suggest that his attention was drawn to the Invalides dome when it was announced that it was to be regilded. One of the clippings reported, "The glistening dome was until a few years ago one of the most beautiful features of the panorama of Paris on a sunlit day" (*New York Herald*, Paris, Sunday, August 11, 1929). The clippings were given to John Rockart with a note: "J.R. This is the item I mentioned about gilding—It may be useful re W. Va. Cap. Dome. CG."

25 Jack, Jenney & Tyler won the commission for the gilding; this letter is found at N-YHS, box 519, folder 5. Among their other projects were the Standard Oil Building in New York City and the ceiling of the Canadian House of Commons. The letter concludes: "The parts not gilded are to receive a third coat of paint of a color to be approved by you. The above figure does not include the furnishing of the necessary scaffolding."

According to Kabler, quoting John Wiseman, project contractor for the dome's restoration, Gilbert "kept $300,000 out of the original construction budget to be spent at his discretion to determine how to do these panels and who would gild them."

26 A copy of the telegram is preserved at N-YHS, box 516, folder 9.

27 N-YHS, box 520, folder 5.

28 N-YHS, box 524, folder 3.

29 Rockart was accompanied by Samuel McGuire from Gilbert's office. No transcript of the October 30 meeting seems to have survived; letter from Gilbert to Conley, N-YHS, box 516, folder 10. The identity of the local consultants is unknown.

30 N-YHS, box 520, folder 5.

31 N-YHS, conservation box 2. Cass Gilbert must have been relieved that the plans were approved and bidding could go forward because now he could receive payment for his and the office's work on the Main Building. A letter from Bonner Hill to Governor Conley dated February 7,

1930, reports that the architect had been paid $150,000 for "services on the main building" as appropriated by the 1927 Legislature. Hill continued: "I understand the Attorney General holds that this amount must be paid back into the general state fund from the five cent direct levy fund. If this is true, I see no reason why it could not be the last payment made from this fund" (Hill to Conley, WVSA).

32 WVSA. The notice was published in the state's newspapers and in national trade journals.

33 Gilbert to Conley, WVSA. In his letter, Gilbert pointed out that this would allow him to choose materials based on "quality, beauty, and cost."

34 Gilbert to Conley, WVSA. Some potential bidders had ordered several sets of drawings.

35 There were three bids for foundations, eleven for electrical work, thirteen for heating and ventilating, ten for plumbing, and three for elevators. Document listing bids received by Gilbert on March 12, 1930, N-YHS, box 512, folder 7.

A document of June 20, 1930, states that the Fuller contract amount was $3,236,000 plus "Additional Alternates accepted in the Contract" of $98,500, for a total of $3,334,500. Fuller Company to Gilbert, June 20, 1930, N-YHS, box 511, folder 9. By this date the following "Authorized Extras" had already been added to the contract: marble: $62,500; and again, marble: $168,000; and "Variegated Limestone" changed to "Select Buff": $125,000, for a total of $3,690,000.

In an attachment, the Fuller Company broke down the expenses as follows:

| | |
|---|---|
| General Conditions | 165,000. |
| Concrete Piles | 160,000. |
| Excavation | 35,000. |
| Waterproofing | 18,000. |
| Concrete Footings, Caps, and Wall | 78,000. |
| Brickwork and Chimney | 167,400. |
| Reinforced Concrete Arches | 170,000. |
| Cement Finish | 65,000. |
| Terra Cotta Partitions | 100,000. |
| Plastering | 65,000. |
| Architectural Terra Cotta | 30,000. |
| Limestone | 950,000. |
| Granite | 10,000. |
| Millwork | 38,000. |
| Carpentry | 25,000. |
| Roofing and Sheet Metal Work | 110,000. |
| Hollow Metal Doors and Trim | 7,500. |
| Glass and Glazing | 17,500. |
| Painting | 24,000. |
| Ornamental Iron and Bronze | 110,000. |
| Structural Steel | 283,000. |
| Metal Sash and Frames, erected | 65,000. |
| Marble | 460,000. |
| Tile Work | 12,000. |
| Guastavino | 4,500. |
| White Glass | 29,000. |
| Mail Chute | 2,000. |
| Allowances | 352,100. |
| Perete | 17,000. |
| Gunite | 20,000. |
| (Total) | $3,690,000. |

Damron reports that the Fuller Company used more than forty subcontractors, several of which were from West Virginia (*West Virginia Capitol*, 15–16). The reinforcing bars were provided by a firm from Huntington. One Wheeling firm was responsible for excavation, another for erecting the steel structure, and a third for painting it. Some of the cement and concrete pilings were provided by companies from Kanawha County.

36 Meyers Brothers' bid on heating and ventilation was $191,021; the low bid, from James McCrea & Son of Baltimore, was $138,523. Meyers Brothers' bid for plumbing was $71,200; the low bid of $64,900 came from Hutter Construction Co. of Fond du Lac, Wisconsin (which was "subject to Gen. Contract," meaning that the bid did not hold if they did not receive the contract for general construction). Between the two was a bid of $65,940, from James McCrea & Son. The high bid for plumbing was $99,167, from A. R. Brueggeman Co. of Cleveland.

37 Telegram from Gilbert to Rockart, N-YHS, box 516, folder 10. Gilbert asks Rockart to "inquire closely if bidders include such major items as piling steel, etc.... If found satisfactory urge closing contract immediately against the chance of withdrawal of low bids." The bids were so low that he wrote that he "would like to include the terraces and the sculpture in the pediments.... Get authority for so doing if funds permit.... We must reserve an amply sufficient sum for contingencies expenses."

38 A document of June 20, 1930, states that the contract amount was $3,236,000 plus "Additional Alternates accepted in the Contract" of $98,500, for a total of $3,334,500. Fuller Company to Gilbert, June 20, 1930, N-YHS.

In his Biennial Message to the Legislature (N-YHS, box 524, folder 3), Governor Conley outlined the contracts that were let:

1. To George A Fuller & Company, Inc., for general construction, $3,236,000.00; alternates for marble, $329, 000.00; exchange select variegated for select buff limestone, $125,000.00; extra concrete piles, concrete mat and steel reinforcing in foundation to insure safety of building, $19,431.50; extra marble for corridors and legislative chambers, $286,662.00; total, $3,996,093.50.
2. To James McCrea and Son, Inc., for plumbing, heating and ventilating, $217,131.00.
3. To Rigs Distler and Company, Inc., for electrical work, $103,725.00.
4. To Otis Elevator Company, for elevators, $38,545.00

Total contract price for the building, $4,355,494.50.
This total is without the architect's fee.

The list of subcontractors is preserved at WVSA.

39 N-YHS, letterbook, West Virginia State Capitol.

## Chapter Seven
## COMPLETING THE "MOUNTAINEERS' MONUMENT"

1 A slightly later document, from July 12, 1930, reveals the significant difference between the cost of carved stone versus cast plaster. Cast plaster decoration for the "Senate, Senate Entry, and Rostrum" would cost $1,800; carved granite would cost $29,500 (minus a credit of $1,800 for the plaster); replacing cast plaster with carved marble in the same area would cost $32,962, only slightly more than carved granite. The additional cost for substituting marble for the "Cornices in Rotunda, and Architraves in House and Senate Foyers," with the credit for the plaster and the "extras" would be $114,737. Fuller Company to Gilbert, July 12, 1930, N-YHS, box 511, folder 9.

2 The *Keyser Mineral News* article, dated November 15, 1930, is at N-YHS, box 516, folder 10. Gilbert's letter to Conley, dated November 28, 1930, is at N-YHS, box 516, folder 10. Criticism of the six commissioners who supported the increased fee was also found in an editorial published in the December 3 *Parkersburg Sentinel*; the writer reveals that it was Bonner Hill who pointed out that "the fee which Gilbert charged

for recommending use of marble is the astounding figure of $17,220." The writer added, "This fee is presumably charged for work done by Gilbert's underlings on re-vamping of the plans and specifications for the additional marble." It was probably Hill who told the writer that "Gilbert's ample fee ... is said to be $261,419.95 for the main unit plans" (N-YHS, box 524, folder 3).

3 Hill to Conley, April 25, 1930, WVSA. Hill suggested that knowing the lettering in advance was important because "Mr. Gilbert had some lettering done in the Supreme Court room in Office Building number two which did not meet with the approval of a number of republicans as well as some members of the Capitol Building Commission and he was requested to make certain changes in it, which he did." We have not found evidence that this was the case, nor is this episode documented in the archives of the Supreme Court of Appeals. Thanks to Rory Perry for confirming this.

4 Gilbert to Conley, May 1, 1930, WVSA. The full passage reads:

> I have as yet made no drawings or designs of the sculpture for the pediments of the north and south porticoes of the Main Unit.... As this sort of work is sculpture requiring a very high degree of skill and artistic ability, it is usually the custom for the architect to select a sculptor and confer with him in regard to it, and evolve from such conferences designs that will best fit the conditions and make the best composition in the space. I would of course convey to the sculptor my ideas of the design through conferences and such illustrative free-hand sketches as might be necessary. I should like to follow this method in this instance.
>
> It has been usual for my clients to authorize me to select the sculptor, and I hope you will authorize me to do so in this case. There is no more satisfactory adornment of a building than good sculpture and no more worthless form of art than bad sculpture (unless it be bad painting) and it can only be acquired through the employment of a sculptor of established experience and ability.

A letter of July 3, 1931, from Conley to Gilbert states: "Your letter of the 1st is received, suggesting inscriptions on the exterior of the Capitol dome. The ones selected by you, in my judgment, are splendid, and I heartily agree with them" (N-YHS, box 514, folder 1).

5 On the cornerstone ceremony, see Damron, *West Virginia State Capitol*, 15. The architect, the governor, and members of the Capitol Building Commission were present. The copper box deposited in the cornerstone held artifacts and documents representing the state, including the state directory, the Constitution, and the birth certificate of one of the babies born that year in West Virginia. Other interesting inclusions pertained to West Virginia's medical history: "literature outlining the latest methods of preventive medicine, a copper seal used in marking safe drinking water along the public highways, a bottle of 'neo-salvarsan' used in treating venereal disease, ... a vial of typhoid vaccine." Neosalvarsan was a modern drug being used in the state's free clinics; its inclusion demonstrated West Virginia's commitment to using the latest methods to ensure the well-being of its citizens.

For the eighteen "Masterpieces," see Hoak and Church, *Masterpieces*. The Society of Arts and Sciences event was reported in detail in the *New York Times*, January 31, 1931.

6 John Donnelly Jr. to Gilbert, January 26, 1931, N-YHS, box 514, folder 3. The firm also worked on the Woolworth Building, see Fenske, *Skyscraper*.

7 The architect's engagement with even minor details of engineering is obvious in a letter assuring him that issues of "anchoring and bonding" for the rotunda frieze have been revised "in accordance with the discussion which took place between our Mr. Moore and Mr. Rockart several days ago." Letter from the New York Drafting Annex of the Vermont Marble Company to Gilbert, March 13, 1931.

8 The results of the May 26 meeting of the Board of Public Works were reported in a newspaper clipping preserved at the WVSA. The article also reports that "Miss Mary Pratt of Wheeling and Charleston assisted in an advisory capacity in the selection of the draperies and furnishings."

A letter dated August 13 lists twenty-seven different pieces of furniture, from revolving chairs to desks and marble benches and signboards (George Reinhard to Gilbert, August 13, 1931, N-YHS, box 515, folder 6). Another letter from Reinhard concerning "Nail Trimmings" informed Gilbert: "We propose to use large antique brass nails, ¾" in diameter, placed closely together with a ⅛" space between these nails, which in our opinion is the finest possible type of finish on top grain leather upholstery."

9 For the General Bronze Corporation's "candelabras," see Hill to Conley, July 10, 1931, WVSA.

For the fireplace equipment, see the letter from New York Art Iron Works to George P. Reinhard Co., August 31, 1931, N-YHS, box 515, folder 6. The letter from George Reinhard to Gilbert estimated the cost of the same items at $676.50; the Reinhard Company seems to have negotiated a cut in the price. Interestingly, they did not mark up the price of the goods they were supplying for the Capitol. Since the amount budgeted for these furnishings was $825, this would result in a savings to the state of $148.50. Reinhard informs the architect that unless a special metal finish is requested, these would be finished in "naturelle."

The rugs needed for the governor's reception room measured 60'9" by 23'6" and 18'6" by 6'6". Reinhard to Gilbert, September 21, 1931, N-YHS, box 515, folder 6. On September 26, the Reinhard Company reported that the color for the House reception room was being changed from crimson to rust and gold, in the same pattern used for the Senate reception room. Reinhard to Gilbert, September 26, 1931, N-YHS, box 515, folder 6.

For Black & Boyd, see their letters to Gilbert dated September 10, 1931, and September 29, 1931, N-YHS, box 513, folder 9. On October 9, 1931, the Fuller Company wrote to Gilbert to point out that Black & Boyd were "materially delaying the completion of the job." The letter listed eleven kinds of fixtures that were going to be late in arriving, with delays listed from two weeks to three months. The crystal fixtures were not going to be delivered until November, and the forty-eight "Marble & Alabaster Standards coming from Italy" were not expected until January 1932.

For the Reinhard Company delivery, see Reinhard to Gilbert, November 10, 1931, N-YHS, box 515, folder 6. The itemized list that accompanied this bill inventories 324 chairs, 42 tables, 21 sofas and settees, 18 benches, 12 circular stands, 7 desks, and 1 chaise longue ("for Women's Retiring Room #26"), as well as draperies, valances, and "all special rugs and carpets."

10 Hill to Gilbert: July 15, 1931; July 21, 1931; July 22, 1931; July 23, 1931; August 13, 1931; September 8, 1931; and September 16, 1931; N-YHS, box 515, folder 3.

11 Plan is preserved at WVSA.

12 Conley sent a copy of Lowe's article to the architect, commenting: "Not knowing about Greek art or other kinds of art myself, I am not in position to know whether the article correctly describes the building or not." N-YHS, box 514, folder 2.

13 To the best of our knowledge, none of these plaster models survive. While none of the city's art teachers and students initially surveyed by our Charleston friends Wayne and Carol Eich had any memory of these works, Charleston artist Betty Warner remembered drawing from the models when she studied at the high school with Agnes Huston, whom she praised highly as a teacher and an inspiration to young artists.

14 This fact was repeated in an editorial of November 30, 1931, in the *Charleston Daily Mail*: "The cost was not so much in the gold itself as in

its preparation and application and the other material used" (N-YHS, box 514, folder 2).

15 Gilbert to Conley, November 11, 1931, N-YHS, box 514, folder 2.

16 Gilbert also pointed out that each unit had cost less than the appropriation: the West Building had cost $32,000 less, the East Building about $50,000 less, and the Main Unit would probably be "about $400,000.00 less than the appropriation, the final accounting not having been completed."

17 Frederick J. Wiley to Gilbert, December 10, 1931, N-YHS, box 515, folder 6. The decorative painting firm of Paris & Wiley had been used by Gilbert for other projects, including the Detroit Public Library and the West Side Building.

18 *Charleston Daily Mail*, December 7, 1931. "GILBERT PRAISES NEW CAPITOL BUILDING ON INSPECTION VISIT," WVSA. Blue laws were in effect in West Virginia at the time.

19 Gilbert received another telegram from the Fuller Company on December 14: "Have again received several telegrams and letters from subcontractors West Virginia Capitol asking for final payment." On December 16, the Fuller Company asked Gilbert for permission to make final payments to twenty-three subcontractors. Telegrams and letter, N-YHS, box 514, folder 9. The letter listed the subcontractors they were ready to pay. They did not intend to pay Black & Boyd, who were late in providing light fixtures and in December were still trying to provide substitutes as needed. Black & Boyd to Gilbert, December 21, 1931, N-YHS, box 513, folder 9.

20 The document is a small sheet dated January 22, 1932, and signed by R. D. R. (probably R. D. Read, Gilbert's secretary). The back of the sheet lists traveling expenses as $13,051.61 and superintendent salaries as $34,014.27 plus $900 for February and March 1932. Apparently steel inspection for the three buildings had been paid by Gilbert's office because this too is listed as an expense: $498.50 (Building 1: Standard Insp. Co.), $949.77 (Building 2: Robert W. Hunt Co.), and $1953.88 (Main Building: G. Aus Co.), for a total of $3,402.15. The inclusion of the superintendents' salaries on this list is an error, however, for Gilbert's contract included the concession that he would pay these salaries.

It is not clear how "cost to date" was calculated, but another sheet of figures had three columns recording the annual amount for each building in the middle and miscellaneous on the right. The middle-column was totaled and then 60 percent overhead and the total of the right-hand column were added to this, as indicated below:

| | | |
|---|---:|---:|
| 1921 | 1,374.45 | 1,420.55 |
| 1922 | 6,581.63 | 1,073.24 |
| 1923 | 13,378.11 | 3,216.04 |
| 1924 | 12,193.38 | 1,689.61 |
| 1925 | 6,300.61 | 326.07 |
| 1924 (#2) | 6,613.23 | 1,642.13 |
| 1925 (#2) | 2,821.50 | 145.34 |
| 1926 (#2) | 10,803.75 | 3,831.19 |
| 1927 (#2) | 10,637.01 | 1,833.59 |
| 1928 (#2) | 2,811.16 | 630.97 |
| 1927 (Main Bldg.) | 1,479.50 | 45.50 |
| 1928 (Main Bldg.) | 4,024.72 | 447.94 |
| 1929 (Main Bldg.) | 34,481.27 | 7,653.17 |
| 1930 (Main Bldg.) | 38,785.79 | 11,719.53 |
| 1931 (Main Bldg.) | 14,174.96 | 2,542.25 |
| | *(to 11/1/31)* | *(to 11/1/31)* |
| | 166,461.07 | 38,217.12 |
| 60% overhead | 99,876.64 | |
| Miscl. | 38,217.12 | |
| | 304,554.83 | |

21 The letter, dated January 31, 1932, is quoted in its entirety in the transcript of the Commission meeting of February 9, 1932. WVSA.

22 Gilbert's letter of February 2, 1932, is quoted in full in the transcript of the Commission meeting of February 9, 1932. WVSA.

23 N-YHS, letterbook, June 17, 1932. The drawing illustrated on pages 86–87 of Cohen and Andre, *Capitols of West Virginia*, which is dated June 20, 1932, in honor of the dedication, was a part of this package. Gilbert was still hoping that the property north of the Capitol could be acquired for parking—again hidden behind trees—and for a parklike extension over the railroad tracks and up the hill to the north.

24 WVSA.

25 *Charleston Daily Mail*, Sunday morning, June 19, 1932, page 43; advertisement for Kresge Stores.

26 *Charleston Gazette*, June 20, 1932.

27 Colonel Guy D. Goff, "Dedication Address," from a typed version marked "Speech of Honorable Guy D. Goff at the Dedication of the West Virginia State Capitol," WVSA. He also referred to education: "We are consciously proud of our schools, our colleges and our university.... The children in our schools today are the future citizens of the state and nation."

28 Governor Conley's address is found in the West Virginia State Archives, *State Papers and Public Addresses of Governor William Conley*, 210–13.

29 We have been unable to locate souvenirs such as cups, pitchers, plates, or pins that are sometimes sold at such celebratory events. Perhaps this seeming lack is explained by the weak economy at the time of the Capitol's dedication.

"Our Capitol," a lengthy laudatory poem by T. J. Honaker, may have been available at the dedication. It begins with references to Greece and Rome ("The lovely Grecian temples on Acropolis / have been an inspiration to the world of Art.... We recall the grandeur that was ancient Rome") and glorifies how West Virginia's Capitol was inspired by antiquity. (The poem, printed on a sheet that includes a photograph of the Capitol, seems also to have been read at a dinner in Morgantown on December 5, 1934. See State Capitol Miscellaneous Poems and Tributes, WVSA.)

30 Below this explanation is the following: "The advertisers who have made this booklet, and help to underprivileged children, possible have done so voluntarily and individually through a splendid spirit of cooperation."

31 "My dear Mr. Gilbert, It gives me great pleasure personally as well as officially to inform you that the Board of Trustees at the meeting today decided unanimously to invite you to attend the Commencement Exercises of the University on Tuesday, June 21st, and at that time to receive the honorary degree of Doctor of Letters. I hope that your engagements will make it possible for you to be present on this occasion." Gilbert received the invitation, dated January 14, 1932, the next day. His acceptance, penned on January 19, expressed his appreciation: "I am highly honored by this invitation and I accept it with most cordial appreciation of all that it means. I cannot tell you how gratified I am at this kind action of the Board and at your own cordial expressions concerning it."

32 That ceremony also was marked by a festive celebration held at the Capitol and in words reminiscent of those spoken and printed at the original dedication. At the top of the program is Governor Jay Rockefeller's message to his "Fellow West Virginians": "Today is a day to reaffirm our faith in the future of our state as we reflect upon its past. As West Virginians we share in the heritage of this great state and the principles upon which it was founded.... Exactly fifty years ago today, some 15,000 West Virginians gathered ... to celebrate the dedication of a brand new State Capitol building, sitting majestically on the Kanawha River. After fifty years of wear and tear the Capitol still

catches the eyes of those who pass by." He continued with reference to the architect: "We were given a message in 1932 from architect Cass Gilbert which serves today as an important charge: 'The State Capitol ... should be an example of how a building can be properly developed and preserved, for it will set an example to other states. It inspires confidence in the state on the part of both its own people and of all who visit it.'"

According to the printed program, many activities were available for enjoyment before and after the ceremony, a number of them reconstructing life at the time of the dedication: movies and fashions of the 1930s (including "1932 bathing beauties"), and a "pre-war auto show" as well as concerts, games, parachute jumps, and demonstrations of glass blowing, marble shooting, and horseshoe pitching.

A handsome publication, *The West Virginia Capitol: A Commemorative History*, elucidated many aspects of the complex and contributed to the celebration (published by the Legislature of West Virginia; first printing June 20, 1982; subsequent printings 1990, 1995, 2006).

33 For the earlier tabulation, made in January 1932, see page 178. The new totals are $13,012.24 for travel expenses, $34,914.27 for superintendents' salaries, and $3,402.15 for the steel inspections for all three buildings; the grand total was $51,328.66. As noted previously, the inclusion of the superintendents' salaries on this list is an error because Gilbert's contract included the concession that he would pay these salaries.

To these sums, Gilbert added others in pencil, some of which are difficult to read:

| | |
|---|---|
| Interest on delayed overdue payments should be added in, say | 10,000 |
| (a) I should not be deprived of architect's fees on the amount saved | 28,200 |
| (b) I should receive fee on the amount saved to the same extent as though it was a "change order" "extra" | 28,200 |

or alternative should receive (a) plus actual cost of changes in plans to reduce cost—amt to be determined

see also [illegible] marked x–x page 5. Contract compensation for changes and delays

A charge for services in preliminary sketches for various sites & report thereon (see pages 1 & 3 [of contract]) "site or sites"

A charge for per diem in time occupied in traveling and personal attendance at Charleston of say $100 to $200 per day

A charge should be made for study of office floor space, assignments, which was to have [illegible].

34 Gilbert to Conley, November 26, 1932, WVSA.

35 Letter from Gilbert to Conley in response to Conley's telegram: "Please advise how and to what extent West Virginia State Capitol has been advertised by you and the several contractors." N-YHS letterbook, December 30, 1932. The periodicals in which the Capitol had been advertised included *Architectural Record, Architectural Forum, Copper & Brass, Successful Construction Methods, Stone, Manufacturers' Record,* and *Heating & Ventilating* (N-YHS, letterbook, 1933).

36 N-YHS, box 524, folder 3.

The "Total Maximum Authorized" is listed as follows:

*Authorized to Be Expended*

| | |
|---|---|
| General revenue appropriations by 1921 Legislature | $2,250,000.00 |
| General revenue appropriations by 1923 Legislature | 500,000.00 |
| General revenue appropriations by 1925 Legislature | 968,000.00 |
| General revenue appropriations by 1927 Legislature | 240,000.00 |
| General revenue appropriations by 1929 Legislature | 13,809.60 |
| Total General Revenue | $3,971,809.60 |
| Appropriated by 1923 Legislature, proceeds of sale of Capitol Annex property | $500,000.00 |
| Interest on same | 1,256.59 |
| Appropriated by 1925 Legislature, proceeds of sale of Temporary Capitol and Governor's Mansion | 350,000.00 |
| Interest on same and $250.00 for old Governor's Mansion | 2,223.84 |
| Total, Including Special Collections | $4,825,290.03 |
| In addition to above the 1929 Legislature authorized an annual direct levy of not to exceed five cents for period of not to exceed five years to be used for the main unit or building, aggregate cost of which is not to exceed | $5,000,000.00 |
| Total Maximum Authorized | $9,825,290.03 |

37 Conley to Gilbert, January 24, 1933, N-YHS, box 516, folder 1. In December 1933, Governor Kump informed Cass Gilbert that "previous legislation had passed taxation laws that were judged by the courts as illegal, and consequently no taxes had been collected for about two or three years." Transcript of meeting of Gilbert and Rockart with Kump, dictated December 28, 1933, N-YHS, box 521, folder 1.

38 Gilbert to Conley, February 3, 1933, WVSA.

39 Transcript of meeting of Gilbert and Rockart with Governor Kump, dictated by Rockart on December 28, 1933, N-YHS, box 521, folder 1. Gilbert had been in Washington attending meetings of the Executive Committee of the Carnegie Institution, and Rockart joined him there. Distler's letter to Gilbert, dated December 14, 1933, is at N-YHS, box 516, folder 1. The letter contains a reference to a modest cost-saving measure, indicating that even a vice president of the Fuller Company understood the need to economize during the Great Depression: "May I call your attention to the fact that Christmas rates are now in effect, and for a fare-and-a-ninth you can get a return trip from Washington to Charleston for $15.45; and at the same time, you can buy the Pullman going and coming for $6.75, against the usual fare $9.00."

40 That Bonner Hill would send such a telegram is curious, as by December he had "relinquished his desk," suggesting that he was no longer serving as secretary to the Capitol Commission.

41 This led to another problem, as recorded in the transcript:

> Gov. Kump stated that they had made a search for the drawings and could not find them and had been informed that Mr. Martens had entered Mr. Hill's office after Mr. Hill had relinquished it and had taken some of the drawings away with him. He said that Mr. Martens was called in and admitted he had done so, apparently with the idea of preparing drawings for terraces and landscaping. The Governor demanded the return of the drawings immediately. Mr. Martens stated that he would return them in two or three days. He was threatened with arrest and produced the drawings, but none of them were the drawings of the terraces and landscaping.
>
> NOTE: In a subsequent conference with Mr. Payne in the evening at the Kanawha Hotel, we learned that the drawings

referred to in our letter to Gov. Conley on June 17, 1932, were found in a flat package in the governor's vault.

Later in the transcript, Gilbert told the governor that terraces and landscaping "could not be undertaken by incapable architects, and certainly not by Mr. Martens."

42 During their visit, Gilbert and Rockart also requested to meet the new custodian, who is identified in the transcript as "Major Davis." Rockart reported: "It was evident from [Major Davis's] remarks that he had no experience in building or the maintenance of buildings." Gilbert and Rockart assured him of their assistance in the future if he had questions. This meeting is another demonstration of Gilbert's concern with the buildings he had designed and confirms his promise that he took "almost the same interest that a parent would in his children" (Gilbert to Walter E. Clark, then editor of the *Charleston Daily Mail*, April 8, 1932, N-YHS letterbook, 1932).

43 Both letters: N-YHS, box 516, folder 1.

## Chapter Eight
## SYMBOLS OF DEMOCRACY: "THE BEST EVIDENCES OF THE … CULTURE AND CIVILIZATION OF A STATE"

1 The quotation in the chapter title is from a letter Cass Gilbert wrote to Walter E. Clark, editor of the *Charleston Daily Mail*, April 8, 1932, WVSA.

2 The same is true of the swastika, which had been used by Native American and ancient Greek cultures before it became a Nazi symbol. It is interesting that while fasces have been discredited because of Fascism, eagles—symbolic of the United States since the late eighteenth century—have not, although they were connected with Fascism as well and often represented in Nazi symbolism.

3 But note Gilbert's comment: "I think the State of West Virginia has followed a wise middle course in building a group of monumental buildings of adequate character but without extravagance or lavish expenditure" (Gilbert to Clark, April 8, 1932, WVSA). More colors and types of marbles were used in his Minnesota State Capitol. At West Virginia, restraint in the choices of marble may be an indication of the change in Gilbert's preferences as well as of the financial limitations of this project.

4 Stutler, "West Virginia's Magnificent State Capitol," 403.

5 Gilbert to Walter E. Clark, documented in Damron, *West Virginia Capitol*, 25–26.

6 Cass Gilbert's description in the "Dedication of West Virginia Capitol" program, June 20, 1932.

7 Gilbert to Governor Conley, November 11, 1931, N-YHS, box 514, folder 2. See Gilbert's further comments in the letter that the dome "would be, in that climate, susceptible to expansion and contraction and the joints would have to be constantly repaired." There are details about cost, for instance: "In other words, the bell of the dome of this dimension in marble might easily have cost $500,000, whereas the comparatively modest expense for covering it with newly developed material of lead coated with copper and using gilding, has reduced the cost to a minimum."

8 For detailed information on the various stages of the appearance and condition of the dome, see "A Capitol Idea: West Virginia's Capitol Dome $4.5 Million Restoration," *West Virginia Construction News*, January/February 2006, 6–14.

9 Cass Gilbert to William G. Conley, November 11, 1931, N-YHS, box 514, folder 2. Another letter reinforces this: replying to a request from Miss Lucille Scott, the valedictorian of Thomas Jefferson Junior High School in Charleston about to speak at her graduation, on May 16, 1930, Gilbert wrote:

> I hope you will mention the symmetrical plan of the Capitol and the fact that the design is of serious and classical character, in harmony with the dignity of a great state. In the early days of the Republic under the influence of Washington and Jefferson the public buildings were given great distinction and beauty by following classic precedent, and it is fortunate that in our time there is a tendency to return to these noble examples as models of good taste. (N-YHS, box 513, folder 5)

10 Gilbert to Walter E. Clark, documented in Damron, *West Virginia Capitol*, 23–24. See also Gilbert to Governor Conley, November 11, 1931 (N-YHS, box 514 folder 2).

11 Stutler, "West Virginia's Magnificent State Capitol," 401.

12 See Stutler, "West Virginia's Magnificent State Capitol," 402, regarding the comparison of dimensions and cost with that of the National Capitol. Gilbert's drum is 75 feet in diameter, while that of the National Capitol is 88 feet.

13 Mansart, King Louis XIV's architect, designed the building in 1680; it was completed in 1709. For a study of the dome with excellent photographs and drawings, see Poche, *Le Dôme des Invalides*. Similar panels are also found at the Palace of Versailles, where the motif is used to decorate pilasters in the Hall of Mirrors and the flanking Rooms of War and of Peace, all of which were designed by Mansart. The same architect employed military motifs for the coffers of the interior of the dome above the grand staircase at the Château de Blois; see Babelon and Mignot, eds., *François Mansart*, 71. The motif is repeated in the late eighteenth-century Library of Louis XVI at Versailles, designed by Ange-Jacques Gabriel.

14 A similar standard, carried on a staff, can be seen on the Arch of Titus in Rome in the relief depicting the spoils from the Temple of Solomon in Jerusalem being brought to Rome. The standard on the dome is supported in the ancient manner, on a pole with a crossbar, over which are draped swags of cloth. For an ancient representation of a staff with such a crossbar, see the reliefs on the Column of Trajan in Rome. The motif of the crossbar supporting a cloth banner is repeated in Mantegna's paintings of the Triumph of Caesar (Hampton Court Palace) and their engraved copies.

15 A newspaper article from 1931 states that the letters were originally included: "On the gilded panels of the dome we see an emblem, 'S.P.Q.R.'" ("State's Capitol, Greek In Style, Combines Building And Setting," *Charleston Gazette*, Sunday, November 8, 1931). In the "Official Souvenir Program and Directory" for the dedication there is another reference to presence of the Latin abbreviation with an unusual translation: "High on the crest of the great bell of the dome, where only an eagle in its flight might see, is a legend inscribed, dedicatory to that for which the beautiful building was brought into being. This legend is in the Latin letters, 'S.P.Q.R.,' and breathes the spell of Caesar, father of a common government by the people, over this State's governmental temple. The legend means, 'The Senate, The People, The Quirinal, and Rome.'" Despite these references, it is difficult to believe that the letters were placed on the dome and then replaced by the elaborate raised design we see today. There seems to be no documentation that would explain such a change.

16 A peltoid shield with a female apotropaic head is found in the reliefs on Palladio's Loggia del Capitaniato, see Venditti, *Loggia del Capitaniato*, plates 29, 31. Similar shields are found in Gilbert's Minnesota Capitol as part of the decorative motif on the wainscoting in the governor's reception room. They appear in conjunction with helmets and Roman standards. Another example of this shield in Gilbert's work is in the spandrel of the entrance to the United States Custom House; the other spandrel there has a standard similar to the one seen above the window on the West Virginia dome.

17 These military motifs are related to mottoes on the structure that refer to the Battle of Lepanto. For detailed photographs and drawings of Palladio's use of military trophies on the Loggia, see Venditti, *Loggia del Capitaniato.* Palladio also used this motif to flank windows on the second floor of the Palazzo Barbarno da Porto in Vicenza; see Palladio, *Four Books of Architecture*, book 2, plate 16.

18 Gilbert used this motif in the Minnesota Capitol for the pilasters of the wainscoting of the governor's reception room. At the United States Capitol, the motif is found on the doorframe of the rotunda door by Randolph Rogers, cast in Munich in 1860 (for an illustration see Reed, *United States Capitol*, 70); in this version wreaths, helmets, trumpets, axes, and quivers are shown hung from a continuous vertical chain. Another example can be seen at the National Capitol, where cascades of military implements decorate the painted wall panels originally designed for the Military Affairs Committee; see *Art in the United States Capitol*, S-128: 322.

Another example of the motif is found at Whitehall, the Palm Beach mansion of Henry Flagler designed by Carrère & Hastings and completed in 1902; here similar designs are used for the panels that flank the doors in the hallway near the ballroom; among the military motifs is the peltoid shield also used in Charleston.

19 Kabler, "Mystery of the Dome," *Charleston Gazette*.

20 In a letter to Governor Conley, Gilbert stated: "I have given very careful thought to the subject and have selected, subject to your approval, the following two inscriptions.... I think we would all agree that the great factors of good government are wisdom, patriotism and diligence, and the most effective of these would be wisdom" (July 1, 1931, WVSA).

21 Inside the circle of Corinthian columns, grilles, reminiscent of those used in Roman baths, complete the decoration. Like that of the United States Capitol, Gilbert's lantern is of tholos style with a walkway below and a balustrade. The base of the lantern is similar to that of Les Invalides.

22 The theme of the west pediment of Gilbert's United States Supreme Court is "Equal Justice under the Law." Among the sculpted portraits are those of Gilbert and Robert Aitken, the sculptor. The subjects of the three pediments on the National Capitol are (1) allegorical figures of America, Justice, and Hope, (2) "The Progress of Civilization," with an allegorical figure representing America in the center, and (3) "The Apotheosis of Democracy," the central figures of which are Peace protecting Genius.

23 An examination of the many garlands on the Capitol reveals both subtle and obvious differences among them: while fruited garlands appear on the lions' head vases below the dome, for example, fasces figure prominently in those around the dome's base (see fig. 75).

24 "The Capitol Guide Courtesy of the West Virginia Senate" states that the "35 Steps Leading to Capitol [on the north side] Signify 35th State of the Union." As visitors to the Capitol we were told that it had been suggested that the forty-eight steps on the south side might refer to the number of states in the Union when the complex was completed. While these numbers are accurate and the symbolism is possible, we have no way of verifying if this was intentional.

25 The ceiling of this porte-cochère is made of Guastavino tile. For the history of this tile, see Ochsendorf, *Guastavino Vaulting*.

26 While the ancient sources for Gilbert's boars and bulls also include representations of rams, the Doric vestibule reliefs do not. Biennial reports of the West Virginia Department of Agriculture for 1925–26 and 1927–28 reveal that cattle, pigs, and sheep were all important; Gilbert's omission of sheep, therefore, seems not to be based on any idea of their irrelevancy for the state. Perhaps he was simply following his aesthetic sensibilities; using only two species allows for easier symmetry, and boars and bulls are more similar anatomically and in the texture of their coats. We thank Carol and Wayne Eich for their research and suggestions on this topic.

27 These rituals are recorded in Cato the Elder's *De Rustica* (*On Agriculture*).

28 Two articles in the *American Journal of Archaeology* (in 1901, "The 'Trajan Reliefs' in the Forum," and 1910, "The So-Called Balustrades of Trajan") announced and interpreted the discovery. Cass Gilbert's reliefs may have been based on the illustrations in Hector d'Espouy's 1905 book, *Fragments d'architecture antique d'après les relevés et restaurations des ancient pensionnaires de l'Académie de France à Rome*; d'Espouy was professor of ornamental design at the École des Beaux-Arts. Other representations of the *suovetaurilia* can be found at the Louvre (a relief from the Temple of Neptune, on an ancient Roman cup representing Tiberius's Nuncupatio Votorum at the Capitolium (current location unknown), and on the Triumphal Column of Trajan.

29 Gilbert's memo of May 1932 is titled "West Virginia State Capitol Symbolism of Carved Heads," WVSA. For illustrations of all the heads, see Damron, *West Virginia Capitol*, 28–29.

30 Gilbert incorporated a head/keystone over the main entrance of his United States Customs House in New York City (1899–1907), for instance. There are also human and animal heads in the cornice decoration of the Broadway-Chambers Building. A rare Etruscan example of this motif is seen at the Porta all'Arco in Volterra, and Roman examples are found at the Temple of Hadrian in Ephesus and at an arch in the city wall of ancient Saepinum, near Naples. Palladio incorporated this motif in various buildings published in the *Four Books of Architecture*. See his Basilica, Loggia del Capitaniato, Palazzo da Porta Festa, the Palazzo Iseppo Porto, the Palazzo Thiene-Bonini Longare, and the Villa Barbaro (book 2, plates 5, 6, 10, 12, 16, and book 3, plate 20). The motif had been used earlier by Giulio Romano at the Palazzo del Te, Jacopo Sansovino at the Loggetta in Piazza San Marco, Michele Sanmicheli at Palazzo Bevilacqua in Verona, and Giovanni Maria Falconetto at the Porta Savonarola and the Porta San Giovanni in Padua. It was also used by Antonio da Ponte for the Rialto Bridge in Venice. Later, frontal, male, helmeted heads were incorporated in the memorial arch at Bozen-Bolzano, Italy, a Fascist monument dated 1928. An American example is the bronze mask that decorated the keystone over the north entrance of the House chamber of the National Capitol from 1857 to 1950. See *Art in the United States Capitol*, SB-14, 370. Also, thirty-three "ethnological heads" decorate the keystones of the first floor windows of the Library of Congress in Washington (completed 1897).

31 Stutler, "West Virginia's Magnificent State Capitol," 403.

32 The West Virginia chandelier is similar to that of Gilbert's earlier Minnesota State House. West Virginia's, however, is larger (eight rather than six feet in diameter) with larger crystals as well. The example in St. Paul is less well proportioned to the vast spaces defined by the dome and rotunda.

33 Drawings reveal that the chain was designed by the architect.

34 We thank the Gilbert family, particularly Jeannette Gilbert Allyson, for use of photographs—including this one—from c. 1950, recently discovered and given to the WVSA. There are currently plans to restore eagles to the lamps.

35 See Goodsell, *American Statehouse*, 129–35. It was not uncommon at that time for the Senate and House to be at the peak of the hierarchy; this order eventually began to change, evidenced in placing the legislative chambers and governor on the same floor. In Gilbert's Minnesota State House, the Senate chamber is opposite that of the Supreme Court, with the larger House chamber on the same floor between them, on the north side of the rotunda. The governor's office is located beneath the Senate chamber. The West Virginia solution might be considered

more successful since placing the chambers directly opposite one another makes the Senate and House of equal importance.

36 It has been stated that there are fifty-five lamps, one for each of the state's counties. See "*The Capitol Guide*, courtesy of the West Virginia Senate": "Lining the long hallway which separates the two chambers are smaller columns of black Georgian marble, one for each of WV 55 counties, each crowned with an Italian alabaster urn." A letter from W. G. Distler, vice president of the George A. Fuller Company to Cass Gilbert, dated October 9, 1931 (N-YHS, box 541, folder 9), refers to forty-eight "Marble and Alabaster Standards coming from Italy," the delivery of which was to be delayed. There are forty lamps in the foyers, four pink Georgian lamps in the House chamber and four Brown Italian marble ones in the Senate.

37 When the Capitol was constructed, only the state flower had been designated; the state tree had yet to be named. The rhododendron was adopted as the flower in 1903; the tree, the sugar maple, not until 1949. It is possible that the flowers depicted above the metopes in the foyers represent rhododendrons. The use of botanical details in state capitols has its precedent in Benjamin Henry Latrobe's use of corn and tobacco as decorative motifs at the National Capitol. At Gilbert's Minnesota State Capitol, ladyslippers decorate some of the Corinthian-style capitals and gophers are hidden in the design of the bronze railings.

38 West Virginia's Capitol is one of only twelve in which the Supreme Court chamber is housed in the Capitol building. In other states the courts are in separate buildings, although in the Minnesota Capitol, the elegant chamber originally designed for the Supreme Court by Gilbert in the Main Building is now used only during the first week the court is in session. The United States Supreme Court was located in the National Capitol until it moved in 1935 to its purpose-built structure designed by Cass Gilbert. See Goodsell, *American Statehouse*, 144.

39 Gilbert seems to have selected maxims for specific locations rather than repeating those he had used elsewhere. Neither of these quotations is found at his Minnesota Capitol, in which several dozen are located throughout the interior; see Gauthier, *Minnesota Capitol*, 49–51.

40 It is possible that the source for these chambers with their surrounding freestanding columns was Benjamin Latrobe's original House of Representatives chamber at the National Capitol. Gilbert's other state Supreme Court chamber, in Minnesota, has columns on only one side.

41 There are no inscriptions in the courtroom of Gilbert's United States Supreme Court Building in Washington; it is reported that an inscription was planned, but that "Cass Gilbert Jr. decided that it would be superfluous since 'the Court speaks for itself.'" See Maroon, *Supreme Court of the United States*, 134.

42 Transcript, "A Moving Monument," 13.

43 A detailed description of the governor's office is found in "Handsome Suite For Use of Governor" on page 8 of the *Charleston Daily Mail*'s special section on the Capitol's dedication, June 20, 1932.

44 Gilbert to Walter E. Clark, documented in Damron, *West Virginia Capitol*, 26.

45 Gilbert to Walter E. Clark, documented in Damron, *West Virginia Capitol*, 26. Also of note is the "broad fireplace ... in which huge logs may be burned to provide a comforting effect, if not actual comfort" ("Handsome Suite For Use of Governor," *Charleston Daily Mail*, June 19, 1932, 8).

46 Gilbert to Governor Conley, February 15, 1932, WVSA. This letter was written in response to a letter from Conley that expressed concern about his own portrait: "Before engaging the services of anyone I would like to know approximately what it would cost for a painting about the size of those now hanging in the Governor's office. I would want a first class job or none at all. As you know the funds are very limited for such matters, no special appropriation being made, but paid out of the Governor's civil contingent Fund, which fund is always burdened. I want you to know that I greatly appreciate the interest you and your son take in the matter and I hope that together we may be able to get a good portrait of myself although the subject is a very poor one to spread on canvas." (Conley to Gilbert, February 4, 1931, N-YHS, box 514, folder 1).

47 See Cole and Reed, *Library of Congress*, 152 and 171, for the paintings on a flat red background representing eight virtues made by George Willoughby Maynard at the Library of Congress. In the National Capitol, "floating female figures" by Brumidi are located in what is now the Senate Committee on Appropriations Room. Reed, *United States Capitol*, 146–49.

48 Cass Gilbert, "Supervision for Capitol Needed To Preserve Its Beauty," (with prefatory remarks introducing the architect), *Charleston Daily Mail*, June 19, 1932. For scholarship on murals, see the work of Bailey van Hook, especially *The Virgin and the Dynamo*.

49 Stutler, "West Virginia's Magnificent State Capitol," 426.

50 "Our New Capitol," the *Charleston Daily Mail*, Monday November 30, 1931, 6.

51 "An Address by Cass Gilbert on the Presentation of the President's Medal of the National Academy of Design to Edwin Howland Blashfield, New York, January 4, 1934," as found in Julia Finch Gilbert, *Cass Gilbert*, 115. In an earlier letter, to Arkansas governor George Donaghey, written on October 12, 1914, Gilbert stated: "In our own time, the arts of mural decoration and sculpture have been employed to record the history of our country and to express the importance of its commerce, its industries, and to put in visible form its aspirations for the finer things of life." Further, "John Sargent and ... Edwin H. Blashfield in the State Capitols of Minnesota, Iowa, and Wisconsin ... have demonstrated what Americans of the present time can do." And "For a State to adorn its Capitol with mural paintings of the first rank is to give its people lasting pleasure, to educate the young as nothing else will and to register itself as among those States where civilization is regarded as worthwhile." Donaghey, *Building a State Capitol*, 368–79.

52 Gilbert to Keatley, January 6, 1922, N-YHS, box 504 folder 4.

53 Gilbert's presentation of the president's medal to Blashfield, as found in Julia Finch Gilbert, *Cass Gilbert*, 116.

54 Gilbert to Walter Clark, April 8, 1932. He continued: "We have no right to experiment with public money ... nor to speculate with such funds on the theory that we may discover a genius.... The most competent artists do not solicit business nor do they enter into competitions and they do not indulge in political intrigue.... The architect who develops the design is best qualified to select the artists and experts who would carry it out sympathetically."

55 William De Leftwich Dodge to Gilbert, May 26, 1930, N-YHS, box 511, folder 4.

56 Mrs. Homer Wilson to Gilbert, June 4, 1930, N-YHS, box 513, folder 7.

57 Capitol Building Commission file, May–November 1930, WVSA.

58 From the office of Cram and Ferguson, Boston, September 9, 1931, to Mr. Rockart in Cass Gilbert's office, N-YHS, box 513, folder 7.

59 N-YHS, box 515, folder 8. Another letter praised A. J. Bogdanove: "My dear Mr. Gilbert: I am taking the liberty of addressing you on behalf of a young artist, Mr. A. J. Bogdanove ... in whom I have taken an interest, and who, in reality is a genius. He is very desirous of doing the work on the State Capitol ... and I would appreciate it if you would grant him an interview" (N-YHS, 503–8 #147, November 3, 1921). Gilbert responded to Professor William H. Goodyear regarding another artist: "I note what you say about Mr. Conrow's ambition to paint a picture or decoration for the West Virginia State Capitol. It is too soon to take that subject up. We are a long way from it and the

money available for the Capitol building may not be sufficient to permit of any extensive decoration. The subject therefore must necessarily be deferred." A rather accusatory letter from Jules Askin to Governor Conley states clearly what he maintains to be crucial for the Capitol: "The subject of Mural decoration is what I would like to bring to your attention.... From my preliminary conversations I was led to believe that your building commission did not know a great deal about the use of Mural decorations and so far had made no provision to use them in your new buildings. To overlook such a vital and important item would be nothing short of a serious blunder. Any building which proposes to be monumental in the least sense should certainly take into consideration a series of Murals done in the traditional manner of the Fine Arts, on canvas, mounted on the walls, depicting a choice and memorable slice of history. Your state has certainly made its contribution of American history and it is only proper that the memory of such events be perpetuated in paintings mounted in dignified wall-spaces" (April 29, 1931, WVSA).

60 Not everyone was happy with the building's progress given this economic condition. Note from the *Wheeling Register*, Wheeling, West Virginia, Sunday, November 16, 1930:

> MORE GOP EXTRAVAGANCE.
>
> For unmitigated, concentrated nerve, brass and downright disregard for a harassed people—we point [*sic*] the State Capitol Building Commission overwhelmingly Republicans.
>
> On Friday the Commission met and decided to add $300,000 MORE TO THE COST OF THE OUTRAGEOUSLY COSTLY CAPITOL THAT MORE DECORATIVE MARBLE MIGHT BE SECURED FOR THE LEGISLATIVE HALLS, CORRIDORS AND FLOORS [capitalization in the original].
>
> And this in the face of the worst political trimming the Republicans have received in West Virginia since 1910!
>
> What is to be done? What can be done with such wastrels? The Capitol Commission knows the taxpayers of the State are suffering as they have never suffered before, that they cannot pay their taxes and are forfeiting their homes and farms because of hard times—and yet, capitol costs are increased $300,000.
>
> Such lack of consideration actually makes the blood boil!

61 For a discussion of the 2010 proposal to add murals to the Capitol, see Wallace, *House of State*, 45–46.

62 A brief look at two state capitols that include murals and pedimental sculpture illustrates how the Charleston complex might have appeared. Gilbert's Minnesota Capitol, completed sixteen years before he received the West Virginia commission, does not have a Classical pediment; instead he placed a monumental quadriga at the dome's base, an allegory titled *Progress of the State*. The sculptor was the well-known Daniel Chester French. See Thompson, *Minnesota's State Capitol*, 56. See Thrane and Patterson, *State Houses*, for further information on the sculpted and painted decor of the Minnesota Capitol. The extensive paintings inside include allegorical murals, such as *The Moral and Divine Law*, and those representing history, *The Discoverers and Civilizers Led to the Source of the Mississippi*, by Edwin Blashfield, for example. The latter, incidentally, includes portraits of Gilbert and the chair of the Capitol Commission, each dressed in contemporary garb. West Virginia's rich history could certainly have provided equally appropriate subject matter.

Missouri's Capitol, completed in 1917 by Tracy & Swartwout, boasts pedimental sculpture of allegorical figures: Lady Missouri is surrounded by Learning, Agriculture, and the Spirit of Progress, among others. The best known paintings inside are murals by Thomas Hart Benton, exemplified by *A Social History of the State of Missouri*. Benton, of course, is an artist whose style and interpretations would not have appealed to Gilbert. See Thrane and Patterson, *State Houses*, 11–16, for the sculpted and painted decoration of this capitol.

Several sculptures in the round were added to the interior and the grounds after 1932. The four niches around the rotunda on the main floor were intended for sculpture; in 1998, the first of these was filled with a larger-than-life-size figure of Senator Robert C. Byrd. The sculptor was Bill Hopen, assisted by Kathy Brunt. The sculpture was cast in West Virginia at the foundry of George Houston. Evidently Gilbert had ideas about what to display: "Niches in the first floor rotunda of the main unit of the capitol building would be used in which to display the state's rarest historical objects if recommendations of [the architect] are followed.... [He] suggested that the niches be covered with glass and used as cases for the display of state flags and other things of historical interest" (*Charleston Daily Mail*, June 19, 1932).

In the rotunda on the floor below is a bust of Anna Jarvis, West Virginia native who founded Mother's Day, sculpted by Lorna Vincent-Venter and dedicated in 2001. Busts of General Thomas "Stonewall" Jackson and Congressman Cleve Bailey are also located on this level. Empty niches and documents contemporary with the Capitol's completion confirm that there were to be additional sculptures.

63 Cass Gilbert, "The Greatest Element," *American Architect*, 144.

64 For descriptions of this and other sculptures on the grounds, see Cohen and Andre, *Capitols of West Virginia*, 102–4 and Wallace, *House of State*, 87–116. The sculpture's unveiling was reported in the *New York Times* on September 27, 1910, and noted in the June 19, 1932, *Charleston Daily Mail* as being "by one of the world's most famous sculptors ... a cadet under Jackson." Moses Jacob Ezekiel (1844–1917), who worked in Rome, had served in the Confederate army. Although decorated by King Umberto I and knighted by King Victor Emmanuel III, he was never knighted by a British monarch and thus should not be called "Sir Moses Ezekiel," as he is in several publications. A copy of *Stonewall Jackson* can be found at Virginia Military Institute in Lexington, Virginia.

65 Henry Kirke Bush-Brown (1857–1935), educated at the National Academy of Design in New York City, is well known for his war memorials at the Gettysburg National Military Park. It is said that it took the sculptor two years to find the right mountaineer to serve as the model for his figure. See Cohen and Andre, *Capitols of West Virginia*, 103.

66 April 22, 1922, *CCC*, 754 and May 2, 1922, *CCC*, 754–55.

67 The Friedley-Voshardt Company cast the figure.

68 See Cohen and Andre, *Capitols of West Virginia*, 103, for relevant information as well as the *Charleston Daily Mail*, June 19, 1932. Gilbert's letter to Walter E. Clark of April 8, 1932, clarifies his determination for the architect to be in charge of choice of sculpture: "without this [planning by the architect] there will be intrusions of incidental sculpture in questionable taste."

69 For further discussion of these sculptures and others that were added to the grounds and the interior after 1932, see Wallace, *House of State*, 87–116.

## Chapter Nine
## CASS GILBERT'S WEST VIRGINIA CAPITOL IN CONTEXT

1 Julia added: "A letter dated April 10th 1929, records very simply this momentous fulfillment of his anticipation: 'this is just to record that the agreement for my services as architect of the S C Building was signed about 10:30 this morning in the conference room of the S C in the National Capitol building by Chief Justice Taft, Justice Van Devanter, Senator Keyes and Mr. David Lynn and myself.'" She also referred to the many articles written about her husband, for instance one from the *Herald Tribune* of New York, written by the critic Royal Cortissoz:

"but a groundswell of his career, so to say, had its origin in classical ideas, and how faithful to them he was is shown by the great building which is still in the process of erection. The one for the Supreme Court in Washington. In its majestic dignity it sums up his characteristics as an architect. They were the characteristics of a designer who drove at refinement, simplicity, just proportion, in short the elements of the grand style" (Julia Finch Gilbert, *Cass Gilbert*, 11, 13).

2 Kirkham, "Master of Style," *Pencil Points*, 547.

3 Hitchcock and Seale, *Temples of Democracy*, 217.

4 F. E. Bennett, "Mr. Cass Gilbert," *Architects' Journal* 65 (1927), 791–97.

5 The commissioner was Fred M. Staunton, who conveyed these opinions to John Rockart when he stopped by Gilbert's New York office on September 18, 1922. Rockart replied that Gilbert wanted the Capitol to be "as simple as possible but in good proportion and to retain the impressiveness from the latter" (transcription by Rockart, N-YHS, box 9, folder 18).

6 It is significant that Vitrolite was produced in Parkersburg, West Virginia, since the promotion of local materials was a consideration throughout the planning and construction phases. Opaque structural glass treatments were not new in the 1920s; Cass Gilbert himself had used such treatment in the Woolworth Building's bathrooms. Vitrolite, however, became well known in the 1920s and has since been closely connected with Art Deco decor.

Compressed cork flooring was not widely used at the time; Frank Lloyd Wright used this floor treatment in Fallingwater, his iconic Pennsylvania retreat for the Kaufmann family. The cork floor in the Supreme Court chamber was for many years covered with dark red carpeting, but in 2011 a new black and beige cork floor returned the Supreme Court conference room to its original appearance, and in 2012 the cork floor in the Supreme Court chamber was restored. In addition, a recently developed material, copper-coated lead, was used in the Capitol's dome.

7 Italian Fascist architecture, which in many cases recalled the vocabulary and magnificence of its ancient Roman predecessors in greatly simplified form, is another indication of the modernist direction European architecture was taking. Architects a generation younger than Cass Gilbert, including Marcello Piacentini, Enrico Del Debbio, and Vittorio Ballio Morpurgo, changed the face of Rome while not abandoning its Classical heritage.

8 On the Nebraska State Capitol, see Luebke, ed., *Harmony of the Arts*, for discussion and illustration. The quotation is from Hitchcock and Seale, *Temples of Democracy*, 272. The European models are Finnish; see Lars Sonck's Kallio Church Tower (1908–12) and Eliel Saarinen's Railroad Station (opened in 1919), both in Helsinki. Hitchcock and Seale, 272–73. On the role of the tower see Hitchcock and Seale, 273–75. The tower was originally intended to be aesthetic rather than functional, but Goodhue eventually incorporated library stacks into its interior space, and later offices were added (279). See Greenberg for discussion of interior space defined by a dome. Lee Lawrie was responsible for most of the sculpture in the Nebraska Capitol.

9 As in West Virginia, funding proved to be a problem; while we see extensive decoration today, Nebraska's murals were not completed at the time of the Capitol's dedication. Only in 1949 did the Legislature appropriate funding for their continuation, and some were not completed until the 1960s.

10 See Remele, ed., *North Dakota State Capitol*, 7, 51.

11 See Remele, ed., *North Dakota State Capitol*, 48, for illustrations of the intended finish on the tower and the finished one.

12 Lorimer Rich, in "Capitols and Legislative Buildings," *Forms and Functions of Twentieth-Century Architecture*, illustrates his discussion of space with the four buildings referred to here. It is interesting that he chooses West Virginia's Capitol: "The monumentality and impressiveness of a capitol depend largely upon the use of simple and sound shapes, good proportions, and a sense of spaciousness in the building and its surroundings" (772–73).

13 Yet during the same period there was also great interest in reviving the past, as witnessed in John D. Rockefeller Jr.'s restoration of colonial Williamsburg in 1928. See also the Colonial Capitol of Delaware (1931–33), by W. William Martin. Rather than choosing a more modern plan, the Commission decided that the new buildings would re-create Colonial architecture. Another interesting example is Tennessee's dedication to the preservation of its Parthenon. The original, temporary building was created for the Tennessee Centennial Exposition of 1897. In 1920 the city decided to reconstruct it as a permanent representation of the Athenian fifth-century BCE temple. The reconstructed Parthenon was opened to the public in May 20, 1931.

14 Gilbert to William E. Harmon, writing as Jedediah Tingle of Brooklyn, April 2, 1923, NYHS, box 504, folder 4.

# GLOSSARY OF RELEVANT ARCHITECTURAL TERMS

This glossary is not intended to be universal. Its definitions are related specifically to the West Virginia Capitol complex (figs. 97–99). Words within definitions in CAPITAL LETTERS are defined elsewhere in the glossary.

ACROTERION (ACROTERIA): an ornamental or figural decoration placed at the apex and/or end of a PEDIMENT (figs. 75, 98).

BALUSTRADE: a railing or barrier formed of elaborate uprights (balusters) topped by a rail (figs. 44, 99).

BEAUX-ARTS: the popular and elaborate revival style and a particular system of architectural education taught at the École des Beaux-Arts in Paris and copied in some American schools of architecture; Cass Gilbert's Minnesota Capitol (fig. 13) is a prime example of how the style could be adapted to an American public building by an architect who did not study in Paris. The public spaces of the interior are especially rich in the use of Beaux-Arts motifs.

CAPITAL: the decorated top of a COLUMN or PILASTER in one of the Greek ORDERS (figs. 77, 98, 99).

CLASSICAL/CLASSICIZING ARCHITECTURE: Architecture based on the precedents, elements, and decorative motifs, as well as the proportions of the architecture of Ancient Greece and Rome, often as reinterpreted by the architects of the Renaissance, especially Palladio. The West Virginia State Capitol is a prime example (fig. 1), as is the US Supreme Court (fig. 20).

CLERESTORY: an area elevated above adjacent rooftops, usually along a central axis; a clerestory would allow light into the interior, as in one of Cass Gilbert's alternative plans for the Charleston Capitol (figs. 34, 35).

COFFERS: recessed square panels that decorate the interior surface of a ceiling or vault. Seen in the legislative chambers and their foyers and in the dome (figs. 55, 65, and gallery 5–7). There are also coffers in the ceilings under the porticoes. Most of the coffers at the Charleston Capitol are decorated with a stylized flower or ROSETTE (fig. 82 and gallery 5–7), but those in the interior dome at Charleston are left plain as at the Pantheon in Rome. The manner in which they become progressively smaller toward the top makes the interior dome seem more spacious than it really is.

COLONNADE: a continuous row of COLUMNS, as seen in the south and north PORTICOES (fig. 1) and in the exterior DRUM of the DOME (figs. 1, 31, 97).

COLUMN: a freestanding cylindrical support, sometimes FLUTED, with a CAPITAL (figs. 1, 53).

COLUMNS IN ANTIS: see IN ANTIS.

CORINTHIAN ORDER: see ORDER.

CORNICE: the projected molding, often decorated, at the top of a wall (fig. 99 and gallery 3, 4).

CURTAIN WALL: the outer covering of a building when that covering is attached to internal supports. At Charleston, the stone wall of the exterior is suspended from the steel structure (figs. 41–44 show the curtain wall being attached during construction). It is called a "curtain wall" because it is neither structural nor self-supporting.

DIOCLETIAN WINDOW: a semicircular window, often very large, that is divided into three sections by vertical mullions (fig. 35); also known as a thermal window because it was often found in Roman public baths (*thermae*), including the Baths of Diocletian.

DOME: a structural element, arched and shaped like half a sphere. The Capitol in Charleston has two domes: the interior dome, which is visible from the rotunda, and the exterior dome, which is elevated above the interior dome and is crowned with a LANTERN, a spire, and, ultimately, an eagle (figs. 70, 97). A specification drawing shows the shape of the exterior, elevated dome and the interior, hemispherical dome (fig. 55).

DORIC ORDER: see ORDER.

DRUM: the cylindrical structural system below the DOME (figs. 31, 56, 97); at Charleston, the exterior drum is surrounded with a COLONNADE. On the interior, the area of the drum is lined with PILASTERS between windows (fig. 55 and gallery 1, 3).

DRUMS: the individual cylindrical sections that, when superimposed, create the COLUMNS of the PORTICOES and side porches at Charleston. Figure 42 shows drums sitting on the ground prior to being put into place.

ELEVATION: an architectural diagram that shows the exterior and/or interior surfaces and their decoration diagrammatically, without the recession and distortion that results from a single viewpoint (figs. 33, 55, 56). Elevations for the chamber of the Supreme Court at Charleston (figs. 51, 52), for example, show not only the four walls but also the decorative motifs planned for the floor and ceiling. Figures 51 and 52 demonstrate how much information Gilbert's office could squeeze onto a single sheet. While elevations can be informative, they do not convey how a building or a room will look when completed.

FASCES: an ancient Etruscan/Roman motif composed of a bundle of rods bound with straps and sometimes incorporating an ax (figs. 70–72, 75, 76, 83). Fasces symbolize authority, order, and unity and were a common emblem of American democracy before they were appropriated as a symbol by the Italian Fascists in the 1920s.

FEDERAL STYLE: the term used to describe the Classical Revival style that flourished in America from about 1790 to 1830.

FESTOON: see GARLAND.

FLUTES, FLUTED, FLUTING: shallow vertical grooves on the shaft of a COLUMN that accentuate the column's cylindrical quality. Seen in Charleston only in the Doric vestibule (gallery 9). The columns of the PORTICOES (figs. 1, 98), of the side entrance porches (figs. 42–45), and of the Supreme Court (fig. 53) are unfluted.

FRIEZE: The horizontal element below the cornice in the Greek ORDERS, which can be decorated or left plain (fig. 97, 99). A Doric frieze with TRIGLYPHS and METOPES lines the rotunda and the legislative foyers (fig. 68 and galleries 3–5).

GARLAND: A decorative motif from antiquity, revived in the Renaissance, that combines abundant leaves, flowers, and/or fruit into long rows. Garlands are usually represented as if draped in swags (figs. 75, 76, 99).

GIANT ORDER: PILASTERS (or COLUMNS) that span more than one story of a structure; see the pilasters on the wings and sides of the Main Building (fig. 98).

GREEK KEY MOTIF: an ancient decorative motif formed of continuous lines that change direction at ninety-degree angles (fig. 99).

GROUND PLAN: an architectural diagram that shows how a building would look from directly above if it were truncated by a horizontal plane slightly above floor level. Often used to demonstrate the interior

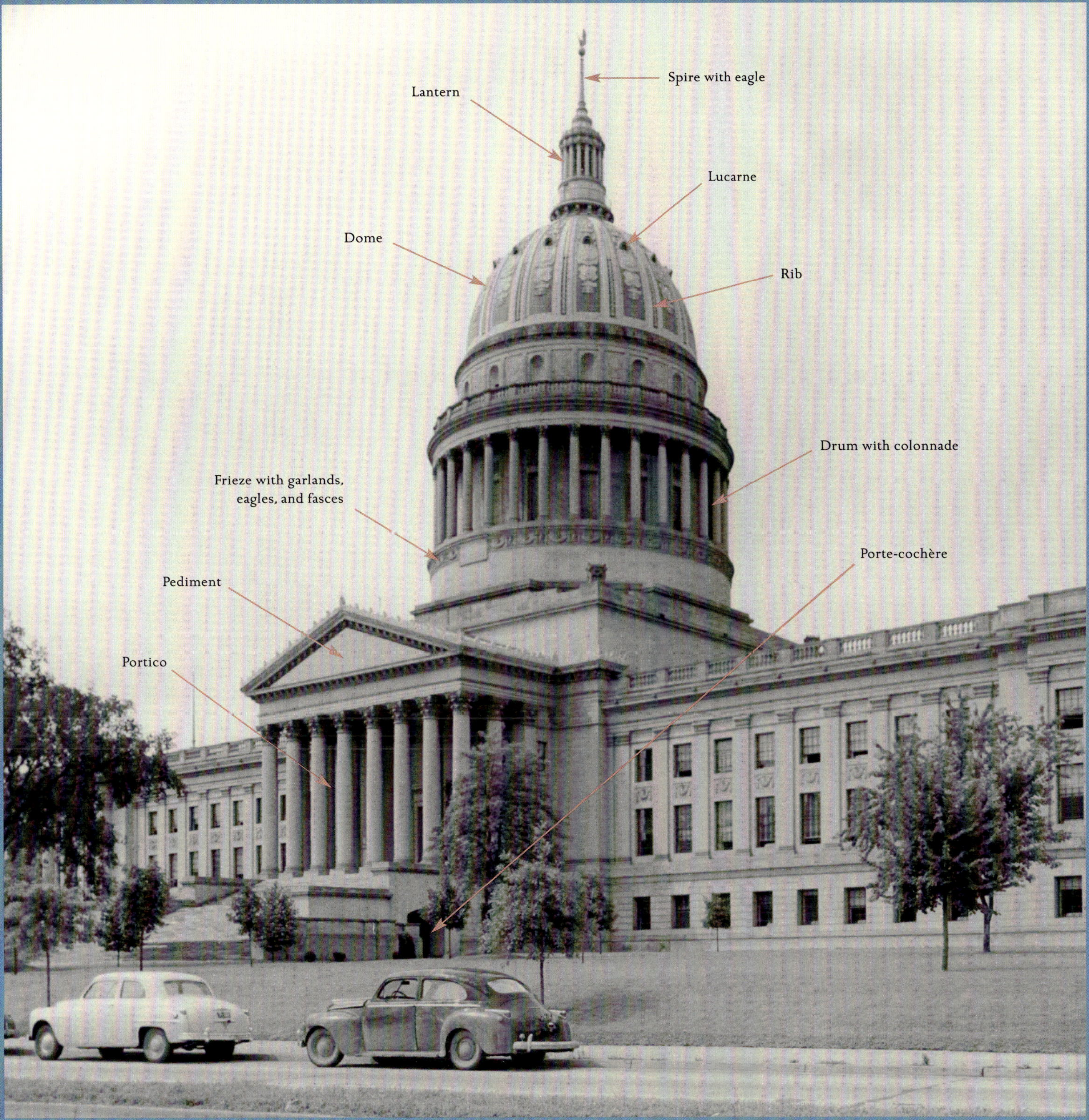


Fig. 97. View of the West Virginia Capitol, c. 1950, Gilbert Family Collection.

Fig. 98. Portico, West Virginia Capitol, c. 1950, Gilbert Family Collection.

Fig. 99. Detail of the Main Building, West Virginia Capitol, c. 1950, Gilbert Family Collection, Gift to the WVSA.

layout of the corridors and other spaces. There is a quick sketch for a partial ground plan for the West Virginia Capitol in Gilbert's diary (fig. 32); a finished ground plan that is similar to, but larger than, the finished Capitol is shown in figure 38. The ground plan of the Supreme Court chamber is seen in figure 51. Some of many other ground plans proposed for the Capitol are illustrated in figures 25, 27, 28, 34.

IN ANTIS: a row of two or more columns framed by walls, as are those above the main entrances to the East and West Wings and those framing the entrances to the legislative foyers and chambers (gallery 3–5).

IONIC ORDER: see ORDER.

KEYSTONE: a wedge-shaped block at the apex of an arch. Sometimes decorated with a sculpted head, as at the side entrances at Charleston (figs. 45, 79).

LANTERN: the cylindrical, windowed structure at the top of the DOME (figs. 31, 70, 97).

LUCARNE: a window on a pitched roof, like those on the dome of the West Virginia State Capitol dome (fig. 70, 97).

METOPE: the square areas between the TRIGLYPHS in the FRIEZE area of the DORIC ORDER. At Charleston, as often in antiquity, the metopes are decorated with relief sculptures (fig. 81 and gallery 3, 4).

MODERNISM: a radical new style that gradually became more popular during the 1920s and 30s. Architects eventually abandoned the references to historic architecture that were so important for the BEAUX-ARTS style and based their designs on pure geometry and exposed, modern materials. Some architects developed distinctly personal styles. Some state capitols built in the 1920s and 1930s are modern in style (figs. 88–91).

OCTOSTYLE COLONNADE OR PORTICO: A row of eight columns, as on the South and North Porticoes (figs. 1, 33, 98).

ORDER: a series of several Greek and Roman architectural styles—revived in the Italian Renaissance—that are based on the use of COLUMNS supporting an entablature. The basic components are the COLUMN (usually including base, shaft, and CAPITAL) and its entablature (including FRIEZE and CORNICE). The relevant orders for the Capitol in Charleston are the three traditional ones, the DORIC, seen in the Doric Vestibule (gallery 9); the IONIC, seen in the chamber of the Supreme Court (fig. 53); and the CORINTHIAN, seen in the grand PORTICOES of the exterior and the columns that surround the DRUM (figs. 1, 19, 98).

PALMETTE: an ancient motif composed of stylized palm fronds fanned out to form a decorative pattern (figs. 75, 76, 98).

PEDIMENT: the low-pitched triangular gable above the south and north PORTICOES (figs. 1, 97, 98). In Cass Gilbert's early designs for the Charleston Capitol, these areas show allegorical or historical sculptures (figs. 33, 31); raised stone blocks installed there suggest that only the financial constraints of the Great Depression prevented the completion of this ancient-inspired decoration.

PILASTER: shallow, flattened versions of the COLUMNS of the Greek and Roman ORDERS, as seen on the exterior walls of the Charleston complex (fig. 99) and lining the interior of the rotunda (gallery 3), the drum (figs. 65, gallery 1, 3), the legislative foyers (gallery 5), and both legislative chambers (gallery 6, 7). Pilasters are decorative rather than structural.

PORTICO: the porches with COLONNADES that mark the south and north entrances at Charleston; porticoes often include PEDIMENTS, as here (figs. 1, 97, 98).

PORTE-COCHÈRE: a covered entrance large enough for a vehicle to drive through and discharge passengers. Cass Gilbert placed a virtually hidden porte-cochère for cars under the steps leading to the South Portico at Charleston (fig. 97).

QUADRIGA: a sculpted group consisting of a chariot, a driver, and four horses. Cass Gilbert placed a gilded quadriga by Daniel Chester French above the PORTICO of his Capitol in St. Paul (fig. 13).

RIB: long narrow, usually arched elements originally designed to provide support internally or externally for a vault or dome. The vertical ribs on the exterior of the dome at Charleston are purely decorative (fig. 70, 97).

RICHARDSON ROMANESQUE STYLE: characterized by low, heavy arches and heavy rustication, this revival style was made popular by the Boston architect H. H. Richardson, who had studied at the École des Beaux-Arts in Paris.

RINCEAU: an ancient decorative motif composed of the leafy tendrils of a vine, usually arranged to form a pattern of repeated spirals (fig. 75).

ROSETTE: a stylized blossom used repeatedly as a decorative motif, especially in COFFERS (fig. 82) or in combination with a GARLAND (figs. 75, 76, 99). Rosettes can vary in design depending on the sources in nature, but they are often so stylized that it is difficult to trace the particular botanical inspiration.

TERRACE: the terraces that Gilbert intended for the West Virginia Capitol were elevated platforms around the base of the structure. They were never built, but the manner in which they would have visually "finished" or "framed" the building is evident in his competition-winning design for the Montana State Capitol (fig. 14).

THERMAL WINDOW: see DIOCLETIAN WINDOW.

TRIGLYPH: the area decorated with vertical grooves between the METOPES in the DORIC FRIEZE. Seen at Charleston in the friezes of the rotunda and legislative foyers (gallery 4).

TRIPOD: the term for an ancient three-legged vessel, often highly decorated. The large decorative elements with lions' heads, palmettes, and garlands on the corners of the terrace below the drum (fig. 75) are based on the design of ancient tripods, although in this case the design has four legs rather than three.

UNFLUTED COLUMNS/PILASTERS: see FLUTES, FLUTING.

VICTORIAN STYLE: the elaborate architectural style, based on earlier architecture and often eclectic, that became popular in Britain, America, and then around the world during the reign of Queen Victoria.

VICTORIAN GOTHIC: the elaborate and eclectic style, based on the medieval Gothic style, that became popular worldwide. The Fourth West Virginia Capitol is a typical example (fig. 11).

# BIBLIOGRAPHY

ABBREVIATIONS

| | |
|---|---|
| *CCC* | *Correspondence: Capitol Commission, Printed as Provided by Resolution of January 12, 1923, by Mr. Underwood.* Charleston, WV: Capitol Commission, 1923 |
| Gilbert Papers, LC | Cass Gilbert Papers, Manuscript Division, Library of Congress, Washington, DC |
| LC | Library of Congress, Washington, DC |
| N-YHS | New-York Historical Society, Cass Gilbert Archive |
| "Report to House of Delegates" | "State of West Virginia Capitol Building Commission: Report to the House of Delegates," with introduction "To The People of West Virginia," Charleston, WV, January 18, 1923 |
| WVSA | West Virginia State Archives, Cultural Center, Charleston, WV |


Ackerman, James S. *Palladio.* Harmondsworth: Penguin, 1966.

Alberti, Leon Battista. *The Ten Books of Architecture: The 1755 Leoni Edition.* New York: Dover Publications, 1986.

Alexiou, Alice Sparberg. *The Flatiron: The New York Landmark and the Incomparable City That Arose with It.* New York: St. Martin's Press, 2010.

Appelbaum, Stanley. *The Chicago World's Fair of 1893: A Photographic Record.* New York: Dover, 1980.

*Art in the United States Capitol* (House Document Number 91–368). Washington: United States Government Printing Office, 1976.

Aylesworth, Thomas G. *State Capitals.* New York: Image Bank, 1990.

Babelon, Jean-Pierre, and Claude Mignot, eds. *François Mansart: La genie de l'architecture.* Paris: Gallimard, 1998.

Betts, Mary Beth. "Cass Gilbert: Twelve Projects." In *Inventing the Skyline: The Architecture of Cass Gilbert,* edited by Margaret Heilbrun, 83–176. New York: Columbia University Press, 2000.

———. "From Sketch to Architecture: Drawing in the Cass Gilbert Office." In *Inventing the Skyline: The Architecture of Cass Gilbert,* edited by Margaret Heilbrun, 35–82. New York: Columbia University Press, 2000.

Blodgett, Geoffrey. "Cass Gilbert, Architect: Conservative at Bay." *Journal of American History* 72 (1985), 615–36.

———. *Cass Gilbert: The Early Years.* St. Paul: Minnesota Historical Society Press, 2001.

———. *Oberlin Architecture: College and Town; A Guide to Its Social History.* Oberlin: Oberlin College, 1985.

———. "Oberlin: The Grand Collaboration." In *Cass Gilbert, Life and Work: Architect of the Public Domain,* edited by Barbara S. Christen and Steven Flanders, 206–19. New York: W. W. Norton, 2001.

———. "The Politics of Public Architecture." In *Cass Gilbert, Life and Work: Architect of the Public Domain,* edited by Barbara S. Christen and Steven Flanders, 62–72. New York: W. W. Norton, 2001.

Boyd, Julian P., ed. *The Papers of Thomas Jefferson,* vol. 8. Princeton: Princeton University, 1950.

Bragdon, Claude. *Architecture and Democracy.* New York: Alfred A. Knopf, 1918.

Broderick, Mosette. *Triumvirate: McKim, Mead & White: Art, Architecture, Scandal, and Class in America's Gilded Age.* New York: Alfred A. Knopf, 2010.

Brownell, Baker, and Frank Lloyd Wright. *Architecture and Modern Life.* New York: Harper, 1938.

Bryan, John M. *Robert Mills: America's First Architect.* New York: Princeton Architectural Press, 2001.

Byard, Paul Spencer. "Representing American Justice: The United States Supreme Court." In *Cass Gilbert, Life and Work: Architect of the Public Domain,* edited by Barbara S. Christen and Steven Flanders, 272–87. New York: W. W. Norton, 2001.

Capitman, Barbara Baer, Michael D. Kinerk, and Dennis W. Wilhelm. *Rediscovering Art Deco U.S.A.* New York: Penguin, 1994.

Cass Gilbert Papers. Cass Gilbert Collection, LC.

Chambers, S. Allen Jr. *Buildings of West Virginia.* New York: Oxford University Press, 2004.

Cheney, Sheldon. *The New World Architecture.* New York: Tudor, 1930.

Christen, Barbara S. "The Architect as Planner: Cass Gilbert's Responses to Historic Open Spaces." In *Inventing the Skyline: The Architecture of Cass Gilbert,* edited by Margaret Heilbrun, 177–228. New York: Columbia University Press, 2000.

———. "Cass Gilbert and the Ideal of the City Beautiful: City and Campus Plans, 1900–1916." PhD diss., City University of New York, 1997.

Christen, Barbara S., and Steven Flanders, eds. *Cass Gilbert, Life and Work: Architect of the Public Domain.* New York: W. W. Norton, 2001.

Cochran, Edwin A. "The Cathedral of Commerce: The Highest Building In The World" (souvenir booklet). 1918. Reprint, Whitefish, MT: Kessinger Publishing's Rare Reprints, 2007.

Cohen, Stan, and Richard Andre. *Capitols of West Virginia: A Pictorial History.* Charleston, WV: Pictorial Histories Publishing Co., 1989.

Cole, John Y., and Henry Hope Reed, eds. *The Library of Congress: The Art and Architecture of the Thomas Jefferson Building.* New York: W. W. Norton, 1997.

Corbin, David Alan. *Life, Work, and Rebellion in the Coal Fields: The Southern West Virginia Miners, 1880–1922.* Urbana: University of Illinois Press, 1981.

Damron, Robert A. *The West Virginia Capitol: A Commemorative History Celebrating the 50th Anniversary of Its Dedication.* Charleston, WV: The Senate, 1982 (reprinted 1990, 1995, 2006).

Daniel, Jean Houston, and Price Daniel. *51 Capitols of America and Executive Mansions.* Waukesha, WI: Country Beautiful, 1969.

David, Harvey G. "Charleston Today." *The West Virginia Review,* December 1924, 26, 45–46.

Dearinger, David B., ed. *Paintings and Sculpture in the Collection of the National Academy of Design,* vol. 1, 1826–1925. New York: Hudson Hills Press, 2004.

d'Espouy, Hector. *Fragments d'architecture antique d'après les relevés et restaurations des ancient pensionnaires de l'Académie de France à Rome.* Paris; C. Massin, 1905. Reprinted as *Greek and Roman Architecture in Classic Drawings.* Mineola, NY: Dover, 1999.

Donaghey, George W. *Building a State Capitol.* Little Rock: Parke-Harper Company, 1937.

Ehlert, Willis J. *America's Heritage: Capitols of the United States.* Madison, WI: State House Publishing, 1999.

Federman, Peter. "The Detroit Public Library." *Classical America* 4 (1977): 85–111.

Fenske, Gail. "Cass Gilbert's Skyscrapers in New York: The Twentieth-Century City and the Urban Picturesque." In *Inventing the Skyline: The Architecture of Cass Gilbert*, edited by Margaret Heilbrun, 229–88. New York: Columbia University Press, 2000.

———. *The Skyscraper and the City: The Woolworth Building and the Making of Modern New York.* Chicago: University of Chicago Press, 2008.

Ferriss, Hugh. *Power in Buildings: An Artist's View of Contemporary Architecture.* New York: Columbia University Press, 1953 (republished by Dover Publications in 2008 as *The Power of Buildings, 1920–1950: A Master Draftsman's Record*).

Fletcher, Rachel. "An American Vision of Harmony: Geometric Proportions in Thomas Jefferson's Rotunda at the University of Virginia." *Nexus Network Journal, Architecture and Mathematics Online* 5, no. 2 (2003): 4–8. http:// nexusjournal.com

Frary, Ihna Thayer. *They Built the Capitol.* Manchester, NH: Ayer Publishers, 1940.

Frelinghuysen, Alice Cooney. *Louis Comfort Tiffany and Laurelton Hall: An Artist's Country Estate.* New York: Metropolitan Museum of Art, 2006.

Gebhard, David. *The National Trust Guide to Art Deco in America.* New York: John Wiley & Sons, 1996.

Gibson, Richard R. *A Celebration of State Capitols.* Self-published, 2010.

Gilbert, Cass. "The Greatest Element of Modern Architecture." *American Architect* 136, no. 2574 (August 5, 1929): 141–44 (original typescript is titled "Memorandum Relative to a State Capitol" and dated December 11, 1927; preserved at N-YHS, box 516, folder 8).

Gilbert, Julia Finch. *Cass Gilbert: Reminiscences and Addresses.* Privately published, 1935.

Goodsell, Charles T. *The American Statehouse: Interpreting Democracy's Temples.* Lawrence: University of Kansas Press, 2001.

Graves, C. H. "Introductory Address." In *Proceedings at the Laying of the Corner Stone of the New Capitol of Minnesota*, 14. St. Paul: Pioneer Press Company, 1898.

Gauthier, Julie Celina. *Minnesota Capitol, Official Guide and History.* St. Paul: Pioneer Manufacturing Departments, 1907.

Hartman, George E., and Jan Cigliano, eds. *Pencil Points Reader: A Journal for the Drafting Room, 1920–43.* New York: Princeton Architectural Press, 2004.

Hauck, Eldon. *American Capitols: An Encyclopedia of the State, National, and Territorial Capitol Edifices of the United States.* Jefferson, NC: McFarland & Company, 1991.

Heilbrun, Margaret, ed. *Inventing the Skyline: The Architecture of Cass Gilbert.* New York: Columbia University Press, 2000.

Hind, Charles, and Irena Murray, eds. *Palladio and His Legacy: A Transatlantic Journey.* New York: Marsilio, 2010.

Hitchcock, Henry-Russell, and William Seale. *Modern Architecture: Romanticism and Reintegration.* New York: Payson and Clarke, 1968.

———. *Temples of Democracy: The State Capitols of the USA.* New York: Harcourt Brace Jovanovich, 1976.

Hoak, Edward Warren, and Willis Humphrey Church. *Masterpieces of American Architecture: Museums, Libraries, Churches, and Other Public Buildings.* New York: Charles Scribner's Sons, 1930.

Irish, Sharon. "A 'Machine that Makes the Land Pay': The West Street Building in New York." *Technology and Culture* 30 (April 1989): 376–97.

———. *Cass Gilbert, Architect: Modern Traditionalist.* New York: Monacelli Press, 1999.

———. "Cass Gilbert in Practice." In *Inventing the Skyline: The Architecture of Cass Gilbert*, edited by Margaret Heilbrun, 1–34. New York: Columbia University Press, 2000.

———. "'Great Gray Buildings': The United States Army Supply Base in Brooklyn, New York." In *Cass Gilbert, Life and Work: Architect of the Public Domain*, edited by Barbara S. Christen and Steven Flanders, 163–74. New York: W. W. Norton, 2001.

Johnston, Norman J. *Washington's Audacious State Capitol and Its Builders.* Seattle: University of Washington Press, 1988.

Kabler, Phil. "Mystery of the Dome." *Charleston Gazette*, October 14, 2005, 1A, 11A.

Kemp, Martin. *Leonardo da Vinci: The Marvelous Works of Nature and Man.* Cambridge, MA: Harvard University Press, 1981.

Kidney, Walter C. *Henry Hornbostel: An Architect's Master Touch.* Pittsburgh: History and Landmarks Foundation, 2002.

Kirkham, Guy. "Cass Gilbert, Master of Style." *Pencil Points* 15 (November 1934): 541–56.

Kostof, Spiro. *A History of Architecture: Settings and Rituals.* Oxford: Oxford University Press, 1985.

Kruft, Hanno-Walter. *A History of Architectural Theory from Vitruvius to the Present.* Translated by Ronald Taylor, Elsie Callander, and Antony Wood. New York: Princeton Architectural Press, 1994.

Lambert, Kirby, Patricia M. Burnham, and Susan R. Near. *Montana's State Capitol: The People's House.* Helena: Montana Historical Society Press, 2002.

Larson, Paul Clifford. *Cass Gilbert Abroad: The Young Architect's European Tour.* Afton, MN: Afton Historical Society Press, 2002.

Loeffler, Jane C. *The Architecture of Diplomacy: Building America's Embassies.* Princeton: Princeton Architectural Press, 1998.

Luebke, Frederick C., ed. *A Harmony of the Arts: The Nebraska State Capitol.* Lincoln: University of Nebraska Press, 1990.

Maroon, Fred, and Suzy Maroon. *The Supreme Court of the United States.* New York: Thomasson-Grant & Lickle, 1996.

Minnesota Legislature, House Committee on Public Accounts and Expenditures. "Report of the Investigation of the Capitol Commission." St. Paul: McGill-Warner, 1903.

Moore, Charles. *Daniel H. Burnham: Architect, Planner of Cities.* Boston: Houghton Mifflin, 1921.

Morgan, E. F. "Inaugural Address of Governor E. F. Morgan," March 4, 1921. West Virginia Department of Culture and History website. *http://www.wvculture.org/history/morgania.html*

"A Moving Monument: The West Virginia State Capitol," transcript of documentary; available at http://*www.movingmonument.org/Transcript.pdf*

Mumford, Lewis. *Sticks and Stones: A Study of American Architecture and Civilization.* New York: Dover, 1955.

Murphy, Patricia Anne. "Architectural Education and Minnesota Career." In *Cass Gilbert, Life and Work: Architect of the Public Domain*, edited by Barbara S. Christen and Steven Flanders, 27–45. New York: W. W. Norton, 2001.

Nichols, Frederick Doveton. *Thomas Jefferson's Architectural Drawings.* Boston: Massachusetts Historical Society, 1961.

Ochsendorf, John. *Guastavino Vaulting: The Art of Structural Tile.* New York: Princeton Architectural Press, 2010.

Oxendorf, Eric, and William Seale. *Domes of America.* San Francisco: Pomegranate, 1994.

Palladio, Andrea. *The Four Books on Architecture, The 1738 Isaac Ware Edition.* New York: Dover Publications, 1965.

Peterson, Merrill D. *Thomas Jefferson and the New Nation: A Biography.* Cambridge, MA: Oxford University Press, 2008.

Pfeiffer, Bruce Brooks, ed. *Frank Lloyd Wright: Collected Writings*, vol. 3. New York: Rizzoli, 1993.

———. *Essential Frank Lloyd Wright: Critical Writings on Architecture.* Princeton: Princeton University Press, 1970.

Plato. *Timaeus.* Translated by G. Burry. Cambridge, MA: Harvard University Press, 1952.

Poche, François. *Le Dôme des Invalides: un chef-d'oeuvre restauré.* Paris: Éditions d'Art Somogy et Musée de l'Armée, 1995.

Pollitt, J. J. *The Art of Ancient Greece: Sources and Documents.* Cambridge: Cambridge University Press, 1990.

Preisler, Julian H. *Jewish West Virginia.* Charleston, SC: Arcadia Publishing, 2010.

Reed, Henry Hope. *The United States Capitol: Its Architecture and Decoration.* New York: W. W. Norton, 2005.

Remele, Larry, ed. *The North Dakota State Capitol: Architecture and History.* Bismark: State Historical Society of North Dakota, 1989.

"Report of the Special Senate Committee on Capitol Commission," submitted to the State Senate March 21, 1923 (Cass Gilbert's copy at N-YHS, box 516, folder 6).

Rich, Lorimer. "Capitols and Legislative Buildings." In *Forms and Functions of Twentieth-Century Architecture*, edited by Talbot Hamlin, 3:771–77. New York: Columbia University Press, 1952.

Riddel, Frank S. *The Historical Atlas of West Virginia.* Morgantown: West Virginia University Press, 2008.

Roth, Leland M. "Cass Gilbert." In *International Dictionary of Architects and Architecture.* Detroit and London: St. James Press, 1993.

Ruggiero, Francis Pio. *State Capitols: Temples of Sovereignty.* Milford, PA: Excelsior, 2002.

Saylor, Henry H. "The A-I-A's First Hundred Years." *Journal of the American Institute of Architects* (May 1957). http://www.aia.org/aiaucmp/groups/ek_members/documents/pdf/aiap014824.pdf

Scott, Pamela. *Temple of Liberty: Building the Capitol for a New Nation.* Washington, DC: Library of Congress, 1995.

Severin, Don. *The Encyclopedia of State Capitols.* Self-published, 1999.

Solomonson, Katherine. *The Chicago Tribune Tower Competition: Skyscraper Design and Cultural Change in the 1920s.* New York: Cambridge University Press, 2001.

Speck, Lawrence W. "The University of Texas: Vision and Ambition." In *Cass Gilbert, Life and Work: Architect of the Public Domain*, edited by Barbara S. Christen and Steven Flanders, 192–205. New York: W. W. Norton, 2001.

Speck, Lawrence W., and Richard L. Cleary. *The University of Texas at Austin.* Princeton: Princeton Architectural Press, 2011.

Starrett, Paul. *Changing the Skyline: An Autobiography.* New York: McGraw-Hill, 1938.

"State of West Virginia Capitol Building Commission: Report to the House of Delegates," with introduction "To The People of West Virginia." Charleston; January 18, 1923 (copy at WVSA, Cass Gilbert's copy at N-YHS, box 522, folder 2).

Steel Jr., Edward M., ed. *The Court-Martial of Mother Jones.* Lexington: University Press of Kentucky, 1995.

Stembridge, Jim. *Fifty State Capitols: The Architecture of Representative Government.* Salem, OR: Coho Publishing, 2011.

Stern, Robert A. M. "Introduction." In *Cass Gilbert, Life and Work: Architect of the Public Domain*, edited by Barbara S. Christen and Steven Flanders, 15–16. New York: W. W. Norton, 2001.

Stickel, Frederick G. "The Passing of Cass Gilbert." *Pencil Points* 15 (November 1934): 556.

Stutler, Boyd B. "The Capitals and Capitols of West Virginia." In *West Virginia Legislative Handbook and Manual and Official Register, 1922*, 706–23. Charleston: Tribune Printing Co., 1922.

———. "West Virginia's Magnificent State Capitol." *West Virginia Review* 9 (1932): 400–403, 425–26.

Swartwout, Egerton. "Cass Gilbert." In *Dictionary of American Biography*, supplement 1, 21: 341–43. New York: Charles Scribner's Sons, 1944.

Thompson, Neil B. *Minnesota's State Capitol: The Art and Politics of a Public Building.* 2nd ed. St. Paul: Minnesota Historical Society Press, 2005.

Thrane, Susan W., and Tom Patterson. *State Houses: America's 50 State Capitol Buildings.* Erin, Ontario: Boston Mills Press, 2005.

Tucker, Garland S., III. *The High Tide of American Conservatism: Davis, Coolidge, and the 1924 Election.* Austin, TX: Emerald Book Co., 2010.

Van Hook, Bailey. *The Virgin and the Dynamo: Murals in American Architecture, 1893–1917.* Athens: Ohio University Press, 2003.

Venditti, Arnaldo. *The Loggia del Capitaniato.* University Park: The Pennsylvania State University Press, 1971.

Vitruvius. *The Ten Books on Architecture.* Translated by Morris Hicky Morgan. New York: Dover Publications, 1960.

Wallace, Jim. *A History of the West Virginia State Capitol: The House of State.* Charleston, SC: History Press, 2012.

*West Virginia Legislative Handbook and Manual and Official Register*, published annually by the Legislature. Years consulted, 1922, 1929

White, Norval, and Elliot Willensky, with Fran Leadon. *AIA Guide to New York City.* Oxford: Oxford University Press, 2010.

White, Theo B. *Paul Philippe Cret: Architect and Teacher.* Philadelphia: The Art Alliance Press, 1973.

Wilson, James. Speech before the Pennsylvania Ratifying Convention. In *The Founders' Constitution*, edited by Philip B. Kurland and Ralph Lerner, vol. 1, chap. 7, doc. 17. Chicago: University of Chicago Press, 1987. http://press-pubs.uchicago.edu/founders/documents/v1ch7s17.html

Wittkower, Rudolf. *Architectural Principles in the Age of Humanism.* New York: W. W. Norton, 1971.

Woods, Mary N. "The First American Architectural Journals: The Profession's Voice." *Journal of the Society of Architectural Historians* 48 (1989): 117–38.

———. *From Craft to Profession: The Practice of Architecture in Nineteenth-Century America.* Berkeley: University of California Press, 1999.

———. "In the Camera's Eye: The Woolworth Building and American Avant-Garde Photography and Film." In *Cass Gilbert, Life and Work: Architect of the Public Domain*, edited by Barbara S. Christen and Steven Flanders, 149–62. New York: W. W. Norton, 2001.

Woolworth, F. E. & Co. *The Dinner Given to Cass Gilbert by Frank W. Woolworth, April 24· MCMXIII.* Baltimore: Munder-Thomsen Press, 1913.

# ABOUT THE AUTHORS

CHAD N. PROUDFOOT is a native of Grafton, West Virginia. He holds a BA in Political Science, a Master of Public Administration with a Graduate Certificate in Cultural Resource Management, and an MA in History, all from West Virginia University. He has a life-long interest in the history of the West Virginia Capitol Complex. In 2002, at age nineteen, he was appointed by Governor Bob Wise as a member of the West Virginia Capitol Building Commission, serving until 2009. He was Vice-Chairman of the Capitol Building Commission from 2004–2009 and served as Acting Chairman in 2006. He currently is Program Coordinator for the Community Resources & Economic Development Program of the West Virginia University Extension Service.

BERNARD SCHULTZ is Professor of Art History and Director of Education and External Affairs for the Art Museum of West Virginia University. From 2000 to 2011 he served as Dean of the College of Creative Arts at WVU. Professor Schultz is the author of *Art and Anatomy in Renaissance Italy* and has co-authored, with David G. Wilkins and Katheryn M. Linduff, six editions of *Art Past/Art Present*, a popular Art History survey book. He has been recognized for outstanding teaching and has written a number of pedagogical study guides in Art History. Professor Schultz currently serves as a member of the West Virginia Commission on the Arts.

MARY LOUISE SOLDO SCHULTZ is a faculty member in the Honors College at West Virginia University where she has received numerous awards for her teaching. She is also the recipient of grants including an Independent Fellowship from the National Endowment for the Humanities and a West Virginia Humanities Council Fellowship for her research on Blanche Lazzell. She wrote the chapter "Studies in France, 1912–1913," in *Blanche Lazzell: The Life and Work of an American Modernist*, 2004, and has written several pedagogical study guides for the study of French and art history.

ANN THOMAS WILKINS was Associate Professor of Classics at Duquesne University until her recent retirement. She continues to teach periodically on Duquesne's Rome campus. She is the author of *Villain or Hero: Sallust's Portrayal of Catiline* and a number of papers on various topics, including Bernini's mythological works and Mussolini's appropriation of Augustan architecture; the latter appeared in *Donatello Among the Blackshirts: History and Modernity in the Visual Culture of Fascist Italy*. In collaboration with David Wilkins she has published on immigrant religious structures and presented papers on a number of subjects, including the architecture of Counter-Reformation libraries in Rome. Together they are collaborating on a book about New Hampshire's public libraries.

DAVID G. WILKINS is Professor Emeritus of the History of Art and Architecture at the University of Pittsburgh. He served as the Director of the University's Art Gallery from 1976 to 1992 and was Chair of the department for nine years. In 1987 he won the Chancellor's Distinguished Teaching Award at the University of Pittsburgh, and in 2005 he was honored by the College Art Association with their national 2005 Award for the Distinguished Teaching of Art History. He teaches periodically on Duquesne University's Study Abroad Program in Rome. He has authored, edited, and contributed to many books, including *Donatello, Art Past/Art Present, History of Italian Renaissance Art, Beyond Isabella: Secular Women Patrons of Art in Renaissance Italy, The Art of the Duquesne Club*, and *A Reflection of Faith: St. Paul Cathedral, Pittsburgh, 1906–2006*.

# ILLUSTRATION CREDITS

Authors' collection: figs. 10–13, 20, 21, 40, 63, 67–69, 87–92, 95, 96
Carnegie-Mellon University, Courtesy Martin Aurand: figs. 15, 37, 86
Drawings by Raymond Agius: figs. 74, 78, 81, 82
Gilbert Family Collection, Gift to the WVSA: figs. 65, 80, 84, 85, 94, 97–99
Keeler Tavern Preservation Society, Inc.: fig. 19
Library of Congress: figs. 4, 16, 17, 22, 23, 32
Library of Virginia: fig. 3
Ministero per I Bene e le Attività Culturali / Biblioteca nazionale Centrale, Firenze: fig. 7
Minnesota Historical Society: fig. 18
New-York Historical Society: figs. 14, 23, 24, 31, 33–35, 54, 57
Photography by Benh: fig. 73
Photography by Brandon Bigheart: fig. 72
Photography by Edward Crim: gallery 5, and fig. 77
Photography by Frank Ceravalo: gallery 2, and fig. 1
Photography by David G. Wilkins: figs. 75, 76
Photography by Thorney Lieberman: gallery 3, 6–9, and figs. 53, 70, 83
Photography by Jeff Lively: gallery 1, 4
Photography by O. Palsson: fig. 93
RMN–Grand Palais / Art Resource, NY: fig. 2
Scala / Art Resource, NY: figs. 5, 6
Smithsonian American Art Museum: fig. 8
West Virginia State Archives: figs. 9, 25–30, 36, 38, 39, 41–52, 55, 56, 58–62, 64, 66, 71, 79

# INDEX

*Illustrations are indicated by page numbers in italics.*

## A NOTE ON THE TYPE

The text of *Cass Gilbert's West Virgina State Capitol* is composed in Golden Cockerel, a type designed by Eric Gill (1889–1940). Born in Brighton, England, Gill attended the Chichester School of Art and later studied calligraphy with Edward Johnson. He embarked on a career as a stone carver and letterer in league with the Arts and Crafts movement, and in 1925 was invited by Stanley Morison to design his first typeface, Perpetua, for Monotype Corporation. Three years later, Robert Gibbings of the Golden Cockerel Press commissioned Gill to create the type and wood-engraved illustrations for *The Four Gospels*, now recognized as one of the truly outstanding books of the twentieth century. While similar in appearance to Perpetua, the Golden Cockerel type possesses wider, more Classical proportions and a greater evenness in its stroke weights. Golden Cockerel was adapted digitally by Dave Farey and Richard Dawson in association with Colin Brignall for the International Typeface Corporation in 1996.